Penguin Books

FIVE AGAINST ONE

For ten years Kim Neely covered hard rock and alternative music for *Rolling Stone.* Currently a freelance writer, she lives in New York City.

Five Against One

One

The Pearl Jam Story

Kim Neely

Penguin Books

PENGUIN BOOKS
Published by the Penguin Group
Penguin Putnam Inc., 375 Hudson Street,
New York, New York 10014, U.S.A.
Penguin Books Ltd, 27 Wrights Lane,
London W8 5TZ, England
Penguin Books Australia Ltd, Ringwood,
Victoria, Australia
Penguin Books Canada Ltd, 10 Alcorn Avenue,
Toronto, Ontario, Canada M4V 3B2
Penguin Books (N.Z.) Ltd, 182–190 Wairau Road,
Auckland 10, New Zealand

Penguin Books Ltd, Registered Offices:
Harmondsworth, Middlesex, England

First published in Penguin Books 1998

1   3   5   7   9   10   8   6   4   2

LIBRARY OF CONGRESS CATALOGING IN PUBLICATION DATA
Neely, Kim.
Five against one: the Pearl Jam story/Kim Neely.
p.   cm.
ISBN 0 14 02.7642 4 (pbk.)
1. Pearl Jam (musical group).   2. Rock groups—United
States—Biography.   I. Title.
ML421.P43N44   1998
782.42166'092'2—dc21
[B]   98–12196

Printed in the United States of America
Set in Melior
DESIGNED BY BETTY LEW

For my beautiful mom, Linda, whose strength and

generosity of spirit——and utterly sick and twisted sense of

humor——have always made her the brightest star in my sky . . .

and for my true love, Mark, who walked into my life just

after I began writing this book, got a glimpse of what

he was going to be in for, and stayed anyway.

Acknowledgments

For the significant roles they played in making this book a reality, my heartfelt thanks go out to the following individuals:

Mark "I'm Not Worried" Kelley, my fearless agent, devoted massive quantities of blood, sweat, and tears to this project. From the beginning, Mark cared about this story as much as I did, and throughout its passage into print—a process that was lengthier and more fraught with complications than either of us ever could have imagined—he remained a tireless advocate, a trusted advisor, and, above all else, a true friend. This book is as much his accomplishment as it is mine. (Special thank you's directly from Mark go out to Rita and Roger Kelley and Karen Reilly.)

David Stanford at Viking Penguin emerged as a knight in shining armor at a crucial point in the life of this book, and has proven himself to be a true writer's editor—not to mention a very cool guy—ever since. I'm very fortunate to have had someone like David in my corner.

Rolling Stone has provided me with pages to fill for nearly a decade, and I'm grateful to a number of current and former staffers for their advice and support, among them Bob Love, Mary MacDonald, Jodi Peckman, Fred Goodman, Karen Sioris, Barbara O'Dair, Bob Wallace, and Jann Wenner. I'd especially like to thank former *RS* music editor (and current Rock & Roll Hall of Fame curator) Jim Henke, under whose tutelage I did some of my best work at the magazine—and without whose insistence that I fly to Seattle to interview a new band called Pearl Jam in 1991. . . . Thanks, Jim.

My beloved kin—camps Neely, Martinez, Cunningham, and Abene—and the ultra-classy Mikal Gilmore, Henry Rollins, David Weber, Leslie Tucker, and Del James, dragged me kicking and screaming over the Great Wall of I-Can't-Do-This. Two of my most cherished family members assumed guardian angel duty before the book was finished. Paul "Fats" Barclay and Samson: R.I.P.

My thanks to Dave Abbruzzese and Sheri Fineman for their generosity, hospitality, and the weeks upon end they spent letting me plumb the depths of their memories. Alex Protzel sniffed out virtually every existing bootleg and fanzine in Jamdom. Richard Price and Associates in Salt Lake City, genealogists extraordinaire, embarked upon the Search for Great Grandma Pearl with astonishing zeal. Peter and Rose Mueller provided me with reams of documents and letters, hours of their time, and *carte blanche* with their family photo album, all of which were a godsend when it came to piecing together the puzzle of Eddie's early years. Chris Cuffaro, who was there in the beginning and looks back on those days with as much fondness as I do, not only broke rank to speak with me for the book, but let me say so. Thanks, Chris.

Dozens of writers in recent years have attempted to document the sprawling, confusing genesis of the Seattle scene, and many times as I inched my way through the Pearl Jam saga, I found myself referring to their work. I'd especially like to thank Clark Humphrey, whose meticulously detailed 1995 book, *Loser: the Real Seattle Music Story*, was an enormous help when it came to pinning down names, dates, and places in the pre-Grunge Northwest; Jo-Ann Greene, whose voluminous August 1993 thesis in *Goldmine*, "Intrigue and Incest: Pearl Jam and the Secret History of Seattle," was similarly valuable in helping me trace the gnarled, twisted branches of the Seattle family tree; and Michael Azerrad, who, with his profiles in *Rolling Stone* and his fine 1993 Nirvana biography, *Come As You Are*, provided a wealth of insight into the Aberdeen set. Jeff Gilbert, Richard T. White, Katherine Turman, Allan Jones, Steve Hochman, and Robert Hilburn have also done some wonderful reporting on Pearl Jam over the years. I'm grateful to all of these writers, whose stories on the band were a tremendous resource.

For always making me feel welcome during the time I've spent with them over the years in and out of Seattle, I'm indebted to Susan Silver, Chris Cornell, Kim Thayil, Ben Shepherd, Matt Cameron, D. C. Parmet, Randy and Lisa Biro, Cameron Crowe, Eric Johnson, Kelly and Peggy

Curtis, Beth Liebling, Tim "Skully" Quinlan, Keith Wismar, Lance Mercer, Ellyn Solis, and Michael Goldstone.

Finally, for their openness and generosity in the early days, and a body of work that has never failed to inspire me, my sincere thanks to Pearl Jam: Jeff Ament, Stone Gossard, Jack Irons, Mike McCready, and Eddie Vedder.

K.N.
January, 1998
New York City

Contents

Contents

PART FOUR: Around the Bend

Prelude
San Francisco, June 24, 1995

There was a sudden, awkward silence—*Did he say what I think he just said?*—and then came *that* sound, the low, buzzing hum that is the single most dread of every performer who has heard it even once: the sound made by fifty thousand people when they turn their attention away from the stage and start talking to their friends.

Stone and Jeff's eyes met ever so briefly, worry passing between them in the sort of mute, telepathic exchange that's second nature to two musicians who've worked together for a decade. Up until now, it had seemed as if they just might pull it off. Saturday had broken warm and sunny in San Francisco, not a single cloud marring the brilliant blue sky over Golden Gate Park. Fans had been lined up since six in the morning, and by eleven, Monkey Wrench Radio, the pirate station from which Eddie and a few pals had been broadcasting punk songs and commentary at recent Pearl Jam shows, had crackled to life from a white tent on Polo Field. The crowd had been good-natured and enthusiastic, even gracing opening act Bad Religion with a semirespectable mosh pit. Better yet, Neil Young had rumbled through the gates on his Harley a few hours ago, to enjoy the day and, more important, to sit in with Pearl Jam for a few songs from *Mirror Ball*, the album they'd just recorded together.

Eddie's status had been iffy this morning. Stuck with what appeared to be a nasty stomach flu (later it would be diagnosed as food poisoning, contracted from a room service tuna sandwich), he'd been in the emergency room at three A.M., and this afternoon when Young had arrived, there'd been Eddie, looking distinctly green, lying facedown on the floor of the band's dressing room. Still, by the time two o'clock rolled around and it was time for Pearl Jam to go on, Eddie had been convinced he'd make it through the set. It might not be the *best* show he ever did, but he ought to be able to manage *a* show, at least. Who wanted to disappoint a mob like this?

Certainly, Pearl Jam didn't. There was much more at stake today than the newspaper reviews tomorrow. This whole wretched excuse for a tour had been plagued by screwups from the beginning, and in the last couple of weeks, even some of the band's staunchest supporters had begun to question their loyalty. Faced with the thought of what might result from yet another cancellation, Eddie didn't even feel he *had* a choice, other than to give a shaky go-ahead.

He'd come through, too, once they were in front of the crowd, not holding anything back, refusing to wimp out on the planned set list even though the first segment was stacked with energy gobblers, among them "Last Exit," "Spin the Black Circle," "Go," and "Animal."

He made it through seven songs.

In the middle of the last—"Not for You," Eddie's scalding message to the press, industry types, and money men he felt should be excluded from the Pearl Jam experience—the adrenaline wore off. With that, the nausea that had been roiling inside the singer woke up again and issued a cranky ultimatum.

Eddie stepped to the microphone after the song, hands hovering near the waist of his gray T-shirt as if suspended by invisible marionette strings, a peculiar mannerism fans had grown accustomed to ages ago.

"If I could talk to y'all from my heart for a second . . ." he began.

He paused for a moment. People in the crowd down front were shuffling around, craning their necks and stretching onto tiptoe so as not to miss a second of what looked to be an unfolding drama.

"This has been like the worst twenty-four hours I've ever had," Eddie went on. "I got a real bad stomach flu last night at like three in the morning, and I went to the emergency room. . . . I'm just all fucked up. I think that might be it for me for a while. Lucky for you, Neil Young's here, so he's gonna take over for a bit. . . ."

For a second or two, there were scattered cheers, followed by hushed confusion and that low, awful murmuring, rising up from the crowd and gaining in intensity. Then, with dawning horror, the other members of Pearl Jam watched as their singer walked away from the microphone and quit the stage.

They stood there, blinking at each other. Time slowed to a crawl.

The crew was already scrambling, trying to get a handle on Eddie's condition—whether he just needed a breather, or whether this was *it*. Young had been passing the time on a tour bus out back, and he'd begun making his way toward the stage as soon as he heard Eddie's announcement. Still, by the time he'd made it up front and he and the band had formed some semblance of a game plan, twenty minutes had passed. For Pearl Jam, each of those twenty minutes felt like an hour.

Not that the situation was any less daunting for Young, who'd driven down from his ranch in the Santa Cruz Mountains expecting to make a relaxed guest appearance and now found himself responsible for the happiness of fifty thousand fans—not to mention fifty thousand *angry* fans, people who'd waited for two years to see their favorite band and who'd jumped through all sorts of hoops to obtain tickets, people who were so starved for a dose of live Pearl Jam that some of them had even coughed up airfare and planned entire vacations around this show. They'd gone to all this trouble to see Pearl Jam, and Pearl Jam wasn't Pearl Jam without *Eddie*. Who cared about this Neil Young character, this tired, tie-dyed relic from their parents' dippy hippie memories?

Young had his work cut out for him, although you'd never have known it from the easy self-assurance with which he took the stage.

"How ya doin'?" Neil asked, looking out at the sea of faces before him, checking the crowd's pulse. From the sound of things, these were not happy campers.

"Let's just rock a little bit," he suggested, the voice of calm, turning to the remaining members of Pearl Jam and attacking his black Les Paul, banging out the first choppy, serrated chords of "Big Green Country" from *Mirror Ball*. If the decision to begin with this particular song, with its opening lyric about a pack of wolves who want their money back, was a thinly veiled jab at the whinier members of the audience, nobody picked up on it. The energy that had dissipated so quickly with Eddie's departure began to return almost immediately, and before long, flailing arms and legs—surely a blessed sight to Neil and the band—were visible in the pit at the front of the stage again.

Moving in typical herky-jerky style, slashing his fingers down across the strings, face scrunched up with emotion, Young led the band through the majority of the *Mirror Ball* songs they'd recorded together and a clutch of his older favorites, including "Powderfinger," "Cortez the Killer," a fat twenty-minute jam on "Down by the River," and two different versions of "Rockin' in the Free World," a tune covered so often and so well by Pearl Jam over the years that some younger fans likely think theirs is the original version. By the time the festivities chugged to a halt just before five o'clock, they'd also ripped through "Hey Hey, My My" and taken things down a notch with the plaintive *Harvest* classic, "Needle and the Damage Done."

A few writers would later opine that this impromptu two-hour set was the finest they'd ever seen Neil Young play. To be sure, it was a powerhouse performance, and one that at least some in the audience appreciated.

For others, though, it just wasn't enough.

Throughout the show, the members of Pearl Jam had occasionally cast glances toward the wings, as if they weren't sure whether Eddie would reappear. Eventually, they learned that the singer had gone to the hospital in an ambulance not long after he left the stage.

The fans, though they'd been sated enough by the sterling "Neil Jam" performance to hold their tempers in check, hadn't entirely given up on Eddie, either. And when Jeff approached the microphone to announce that Eddie wasn't coming back, things got nasty. No matter Jeff's apology, no matter his promise that the band would try to return to San Francisco and play another show at the end of the tour. When the crowd realized that they'd seen all of Eddie they were going to see that day, the full weight of their disappointment, in the form of a fusillade of loud boos, came crashing down on Jeff.

"Eddie *Cheddar*!" someone on the field hollered. A volley of exasperated catcalls—"Refund!" and "Fuck *you*!" and "Rip-off!"—cut through a lower-level drone of disgruntled muttering that was beginning to rise from the field like steam.

The bassist took a step back, crestfallen.

Jerry Pompili of Bill Graham Presents, who was emceeing the show, moved to the microphone. "This band has spent the last year and a half trying to do right by you," he yelled. "You owe them a thank you, and I want to hear it right now!"

Not exactly the best choice when it comes to soothing the savage beast. The requested show of gratitude, not surprisingly, failed to materialize. Although the more die-hard fans present would later argue in defense of Pearl Jam, the majority who straggled out of Golden Gate Park were less forgiving about having been the victims of a rock & roll bait and switch.

As for Pearl Jam, the fact that they'd faced down a potentially disastrous situation and managed to emerge without a riot on their hands must have seemed a hollow victory at best. This was a band that had always waved an egalitarian flag, always taken pride in putting its fans first. In fact, no stronger reflection of that ethic could be found than this tour itself, organized in alternative venues as a means of sidestepping Ticketmaster and, as a result, keeping concert tickets below the typical asking price. That it was all failing so miserably had to be a heavy blow.

It's not hard to imagine how the members of Pearl Jam felt if they heard the vituperative commentary that peppered the radio airwaves following the concert—fans calling stations to spew I-want-my-money-back diatribes, deejays speculating that Eddie had been drunk as a lord the night before the show and that his "flu" was, in fact, a bad hangover. True, for the last few years, the band—and especially Eddie—had been attempting to turn down the intensity of their fans' worship, to get their audience to relate to them as *people*, not icons. At the same time, though, their intention had been to step off the pedestal *themselves*, not to be knocked off by a roundhouse punch, tossed into the "Down" elevator by the very people who'd pushed the penthouse button on them four years ago.

All of the adulation may have been disquieting at times, but to glimpse the other side of the coin was even more frightening. Just a few months ago, Pearl Jam had been David to Ticketmaster's Goliath, lauded for their efforts on behalf of the little people, blessed with a legion of fans whose appreciation and affection was so ardent that it had sometimes bordered on suffocating.

Now, though, something had shifted. It had been almost indiscernible at first—a snide comment in some late-night comedian's monologue, the occasional catty op-ed piece in the paper—but, in the last few weeks especially, it seemed as if they'd been standing under a gargantuan microscope, squirming under the watchful eye of a public that was inspecting their every move for some fault or imagined slight. The pressure was unbearable.

All they'd ever wanted was to play the music they loved and have people embrace it. And they'd realized that dream, more so than any of them had ever imagined—to the extent that it remained lodged in their grasp even when it began to feel more like a curse and they tried to pry it from their fingers. For four years, they'd seemed incapable of a single misstep; now they were walking on a minefield.

How on earth had it all come to this?

Part One

※◎◎◇非

Come on Down

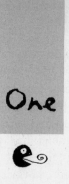

One

Corporate Rock Sucks / Early Days in Seattle: Punks on Parade /
Green River / What, Are They Kidding?

Punk rock was dead in America, or so they said.

Some claimed the last gasp came in 1977, when upscale New York department stores like Saks Fifth Avenue and Bonwit Teller began selling gold-plated safety pins at $100 a pop, and British designer Zandra Rhondes whipped up a collection of ripped, safety-pinned evening gowns—asking price, $1,150 each—for Bloomingdales. Others held out until *Mademoiselle* magazine did a four-page spread on punk fashion, and pop princess Linda Rondstadt got all gussied up with spiked hair for the cover of her *Mad Love* album. No matter when exactly it was that the coroner supposedly arrived, by the end of the Seventies a general consensus had been reached among the mainstream cognoscenti: Punk rock was over.

Americans may have embraced punk fashion, but when it came to the music—such a far cry from the insipid, bloated arena rock prevalent in the Seventies—most of them just hadn't been ready for it. So wide was the gulf between those who "got" punk and those who didn't that the major labels who'd taken a chance and signed groups like the Sex

Pistols and the Ramones had no idea how to sell them to the public. Rather than make any real effort to get the music heard, their solution was simply to cut their losses.

They never counted on the aftershocks. The first wave of punk—from hardcore progenitors like the MC5 and the Stooges and the glitter/glam New York Dolls, to the mid-Seventies CBGB contingent led by Television, the Dead Boys, and the Ramones, to the Sex Pistols and their British successors the Damned and Generation X—was deemed a commercial failure by the mainstream industry before many teenage rock fans in the United States even got to *hear* it. Actual, vinyl proof of what had come roaring and spitting out of New York and Britain wouldn't filter down to fans in smaller U.S. towns until a few years later, about the time MTV was looming on the horizon to peddle the Go-Go's as a fluffy pop "girl" group. In their haste to stage a funeral and move on to the next money-making trend, the industry had also overlooked punk's most powerful, populist element: It was easy to *play.* So it was that, even as the mainstream tastemakers were tying on punk's toe tag, the first stirrings of a response to the New York and British wave were already being heard on the West Coast. By the end of the Seventies, trailblazing bands like Black Flag, X, and the Dead Kennedys, who put an angrier, darker spin on punk, had formed and were making records, and before long other bands had cropped up in their wake in cities across the United States, among them the Minutemen, the Circle Jerks, Fear, and Flipper from California; Hüsker Dü and the Replacements from Minneapolis; and Minor Threat from Washington, D.C.

Not that any of these bands were welcomed into the fold with open arms. Ignored by the mainstream music industry, by the media, by radio, and by the majority of rock club proprietors, the early torchbearers were forced to rely on nontraditional means of recording, distribution, and promotion. They formed their own labels and sold their records via mail order, spread the word via homemade fanzines, and painstakingly built their followings with incessant touring, mapping out routes that hit the small-town clubs that would have them, and sharing the names of hospitable club owners with their friends in other bands. Within a few years, they'd created their own infrastructure and were nurturing small pockets of fans across the country, many of whom would go on to start *their* own bands.

One such fan, as fate would have it, was twenty-year-old Jeff Ament. The strapping, contemplative son of a barber, Jeff had grown up in a town called Big Sandy—population 740—a mere speck on the map not far from his birthplace of Havre, Montana. During his early years, Jeff's exposure to music was rather limited. There were the dreaded piano lessons foisted upon him by his mom—to add insult to injury, he had to pay for them by mowing his teacher's lawn—and there was church music: The Aments were strict Catholics, and Jeff served as an altar boy. But when it came to rock & roll, Big Sandy's offerings were paltry. The town didn't even boast a single record store, and for years Jeff subsisted on radio and on hand-me-down singles given him by his uncle, Pat.

"He gave me 'Help,' with 'I'm Down' on the other side, which I thought was an amazing song, and also 'Proud Mary,'" Jeff recalled. "I thought Uncle Pat was one of the coolest people in the universe—he had long hair and sideburns, and his room had candles all over the place and Santana posters on the walls. I probably got as excited about hanging out with my uncle as I did about anything."

In the eighth grade, having discovered Kiss, Jeff bought a guitar and began taking lessons. He liked the way he looked when he practiced his Gene Simmons moves in front of the mirror—his guitar, a cheap SG copy, even looked like Simmons's bass—but wringing a respectable noise out of the instrument was another matter entirely. Like so many other children of Seventies album-oriented radio, Jeff had a special place in his heart for riff-rockers—Aerosmith, Led Zeppelin, Black Sabbath, Ted Nugent, and the aforementioned Kiss. He'd also been seduced by the new wave of British heavy metal, bands like Venom and Iron Maiden. These were the bands he wanted to sound like when he strapped on his guitar, but try as he might, nothing he played came close to the majestic *kraaaaaaang* he was aiming for. Unfamiliar with tricks of the trade like distortion boxes and barre chords, all Jeff could manage was a miserly *plink-plink-plink.* This was most unsatisfactory.

After a few months, he abandoned the guitar lessons and focused his ambition on basketball, one of his other loves. An avid fan and accomplished player, Jeff had been the starting point guard for his All-State team at Big Sandy High School, and when he enrolled at the University of Montana in Missoula to study art, he planned to play for that school as well. A month after he moved to Missoula, though, athletics once again took a backseat to his interest in music. He'd found a few basketball-playing, skateboarding, music-loving kindred spirits—among them a guitarist and Circle Jerks fan named Bruce Fairweather—and begun to explore the emerging music underground, collecting records and poring over fanzines. Meanwhile, Jon Donahue, a friend in his dorm who played bass, had invited Jeff to jam. Before long, the two had switched instruments.

"Jon knew barre chords and could play a couple of things on guitar," Jeff remembered, "so we'd spend weekend nights drinking beer, plugged into the same amp, playing Ramones and Clash songs. Later on we went to see a local pop-punk show, and we decided to wear makeup and boots and everything. The crowd in Missoula was all hippies, so they were freaking out about us. After the band finished their set, we asked if we could borrow their drummer and play. We played the Ramones' 'Blitzkrieg Bop' and 'Pinhead,' and also a 999 song called 'Homicide.' Afterwards, the leader from the other band said that if we found a drummer, we could open up for them next time." Hence the shaky genesis of Deranged Diction, whose lineup had shifted by 1982 to feature Jeff on bass, Fairweather on guitar, drummer Sergio Avenia, and vocalist Tom Kipp.

Missoula, despite being a college town, offered pretty slim pickings when it came to gigs for an outfit like Deranged Diction. Most of the bands in town played Top Forty fare, but Jeff and his friends had pooled their influences and were spewing out Dead Kennedys, Circle Jerks, and Flipper covers. Still, they developed a respectable following, thinning out the cover versions in their set and adding more originals as time went on, even recording a half-live, half-studio cassette, *No Art, No Cowboys, No Rules,* that featured titles like "Aspirin," "Kill or Be Killed," "Kokaine," "Pruning," and "I'm an American." In a move he would repeat throughout his career, Jeff hand-designed the cover of the obscure cassette, which the band self-released in a limited edition of 100 copies.

It was a start anyway. But if you're seriously pondering a career in music—which, by this time, Jeff was—Missoula wouldn't exactly be your first choice as a launching pad. On top of that, college was a disappointment. Jeff hated the pervasive frat mentality, and he was equally disillusioned by his art classes, viewing the by-the-book approach of his teachers as a hindrance to his creative imagination. Before long, Jeff had decided to drop out, and he and the other members of Deranged Diction were weighing their options. If they were going to get anywhere with this band, they needed to relocate. Seattle, a hop across Idaho to the west, seemed the closest logical destination. It was a college town that was open to new music, larger and more vital than Missoula, but not so busy that it would be overrun with ambitious bands all fighting for club dates, like New York or Los Angeles. Tom Kipp opted to stay behind, but

Fairweather, Avenia, and Ament were game. In June 1983, they packed up and headed for Washington.

"We moved out because we thought we would actually make it with that band," Fairweather would later remember. "That was kind of ridiculous, but we were really kind of young then."

X◇X

What the trio found when they arrived in Seattle, much to their chagrin, was hardly the new music mecca they'd imagined. There *was* new music being made, but you had to know where to look in order to find it, and the members of Deranged Diction likely spent their first few months in the Pacific Northwest wishing they'd chosen a different destination. The visibility of Seattle's music community, they would learn, seemed to rise or fall in proportion with the level of tolerance displayed by local law enforcement, and when Deranged Diction first set foot on Washington soil, at the tail end of a freak late Seventies, early Eighties punk and new wave boom, patience for young hooligans with guitars was at a low ebb.

In the Sixties, Seattle had been a hotbed of hippie activity, home to a number of psychedelic ballrooms and dozens of biker taverns, and a major tour stop for Woodstock-era musicians, among them Seattle native Jimi Hendrix, who left in 1964 to tour with the Isley Brothers and returned a star in 1968. Outdoor rock festivals were common as well; the most famous of these, held a week after Woodstock, was the 1969 Seattle Pop Festival, which drew fifty thousand fans to hear acts like the Doors, Led Zeppelin, Ike and Tina Turner, Alice Cooper, and Ten Years After.

In 1969, though, with the swearing in of a new mayor who had his heart set on revamping Seattle into a placid baby boomer wonderland, things began to bode ill for the city's rock & rollers. One of Wes Uhlman's first acts as mayor was a vigorous clampdown on Seattle's bar scene. Prior to his whip-cracking influence, officials had tended to look the other way when it came to enforcing the liquor laws; underage drinking and clubs that served alcohol past the legal two A.M. cutoff point weren't considered a major crisis. Under Uhlman, all of that changed. The local liquor statutes were adhered to with religious fervor, and club owners often found themselves hassled by the police or the fire department. Uhlman's successors would carry his no-fun-for-kids torch well into the Eighties, with local laws like the odious Teen Dance Ordinance, a 1985 edict that imposed such excessive insurance and security requirements on all-ages dance events that they became cost prohibitive for many of the city's financially strapped promoters and club owners.

Fewer and fewer nightclubs booked original rock bands, fearing that they'd be raided. The clubs that did book live music usually opted for the inevitable Top Forty cover band approach. By 1977, tired of trying to convince the few club owners in town to book their bands—and raring to kick out the jams, thanks to a recent show by the Ramones, the first (and last) punk band ever to appear in the Georgian Room of the Olympic Hotel—the local teenagers had devised a way to sidestep the oppressive laws. In yet another twist on the DIY ethic, they began renting out halls and organizing their own shows. A string of punk and new wave groups started the trend, and a tiny, tight-knit scene began to revolve around impromptu shows staged in basements and rented party spaces. These self-promoted one-off gigs, advertised by photocopied flyers and word-of-mouth, were for a few years virtually the only means by which young, original bands could reach a live audience in Seattle, unless they happened to luck out and land a job as opening act for one of the touring bands that came through town to play the Paramount.

At least a few sympathetic entrepreneurs recognized the need for regular all-ages venues to showcase original music and set out to fill the void. Jim Lightfoot, the owner of Time Traveler Records on Second Avenue, rented out the Showbox Theater, an old ballroom on First Avenue next to the International Donut House that was currently being used as a bingo hall, and began staging weekly concerts there. After the Showbox began booking national bands—Iggy Pop, the Police, the Ramones, the Cramps, Gang of Four, Squeeze, the Dead Kennedys, Psychedelic Furs, Devo, and Black Flag would all perform there in the next year and a half, usually paired on bills with local favorites like the Blackouts and the Beakers—other Seattle restaurateurs and club owners tentatively began opening their doors to original local bands. The Gorilla Room, set up in the back room of a Chinese restaurant near Pioneer Square, began booking all-ages shows in March 1980. WREX, hastily converted from a gay bar, offered its stage to local bands two or three nights a week beginning in April of the same year.

Meanwhile, local radio had picked up the ball. KAOS, the student-run station at Evergreen State College in Olympia, had been pretty much the lone indie music station in the area since 1976, but in November 1979, KZAM, a Bellevue station, began transmitting a three-hour Monday night show called "Music for Moderns," often giving airtime to tapes and self-recorded 45s submitted by local bands. In 1980, KCMU, the low-power University of Washington station, followed suit, deviating from its usual soft-rock format with nightly new music shows.

Seattle's music-loving writers began setting pen to paper to chronicle the action. *The Rocket*, at first derided as too mainstream by the local punks but in later years recognized as the city's preeminent alternative paper, began life in October 1979 as a monthly music pullout in the *Seattle Sun*. Stacks of regional fanzines, some crudely reproduced, some more slickly designed, proliferated in punk-friendly record stores. *Stelazine, Boy, Strictly Confidential, Twisted, Op* (later to become *Option*), and *Punk Lust* were among dozens of publications championing Seattle indie bands. And then there were *Subterranean Pop*, first put out in 1979 by Evergreen student and KAOS deejay Bruce Pavitt.

Pavitt, one of the prime catalysts for what would happen in Seattle in later years, was an interesting character. He'd grown up in Park Forest, Illinois, an upper-middle-class suburb of Chicago, and attended a progressive high school called the Active Learning Process Center. (Among Pavitt's acquaintances in Park Forest were Kim Thayil and Hiro Yamamoto, who would eventually follow him to Seattle and wind up in Soundgarden, and Tom Zutaut, who would go on to an A&R career and sign Guns n' Roses to Geffen Records.)

Once he was at Evergreen, Pavitt began championing the American independent underground with a vengeance. *Subterranean Pop*, the first cover of which was decorated with crayon, started as project for class credit and was devoted entirely to indie bands. A self-professed regional culture junkie, Pavitt put more emphasis on artists outside major industry centers like New York and Los Angeles. His goal from the beginning, as he put it, was to "decentralize" pop culture.

"People today don't realize how stark the situation really was in regards to media attention," Pavitt said in 1992. "I thought, in my own small way, if I started reviewing some of these records, then something would start to kick in."

By the time he put out his third issue, Pavitt had abbreviated the name of the zine to *Sub Pop* and enlisted sometime-contributor Calvin Johnson, a fellow KAOS deejay who would go on to form the minimalist pop trio Beat Happening and head up the band's influential home, Olympia's K Records. Two issues later, with *Sub Pop 5*, Pavitt began alternating the print format of the zine with an audio format, issuing cassette compilations culled from demo tapes sent to him by indie bands across the country. He also cut quite a dapper figure at gigs.

"He would show up wearing a black jumpsuit with fluorescent traffic-guard stripes, and stand in front of the band with his hand in the air like a Nazi salute, with no expression on his face," one observer recalled. "Then all of a sudden he would start gyrating to the music. When the song ended, Bruce would stop and salute again."

Between 1979 and mid-1981, new bands—like Solger, X-15, the Fastbacks, the Fartz, the U-Men, Maggot Brains, and the Silly Killers—were forming all the time; at one point, there were forty or fifty bands playing around Seattle, each putting their own unique stamp on the punk-new wave-hardcore theme. And for the first time in over a decade, there seemed to be enough willing venues in town to support all of them. It was inevitable, with so many kids having so much in-your-face fun, that the local save-the-children forces would start paying closer attention.

At first, aside from the odd penchant that testosterone-and-beer-fueled punkers seemed to have for ripping restroom sinks off the walls, or the occasional display of really bad taste—like the night when the Refuzors' Mike Lambert hurled a dead cat into the crowd at Danceland USA to punctuate the band's song, "Splat Goes the Cat"—there hadn't been anything taking place at shows that was tangible enough for the authorities to latch on to. But gradually, as more and more teens got turned on to the Los Angeles hardcore bands and misinterpreted the music as a soundtrack for head busting, the scene got rougher and more and more shows became the setting for brawls. Though the band abhorred violence, shows by the Fartz—featuring future Guns n' Roses bassist Duff McKagan, who is jokingly said to have played at one time or another in every band ever to have come out of Seattle—became a constant target for such trouble. One memorable evening culminated in the Gorilla Room's being turned upside down by a chain-wielding Vancouver hardcore gang.

Friction was also arising more and more often from a long-simmering hatred between the Seattle punks and the "donut kids," a rough-and-tumble crew of runaway street kids, prostitutes, and drug dealers who hung out at the International Donut House. Soundgarden bassist Ben Shepherd, who was about twelve years old at the time, still remembers a run-in he and his siblings had with a group of Donut Kids before a Dead Kennedys/Hüsker Dü/Fartz gig at the Showbox.

"There were four guys, and every one of 'em had a knife," Shepherd said in 1994. "We started walking toward the Showbox, and all of a sudden they grabbed my sister and put a knife up to her throat. My brother talked 'em out of it. Then we were waiting in line to get into the show and they started coming back. I was just instantly hating society. We were getting all this shit because they thought we were punk rockers, just because we listened to this music."

Like Shepherd, many of those who went to the early punk shows were irritated by the trendy violence that had infiltrated the scene. They viewed it mostly as a necessary evil that accompanied the real draw: the *music*. The media, though—not just in Seattle, but everywhere that punk had taken root—had already begun playing up any skirmish as if violence were the main attraction, guaranteed to break out at every show. Their target audience was comprised of boomer parents, who'd spent the Sixties and Seventies getting their ya-yas out and were now paying for it with a whopping divorce epidemic. Single-parent households had become twice as common, and even in those families that had managed to stay together, both adults were usually working. With so many parents preoccupied with their careers, unable to supervise their kids as closely as they would have liked, any variation on the Teens-On-The-Rampage theme made for hopping ratings, playing right into every parent's deepest fears.

By 1981, even as Seattle's zine writers were condemning violent incidents at shows and urging their unrulier peers to shape up, the mainstream media were trumpeting out hysterical reports on the Growing Punk Threat. The dreaded Killjoy Kops began turning up at shows again, and the tiny freedoms the local teens had been racking up began falling like dominos. The Gorilla Room was shut down by the Liquor Board in September; WREX bit the dirt five months later, closing its doors in February 1982. Oldies and mainstream hard rock began to squeeze out local bands on the airwaves, and club proprietors returned to their old reluctance to book original bands. Scared off by the threat of violence, even the once-friendly rental hall owners began balking when it came to booking punk bands. Some of the bands resorted to desperate measures to get gigs. The Fartz, in an attempt to ditch their reputation for attracting a rowdy element, changed their name to 10 Minute Warning after a lineup shift. Other local bands gave up on Seattle altogether, fleeing to more youth-tolerant cities.

This was the rather forbidding environment that greeted Jeff Ament and his Deranged Diction cohorts when they arrived in Seattle in 1983, hoping to take the world by storm.

XOX

Jeff took a low-paying job pulling shots of espresso and began sniffing around in search of musically like-minded people. There weren't many of them.

"The scene at the time wasn't anywhere near what it's perceived as," Soundgarden frontman Chris Cornell recalled in 1994. "There were as many effeminate, almost European-influenced bands as there were bands with broken guitars with Kiss stickers on them."

Most of the latter hung around a knot of Pioneer Square venues that hadn't yet been targeted by the authorities—the Gray Door, the all-ages Metropolis (booked at the time by future Soundgarden manager Susan Silver), and the Central Tavern, which primarily offered jazz and R&B but had just begun testing the water with underground rock bands. There were also a few local art galleries—like Ground Zero and Graven Image—that had begun showcasing music. When all else failed, there were always the lifesaving basements and garages, and makeshift all-ages venues like Munro's Dance Palace, a ballroom dance studio where Deranged Diction played one of their earliest gigs.

Diction's sound morphed from straight hardcore into something more like *Paranoid*-era Black Sabbath soon after they arrived in Seattle, and opinion on the band was mixed. Some of the stauncher punk loyalists took delight in ribbing Jeff—who'd grown his hair long and sometimes appeared onstage in eyeliner and a kilt—for his traitorous metal leanings. Among those hurling barbs were the Melvins, a trio from the lumber town of Montesano who would later be credited with infecting Seattle with dirge fever.

"Jeff was a *Venom* fan," the Melvins' drummer, Dale Crover, snickered in 1993. "We used to make fun of him."

Still, Diction piqued the interest of at least three locals: Mark Arm, Steve Turner, and Alex Vincent, whose own bands—Mr. Epp and the Calculations, the Limp Richards, and Spluii Numa—also played on the Pioneer Square circuit.

Mr. Epp, which featured both Turner and Arm on guitar and has been described by Arm as "the worst band in Seattle," nonetheless had the distinction of having made a few records, most notably a 7-inch EP called *Of Course I'm Happy, Why?*, released in 1982 on the Pravda label. The Richards, also featuring Arm, were a jokier outfit led by Dave Middleton, a fellow immortalized by Arm as "the spazziest, freaked out lead singer you could imagine." (Turner joined Arm in the Limp Richards for a few rehearsals, but the band split up before he got a chance to perform with them.) Spluii Numa, the short-lived melodic punk band for which Vincent was drumming, is remembered fondly by many who were around at the time, although the ever-blunt Arm viewed Spluii Numa as a cheap Social Distortion rip-off.

All three bands had petered out by 1984, and Arm, Turner, and Vincent were looking to put together something new. When it came time to recruit a bassist, they began pursuing Jeff Ament. Initially, Jeff shunned their advances, telling Turner quite plainly that he thought Mr. Epp stank. But when Deranged Diction fizzled out in June of '84, Arm and Turner's hounding seemed more welcome, and Jeff finally agreed. After a few basement sessions, the foursome decided to make it official. At Turner's suggestion, they named themselves after a serial killer whose prostitute victims had been turning up on the bank of a nearby river, and the seminal Green River was born.

XØX

Green River had only played a few shows, the first of which saw them serving as opening act for art-rockers Positive Mental Attitude at a private Capitol Hill party, before Arm gave up playing guitar in the band so he could polish up his more crucial role as vocalist and frontman. Reluctant to forfeit their meaty twin-guitar attack, Green River decided to start scouting for a replacement. Conveniently, Turner and Vincent happened to know just the man for the job.

The two had first met Stone Gossard at Northwestern School of the Arts, a tony Capitol Hill private school whose corridors, teachers like to boast, were the real birthplace of grunge. (Headmistress Ellen Taussig, who kept an acoustic guitar in her office for the students' use, would in later years be the proud recipient of one gold and two platinum album awards for Pearl Jam's debut album, *Ten*, courtesy of grateful alumnus Stone.)

Stone (his given name) tended to have a wise-ass sense of humor, but he'd always been a good-natured kid. His father a prominent Seattle attorney and his mother employed by the city government, he'd had a decidedly comfortable, upper-middle-class upbringing, unmarred by divorce or any of the usual unpleasantness. Fond of school, he was quick to make friends. The only real bane of Stone's childhood appears to have been a stuffed chimpanzee with cracked plastic eyes and missing fingers that's on display as part of an exhibit at Seattle's Pacific Science Center. The monkey is accompanied by a card bearing the legend PEOPLE TELL ME I WAS AFRAID OF THIS.

Although in later years Stone would become a rabid fan of rap, Seventies funk, and the Stax R&B and soul bands—and studies in music theory, jazz, and chorus at Northwestern exposed him to a healthy dose of more traditional fare—he was more interested at the time in mastering the canon of the same Seventies hard-rockers that Jeff loved.

"When I met Stoney, he liked commercial hard rock," Steve Turner later remembered. "He was a metal dude and I was a punk dude. He'd play me early Alice Cooper and Mötörhead records, and I'd play him Black Flag. He also got into Southern California punk bands like Bad Religion and Social Distortion."

Inevitably, Kiss was in the mix, too. Gossard was such a huge Kiss fan that at one point he tried to make Kiss shoes for himself, nailing two-by-fours to a pair of thin-soled Capezios. Bob Whittaker, Mudhoney's manager and the gatekeeper of this little snippet of history, has said that he doesn't recall whether Stone ever got up the nerve to wear the things in public.

During their senior year at Northwestern, Turner and Gossard, along with a classmate named Jeff Covell, had formed a band called the Ducky Boys, but the band had never made it out of the basement, only lasting six months or so. After the Duckys had called it quits and Turner moved on to join Arm in Mr. Epp, Ben Shepherd had invited Stone to join *his* band, an abrasive speedcore outfit called March of Crimes.

Stone joined eagerly. Not only were the guys in March of Crimes keeping company with the much-admired Melvins, they were gigging regularly. "We played a lot of shows at the Metropolis," Shepherd recalled. "And we played the very first show at Gorilla Gardens, where Soundgarden played their second show ever. That was like the place where all the out of town bands would play all-ages shows. A total rip-off joint."

Stone's stint in March of Crimes lasted about a nanosecond. Although he and Shepherd got along fine, he clashed with the other band members ("I was trying to have my second-rate Van Halen licks involved," Stone said later), and they fired him the first chance they got. A man without a band, he was pondering his next move when Turner and Vincent approached him about joining Green River. Stone accepted—no doubt gratefully—and, their lineup complete, Green River got down to business.

The band's first show with Stone took place at the Gray Door, a sleazy unlicensed basement club that was notorious for open drug use and lousy plumbing—the lone Porta Potti that sufficed as a restroom was never emptied. A few months later, in October 1984, Green River landed a much more prestigious gig, opening for the Dead Kennedys at the Moore Theater. Some went home that evening impressed, but others in attendance took one look at Jeff's flashy New York Dolls getup—the abundant scarves, the big hair, and all that makeup—and let fly with a hail of ice and popcorn, tossing in an occasional shoe for good measure.

"There were a lot of rules that bands had to conform to as far as tempo and attitude and how they looked," Bruce Pavitt would later recall. "Green River was looser, probably a little more sexual, more rooted in the Stooges than a lot of political dogma. It went against the grain of what was happening at the time, and they stood out because of that."

One individual who took notice was Gerard Cosloy, who'd created the widely circulated fanzine *Conflict* and was now running Homestead Records, the independent New York label that also recorded the U-Men. Cosloy arranged for Green River to make their first record, *Come On Down*. Two months after the Moore Theater show, together with producer Chris Hanzsek, they went into Crow Studios and recorded the half-dozen songs that would appear on the EP.

In later years, after a number of Seattle artists had risen to fame and Green River began receiving credit as one of the scene's pioneering bands, superlatives about *Come On Down* would come spewing out of word processors at an alarming rate, some writers pressing the notion that the album was a thing of brilliance, the Holy Grail of Grunge. In truth, *Come On Down* was remarkable only as a harbinger of things to come. The album captured Green River in the period just *before* the band's sound melded into the cohesive punk and metal marriage they would later be lauded for, and as a result seems more like a song-by-song pissing match between Stone, Jeff, and Alex Vincent, with their headbanging tendencies, and the Arm-Turner contingent, who favored hardcore. Tracks like "Ride of Your Life" are crisscrossed with the scars of Jeff's high school Iron Maiden fixation, while the EP's one caterwauling stroke of brilliance, the Turner-penned "Swallow My Pride," harks back to classic Iggy and the Stooges, Arm doing his sneering best to pay tribute to the World's Forgotten Boy.

Because of scheduling problems at Homestead, *Come On Down* wouldn't be released until late 1985. Turner—a fan of Sixties garage-rock acts who is said to have been disgusted by the metal elements that were threatening to overtake Green River—would no longer be in the band when the EP finally emerged. He quit in August 1985 to attend Western Washington University and was quickly replaced by Jeff's old Deranged Diction band mate, Bruce Fairweather. As it turned out, while Turner was away at school he also missed out on the moment when a number of other bands in the Seattle community decided that Green River were onto something and that it was acceptable to embrace the Seventies hard rock they'd all grown up on.

As recently as 1981, Seattle's punk and metal camps had been split down the middle. "I realize how difficult this is to believe, but I swear it's true," local critic Dawn Anderson wrote in her music paper, *Backlash.* "Heavy metal and punk were thought to have nothing to do with each other at all."

By the time Turner left for college, though, Green River wasn't the only band gigging around Seattle that was infusing punk with hard rock. The Melvins were still around, and, inspired by bands like San Francisco's Flipper, they were experimenting with a mutated version of hardcore, the tempo stopped down to a low, throbbing drone that seemed to ooze out of the amps. Soundgarden had just sprung from the ashes of a goofy, short-lived cover band called the Shemps. Skin Yard, formed in early 1985, was a virtual cornucopia of later Seattle notables, teaming bassist and future C/Z Records owner Daniel House with drummer Matt Cameron (later to join Soundgarden), vocalist Ben McMillan (later of Gruntruck), and guitarist Mike Giacondino, a.k.a. Jack Endino, who would go on to produce most of the records—among them the debut albums of Soundgarden, Mudhoney, and Nirvana—that later put the Sub Pop label on the map. All of these bands had distinctly different sounds, but they were the first to confound local audiences with the dark blend of hard rock and hardcore that caused a major shift in the community.

"It was really bizarre," Dawn Anderson later recalled of an early Gorilla Gardens show that paired Soundgarden and the Melvins with headliner Hüsker Dü. "Everybody was staring at them, going, 'What, are they kidding?' They were playing this wild, really heavy, dense music, and everybody was just staring at them going, 'Duh.'"

Green River, Soundgarden, Skin Yard, and the Melvins weren't the only groups stumping the locals. Hailing from a suburb half an hour from Seattle by ferry was Malfunkshun, led by an incredibly gifted young man named Andrew Wood, who would in the span of a few years change Stone and Jeff's lives irrevocably and who had been industriously executing his own plan for total world domination.

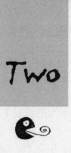

Two

Landrew the Love Child / *Deep Six*
and Sub Pop / Green River Dries Up

About nine miles west of Seattle, within the Puget Sound Basin and just east of the Kitsap Peninsula, is Bainbridge Island, a quiet harbor city that spans three and a half miles at its widest point. A busy logging and shipbuilding center in the late nineteenth century, Bainbridge is a high-rent suburb today, its main thoroughfare carved through heavy forest of fir, maple, and alder. The island has little to offer for thrill seekers, but its popularity with cyclists and nature lovers, along with its fortuitous location—just across the Agate Pass Bridge from the burial site of Chief Sealth, the Suquamish and Duquamish tribal leader who was Seattle's namesake—usually earns it at least a few lines in the travel guides.

In some circles, though, Bainbridge Island's biggest claim to fame will always be that it unleashed Landrew the Love Child upon the world.

By the late Seventies. when Air Force officer David Wood and his wife, Toni, settled their family on Bainbridge, their youngest son, Andrew, had seen more of the world than most boys his age. He had also, by most accounts, already come to the conclusion that it was his to conquer. Andy had always been an outgoing child—a trait that served him well, given the sink-or-swim nature of grade school friendships and the military transfers that had taken the Wood family from his birthplace of Columbus, Mississippi, to Washington, D.C., to Maine, and then to Germany before they moved to Bainbridge. He loved being the center of attention.

When the elder Wood served in Vietnam, one of the "talking" letters on cassette that his boys mailed him featured a song written and sung by a three-year-old Andy. When Andy was ten, he began proclaiming that he was going to be a deejay; his father remembers him carting around a microphone that transmitted through a radio, pestering his siblings for interviews. It was in 1977, though, at the age of eleven, that Andy settled on the showbiz goal he would pursue for the rest of his life. According to legend, the epiphany took place at a Kiss concert at the Seattle Coliseum. Just after opening act Cheap Trick left the stage, Andy turned to his older brother Kevin and said matter-of-factly, "I want to be a rock star."

Four years later, in 1981, he skipped out on his family's Easter dinner and got started.

Malfunkshun—Andrew on vocals, Kevin on guitar, bassist Dave Reese and drummer David Hunt—sprang from that first rehearsal, but they only managed to put on one show, at a party, before Reese and Hunt quit to join another band. Andrew assumed the departed Reese's bass chores, and he and Kevin pressed on, swiping drummer Regan Hagar from Maggot Brains to replace the departed Hunt. Malfunkshun was soon ready to roll again, and by August they'd landed their first real gig, at Bainbridge Island's Blackberry Jam festival.

Within a few years, Andy's world revolved around the band. According to his father, if it hadn't been for an eleventh-hour stint of hard work with his high school counselors, Andy's single-minded pursuit of all things musical would have cost him his graduation. By 1984, Malfunkshun were regularly gigging around Seattle, and their sound had begun to change. In the beginning—mainly because they hadn't yet mastered their instruments—they'd been playing pure hardcore, little more than distortion and screaming. But after Andy's discovery of glam gods T-Rex and the practice afforded by a few years of hard-won gigs (still under twenty-one, they weren't allowed in clubs and were limited to all-ages venues), they'd taken on a more melodic, heavy rock sheen.

Malfunkshun's look had changed, too, after Andy snuck into Bainbridge High's theater department and walked out with a cache of stolen makeup. He experimented with it until he was satisfied with the white-faced, pouty-lipped visage looking back at him in the mirror, and a silver lamé cape, feather boa, and platform shoes completed the ensemble. Later, he would often appear on stage wearing a top hat, or huge sunglasses and a thick fake-fur coat. The new Andrew, he reasoned, needed a new name, and before long, he was referring to himself as "Landrew," short for "Landrew the Love Child."

Landrew wasn't just an empty, visually oriented persona—he came with his own philosophy. At the time, scowling, pseudo-Satanic heavy metal bands were becoming popular, and Andy resolved that Malfunkshun wouldn't be a part of such dour chicanery. Rather, he vowed to anyone who would listen, he and Malfunkshun would make it their life's work to spread "antidevil" sentiment. The antithesis of all the schlocky bands who were building their images around the 666-is-the-number-of-the-beast credo, Malfunkshun was to be Seattle's first "333" band, their music classified by Andy as "love rock."

People weren't sure what to make of Malfunkshun. Andy's androgynous mode of dress caused some confusion, for one thing: At the first Malfunkshun show he witnessed, the Melvins' Dale Crover watched Andy take the stage and thought the fur-bedecked vision of loveliness before him was a "pretty huge" girl. Neither did those on the punk circuit know how to respond to the band's full-out glitter rock feel. "When we opened for bands like the Silly Killers," Andy recalled in 1986, "people thought we were a novelty comedy band."

Before long, though, Andy's giddy, outlandish charm had made a name for him around Seattle. When he wasn't performing with Malfunkshun, he would do solo gigs, performing the Elton John–influenced piano ballads of which he wrote dozens, or singing along to backing tapes. Sometimes, he served as an informal master of ceremonies for other bands at their shows. Always, his enthusiasm and childlike lack of inhibition won over potential detractors in the audience. Only Andy had the nerve to gallop across the stage at a near-empty club and holler, "Helloooooooo, Seattle!" as if he were addressing thousands. He took the arena-rock pretensions of his heroes to such obvious extremes that, whether you thought you were witnessing a campy send-up or a genuine display of Ted Nugent worship run amuck, you couldn't help but like him.

"Andy was just the *greatest* guy," says Sheri Fineman, who was friendly with some of the regulars on the scene and would later work as a nanny for Pearl Jam manager Kelly Curtis and his wife, Peggy. "I worked at this deli downtown, and he worked for the messenger service across the street, and he used to come in all the time. Andy was definitely something. He *was* the show. Andy was always like, 'Hey, let's party, let's smoke pot, let's just everybody be happy.' It was just straight in your face: 'Okay, I'm gonna go on stage now! I'm here to have a good time, let's do it!'"

As upbeat and cheeky as Andrew was, though, the people who were closest to him knew that his game-show-host antics and campy stage wear masked extremely low self-esteem. The sunny disposition Andy had displayed as a child was still there, but bubbling beneath the surface were deep insecurities that had plagued him since adolescence.

"He was scared about simple things—living socially and working," Chris Cornell said of Andy. "He was probably just more afraid of being alive than anybody would realize, because he was so outgoing that you never saw that side of him. He was guarded. He was always 'on.' At his worst times, he was laughing about it."

Those fears made Andy a natural candidate for drug addiction. Worse still, the most numbing illicit drug on the street—and the one Andy probably saw as darkly glamorous, since so many full-blown rock stars had had public battles with it—was also the most insidious of them all.

It's believed that Andrew first began dabbling with heroin in his senior year at high school, introduced to the drug by a new acquaintance, a girl nobody knew who lived in Seattle and had begun to turn up with him at parties in Bainbridge. At first, when his use was minimal, he'd been able to hide it from his friends and family. But by the time he was nineteen and living in Seattle, he'd developed a serious habit, tracks on his arms bearing witness to the frequent mainlining that would soon result in another telltale symptom: hepatitis contracted from dirty needles. In the summer of 1985, jaundiced, sick, and scared, Andrew returned to his parents' home, where his frightened family talked him into entering a drug rehab program at Cabrini Hospital.

When the newly detoxed Andy left Cabrini, he'd planned on moving back in with his parents, but Chris Cornell, who'd just rented a house in Seattle and was scouting for a roommate, presented a second option. Thinking that Andy needed to get back into a daily routine and that holing up on Bainbridge would be depressing for him, Cornell asked Andy to room with him, and Andy welcomed the idea. Once he'd moved in, he returned to his music with an enthusiasm and prolificacy that left

Cornell overwhelmed. Working on a home four-track, Andy often made cassettes of his songs that he sold through local record stores and gave away to friends. According to his brother Kevin, he didn't seriously pursue selling them, but if someone sent money to his post office box, he'd make them a cassette. For one project, which Andy called *Melodies and Dreams*, he made tapes for a few dozen people, the selection of songs and the hand-designed cover on each copy unique from all the others.

Andy lived with Cornell for only a short time; not long after he moved in, he met—and promptly fell in love with—Xana LaFuente, a dark-eyed, dark-haired beauty who worked in a vintage clothing shop. About a month after they met, Andy and Xana rented a house together on Melrose Avenue East, a wooded, rather isolated stretch of Capitol Hill. (In 1986, when Xana and Andy vacated the house to take an apartment in the Queen Anne neighborhood, Cornell moved in, turning the house into a practice space for Soundgarden.)

Malfunkshun, temporarily disabled by Andy's rehabilitation, had regrouped as well, and were a galvanizing fixture on the scene, the swirly, star-festooned posters that Andy drew to advertise gigs now a familiar sight around town. "In my mind, Andy and Malfunkshun were the originators of the alleged 'Seattle sound,' in that that sound is a parody, a send-up of all those Seventies bands and clichés," Jonathan Poneman, future cochair of the Sub Pop label, opined. "No one was more totally into that, or more convincing, than Andy."

By now, it was rare that you went to a Malfunkshun or Soundgarden show without finding members of Green River or Skin Yard in the audience. A feeling of camaraderie had begun to develop among the half-dozen misfit bands that were thumbing their noses at Seattle's punk-and-rock-don't-mix mandate.

"Everyone I knew who moved here from Park Forest would run around with people from Kitsap County, on the other side of the water," Soundgarden guitarist Kim Thayil recalled. "Ben McMillan and Jack Endino from Skin Yard, Andy and his brothers, Ben Shepherd—it was just strange. All of us were kind of weird people who would make friends and then lose them because they thought we were really uncool or no fun. There was a certain trippy specialness, you know? You'd go check out all your friends, the guys in Green River and Skin Yard and the Melvins, and it was just sort of like, 'Wow, this is cool.'"

Sensing something in the air, recording engineer Chris Hanzsek and his partner, Tina Casale, decided to capture it for posterity. In August 1985, they began booking sessions at Ironwood Studios with the bands they saw as being at the vanguard of an emerging scene: Malfunkshun, the U-Men, Green River, Soundgarden, Skin Yard, and the Melvins. Stuck with a meager indie budget, Hanzsek and Casale set up house rules: Each band was limited to only a few hours in the studio, and only one member of each band was allowed to meddle in the control room.

A few of the musicians would bitch about this recording setup later, claiming that their tracks would have been better if they'd had more say in the production. Nonetheless, *Deep Six*, the compilation that arose from those August and September sessions, was groundbreaking.

The U-Men's "They" was a miasma of chugging, mud-coated rocka-billy. Green River contributed "10,000 Things" and "Your Own Best Friend," a pair of dank, dark, rusty-nail scorchers shot through with Arm's creepy moaning and screaming. The Melvins bounced between bludgeoning dirge and breakneck hardcore on "Scared," "Blessing the Operation," "Grinding Process," and "She Waits." Malfunkshun's tracks saw Andy memorializing his bout with hepatitis on the Sabbath-tinged "With Yo' Heart (Not Yo') Hands," and the band nearly buried in the chaotic fast blues and frantic upper-register guitar of "Stars-N-You." Skin Yard were more arty, sporting an obvious Brian Eno influence, their phenomenal "Throb" all dissonance and disembodied vocals, "The Birds" atmospheric and haunting, with a lone, sinuous sax weaving through the mix. Soundgarden offered the sinister "All Your Lies," a spiky, belligerent track called "Heretic," and the blistering hardcore treatise "Tears to Forget." It was all there, showcasing for the first time what the isolation and inbreeding of Seattle's underground scene had wrought. Released on April Fool's Day 1986 on Hanzsek and Casale's new C/Z label (soon to be taken over by Skin Yard's Daniel House), *Deep Six* would later be widely hailed as the definitive first salvo in Seattle's collective assault on the music world.

In October 198, just after they recorded their *Deep Six* tracks, Green River piled into a van and set off for their first "tour," a run of seven shows cobbled together by Jeff, who had by now become the band's de-facto business manager. They all worked to save money for the tour, which was considered big news, earning them a write-up in *Rocket*—in those days, few local bands even made it as far as Portland—but which turned out to be something of a letdown.

Since *Come On Down* hadn't yet been released, nobody outside Seat-tle was even aware of Green River's existence, and it seemed to the band that some in the sparse audiences they played to that fall didn't *want* to know they existed. A pair of shows opening for future Nirvana producer

Steve Albini's band, Big Black, went well, as did a gig at Maxwell's, in Hoboken, New Jersey. But when Green River gave it all they had within the hallowed walls of New York's punk church, CBGB, only six people were in the audience, and two of them were employees. A Halloween date in Detroit, opening for Samhain, Glenn Danzig's post-Misfits outfit, was sheer hell. The band had been excited about playing in the hometown of the Stooges and the MC5, but they quickly realized that they were unwelcome.

"Everyone had this bad-ass attitude," Arm remembered. "These people just wanted everything fast. Jeff was wearing a pink tank top with 'San Francisco' in purple letters, and with his hair . . . well, you can imagine. Midway through Green River's set, the sneering skepticism of the crowd gave way to a more physical show of disapproval, audience members spitting on the band and trying to pull them off the stage. After a husky-looking goon grabbed Jeff and dragged him into the crowd, and the more slightly built Arm made an unsuccessful attempt to jump into the tangle of bodies and rescue him, a policeman had to intervene, and the show ground to a halt.

The band's next tour, following the release of *Come On Down* at the end of the year, saw them faring better: Aerosmith guitarist Joe Perry happened to be in the crowd when they returned to CBGB during the jaunt, a momentous occurrence that delighted the band to no end. For months after Green River returned home, Seattle's rumor mill had it that Perry had kept in touch with the band and was going to produce their next record—scuttlebutt no doubt fueled by the band members themselves.

In March 1986, while they waited for Perry to show up with the promised brass ring, the band teamed with Jack Endino to record a single they would later release on their own ICP label, pairing the Green River original "Together We'll Never" with a cover of the Dead Boys' "Ain't Nothin' to Do." At Arm's suggestion, Green River reportedly attempted to record a cover of the Stooges standard, "Dirt" around the same time, but had to abandon the session when aspiring virtuoso Jeff denounced the bass line as too easy and refused to play it.

Lack of finances would keep the "Together We'll Never" single on the shelf for another eight months. When it was finally released in November, its sleeve would bear a joke production credit of "J. Perry," the band having admitted to the *Rocket* a few months prior that the rumors of Joe Perry producing Green River's next record had been a little premature. They'd glibly intimated to the paper that they would still consider working with Perry "if we're in the right place at the right time with the right kind of money," but in truth, they'd probably given up on any help from Perry at that point, evidenced by the fact that the "next record" in question was already finished.

Dry As a Bone, the five-song EP Green River had recorded in June with Jack Endino at his new Reciprocal Recording, saw the band fulfilling the thrashy, trashy promise they'd only hinted at on *Come On Down*. From the thunderous gothic overtones, whiplash snare and cymbal, and wet-cat shrieks of "P.C.C." to the pensive, dark "Baby Takes," an ode to a vampirish lover from which the EP's title was lifted, to "Unwind," which kicked off with bottom-heavy blues and unspooled into a lost companion to Aerosmith's "Toys in the Attic," *Dry As a Bone* showcased a band that had finally settled into a sense of its own identity. A bonus track, released only on the cassette version, saw them vamping it up on a distortion-laden cover of David Bowie's "Queen Bitch," Arm drawling and stuttering atop the walls of guitars with streetwise aplomb.

The raw, live feel Endino got out of Green River on *Dry As a Bone*—typical of the work that would soon make him the producer of choice around Seattle—was partially a product of limited time and money. Most of the early records Endino helmed were done on eight-track, which made multilayered vocal and guitar tracks unfeasible and served to put the kibosh on self-indulgence. But his skill at capturing the raunchy essence of bands like Green River was also a function of his familiarity with and love for the music he was recording.

"I had a pretty good notion of how to record a grungy, sloppy guitar," Endino told the *Rocket* in 1992, "because that's the kind of guitar I played myself. I realized early on that I had a terrible guitar sound, and how was I going to record it? Then I ended up recording about a hundred bands that had *equally* terrible guitar sounds, and a new aesthetic was born. What sounded horrible back then is now a standard."

Who needed Joe Perry, anyway? If Green River were disappointed over the absence of that hoped-for "Produced by Joe Perry" credit on the sleeve of *Dry As a Bone*, they'd soon get over it. As it happened, the mere timing of the EP's release would reap more notoriety for them than the fabled Joe Perry partnership would have, anyway. When it was finally issued, *Dry As a Bone* would have the distinction of being the first individual band release on a label that would within a few years be perceived as Seattle's Motown.

XOX

Bruce Pavitt hadn't been sitting idle while Green River and friends were slogging it out in the clubs. As always, he'd had his ear to the ground. A few years earlier, in 1983, Pavitt had moved to Seattle and turned his fanzine and cassette series into a monthly column—"Sub Pop U.S.A.: A Guide to U.S. Independents"—for the *Rocket.* He'd also begun doing a weekly "Sub Pop" radio show on KCMU, devoted to independent bands.

Meanwhile, he'd taken a job working in the warehouse at Yesco, a Seattle elevator music company that was about to be bought out by the Muzak Corporation. In the ultimate ironic twist, a number of the city's hardest-hitting musicians did menial work at Yesco, duping tapes or moving boxes to buy guitar strings and pay their rent. Among Pavitt's coworkers were Mark Arm, Ron Rudzitis of Room Nine (later of Love Battery), and Tad frontman Tad Doyle.

"We infiltrated that place," Doyle said later. "I know it sounds funny, but that's where the Sub Pop community really started. A lot of us worked there, and we hung out together. We'd go to the same clubs, play the same places, and support each other."

Perhaps inspired by the release of the *Deep Six* compilation and by his friend Calvin Johnson's K Records, which had become a hub of musical activity in Olympia, Pavitt had decided to reignite the audio arm of his old fanzine, this time as a proper record label under the Sub Pop logo. Using the Yesco offices as home base, he'd scraped up enough money to issue his first vinyl compilation, *Sub Pop 100*, which included tracks by Sonic Youth, Scratch Acid, the Wipers, the U-Men, Skinny Puppy, Shonen Knife, and Naked Raygun, as well as a selection called "Spoken Word Intro Thing" gratis of Big Black's Steve Albini. In one of the quirky touches that would go on to lend Sub Pop a special mystique, the side of the album featuring the Shonen Knife and Skinny Puppy tracks had MACHINES etched into its run-out groove, while the other side, featuring Scratch Acid, the Wipers, Sonic Youth, and the U-Men, was etched with the word GUITARS.

No doubt availing himself of the Yesco mailroom, Pavitt sent *Sub Pop 100*—which boasted a garish black, green, and yellow cover created by one of his *Rocket* acquaintances, contributing designer Dale Yarger—to as many media outlets as he could think of. Enclosed with each was a hand-signed letter ("Love, Bruce," he scrawled in red marker) announcing the label's formation and entreating reporters to "have fun and be sure to write something upbeat and positive about the new *Sub Pop 100* record."

"And hey," Pavitt crowed in his press release, "Sub Pop will also re-lease solo projects from totally cool Seattle bands. Stay tuned for a new Green River LP!!!" As a means of whetting appetites for *Dry As a Bone*, his next scheduled release, Pavitt slipped copies of Green River's "To-gether We'll Never/Ain't Nothin' to Do" 45 ("A total Stooges/Dead Boys rip-off!!! It kills!!!") into some of the *Sub Pop 100* packages he mailed out. You only got one if you were, as Pavitt put it, "one of the lucky ones."

Dry As a Bone, which had been in the can for several months when *Sub Pop 100* was released in late 1986, wasn't the only record Pavitt was itching to put out. Soundgarden were already working with Endino at Reciprocal, laying down the tracks that would wind up on their first sin-gle ("Hunted Down"/"Nothing to Say") and their *Screaming Life* EP. He also wanted to record locals Blood Circus and Swallow. Unfortunately, Pavitt's ambitions at that point were out of kilter with his bank account; it didn't help matters that he blew most of the profit from *Sub Pop 100* on a trip to Amsterdam. Another seven months would pass before he fi-nally borrowed $2,000 from his father to pay for the pressing of *Dry As a Bone* and the Soundgarden 7-inch. Even with the loan, Pavitt managed to swing the July 1987 releases only after a Canadian manufacturer agreed to let him have the Green River album jackets before he'd paid the bill. Subsequent Sub Pop releases, like Soundgarden's *Screaming Life* EP, would be put on hold until late 1987, when Kim Thayil saved the day and suggested that Pavitt hook up with Jonathan Poneman, the financially savvy KCMU deejay and talent booker who had money of his own to invest and who also had a knack for wheedling money out of *other* people. Once Poneman came on board, Sub Pop's release schedule would even out a bit, and eventually the two would be confident enough about the future of the partnership to quit their day jobs, take out a loan, hire a few employees, and rent office space at the Terminal Sales Build-ing, although it would be years before they were solvent.

While they awaited the release of *Dry As a Bone*, Green River con-tinued gigging around Seattle, earning a reputation for goofy chaos that probably served to draw as many spectators as their music did. They got banned from the Central Tavern and stuck with a fine for damages after one show disintegrated into a boisterous food fight, audience members flinging hunks of Spam at Green River and the band dropping their instruments in mid-song to retaliate. Not even decorated punk veterans were spared from their prankishness: When they served as opening act for former Sex Pistol John Lydon's band, Public Image Ltd., at a Paramount gig in late 1986, Arm capped Green River's set by telling the audience to stick around if they wanted to "see what happens to somebody who's completely sold out." While Public Image Ltd. were on stage, Green River crept into Lydon's dressing room and decimated it, smuggling the cherished reclining chair Lydon lugged around on tour with him out of the theater in the bargain.

Not everything was fun and games, though. By this time the tension over musical direction that had been simmering between the members of Green River had begun to cause serious arguments. Jeff, in particular, wanted to push the band in a more commercial direction and lobby for a major label deal, while Mark Arm still adhered to the punk school that saw major labels as the scourge of the earth. Arm was also reportedly incensed when Jeff and Stone casually suggested he might want to think about taking singing lessons. "Jeff and Stone want to be rock stars, and I think Bruce does too," Arm would opine to *Slur* in 1988. "I think they realized that they could not get as famous as possible with a singer like me. I don't have a commercial voice."

Back at Sub Pop, Pavitt had been nudging Poneman for money to record another Green River album, but Poneman was reluctant to fork it over. "I thought they sucked," Poneman recalled. "While I could appreciate their sensibilities and their sense of humor, live, they always came to a point which I associated with jock rock. Originally they were a post-hardcore rock band, but as they developed, they became something which was more immediately derivative of the Seventies. I just didn't get it."

Poneman finally came around after Green River's performance at their record release party for *Dry As a Bone*, held at the Scoundrel's Lair, a club he was booking. "The party was one of those events when it was total anarchy and total control at the same time," he told *Goldmine*. "You had a feeling that if Mark said, 'Destroy the room,' people would have." In July 1987, just after the party, Green River went into Reciprocal with Jack Endino to begin recording *Rehab Doll*, which would be their last album.

The clash between the commercial and anticommercial factions in Green River reappeared during the sessions for *Rehab Doll*. In August, after Endino had recorded the basic tracks, the band switched gears and went into a posher, 24-track studio, Steve Lawson Productions, to finish the album with producer Bruce Calder. Calder's tracks were much more glossy and layered than the rawer, more live-sounding tracks done by Endino, which Arm later claimed he'd been happier with. Although *Rehab Doll*—which wouldn't see release until the following year, after Green River had folded—still successfully captured the band in its element, a few of the tracks suffered from Calder's airbrush treatment, especially "Swallow My Pride." A talk-singing guest appearance by Sonic Youth's Kim Gordon did much to redeem the track, but the sped-up, more metalized version on *Rehab Doll* was much less meaty and thudding than the earlier version included on *Come On Down.*

"Some of the other members of the band started getting the idea they could be popular, and began to think, 'Well, I'm getting to be twenty-four, so what am I going to be doing the rest of my life?'" said Arm. "Green River got into the idea of signing to a major, and *Rehab Doll* was recorded with that in mind. But for me, too many compromises were made. I was listening to far simpler stuff, like basic Stooges."

The rift widened when Green River embarked on their third and final tour, a five-day West Coast trip that saw them open for Jane's Addiction—delicately described by Arm in *Slur* as "one of the worst bands I've ever heard in my life"—at a Los Angeles club called the Scream.

"We had a guest list of ten people, all of whom were from major labels," Arm told the *Rocket* of the show. "Only two of them came. Meanwhile, I wanted to get my friends in and they said, 'No, it's really important that we get these industry people in.' But these people didn't give a shit about us. I'd rather have had my friends come in for free." The argument reportedly culminated in a near-fistfight between Jeff and Mark in the dressing room after the show.

After that outing, it became clear to everyone involved that Green River was on its last legs. Although the band members went through the motions and Green River limped along for another few months, all of them had begun looking for greener pastures. Arm was playing occasional gigs with his old pal Steve Turner in a gross-out band called the Thrown Ups. Jeff, Stone, and Bruce, meanwhile, were hell-bent on success, holding regular meetings in the Cloud Room, a piano bar at the Camlin Hotel. According to one observer, these gatherings "reeked of L.A.-ism, and of chicks who smelled money."

The three had also begun spending a lot of time with Andy Wood. By this time, they knew Andy well. Malfunkshun had been sharing rehearsal space with Green River, sometimes even borrowing Green River's P.A. for gigs. Andy had commercial aspirations more in line with their goals, and as a vocalist and writer, he was better suited for the musical direction they wanted to take. Soon, Stone, Jeff, and Bruce were holding casual jams with Andy and Malfunkshun drummer Regan Hagar, and the results were encouraging. On Halloween 1987, Mark Arm walked into Green River's rehearsal and the others, after some hemming and hawing, broke the news that they were through with the band.

"Okay, cool," said Arm, not very surprised. He'd seen it coming.

Three

Lords of the Wasteland / Mother Love Bone / Go West, Young (A&R) Man / *Shine* / Come Bite the Apple / He Who Rides the Pony / Say Hello 2 Heaven

In late 1987, Jeff, Stone, Bruce, Andy, and Regan dubbed themselves Lords of the Wasteland and began playing shows. The first of these all-ages affairs held in the basement of the Luna shoe store on Broadway, saw them playing mostly Stones, Zeppelin, and James Gang covers. (Arm, for all his supposed acceptance of Green River's demise, couldn't resist the opportunity to take at least one mocking jab at his former band mates' new affiliation: Not long after Lords of the Wasteland began playing around Seattle, Arm and a few friends played a one-off show billing themselves as the Wasted Landlords. Arm would find a more suitable outlet for his energy in 1988, when he teamed with Turner, ex-Melvins bassist Matt Lukin, and Bundle of Hiss drummer Dan Peters to form Mudhoney, a band that would go on to make its own substantial impression on the scene, and would eventually—despite Arm's professed scorn for the corporate world—ink a deal with Reprise, a subsidiary of Warner Bros. and about as major a label as could be found.)

Lords of the Wasteland continued holding loose rehearsals, but apparently not all of them were satisfied with the lineup. In December 1987, former 10 Minute Warning drummer Greg Gilmore, who'd just returned from a trip to Asia, was invited into the fold. "Greg and I were walking on Capitol Hill," recalls Sheri Fineman, "and we ran into Stone. Stone said that he had this band, and he wanted Greg to come jam with them." According to what Gilmore has said, the other members of Lords of the Wasteland neglected to mention to him that they'd already been working with Regan Hagar, and Hagar apparently wasn't aware of Gilmore's involvement. This led to a rather awkward standoff a few days into Gilmore's rehearsals with the band, when Hagar showed up at the practice space to find Gilmore behind the drums. "All of a sudden, everyone got real quiet," Gilmore remembered.

Eventually, Hagar got the hint, and with Gilmore in place, the next order of business was a name change. Stone wanted to call the band the Dum Dum Boys, after an Iggy Pop song, and Bruce was championing Daddy Long Legs—both of which Andy hated. One day on his messenger job, Andy pulled over to the side of the road, as he often did to compose lyrics, and made a list of possible band names. His favorite on the list was Mother Love Bone. When he presented it to them, the others thought the name was horrible, but Andy wouldn't budge. After a week of constant hounding at rehearsals, he finally bulldozed his band mates into accepting it.

In February 1988, Mother Love Bone went into Reciprocal and recorded a demo of their songs, then began plotting their career strategy. For a while, they pondered a move to Los Angeles. At the time, Los Angeles–based glam-metal bands like Poison and Mötley Crüe were just beginning to make an impression on mainstream record buyers, and the proliferation of lipsticked, mascaraed metalites who were springboarding from L.A.'s Sunset Strip clubs to the top of the charts had made Los Angeles a feeding ground for record company A&R staffers, and a magnet for ambitious rock bands looking for major-label deals.

Gilmore, interestingly, had already made a pilgrimage to L.A.—one that had nearly landed him in one of the most successful bands the city had birthed. In 1985, Gilmore and one of his 10 Minute Warning band mates, Duff McKagan, had traveled to L.A., and, during their first week there, had answered a "musicians wanted" ad run by a guitarist named Slash. Gilmore had sat in on a few jams and beat a hasty retreat back to Seattle, but McKagan stuck it out with the scrappy West Hollywood quintet, a move that turned out to be his ticket to fame. Later that year, McKagan brought Guns n' Roses—led by the volatile W. Axl Rose and dishing out a darker, more decadent and punk-infused blend of hard rock than any of the other Sunset Strip bands—through Seattle on a disastrous van tour, where they played a club show in front of thirteen people and got stiffed when it came time to collect their fee. Three years later, when Guns n' Roses returned to Seattle, it was to play the Coliseum: Their first full-length album, *Appetite for Destruction*, was lodged in the Top Ten, the start of a winning streak that would make them the hottest ticket in rock music until the early Nineties.

Perhaps acting on advice from Gilmore, who is said to have been turned off by the Sunset Strip scene, Mother Love Bone decided against a full-scale move to Los Angeles. They did, however, realize that in terms of being noticed by industry types, L.A. was where the action was, and Jeff, as usual, set about trying to get a piece of it for the band, mailing copies of their newly recorded demo to industry contacts he thought might lend a hand or book them for shows.

As it turned out, the batch of demos Jeff sent out netted the band more than bookings. Before they'd even played their second show together as Mother Love Bone, the tapes had captured the attention of their future manager, as well as the interest of Anna Statman, a newly appointed A&R executive at Geffen whom Jeff had met when she'd worked for Slash Records.

Kelly Curtis, a former tour manager and Heart fan club officer who was then a partner at a Seattle management firm called Mark Allen Productions, first heard the Mother Love Bone demo when Jeff sent it to Curtis's associate in the firm, Ken Deans. Curtis's initial interest in managing Mother Love Bone was minimal, although he and Deans began helping the band out on a casual basis, giving them advice and occasionally letting them use the office.

He found himself more closely involved, though, after Anna Statman stepped into the picture. Statman, who'd received a copy of the demo from Jeff and begun placing daily phone calls to the bassist to tell him how much she liked the band, was eager to see them in a live setting, and she phoned Curtis to see if he would accompany her to an upcoming Mother Love Bone show at the Vogue. The Vogue show would prove a turning point, prompting Statman to offer Mother Love Bone $5,000 to record a more professional demo and the band, in turn, to bring Curtis into the fold as their manager.

In June 1988, Mother Love Bone recorded a more polished demo, expressly for Geffen ears. The label's president, Eddie Rosenblatt, liked what he heard, and in early July, Curtis and Mother Love Bone flew to

Los Angeles to meet with him. While there, the band hired a lawyer, and took the opportunity to meet with a few booking agents and other industry movers as well. Then they returned to Seattle, happy with the progress they'd made and feeling relatively secure that the coveted major-label deal was in the bag. What happened next was a shocker for everyone involved.

※◇※

"We thought we were gonna be signed by Geffen, and that became a big movie," Andy later told Josh Taft and Adolfo Doring during an interview for a video press kit on Mother Love Bone commissioned by PolyGram Records. "We waited around and we all quit our jobs, because we thought we were gonna have money. But things kind of fell apart, and we decided that maybe we should listen to what other labels had to say. That's when the whole bidding war started."

If anybody involved knew what prompted the swell of interest in Mother Love Bone just after the band returned from Los Angeles, nobody was talking, but suddenly, they found themselves in the midst of what Wood referred to as the "Mother Love Bone Restaurant Tour."

A&R people turned up in droves at the band's next few shows, and by August, Mother Love Bone, still awaiting a formal offer from Geffen, were fielding calls from other labels, among them Capitol, Atlantic, Island, A&M (which was also actively pursuing Soundgarden and would sign them later in the year), and PolyGram. The latter, represented by an amiable young A&R staffer named Michael Goldstone, would prove the victor, signing Mother Love Bone in November for a reported $250,000 advance—an unusually generous sum for a new band.

Geffen's Tom Zutaut, who had replaced Statman in the label's dealings with Mother Love Bone, had finally made an offer to the band in mid-September, after a gig at the Central Tavern. By that time, though, as Curtis told Richard T. White of the *Rocket*, "it was a whole new ball game, because we felt we owed it to all these people who had come up to listen to their rap. The last time we talked to Zutaut, we told him we were calling him in a week; we called to tell him we were signing and we never heard back from him."

Zutaut declined comment in White's story—an astutely reported piece that appeared in January 1989 under the headline "The Art of the Deal"—but another Geffen source who was quoted accused Mother Love Bone of playing dirty pool. "Their britches became too large for their body very quickly," the anonymous staffer told White. "They tried to get as many labels, as many booking agents, as many scumbag parasitic people as there are in this business, to be as interested in this band as possible, and they blew the whole thing out of proportion."

Maybe. But it's easy to point fingers when you've got egg on your face, and it could also be posited that had Geffen really been on the ball, they'd have signed Mother Love Bone back in July. Thanks to a surprising new acceptance within the mainstream of bands like Guns n' Roses, Jane's Addiction, and the Red Hot Chili Peppers—none of whom would have been predicted as successful a few years previous—major labels were snapping up any group that had anything even remotely in common with those bands, and Geffen would have been wise to realize that, in the current climate, they wouldn't be the only label interested in a band like Mother Love Bone. Although the band's music bore only general similarities to that of Guns n' Roses, their look definitely put them in the same gypsy-hard-rock category, almost certainly a selling point in the eyes of label scouts hoping to sign their *own* version of Guns n' Roses. And of those, of course, there were many.

"There were dozens and dozens of the 'next Guns n' Roses' signed after Guns n' Roses made it, and we were like a Jane's Addiction when we were signed," Chris Cornell of Soundgarden recalled a few years after Seattle had been picked clean by the major labels. "If an A&R guy didn't get the band he was after, he'd go on to the next one that was similar."

Mother Love Bone may have been Seattle's winner in the major labels' "next Guns n' Roses" sweepstakes, but it appears it wasn't for lack of trying on the part of other local bands. Although they probably wouldn't admit to it today—Guns n' Roses' decadent antics and politically incorrect lyrics having made them something of a pariah among the Nineties alternative set—it seems certain that at least a few Seattle musicians took notice of Guns n' Roses' success and the wave of major-label signings it sparked. In 1988, in one of their earliest incarnations as a glam-metal band, Alice in Chains played a number of gigs around Seattle as Alice 'N Chainz, and the band posed for at least one promotional photo in an alley, garbed in the same skin-tight-jeans-and-cowboy-boots regalia favored by Guns n' Roses. Even Mudhoney's Mark Arm, who seemed to take fiendish delight in deriding Mother Love Bone for their arena-rock ambitions, wasn't above a little Guns n' Roses coat-tail riding. As late as 1989, Arm was cannily aligning Mudhoney with Guns n' Roses in interviews. Asked by a *Melody Maker* writer what difference he saw between the two bands, Arm replied, "Not much. There's five of them, and four of us, their hair's a little longer and they're richer. But in terms of coming from the same background, yeah!"

Just as Soundgarden had when they signed to A&M, Mother Love Bone got a tremendous amount of flak from other Seattle musicians when they signed to PolyGram, the standard accusation being that they'd "sold out," tailoring their sound and image in order to make themselves more commercially acceptable. Few of their critics (the loudest of whom conveniently stopped hurling barbs after *their* bands were picked up by major labels) seemed to consider that they'd simply been at the right place at the right time, emerging when the market happened to be the most receptive to what they'd been doing all along.

What some viewed as Jeff and Stone's unseemly pursuit of stardom would dog them in later years, after alternative music—along with its no-frills, anticorporate, antiambition rules—broke into the mainstream, and bands and their fans alike began bickering over who had the most street credibility. For now, though, Mother Love Bone were so excited about their future that the cries of "sellout" didn't especially concern them—least of all Andy, whose dreams now seemed well within his grasp.

"I don't know if everybody's as anxious as me to get into that arena," the singer enthused to Taft and Doring during their interview for the PolyGram video profile. "I want to get on an arena tour with some band—who cares, *Warrant* for that matter.

"What the hell!" Andy beamed. "Go on tour with Warrant, just so we can play arenas. That's the kind of crowd I like; those are easy crowds. You can say *'Your mother smells bad, PEOPLE!'* and they'll just go, *'YEEEAAAAAH!'*"

It's obvious from Taft and Doring's footage—much of which didn't make it into the press kit but would be released by PolyGram in 1993 as a home video, *The Love Bone Earth Affair*—that Andy wasn't naive about the work that awaited the band, nor was he assuming that their future was cemented now that they'd been signed. "It's just a step," he said matter-of-factly, "and it's really not a big deal, 'cause you've gotta *sell* the records once you've made 'em. It's not what everybody thinks."

What was just as obvious, though, was that the singer was prepared to do whatever it took to lead his band to the top—and do it with his customary charm. After commenting that, if nothing else, getting signed was "better than licking boots," Andy turned the full wattage of his smile on his interviewers.

"By the way," he added, "you have nice boots."

XOX

PolyGram was eager for Mother Love Bone to make an album, but the band members—who'd only played fourteen shows together when they signed with the label—saw touring as a bigger priority. The idea that made the most sense to both the band and the label was for Mother Love Bone to record an EP, then spend a few months touring to hone their sound before they recorded a full-length album.

In January 1989, Mother Love Bone spent five days in London Bridge Studios recording *Shine*. The 5-track EP, helmed by Mark Dearnley—who'd engineered a number of AC/DC albums, most notably *For Those About to Rock*—featured "Thru Fade Away," "Mindshaker Meltdown," "Half Ass Monkey Boy," and, perhaps the most haunting example of Andy's spare piano balladry on record, "Chloe Dancer/Crown of Thorns." ("Crown of Thorns," minus the "Chloe Dancer" intro, would turn up on the band's debut LP, *Apple*, in 1990. The entire eight-minute track would also resurface in 1992 on the soundtrack for writer-director Cameron Crowe's Seattle-based film, *Singles*.)

By this time, at least a few major labels were aware of the marketing value of underground cachet. In the past, the majors had tended to watch indie bands until they'd built up word-of-mouth in the underground, signing them only after they'd amassed significant followings who would ostensibly stick around and make things easier when it came to breaking the band into the mainstream. The flip side of that, of course, was that a certain, elitist segment of any given band's earliest followers had a tendency to ditch them once they'd "sold out" to a major label, and move on to look for fresh blood. Eventually, some of the majors caught on to this and began creating boutique labels for the new bands they signed, as a means of easing them into the mainstream gradually, minus the telltale corporate trimmings that wreaked havoc with street credibility.

Interestingly, PolyGram proved much less savvy on this point than the band it had just signed. Perhaps taking a clue from Geffen, which had in 1986 released Guns n' Roses' first EP on Uzi/Suicide, an indie-vibed label created specially for the band, the members of Mother Love Bone hit on the idea of creating their own imprint under the PolyGram umbrella—Stardog Records, after "Stardog Champion," a song from their earliest demos—so that *Shine* wouldn't have to bear the scars of their corporate dalliance. Although the idea was hardly extravagant—simply a matter of slapping a different logo on the packaging—PolyGram reportedly balked, viewing it as unnecessarily self-indulgent until Michael Gold-stone stepped in and explained it to the label heads in terms they could understand, emphasizing its promotional potential. Seen in this light, the idea of issuing *Shine* on a new imprint suddenly made sense, and the company's publicity machine wasted no time in exploiting it, boast-ing that PolyGram "loved the band so much we actually bought the Star-dog label to get them." Such ads may have elicited a few snickers from *Billboard*-reading industry heavies who knew the truth—that Stardog Records was born within the walls of PolyGram for the express purpose of lending an indie feel to Mother Love Bone's first record—but gener-ally those who were wise to the ruse kept it to themselves.

After celebrating the release of *Shine* in March with a bash at the Ox-ford Tavern in Seattle, Mother Love Bone headed for Boston, where they would launch a forty-date club tour pairing them with PolyGram label-mates Dogs D'Amour, a scruffy, eyeliner-sporting quartet of Hanoi Rocks pretenders from England, whose own newly released debut, *In the Dy-namite Jet Saloon*, had also been produced by Mark Dearnley.

From the get go, Mother Love Bone and the Dogs D'Amour did *not* hit it off. Even in the empty clubs that plagued them on the earliest dates of the tour, Andy, with his effervescent, baby-faced presence, managed to upstage the headlining Dogs, and worse, as the tour progressed and the audiences got larger, it became apparent that Mother Love Bone was the bigger draw. By the time the tour reached Los Angeles for a two-night stand at the Club With No Name, the Dogs D'Amour had declared passive-aggressive war and begun setting up their equipment in a man-ner that hogged as much precious stage space as possible. At smaller clubs, this left Mother Love Bone—whose gear had to be set up in front of the Dogs' so that it could be quickly moved off the stage after their opening set—with only a cramped three- or-four-foot patch of stage on which to perform. The rest of the band could make do, but for the larger-than-life Andy, the confinement was unbearable, and eventually he ar-rived at a solution that probably left the headliners wishing they'd left well enough alone: By the time the tour hit the Cat Club in New York City, Andy had armed himself with a wireless mike, which gave him the freedom to leap off the stage whenever the whim struck him, roaming among the crowd and teasing various audience members as he sang.

Pettiness on the part of the headliners wasn't the only glitch in the tour. Perhaps because of the grueling pace, or the claustrophobic reality of traveling from show to show in a stuffy van together, crankiness set in, and Mother Love Bone experienced its share of growing pains.

"There was a lot of tension," Jeff said in 1991. "And there were certain nights when the tension was in the right place, and we had a good show. But it wasn't consistent at all. The tension was between the other four of us, and Andy was the one who made us forget about it. There were certain nights when he was really on and really funny, and that made us loosen up. But some nights, that didn't happen, and it was awful. It wasn't any fun."

Jeff blamed the friction on a "lack of communication" between "certain people" in the band, declining to point the finger at any of his band mates. But Sheri Fineman, whose friendship with Greg Gilmore put her in the position to witness a number of heated arguments, says that most of the rows erupted between Jeff and Greg.

"They were always butting heads," recalls Fineman. "They did not like each other—and the reason was because they were both exactly alike in some respects. Stone was always the one standing between Jeff and Greg, smoothing things out and trying to make it okay for everyone."

All told, the outing didn't exactly match up to the glamorous visions of touring they'd carried around in their heads. Nor was it a financial success for the band. But in terms of building their audience—not to mention prevailing over the Dogs' bottom-of-the-deck tactics—it was a victory. At the end of the tour in May, when they returned to Seattle to play a headlining show at the Oz with openers Alice in Chains, they were jubilant.

After the pace of the tour, the next few months in Seattle were anticlimactic. Although they played a number of local shows and did a bit of recording—a cover of Argent's "Hold Your Head Up" for a compilation of Seventies covers planned by PolyGram that was never released, and some preproduction work for their debut album with producer Davitt Sigerson—most of the summer was spent in an excruciating waiting game. Compared to their earlier experiences making records with tiny indie labels, where they'd often dealt directly with the owners and any snafus could usually be addressed with a single phone call, the band members couldn't believe how much red tape was involved this time around.

"The whole time we were at PolyGram, we spent the entire time educating and reeducating new people," Jeff griped. "I mean, they were going through all these changes and restructuring the whole company, and every day we were talking to somebody different on the phone and they'd be like, 'Who's Mother Love Bone?' It just got really old."

For most of the band, the waiting was tedious, but for Andy, with his proclivity for self-medication when he was plagued by boredom or personal problems, the inactivity was also dangerous. During that summer, he fell back into his old pattern of substance abuse, mostly drinking or smoking pot but occasionally using cocaine or heroin. Xana, who strongly disapproved, argued with him constantly about his drug use, urging him to seek help. Sometimes when she confronted him, Andy was defiant. Other times, he was repentant, confessing that he wanted to stop but didn't know how. It's likely that even Xana would have been unaware of the severity of the problem had she not come home a few times unexpectedly and caught Andy in the act. Ashamed of his addiction, the singer went out of his way to avoid his friends when he was using, a ploy that dated back to his days as Chris Cornell's roommate.

"I never had any experiences, when he lived with me, of him doing drugs," Cornell recalled. "He wasn't someone who had to cop every day, or who would steal your stuff. He wasn't that way at all. The only thing he was dishonest about was when he would actually do it. He would try to hide it." Andy was especially careful around the other members of Mother Love Bone, sometimes failing to show up for rehearsals or band meetings when he had succumbed to temptation, so they wouldn't know he'd slipped up. As summer gave way to fall, Andy was using more and more often, and before long, hiding out from his band mates would not be as easy. They had a record to make.

In September, Mother Love bone traveled to Sausalito, California, where, with Terry Date, who'd just produced Soundgarden's major label debut, *Louder than Love*, they began work on the phenomenal *Apple*, their first full-length LP.

The sessions for *Apple* took nearly three months, the band spending September and October in Sausalito and then returning to Seattle in November to finish the recording at London Bridge Studios. Gilmore had nailed his drum tracks in a matter of days, but the guitars and vocals seemed to drag on interminably, requiring numerous layers and overdubs. Then, four or five of the tracks had to be remixed several times before the band members were satisfied that they were as good as they could be.

Although their perfectionism gobbled expensive studio time, there's no question that it paid off. From beginning to end, *Apple* was an astounding debut, especially on tracks like "Bone China" and "Stardog Champion," both of which shone from the same keen understanding of dynamics that had made Led Zeppelin famous, pitting delicate melodies and vocal nuances against bloozy, lumbering guitar and kick drum foundations. The album was an incredible testament to the band's songwriting skill, leaving no doubt as to the promising future that awaited them.

Unfortunately, it became apparent to the other members of Mother Love Bone as they worked on *Apple* that there was a threat to that future. Andy's drug use had by now become obvious, and they weren't sure how to help him. Although they tried to talk to him about the problems that were at the root of his substance abuse, Andy preferred to keep his troubles bottled inside rather than burden anyone else with them. At one point just after the *Apple* sessions were finished, Jeff learned that Andy—perhaps stoned and afraid to go home and face Xana—had spent the night huddling in sub-zero weather in the parking lot of Ivars, a seafood bar a mere block from Jeff's apartment.

"I was like, 'Dude, you don't know me well enough, you don't have the confidence to come to my door and say I need a place to stay, I need some help?'" Jeff remembered. "That really hurt."

In late November, while *Apple* was being mastered, Andy's band mates confronted him about his drugging, and, together with Xana, convinced him to see Dr. Richard Fields, a therapist who specialized in substance abuse. Fields met with Andy and recommended supervised treatment. Andy went willingly, spending most of December at the Valley General Hospital Alcohol and Drug Recovery Center in Monroe, Washington. He spent the time there filling spiral notebooks with poetry, much of it angry and self-critical, an attempt to explore the fears at the root of his addiction.

Andy emerged from rehabilitation with a renewed sense of enthusiasm and a determination to leave the drugs behind once and for all. Maintaining his sobriety with continued therapy and regular Monday night Narcotics Anonymous meetings, he did a tremendous amount of writing throughout January and February, bringing Stone a number of new piano melodies that the two began working into songs. In anticipation of the release of *Apple*, scheduled for April, Mother Love Bone kicked into high gear, shooting a black-and-white video with Josh Taft for "Stardog Champion," the track slated as their first single, and commencing intensive rehearsals for the upcoming twelve-week tour that would coincide with the album's release. By the time March rolled around, with the tour and the release of *Apple* just around the corner, the members of Mother Love Bone were in a perpetual state of excitement, seemingly walking on air. This time, with a full-length album under their belts and without the Dogs D'Amour around to piss on the parade, they were really going to conquer the road.

"They kept telling me, 'We're gonna be *huge!*'" says Fineman, laughing. "And I'm like, 'Why?' I just thought of them as another stupid band—other than Andy, I didn't think they were that great. But I guess they were. Even now, there are people everywhere who are Mother Love Bone fans."

As a means of helping Andy stay sober on the tour, the band had agreed that alcohol would be barred from their tour bus, and Kelly Curtis began interviewing road managers who'd had experience dealing with addicts. Everyone involved knew that the outing would present a lot of risky temptation for Andy, who was taxed enough as it was. It was nearly impossible for him to go out in Seattle without running into old junkie friends who offered him drugs, and his will was tested constantly.

So far, though, he'd persevered, staying clean for nearly four months. Just after Mother Love Bone had finished rehearsing for their tour, Andy spoke of his sobriety with cautionary pride, in an interview conducted by writer Michael Browning of *RIP* magazine on March 15.

"I'm lucky to be sitting here," he told Browning. "It's a total struggle. When you first get out, you're on this pink cloud, and it's pretty easy. After a while, things start getting more real. You have to just stay straight a second at a time."

During the interview, Andy talked to Browning about the songs on *Apple*, and about his hopes of making a solo record with his brother, Kevin, whom he said he still regretted leaving behind in Malfunkshun. In a thinly veiled reference to the Sub Pop/Mudhoney set, a few of whom had made it clear they disapproved of Mother Love Bone's courting the mainstream, Andy also addressed the elitism that divided mainstream and underground bands and their respective fans, a rift that would widen into a virtual chasm within a few years.

"I'm not going to name any names or anything," he said, "but there seem to be some people who are real concerned about who their fans are, which doesn't make any sense to me. They're all basically rock fans. We want them to be our fans. We don't want to draw any kind of lines."

As the night approached, Andy had to cut the interview short; he and Xana had tickets for an Aerosmith concert at the Tacoma Dome. Andy was scheduled to sit on a panel the following week at the Northwest Area Music Association conference, so he and Browning made plans to meet up at the conference and talk some more there. Neither

would have predicted, as they said their good-byes, that the interview
they'd just done would be Andy's last.

※◇※

On the evening of March 16, while Kelly Curtis sat in his office waiting for Andy to show up for a meeting with a prospective road
manager—substance abuse watchdog, Andy and Xana's upstairs neighbor, Lisa Vanderbeck, was getting up to see what all the commotion was
downstairs.

Vanderbeck, who worked as a barista at Uptown Espresso and had
often served *americanos* to the members of Mother Love Bone, had been
trying to watch television earlier, but for a lengthy, irritating interval she
had not been able to hear it. Someone had been standing outside Andy
and Xana's window, repeatedly yelling *"LANDREW! LANDREW!"* at the
top of his lungs. Eventually, the noise had abated, and Vanderbeck had
forgotten about it. Now, though, a siren was wailing outside, and the reflection cast by red ambulance lights was bouncing ominously around
her living room walls. She went downstairs to investigate and found a
shell-shocked Xana standing in the doorway, watching as the ambulance drove away.

As the details spilled out later, via news reports and the whisperings
that filtered through the stunned community, Xana had arrived home
around 10:30 P.M. and found Andy sprawled facedown on their bed,
unconscious. Next to the bed, an empty syringe bore toothsome, evil
witness to what the county medical examiner would later rule an
accidental and acute overdose of heroin.

Andy lay in a coma at Harborview Medical Center all weekend as
Xana, his family, Kelly Curtis, and his band mates held vigil, praying
that he'd come out of it. After the doctors informed Toni and David
Wood that there was virtually no chance that Andy would regain consciousness, the Woods made the agonizing decision to remove their
twenty-four-year-old son from life support. On Monday afternoon,
March 19, 1990, with the lights lowered and a tape of one of his favorite
albums, Queen's *A Night at the Opera*, softly playing in the background,
Andy's family, Xana, Curtis, and Mother Love Bone formed a close, loving circle around his bed, and let him go.

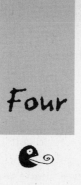

Four

Starting Over / Mike Steps Out of His Shadow / Love Chile and Luv Co. / Temple of the Dog

For the surviving members of Mother Love Bone, the next few days of funeral arrangements and memorials passed in a bewildered haze. None of them could make any sense of the tragedy.

"Everyone was pretty traumatized," says Sheri Fineman. "They were devastated by Andy's death, especially Stone. And I think it really upset Kelly a lot. He keeps journals all the time, and I remember him just writing pages and pages. It was really upsetting—everyone was freaked out."

Losing a cherished friend was difficult enough to deal with, but Andy's band mates were also grappling with the reality that Mother Love Bone—and the band's future, which had seemed so full of promise—had died with him. In the aftermath of Andy's death, their confusion manifested itself in different ways, ranging from numb shock, to heavyhearted resignation, to anger. The question that haunted them— unspoken at first, then posed aloud by their family and friends—was, What would they do *now*?

PolyGram was sensitive in the weeks after Andy's death, allowing the band members the time they needed to decide how, or if, they would continue. Everyone agreed that *Apple* should be released, and the album was issued a few months later, with the words *In memory of Andrew Wood* stamped on its back cover. As to whether Mother Love Bone would carry on, it wasn't as easy to reach a decision.

"Greg wanted to keep going with the band and find another singer," recalls Fineman. "You know, they'd gotten signed and this was going to be it, and 'we can't give up,' and 'fuck Andy.' He was kind of getting angry at him for dying in such a stupid way, and I don't think Jeff and Stone were really ready to hear that. And Jeff and Greg *already* weren't getting along, and Stone was tired of being in the middle of that. So things just kind of fell apart."

Ultimately, Stone and Jeff decided that Andy's personality had been such an integral part of the band that it would be folly to continue without him, and Mother Love Bone officially disbanded. Fairweather and Gilmore played together briefly in a band called Blind Horse, before Fairweather switched to bass and joined Love Battery and Gilmore left Seattle to travel in Mexico and Central America. As for Stone and Jeff, they were adrift, uncertain whether they would play together again or whether they would even continue to play at all.

"I think Stone knew," Jeff mused in 1991, "but I didn't know what I was going to do with my life. I felt like I'd spent a lot of time getting to that point, and the fact that the rug got pulled out from underneath us right when we were about to go on the road was really depressing. 'Cause that's all I'd ever wanted to *do*. Making records is great, but I'd made a lot of records, and in all the years I'd been in bands, I'd never been out for three or four months, six months or a year. So when that got taken away, it was like, 'Oh, man, I've got to start all over again.'"

The world wasn't going to stop and wait for them, either. Soundgarden, now considered *the* Seattle band by mainstream music pundits, had just left to tour Europe, and in February, *Ultramega OK*, the album they'd made for SST before signing to A&M, had been nominated for a Grammy. Columbia had just signed Alice in Chains. Tad and Mudhoney had been crisscrossing the map on various tours, both bands having released a number of Sub Pop singles and LPs. And having seemingly burst into existence from nowhere was Nirvana, a trio from Aberdeen led by an astoundingly talented singer-songwriter named Kurt Cobain, who'd been weaned on the Beatles and later been bitten by the punk bug when he began hanging out with the Melvins. Nirvana were late bloomers compared to the other bands on the scene, but once they got rolling they'd made up for lost time, their fusing of dense guitars with

Cobain's anguished, scream-on-pitch vocals and irresistible pop hooks quickly making them a band to watch—especially after Sub Pop released their first album, *Bleach*.

"We put out *Bleach*, and gosh, it just kept selling," Bruce Pavitt later told Michael Azerrad, author of the Nirvana biography *Come As You Are*. "Never in the history of our company have I seen a record just sell and sell and sell. They did tour, but a lot of bands tour. The word of mouth was there. There was something special there."

A buzz had begun to circulate about the Seattle scene in general, much of it due to the efforts of Pavitt and Poneman, who had spent the past two years tirelessly promoting the bands on the Sub Pop roster. The two were always strapped for cash, pouring every penny of profit from the records they released back into the label. But when it came to hyping their bands—and, some later accused, themselves—they spared no expense. Typical of their extravagance when it came to publicity-generating tactics (a trait that prompted Soundgarden's Kim Thayil to refer to them as the "Don Kings of the Seattle scene") was their decision in the spring of 1989 to fly Everett True, a writer for the British music paper *Melody Maker*, to Seattle.

"Our European agent had a distributor whose publicist said, 'If you're willing to fly this guy over, he'll do a big spread on you,'" recalled Poneman.

"That was the beginning of the hype machine," concurred Pavitt. "*Melody Maker* had this huge spread that said Seattle had the hottest rock scene in the world. It was a legitimate story, but there was enough payola in there to make it good and sleazy." ("Something we respect," Poneman added with a laugh.)

To some, the expense of importing a British journalist might have seemed a careless gamble, but to Pavitt and Poneman, shrewdly cognizant of the number of American bands who'd first received notice in the ever-attentive British press and later parlayed it into success on their home turf, it was simply one more step in a cleverly executed marketing plan. And it paid off. True's first glowing reports on what he called a "rock explosion emanating from one small, insignificant, West Coast American city"—a *Melody Maker* spread on Mudhoney on March 11, 1989, and a similarly gushing roundup on Sub Pop the following week that featured capsule descriptions of the label's most promising artists— had had a significant impact on the scene, sparking a frenzied interest in the Seattle bands that eventually began to filter down to the press and the major labels in the United States. Thanks in large part to their rowdy single "Touch Me, I'm Sick"—considered by many to be the recording that really got the "grunge" ball rolling—Mudhoney reaped the lion's share of attention from the British press blitz, their 1988 EP *Superfuzz Bigmuff* rising to the top of the U.K. independent charts and remaining there for a year. But Tad, Nirvana, and Soundgarden were hardly left in the dark. They, too, had found themselves under a bigger spotlight than they enjoyed previously, especially after Radio One deejay John Peel, one of Britain's most influential tastemakers, heard their contributions on *Sub Pop 200*, a compilation of mostly Seattle bands released by the label in late 1988, and began publicly championing the compilation and the bands that appeared on it.

Another masterstroke was the Sub Pop Singles Club, dreamed up by Pavitt and Poneman in 1988 as a means of increasing their capital while at the same time enhancing Sub Pop's mystique. Subscriptions—$35 annually, in return for which members received monthly limited edition singles, most of them on colored vinyl—began increasing steadily after the Brits took Sub Pop under their wing, and within a few years Pavitt and Poneman would have seven thousand subscribers. The club's first 1,000-copy release, an October 1988 single featuring Nirvana's cover of Shocking Blue's "Love Buzz" backed by the band's own "Big Cheese," now fetches upward of $100 in collectors' circles.

Stone and Jeff hadn't really been part of the Sub Pop clique since the breakup of Green River. Although they were friendly with some of the musicians in the Sub Pop camp, others had ostracized them for their unabashed flouting of the scene's antiambition, antisuccess aesthetic, and Sub Pop and its roster of bands had seemed to be operating in an insignificant parallel universe during the time Stone and Jeff were pursuing mainstream success with Mother Love Bone. Now, though, the tables had turned. It had to be a bitter pill for the two that, just as their band's career was cruelly cut short, so many other Seattle musicians suddenly appeared to be leading charmed lives.

It seems appropriate that when Stone and Jeff did surface from their depression over Andy's death and start testing the water again, they hooked up with an individual who was also something of an outsider to the punkish Sub Pop fold. Since the early Eighties, Mike McCready had been eking out his musical identity in a subset of the Seattle community that was the polar opposite of Sub Pop, a scene dominated by heavy metal bands (TKO, Mace, Culprit, Rottweiler, Metal Church) that had sprung up around the same time as the immensely successful Queensryche, playing most of their early gigs at the Lake Hills Roller Rink.

Mike, a whip-thin, wispy-haired George Carlin fanatic, was a difficult fellow to read. Quiet and almost painfully shy by nature, he tended
to hide his feelings behind a wall of clownish exhibitionism. He could
often morph from a teenage Descartes into a one-man Comic Relief
troupe in the space of a few seconds, running around naked at rehearsals or tossing out strings of one-liners that caused his friends to
collapse helplessly in laughter.

"With Mike, it's either joke after joke, or nothing at all," says one acquaintance. "When there's a spotlight on him, he comes alive. But I've
yet to really get any insight into him. He doesn't share much. That's just
the way he is."

Born in April 1964—his mother, Louise, an elementary school art
teacher and his father, Roy, employed by the city of Seattle—Mike was a
disciple of Kiss, Aerosmith, and AC/DC just as Jeff and Stone had been,
buying his first cheap Les Paul copy at age eleven. For a time, he took
guitar lessons from a local instructor, but the lessons were tedious. He
never learned to read music and eventually opted for the traditional
hole-up-in-your-bedroom route to proficiency.

"Everything I know, I stole directly from Ace Frehley, Angus Young,
and Keith Richards," Mike told Seattle writer Jeff Gilbert in 1995. "I
used to sit for hours and copy every lick on those early AC/DC and Kiss
records."

When he was fifteen, Mike joined with Danny Newcombe and brothers Chris and Rick Friel to form Warrior, a high school Kiss cover band
(they actually played "Black Diamond" in the school lunchroom) that
was renamed Shadow a few years later. Shadow started out on the roller-
rink circuit before graduating to larger all-ages venues, including performances at the Moore Theater's annual Headbanger's Ball festivities
on two consecutive Halloweens. (The response was encouraging at the
1984 Moore show, but the following year, playing on a bill with TKO
and Metal Church, they were booed. The audience, having shown up
to hear speed metal, quickly grew bored with Shadow's more pop
leanings.)

After they came of age, Shadow had moved into the club circuit, on
at least one occasion opening for Green River at Gorilla Gardens. But
their look and sound were worlds apart from what bands like Green
River and Soundgarden were doing at the time. In early promotional
photos, the members of Shadow were always clean scrubbed and precocious, striking kissy-pooh *16* or *Tiger Beat* teen idol poses that once
prompted the *Rocket* to dub them "Seattle's Menudo."

Eventually stripped down to a three-piece—Mike playing lead guitar, Chris Friel on drums, and Rick Friel on bass and vocals—Shadow gigged around Seattle for the next few years, picking up a thrashier, funkier sound and adding some visual pizzaz to their show. Mike's favorite shtick at one point was smashing dolls on stage. In 1987, after they'd recorded a few inexpensive demos, Shadow saved their money and, like hundreds of other ambitious metallists before them, struck out for Los Angeles, which was well on its way to reaching poodlehead supersaturation by that point.

Living expenses in L.A. were much steeper than they had been in Seattle, and although they took jobs, Mike working as a clerk at Aaron's Records in West Hollywood, they were barely scraping by. They got gigs at clubs like Fenders and the Whisky, but with no money to rent a practice space they were unable to work on new material, and their morale began suffering badly. It didn't help when the *L.A. Weekly* gave them a thumbs-down, intimating that they didn't know what they were doing because they were from Seattle. They continued playing, but the competition was steep, and eventually they accepted the fact that Los Angeles was not going to be their path to glory.

"Basically, we weren't that great a band, and we didn't realize it until we got down there," Mike recalled. "I guess we lost our focus. I got really bummed out and came back to Seattle."

The thirteen months the band spent in Los Angeles had almost been disillusioning enough to put Mike off music for good. By the time Shadow returned home in 1988 with their tails between their legs, he was badly burned out, and within six months, he'd quit the band, cut his hair short, taken a job at a video store, and enrolled in some community college classes. Later, he would joke that he veered dangerously close to Republicanism that year, while his sadly neglected guitars gathered dust in a corner. He's always credited Russ Reidner—a friend who would later turn up in a band called the Cheap Ones, along with Shadow's Danny Newcombe—with dragging him back from the precipice of conservatism and reawakening his interest in music. Together with Reidner and a loosely shifting network of other friends, Mike began jamming around, by this time seriously influenced by Stevie Ray Vaughan and beginning to develop the limber blues style that characterizes his playing today. In the spring of 1990, he formed a short-lived psychedelic outfit called Love Chile. The band played only two shows, and at one of them, Stone and Jeff were in the audience.

Stone had known Mike since the early Shadow days—according to

Mike, the two traded rock pictures together before Stone could even play guitar—and he and Jeff had taken note of Mike's finesse back when Mother Love Bone were still together, when they'd stumbled upon him playing along to a Stevie Ray Vaughan record at a house party. "Everybody was just kind of hanging out," Jeff recalled, "and he plugged his guitar into this kid's amp and just started *wailing*." But it was in June 1990, when they saw Love Chile play a show at the OK Hotel supporting Jangle Town—a post-Shadow band formed by Chris and Rick Friel and also featuring Reidner—that Stone and Jeff truly became aware of Mike's potential. "That night was probably the greatest I've ever seen him play," Chris Friel recalled of the show. "He was just on *fire*."

Stone had been doing a lot of writing since the demise of Mother Love Bone, and he recognized in Mike's playing a delicate lead style that would dovetail with his own sense of melody and rhythm. He phoned Mike soon after the OK Hotel show, and when the two got together for a jam, they instantly clicked.

Jeff, meanwhile, had been keeping active with a number of bands, among them the War Babies and an ever-changing aggregation of players who billed themselves as Luv Co. He and Stone hadn't played together since Andy's death, but as summer rolled around, he received a summons from Stone and Mike and began sitting in with them at their rehearsals in the attic of the Gossard home. It wasn't long before they realized they had some material worth recording. Lacking a drummer for the sessions, they enlisted the aid of Soundgarden's Matt Cameron.

"We got together with Matt and went into the studio for two or three days," Jeff remembered. "There was no pressure, because they weren't really songs; they were just song ideas, jams, and that sort of stuff. It was totally cool, because at that point, it was just kind of picking up the vibe and going with it."

The vibe, as it turned out, was stronger than any of them had anticipated. Before long, in a development facilitated by Matt Cameron's involvement, they found themselves working on another project as well.

XOX

Andy's death still weighed heavily on Stone and Jeff's minds. They spoke of him almost daily, occasionally with sadness but more often with laughter, remembering their favorite Andy-isms. Several times that summer, Stone saw blonde strangers on the street or in the store and felt his pulse quicken for a blissful instant—*Andy!*—before reality came crashing back to make him drop the hand he'd been about to raise in greeting.

Stone and Jeff hadn't been the only local musicians hit hard by the tragedy. Soundgarden's Chris Cornell, who'd been especially close to Andy and had often spent time with Xana when Andy was out of town, had been heartbroken over the loss of his friend. And unlike Stone and Jeff, the members of Soundgarden hadn't been able to rely on the supportive Seattle community to ease them through the healing process. Soundgarden had set off for a European tour just after Andy died, and, for Cornell in particular, the tour had been a nightmare.

"It was horrible," Cornell remembered, "because I couldn't talk about it, and there was no one who had loved him around. I wrote two songs, 'Reach Down' and 'Say Hello 2 Heaven.' That was pretty much how I dealt with it. When we came back, I recorded them right away. They seemed different from what Soundgarden naturally does, and they seemed to fit together. They seemed like music he would like."

Cornell had briefly considered rerecording the two songs with the surviving members of Mother Love Bone and releasing them as a single, and just as quickly convinced himself the idea was stupid. But when Matt Cameron played Cornell's tape for Stone, Jeff, and Mike while he was working with them on their demo, they fell in love with the songs and enthusiastically embraced the idea of recording them. Once they were all in the studio together, they experienced such a flood of creativity that Cornell's idea for a single was rapidly left in the dust. Between Cornell (who in addition to the songs he'd penned in Europe contributed "Hunger Strike," "Call Me a Dog," "Wooden Jesus," "Your Savior," and "All Night Thing") and Stone (who weighed in with "Pushin' Forward Back," "Times of Trouble," and "Four-Walled World"), enough new material came into the sessions for a full-length album, later to be titled *Temple of the Dog*, after a line from Andy's song "Man of Golden Words."

Stone, Jeff, and Mike continued recording tracks for their demo with Matt Cameron as well, finally settling on the five instrumentals—early versions of "Alive," "Once," "Footsteps," "Alone," and "Black"—that would be labeled *Stone Gossard Demos '91* and sent around to prospective drummers and vocalists. (It's interesting to note that the melody for "Footsteps" also turned up on *Temple of the Dog*, with lyrics by Cornell, as the song "Times of Trouble.")

Between the cathartic preproduction on *Temple of the Dog*, and the invigorating promise of the songs they were recording with McCready and Cameron, the sessions were a badly needed boost to Stone and Jeff's flagging spirits, providing all the evidence they needed that, as much as it might have seemed like it when Andy died, their best work wasn't behind them. Only one dark cloud hung over them that summer as they put their musical lives back together: When they'd signed to PolyGram with Mother Love Bone, they'd also signed as individual artists, which meant that PolyGram had a lock on any new music they made. That might have been fine, but Michael Goldstone, always their key ally at PolyGram, had just jumped ship to take a job at Epic, and the communication problems they'd experienced with the label in Mother Love Bone had only grown worse since Andy's death.

"They got a new president, and then the company split into three different companies, and there was all this shifting going on and we didn't know where we were," Jeff recalled later. "We didn't know if we were at Mercury or Polydor or the new label, or what. People were telling us, 'Don't worry about it, whatever you guys need,' but nothing was happening, and it just got to the point where that started to take a front seat. All Stone and I wanted to do was concentrate on getting a new band together. We finally just said, 'Look, we want to be cut loose, we don't want a record label looming over our heads and adding all this extra pressure.' So they let us go."

Not without some stiff haggling, though. Freedom left Stone and Jeff in debt to PolyGram to the tune of half a million dollars, and if it weren't for the intervention of Goldstone, who was already angling to sign them to Epic, they would have been stuck where they were. Goldstone was busy convincing Epic to fork over the $500,000 necessary to satisfy Stone and Jeff's financial obligation to PolyGram. While this would still leave them with a whopping piggy-bank deficit—Epic would later charge the sum against their royalties—at least they would be in hock to a label they felt comfortable with.

With the administrative kinks worked out for the time being, Stone, Jeff, and Mike turned their attention to finding a singer and a drummer. On their short list of drummer candidates was Jack Irons, a Californian who'd spent most of his musical career in the Red Hot Chili Peppers and gone on to tour with Joe Strummer, the much-revered former guitarist-vocalist for the Clash.

Stone and Jeff had seen Irons play a couple of times and thought he had a "pretty cool vibe," but it's also possible that they felt a kinship with him on a nonmusical level. In June 1988, Irons, too, had lost one of his dearest friends—the Chili Peppers' first guitarist, Hillel Slovak—to heroin, and it was fairly well-known that Irons had always maintained a devoutly antidrug stance. During his tenure in the Chili Peppers, at times when both Slovak and the band's vocalist, Anthony Kiedis, were using, Jack had made his disapproval so clear that he later said they may have found it difficult to talk to him about their addictions.

"Trying to talk to me about drugs, or drug problems, was a very painful thing to do," Irons recalled. "I was so against the whole thing that nobody even wanted to hear my shit."

Slovak's death had sent Irons into a mental collapse so severe that his family had committed him to a psychiatric hospital. He'd been there for a few months, convinced that he was going to leave music behind him for good, when he got the phone call from Strummer that finally drew him out of his shell. He'd been active again for a few years by the time Goldstone, at the request of Stone and Jeff, passed him a copy of the now-infamous *Stone Gossard Demos '91* tape.

Jack liked the songs, but for him, the timing was all wrong. He was in the process of putting together his own band, Eleven, and also preparing for a tour with Red Kross. On top of that, his wife was pregnant, and Stone, Jeff, and Mike were based in Seattle. He could hardly pack up and move at the moment, and although the band suggested that they might consider relocating to California, he reluctantly turned them down. Disappointed, the three resigned themselves to continuing their search, asking Irons to let them know about it if he happened to come across anyone who might fit the bill.

"One of the last things we said," Jeff recalled of the conversation, "was, 'Here's a couple of extra tapes; if you know of any other drummers or singers, give 'em to whoever you think.'

"And Jack said, 'I know this one guy down in San Diego who might be cool. . . . '"

Five

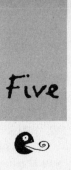

Bad Radio / Crazy Eddie Goes Camping / *Mamasan* / Mookie Blaylock

"I was going to try, or die trying. I felt like it wasn't gonna happen if you didn't *make* it happen. If you were gonna get your music out there, you really had to be full-fledged."

Certainly, nobody who knew twenty-five-year-old Eddie Vedder in San Diego would have accused him of being less than full-fledged. In 1990, the ambitious young singer was living in an apartment complex on Lake Murray Boulevard in the San Diego suburb of La Mesa, sometimes spending nights at the Mission Beach apartment of his girlfriend, Beth Liebling. He worked at a Chevron tank farm, pulling sixty-hour weeks on the graveyard shift as what he called "a glorified gas pumper." Prior to the Chevron job, he'd worked nights doing security at the posh La Valencia hotel in La Jolla, an old-world, Mediterranean-style resort situated right on the Pacific, where celebrities often stayed.

"It was really great, because I'd meet all these cool people," Eddie said of the hotel job. "Like, Richard Thompson would stay there. But I didn't have to kiss ass. I wasn't waiting tables—they'd need my help or something."

The La Valencia and Chevron jobs had appealed to Eddie because they afforded him plenty of on-the-clock songwriting time, a crucial requirement for someone who was as certain as Eddie was that a career in music was his destiny. To him, music had always been more than a hobby. Rather, he was fond of telling people, it was what he lived for. Having his songs heard was a goal that dominated his every waking moment—and in those days, Eddie enjoyed more waking moments than most. He was known around San Diego, he has said, as "the guy who never slept."

"I was pretty much a madman," he recalled. "I knew what I wanted to do, and I felt like I could sing a song better than anybody else. I wasn't a security guy—I wasn't gonna own my own security company or whatever. But if you're gonna work forty hours a week, try to work somewhere where there's some benefit, you know what I mean? I had jobs where I could write or read, even listen to music, for at least four or five hours a night, unbothered. I was just living up to what I felt was some sort of destiny to be an artist."

To that end, the self-described "little surfer with really big ideas" had kept to a punishing schedule ever since 1984, when he'd migrated to the sunny beach community from his native Chicago. Usually, he would work all night, guzzling coffee toward the end of his shift to see him through the drive home, where his beloved four-track awaited. Once home, he'd work on his songs, then grab a beer and an hour of sleep and head out to the clubs, usually the Bacchanal, where he became a fixture, pestering the manager for tips about how to make it in the music business and meeting as many of the successful rockers who played there as he could. If he wasn't at the Bacchanal he could often be found at Winter's, a college hangout on El Cajon Boulevard where he and Beth helped to organize a weekly gothic-rock night called Red Tape. Other nights and some weekends, Eddie logged time as a runner for Avalon Attractions, a local promoter, helping out at major concerts on the campus of San Diego State University, where Beth was attending classes.

"I'd work for free as a roadie, just to be closer to the whole pulse of what was going on," he said of those days. "Even years back, I'd put myself in positions where I got to, like, hang out with Sting right before he went on stage. Whatever it was, I'd get pretty much the ultimate experience."

When he wasn't lugging gear for another band on his free evenings, he was gigging with his own band. For six years, he'd been trying to make an imprint on the world in a series of groups whose drive, frustratingly, had never seemed to equal his. He'd worked his way through a number of short-lived bands—Surf and Destroy, the Butts, and Indian Style (a punk outfit that also featured future Rage Against the Machine drummer Brad Wilk)—before settling in as frontman for Bad Radio, a position he won in 1986 after answering a want ad in the *San Diego Reader* and auditioning with a cover of the Rolling Stones' "Paint It Black."

"There were two other singers who auditioned," recalled Valery Saifudinov, the owner of Bad Radio's Carlsbad rehearsal studio. "I told the band that Eddie was the guy they should get. He was a young songwriter who already had a good sense of what he wanted to do. He had the right taste—Springsteen, U2, people who mean something."

Between 1987 and 1989, Bad Radio practiced a few times a week at Saifudinov's studio, growing into one of the top bands on the San Diego scene, in large part due to Eddie's involvement. Judging from demos the band made that are floating around today in collectors' circles—which were obviously, to be fair, recorded under less-than-ideal circumstances—most of Bad Radio's material wasn't all that exceptional. But even backed by a band that was clearly no match for his powerhouse of a voice, Eddie was an arresting presence. The sheer beauty of his ragged tenor did much to redeem the band's weaker songs, and on the more solidly crafted compositions, he positively shone.

Eddie's input wasn't just musical. He'd quickly taken charge of the band's business affairs, photocopying hand-designed promotional fliers to plug their gigs and networking with anyone who could book them or give them a leg up. He also steered Bad Radio in a more socially conscious direction after joining Musicians Who Care, an Encinitas-based network of charity-minded artists that sponsored a number of benefits Bad Radio played, including a November 1989 Human Rights Now! concert at the La Jolla Teen-Senior Center, staged to raise money for Amnesty International. At times, Eddie was so broke that Patricia Grimes, the cofounder of Musicians Who Care, had to hound him for his dues, but what he lacked in funds, he made up for with charisma.

"Eddie walked in a room, and he had this illumination," Grimes later told the *San Diego Blade Citizen*. "He had this essence, something that stands out. The first time I met him, he walked up and hugged me and thanked me for what we were doing with Musicians Who Care. I remember thinking he had a very positive spirit. Eddie was the kind of person who created a large amount of impact in a short space of time."

As a lyricist, too, Eddie packed a keen social awareness that gave Bad Radio's material more resonance than was typical for the party-time bar circuit they were a part of. At this early stage his songwriting had yet to be informed by the poetic subtlety and gift for entendre for which he would later be known, but his heart was in the right place. Early on, he was tackling problems like homelessness ("Homeless") and domestic discord ("Better Man," which would resurface in 1994 on Pearl Jam's third album, *Vitalogy*); other songs from the same period, like "Believe You Me" and the distinctly U2-influenced "Crossroads," were less specific, more like apocalyptic snapshots of a world going downhill fast. Whatever the topic, though, most of Eddie's songs had protagonists with one trait in common: They were all fighters.

As was Eddie himself, judging from what he said about his background later, after he was in the public eye. He gave the impression that nothing had ever come easily to him, and sometimes you got the sense that his ambition had had as much to do with fleeing his past as it had with pursuing his dreams. When he spoke of his upbringing—something he rarely did in much detail, at least to reporters—it was often with a dismissive bitterness, as if he'd drawn the short straw in that department and, lacking any real support from his parents, been fed into the viselike jaws of adult responsibility well before he was ready to handle the pressure.

"I was on my own pretty early, like by the time I was sixteen," he said in 1991. "There never was just *life*—it was always just dealing with it. I spent a long time only having negative things to deal with. There was a lot of determination involved to keep myself afloat, and it was always singular. There was never anything to fall back on. There was never a parent with a credit card, never anything. It gets intense. That's why I understand people in the street."

This was the Eddie Vedder that fans worldwide would come to know in a few years, through his songs and through the press: earnest and sincere, conscientious, empathetic about the misfortunes of others, and haunted himself by what appeared to be a walk-in closet full of old ghosts and bad memories. It's difficult to reconcile this individual with the Eddie who can be seen in video bootlegs of old Bad Radio shows—the gregarious fellow with a trendy bi-level haircut, sporting a leather cap and loud, baggy trousers, who reminds club goers at the end of the set that there's a "party at my house, tonight and every night." In fact, some who knew Eddie in San Diego claim never to have seen the troubled, world-weary side he displayed in later years.

Rob Jensen, who worked with Eddie at Chevron in 1988, described him in a piece he wrote for the *San Diego Reader* as "a funny, outgoing, smiling guy," a "great storyteller" who seemed "happy to be doing what he was doing." According to Jensen, the Eddie he saw just a few years later on MTV—"angry, hushed, distant, wearing a constant expression of grave concern," and conveying "deep disappointment with his success"—had little in common with the coworker he knew in San Diego. The Eddie he knew, Jensen wrote, had boasted about snagging an invite to a Hollywood party, enthused endlessly about his band and his exploits as a roadie, and had made it clear that success as a professional musician, taking his career "all the way," was exactly what he wanted. Whether the real Eddie in 1990 was the happy-go-lucky individual captured on video and remembered by Jensen, or the tortured artist with the perpetually furrowed brow the world would come to know a few years later—or, most likely, a little of each—what's certain is that he hadn't found what he was looking for in Bad Radio.

For a while, it had seemed that the band had real potential. They were packing clubs, and they'd made a four-song cassette that they sold at a local Tower Records. Marco Collins, then a deejay at 91X, a local station that had a soft spot for San Diego bands, later said that he remembered Eddie calling the station and pestering him to play Bad Radio's tapes. The band had even aroused a little major-label interest, according to the *Los Angeles Times,* which reported in August 1989 that they were setting up a showcase at Los Angeles's Club Lingerie to audition for MCA Records executives. But despite the attention Bad Radio was getting, for Eddie, something was missing. By late 1989, he'd had to face the reality that, once again, his band mates weren't as committed as he was—at least not for the right reasons.

"We'd win 'battle of the bands' on intensity alone, but it was coming from *me*," Eddie recalled. "I couldn't get anybody else to give up their fucking bullshit. As far as songs and stuff, they weren't reading, they weren't *living*. They knew how big [Mötley Crüe drummer] Tommy Lee's new drum kit was, but, you know, fuck that."

By the summer of 1990, Eddie had quit Bad Radio and was pondering his next move. It was at this point that Jack Irons stepped into the picture.

XOX

"It was the weirdest thing," the Red Hot Chili Peppers' bassist, Flea, said in 1994, of his first meeting with Eddie. "We went backpacking up in Yosemite, and Jack brought him along. He was like, 'This is Eddie.' Then two years later, we go on tour, and there's this band that's gonna open for us called Pearl Jam, I never heard of 'em. And it was the guy from the backpacking trip. I was like, 'Oh *wow*, we spent two weeks together in the mountains.' Eddie goes from being an obscure figure on a backpacking trip to, you know, the world's largest rock star. Man, that was *intense*."

Intense is a word that invariably surfaces when people talk about Eddie, and, just like everybody else, Jack Irons hadn't found it easy to dismiss the short, earnest fellow he'd met backstage at the Bacchanal in the fall of 1989, where Irons was appearing with Joe Strummer's band. On the evening in question, Eddie had played hooky from his Chevron job so he could do some volunteer roadie work and, hopefully, meet Strummer.

"I forwent my paycheck that night to go hang out at sound check, because to me, just to look at Joe Strummer's guitar was cool," Eddie said later. "And that night the power went off and I sat in a tiny room with Joe Strummer for like an hour with just this big Mag-Lite on his face. It was a totally surreal experience. I remember he gave me a hit off his cigarette and it was half pot and half tobacco, and I nearly puked."

Eddie had spent a lot of time talking to Jack Irons that night, and in the year that had passed since, the affinity that had sprung up between them had developed into an easy friendship. They'd kept in touch by phone, and often, when Jack wasn't touring, Eddie would drive to Los Angeles to shoot hoops with him. One mutual acquaintance says that Eddie looked up to Jack so much that "Eddie *was* Jack Irons—facial expressions, talking, everything. Everything he did was modeled after Jack."

Whether or not Eddie's idolatry of Jack was as blatant as some claim, it is easy to see how he might view Jack, with his unquestionable punk pedigree, as a mentor of sorts, a direct link to a members-only club that Eddie himself badly wanted to join. A decorated punk veteran who'd toured the world and who'd made records with the Chili Peppers and Strummer, Jack knew his way around the industry, and his best buddies were people Eddie knew only from pictures in magazines. It was through Jack that Eddie would first meet some of the musicians who would later be regarded as his peers, a circle of friends—among them Flea and the Chili Peppers, and Alain Johannes and Natasha Schneider of Eleven, Jack's new band—that had first formed within the walls of the illustrious Fairfax High School, the Los Angeles breeding ground for countless musical talents throughout the decades, from legendary producer Phil Spector right on up to the Peppers. Eddie's first interaction with some of these musicians as an equal as opposed to a fan took place in July 1990, when he accepted Jack's invitation to accompany him and a handful of others on a ten-day backpacking trip at Yosemite National Park. The Yosemite excursion had such a significant impact on Eddie that he would still be talking about it a year later.

The way he told it, the trip was a revelation for him, awakening the slumbering daredevil inside him and giving him a heightened sense of his own possibility. It's likely that the identity that would be so closely associated with Eddie later on—that of a risk taker, hell-bent on living for the moment, intent on pushing himself to the limit and making the most of every opportunity—first took root during those ten days in the wilderness. Eddie had gone out of his way to make an impression on the others with his antics, diving off cliffs and caroming down steep rock slides that nobody else would risk. Receiving a standing ovation from his fellow campers after he grew a bit too bold and only narrowly escaped being carried over a cliff by some rapids, he said later, had made him feel *alive.*

"It was so exciting," Eddie enthused about the trip. "I was nick-named 'Crazy Eddie' by Flea and everybody else. It was partly because I was with these people I respected so much, people who were so intense. They were questioning doing certain things, and I'd think, 'I could do that, my body could withstand that.' If you ever bump into Flea, tell him you know Eddie, and he won't know who I am. But tell him you know Crazy Eddie and he'll go, 'Crazy Eddie—he's *crazy.*' After that, I was expected to do *everything crazy.*"

The Yosemite trip was a significant one for Eddie on another level, as well. During the drive back, Jack popped a cassette into the tape deck that Eddie had never heard before, one he proclaimed to be "cool, really cool." Only later would Eddie reflect on that day and realize that the music he'd heard contained the seeds of his future. The next time he heard the name of that particular band, it was in September, two months after the camping trip.

"Jack called and said, 'You know those guys from that tape, Mother Love Bone?'" Eddie remembered later. "He explained the whole story to me. He said they'd asked him to play drums, and also asked him about singers. He said he'd talked to them and said, 'Well, I could never move to Seattle,' and they'd said maybe *they'd* move. So I thought that if all went well, I would be playing with Jack. He was a great friend, and that meant a lot to me, that maybe I could be playing with Jack."

Jack put Stone and Jeff in touch with Eddie, and not long afterward, during a trip to Los Angeles, they met with him. "He gave us a tape of some of the stuff he'd done, and we thought it was pretty cool," Jeff remembered.* The clincher, though, was what Eddie would do with their demo. Back in San Diego after his meeting with Stone and Jeff, Eddie took the tape to work with him one night so he could absorb the songs. The following morning after his shift, with the instrumentals still in his head, he went surfing. As usual, he was on the brink of exhaustion—which, he would say later, heavily influenced what happened next.

"The sleep deprivation came into play," Eddie recalled. "When you haven't slept for days, you get so sensitive that it feels like every nerve is directly exposed. You can watch a mother with her child walk across the street, or see a little article in the newspaper, and you'll just start to weep.

"I went surfing in that sleep-deprived state, and totally started dealing with a few things that I hadn't dealt with. I was really getting focused on this one thing, and I had this music in my mind at the same time. I was literally writing some of these words as I was going up against a wave or something. I got out of the water, and I went right into the house and recorded three songs. I didn't even write down the lyrics. I just wrote an outline and sang it, and the only time I even listened back to it was when I was mixing it down from four-track. I listened to it, got it right, and then listened to it again, and then just sent it off. I didn't really think about it. When I think back, it's pretty weird, because it was like a three-song mini opera, this story that was really intense. Pretty much half of it was real, and half of it was extensions of reality."

The story behind Eddie's mini opera—or *Mamasan*, as it's known, after the title he gave the tape he returned to Jeff in Seattle—would become a rabidly discussed component of Pearl Jam lore a few years later, after Eddie divulged what the lyrics he'd written for "Alive," "Once," and "Footsteps" meant to him and explained how the three songs fit together. But at the time, he never imagined that anyone else would even care.

"I didn't think about it as being an opportunity or anything," he re-

---

*Conflicting versions of this incident have been offered by the members of Pearl Jam. Eddie's account omits an initial meeting with Stone and Jeff entirely. But Stone and Jeff have both spoken of a face-to-face meeting with Eddie prior to his now-mythical trip to Seattle in October 1990, Jeff in the conversation with this reporter excerpted above, and Stone in a 1991 radio interview in which he recalled that he and Jeff "met [Eddie] in Los Angeles and flew him up [to Seattle] about two weeks later." A first meeting in Los Angeles would have made sense, as Stone and Jeff were frequently in Los Angeles at the time promoting Mother Love Bone's *Apple*, and Eddie was often there visiting Irons.

called. "At the time, it didn't matter to me. The coolest part was that it was helping me get a few things out of my system. The music was bringing things out of me that hadn't been brought out. It was really natural with this music. Before, it had always seemed forced."

Eddie didn't think about the tape again until later that week. He treated himself to a movie one afternoon—David Lynch's *Wild at Heart*—and then piloted his Toyota truck down to the beach to play some guitar. While there, he bumped into a friend who had the latest issue of *Rolling Stone,* and in it was an item about Stone and Jeff's search for a singer. Eddie examined the magazine. He said nothing to his friend, but the article left him feeling self-conscious about the tape he'd just put in the mail.

"It was like, 'Aw, *fuck*—those are the Love Bone guys right there, I should've paid more attention to that tape,'" he recalled, laughing. "You know, you'd think I would've written a better hook, something about 'Meet you on Saturday night.'"

He needn't have worried. Back in Seattle, probably right about the time Eddie was sitting on the beach in San Diego and wringing his sandy hands, Jeff Ament was sitting in his Seattle apartment, listening to the *Mamasan* tape. Jeff played it through three times. Then he got on the phone.

"Stone," the bassist told his longtime partner, "I may be totally whacked out, but I think this guy is amazing."

※◇※

Eddie left town for a few days and returned home to a series of answering machine messages from Jack, each sounding more urgent than the last.

"*. . . These guys are looking for you, and you really should call them.*" Beeeeep. "*Hey Eddie, really, call these guys—they want to fly you up and all this weird stuff. . . .*"

Within days, Eddie and Jeff were talking at length on the phone, and Eddie quickly agreed to take a week off work in October and travel to Seattle. Stone, Jeff, and Mike, meanwhile, having resigned themselves to the fact that Jack Irons wasn't going to budge, had been busy auditioning drummers. Among the candidates was Dave Krusen, a slight, dark-haired fellow hailing from Gig Harbor, Washington. Krusen, despite stints in numerous local bands since 1979—among them Outrigger, Agent Boy, and a new wave outfit called the Boibs—was something of an unknown quantity in Stone and Jeff's circles when Tal Goettling, a mutual friend, told him about the auditions. Still, his hard-hitting style put him ahead of the competition, and two weeks after he auditioned—the same week Eddie was due from San Diego—Krusen was invited into the fold.

Later, the band members would describe their first week together in near-mystical terms, clearly overwhelmed by the speed with which they'd come together and the creative explosion that had ensued once they had. On the day he arrived in Seattle, Eddie went directly from Sea-Tac airport to the band's rehearsal space, then in the basement of Galleria Potatohead, a Belltown art gallery not far from the Crocodile Cafe. As planned, the others were already set up, and when Eddie got there, rather than fritter away any time on getting-to-know-you chitchat, they simply cranked up the amps. By all accounts, the connection was immediate, and powerful.

"Everything happened so *quick*," Jeff recalled in 1991. "When we got together those first few days, I knew that that's what I was supposed to be doing. I don't think you're ever sure of anything you're ever doing, but that week was one of the greatest weeks of my life."

Eddie, similarly astounded by his new band's prolificacy, later described that first week as "just a totally magical thing, the most intense musical experience I'd ever been involved in. I'd written three more songs before I left San Diego, and then we wrote more from scratch while I was in Seattle," he remembered. "All of a sudden, we had eleven songs."

From home, Eddie had brought a box of ten cassettes by Kipper Jones, an R&B artist on Virgin Records, where Beth was working in the publicity department. As they practiced, the band recorded over these, making cheap tapes of their rehearsals courtesy of Virgin and Mr. Jones. Some of the songs captured on those tapes, like "Release," were complete improvisations that seemed to flow out of their own accord, emerging full-blown and requiring no tinkering or editing after the fact. Although a few words here or there would be changed, most of the off-the-cuff lyrics Eddie supplied for "Release" the first time the band played it would still be intact when the song turned up on their debut album. A little superstitious about the ease with which the words had come out of him, Eddie honored his muse by refusing to commit the lyrics to paper.

"On 'Release,' everyone plugged in their guitars and started this kind of tinkling," Eddie recalled, "and I started humming, moaning or whatever, and then all of a sudden it was like a six-minute song that totally rolled and peaked. Those words—I still refuse to write them down, even if they need them for publishing. I won't write 'em down. That was just something I hadn't experienced, it was so intense."

After five days of rehearsals, energized by the productive week they'd had and wanting to test their new lineup in a live setting, Stone and Jeff finagled a slot for the band on a bill at the Off Ramp Café. In need of a moniker to perform under, they named themselves after one of their basketball heroes, then–New Jersey Nets point guard Mookie Blaylock. The choice wasn't as random as it sounded: During rehearsal breaks that week, they'd been swapping basketball trading cards, and at one point, someone had slipped Blaylock's card into the cover of one of their rehearsal cassettes. "Ultimately, it was kind of goofy," Eddie admitted. "But that first week, we were too busy working on songs to think about a name."

The hour-long set that the newly christened Mookie Blaylock performed at the Off Ramp hardly qualified for entry in the Greatest Rock Show Ever Played sweepstakes, but given that the five musicians who filed onto the club's tiny stage had worked together for less than a week, the coming out witnessed by those present was nothing short of astounding.

The band had been running late for the unannounced gig and was still sound checking with "Even Flow," a funkified riff of Stone's paired with a typically stark Eddie lyric about homelessness, when the Off Ramp opened its doors. Eddie, bundled in a shabby blue windbreaker and wearing a rather goofy hat—a cylindrical, brimless creation that would have been more at home on an aging lodge brother—took the stage, glanced around the empty club, and launched into the song with his eyes tightly closed. When he came to at the end of the song, he was standing in front of a crowd.

"I opened my eyes and it was full, and everyone was just clapping and going nuts," Eddie said later. "It was the weirdest thing—it was like a fucking serious dream."

Pausing occasionally for emergency retunings or water breaks, the band went on to debut—to a clearly appreciative audience—the strongest of the songs they'd composed earlier in the week. There was "Alone," a thunderous ode to either companionship or solitude, depending upon how you interpreted it; "Once," the second chapter of Eddie's *Mamasan* trilogy, the rolling, angry rant of a man whose desperation has transformed him into a sociopath; "Black," a haunting, beautifully crafted soliloquoy by a heartbroken Romeo who's remembering his absent lover; "Breath," plaintive and comforting, a paean to exploration both mental and geographical, whose protagonist asserts that "there's much more than this" and entreats the listener to "run away, my son" and "see it all, see the world"; and "Just a Girl," a dissonant, chordally

rich tale that appears to have been Eddie's first attempt to address the
abortion debate. A staunch pro-choice advocate for reasons his new
band mates had yet to learn, the singer would speak out on the issue
countless times in the years to come.

At that early stage, Eddie clearly hadn't developed the sense of his
own power that would be apparent in his later performances. He appeared insecure and withdrawn through much of the Off Ramp set,
hands jammed in his pockets, eyes either squeezed tightly shut or cast
toward his shoes. Sometimes, he retreated to the darkened corners of the
stage, as if he liked the sanctuary the shadows provided from the prying,
judgmental eyes of the crowd.

There were a number of striking glimpses during the show, though,
of the mesmerizing, almost evangelical frontman Eddie would later become. Occasionally, he appeared to lose his inhibitions in the wash of
sound that supported him, and at those moments, he emerged as a man
possessed—pacing like a caged animal, tearing at his hair, his face red-
dened and his features distorted, his earlier, measured delivery of the
lyrics transformed into something spine-chilling and almost other-
worldly. During certain numbers, veering between a tortured, broken
tenor and a lullaby croon, clutching himself at the waist and bending as
if injured, letting fly with a low moan or a bloodcurdling shriek, he gave
the impression that getting the words out required every atom of physical energy and emotional strength he had in him.

To anyone paying close attention that night, it might have been apparent that two songs in the set—"Alive" and "Release"—held more
emotional resonance for the singer than any of the others. "Alive," the
first song Eddie had put on his *Mamasan* tape and the first song the
quintet had played in the basement of Galleria Potatohead the day he arrived in Seattle, was the story of a boy whose mother informs him that
the man he's always believed to be his father, in fact, isn't—and that,
even worse, his real father is long dead. On "Release," the boy reveals
his primal yearning for the father he never got to know, Eddie's delivery,
at first calm and liquid, building to an impenetrable wall of angst as
he approaches the last verse: "I'll wait up in the dark for you to speak to
me / I'll hold the pain, release me. . . ."

Eventually, Eddie's band mates, and later his audience, would learn
that the story he'd recounted on "Alive" and "Release" was in fact his
own—that *he* was the boy whose family had kept secrets from him, the
boy who'd learned too late who his father was. By the time the truth
came out, though, both songs would already carry entirely different con-

notations in the minds of listeners. Eddie could hardly have predicted, that night at the Off Ramp when he sang it before an audience for the first time, that "Alive," the song he'd written to commemorate the most emotionally wrenching day of his life, would within a year be widely interpreted as an *anthem*, its refrain of "I'm still alive" destined to be taken up like a gaudy, celebratory flag and waved tauntingly in his face by legions of unknowing fans.

XOX

All told, it had been an incredible week. The day after the Off Ramp show, Mookie Blaylock went into London Bridge Studios and made a rough demo of all the new songs they'd written. That night, with the recording finished, Eddie and Jeff enjoyed a basketball bonding session at the Seattle Kingdome, watching the Chicago Bulls tap-dance all over the Seattle Supersonics in an exhibition game. Two days later, a rather shell-shocked Eddie found himself back in San Diego.

"I'm at work, and everything's just the same," he recalled. "I'm punching the time clock and doing that whole thing, and it was as if I'd fallen in love with a girl over the summer and now she was back at home. It was like this thing that you could remember so well, but you couldn't grasp. I'd be feeling that way, but then I'd put in this tape. It was so intense to hear that it really happened. I'd listen to 'Release' and just go, '*Jesus.*'"

It took the singer a month to get out of his job and tie up loose ends. By December, he was back in Seattle for good, ready to relive the dream.

Six

Singles / Ten / Great Grandma Pearl and the Power of Myth / Exit Krusen / Dave Abbruzzese Gets a Hot Tip / How to Shoot a Video and Scare the Suits in One Easy Lesson

An unusually severe winter storm blew into the Puget Sound from British Columbia the same week Eddie returned to Seattle, announcing its icy presence five days before the singer's twenty-sixth birthday. By late evening on December 18, what came to be known as the "Great Seattle Snowstorm of 1990" had dumped between eight and fourteen inches of wet, compact snow on Seattle and its suburbs—hardly a blizzard by New York or Chicago standards, but every bit as paralyzing for a city accustomed mostly to rain.

The storm gifted Seattle with a heightened sense of community for a few days, as citizens pulled together to exclaim over the odd weather, help each other dig out, and giggle at the handful of sour-faced types who insisted on going about their business as if nothing unusual had taken place. One afternoon that week, Eddie, Jeff, and Chris Cornell lingered over coffee at a restaurant near Seattle Center, laughing as they watched the slick streets hoodwink unsuspecting motorists. For Eddie, sitting outside in the cold with his two new friends and enjoying the aftermath of the storm, the frostbitten camaraderie emanating from the

packed cafes of his new home seemed the perfect welcome. But Chris
Cornell had an even better welcome in mind.

Back in October when Eddie had first come to Seattle, preproduction
work on the *Temple of the Dog* album had been underway, and on a few
nights after Mookie Blaylock had finished their rehearsals, Cornell and
Matt Cameron had shown up at the band's practice space to work on
Temple material. Eddie, on hand but not a participant, had for the most
part contented himself with recording the *Temple* rehearsals on his
cache of Kipper Jones tapes. But at one point, as Cornell was trying to
work out an overlapping vocal on a song called "Hunger Strike," Eddie
had stepped in to help out.

Cornell had been impressed with the shy singer's improvised contri-
bution, and as it happened, he and the others were finishing up the
recording of *Temple of the Dog* when Eddie returned to Seattle. Wanting
to include Eddie in the project, Cornell phoned Eddie and invited him
to supply background vocals on a few of the *Temple* tracks—and also to
duet with him on "Hunger Strike." The gesture, which Eddie described
as "a beautiful way to be introduced to the whole family," touched the
Seattle newcomer deeply, marking the start of a close bond between the
two vocalists that has been intact ever since.

Not everything was this idyllic during Eddie's first week back in
Seattle. After Mookie Blaylock opened a show for Alice in Chains at the
Moore Theater on December 22, the *Seattle Times* declared that they
played "bad Seventies country rock" and opined that "not even a cameo
appearance by Soundgarden's Chris Cornell and Matt Cameron made
Blaylock interesting." But the band had too much to do to let a snotty review spoil their enthusiasm. They'd wasted no time in adding to their
repertoire of new songs, and they'd already begun discussing their
agenda with Michael Goldstone and other key personnel at Epic.

"We wanted to make a record, and we didn't want it to come out in,
like, 1993," Jeff recalled later. "We told the record company, 'This is
when we want to make a record, and we want to be on the road this summer—that's a huge priority. And we're not gonna overthink this thing,
we're not gonna get caught up in the game and the bullshit. We're gonna
make a record the way people are supposed to make records.'"

On January 29, Mookie Blaylock went into London Bridge Studios
with Rick Parashar and recorded a more polished demo of the best of the
songs they'd written, as well as a cover of the Beatles' "I've Got a Feeling." A few days later, wanting to get more live experience under their
belts before they began recording their debut, the band set off on a two-

week West Coast club tour opening for Alice in Chains, who were then being comanaged by Soundgarden's manager, Susan Silver and Kelly Curtis. For Eddie, who hadn't yet picked up his now-notorious disdain for the press, one high point of the tour was a mention the band got in the *New York Times* sports section.

"That was the ultimate," Eddie said of the item. "I mean, to be in the *New York Times* was great, but to be in the *sports* section! They had a whole thing about 'Mookie Blaylock is playing against the New York Knicks tonight; Mookie Blaylock is also opening for Alice in Chains in California.' And then it went on to talk about how we got the name. It was totally amazing."

Meanwhile, the Seattle music scene was about to be immortalized on film. In the spring of 1990 when Andy Wood had died, Cameron Crowe, the affable young writer-director behind *Fast Times at Ridgemont High* and *Say Anything* and a longtime friend of Kelly Curtis's (the two had met through Crowe's wife, Heart songstress Nancy Wilson), had been in the process of rewriting an old script called *Singles.* In a 1992 essay for *Rolling Stone*, Crowe described how the screenplay had taken a different course following a gathering he attended at Curtis's house on the night of Andy Wood's death:

> Inside the small house were Andy Wood's friends, his band mates, members of other bands from throughout the city. The same odd look on all their faces—*I've never had a close friend die before.* And still they kept arriving, these dazed Seattle musicians—a breed all their own, the inspired children of pro basketball and Cheap Trick and Led Zeppelin and Black Flag and Kiss.
>
> In the coming years, many of the musicians in that room would see success far beyond their early dreams, beyond even the arena dreams of Andy Wood. But that night it was mostly about staying warm, pulling together. It was almost instinctual. And I thought about Los Angeles, where musicians would already have slipped audition tapes into Kelly's pocket.
>
> I wanted to write something that captured the feeling in that room. Not Andy's story but the story of how people instinctively need to be together. Is anybody truly single? I knew I'd soon be rewriting the rewrite of my script, and I knew I had to direct it, too.

At the center of Crowe's script was the relationship between a Seattle traffic engineer named Steve (played by Campbell Scott) and an environmentalist named Linda (Kyra Sedgewick). But it was the secondary characters, Steve's neighbors, who would prove the real draw when *Singles* hit the theaters. Matt Dillon had been cast as a Seattle rock musician named Cliff Poncier, which gave Crowe the opportunity to write in cameos for real Seattle musicians and set a number of his scenes in local clubs, with bands like Soundgarden and Alice in Chains performing in the background. The soundtrack, too, would almost exclusively feature Seattle artists.

Known for a near-obsessive attention to detail when it came to research, Crowe had shadowed Jeff and Stone as he worked on the rewrite, soaking up their mannerisms, meeting their friends, and injecting bits and pieces of what he saw into his script to lend it realism. In the end, Crowe found his interaction with the musicians so valuable that Kelly Curtis would receive credit as an associate producer on the film; Crowe based his Cliff Poncier character almost entirely on Jeff—right down to Poncier's clothes, which were the real item, straight out of Jeff's closet, and his cluttered room, modeled on the bassist's own. (Jeff was happy to admit to reporters that Poncier's appearance and living quarters had been modeled after his, but he was quick to point out that he hadn't been the inspiration for Poncier's more buffoonish character traits, such as his cavalier treatment of his onscreen girlfriend, Janet, played by Bridget Fonda. "Maybe that's more based on Mark Arm," Jeff coyly suggested to one interviewer.)

In preparation for his role as Poncier, Matt Dillon also spent some time with Stone, Jeff, and Eddie, and eventually Crowe decided to cast the three in bit parts as members of Poncier's band, Citizen Dick. Rehearsals for *Singles* began on February 25, just after Mookie Blaylock and Alice in Chains returned home from their West Coast tour. The cast met for the first time that evening, at a show the two bands played at the Off Ramp. Crowding into a corner booth at the sweaty, packed club to soak up the scene that was supposed to provide the backdrop for the film, Campbell, Sedgewick, Dillon, and Fonda had no idea that by the time *Singles* saw release, *they* would be perceived as the window dressing.

Interest in the Seattle scene was still gathering momentum, much of it generated by—and associated with—Sub Pop. But, ironically, the majority of the bands who would later be identified with the so-called "grunge" movement had already departed Sub Pop for greener pastures. And in January, the label had lost the most precious jewel in its crown: Nirvana.

One reason that some of Sub Pop's artists had become disenchanted with the label was the way Pavitt and Poneman had been hyping their roster to the press. The two had built on the initial interest in Britain by perpetuating stereotypes they knew the condescending U.K. music weeklies would eat up, painting the Seattle scene as a backwoods, white-trash community populated by dumb, lumberjack lunkheads who just happened to have some musical talent. Much was made, for example, of Tad Doyle's former occupation as a butcher, Pavitt and Poneman even convincing the singer to pose with a chain saw for some eager photographers. The real story—that Doyle was well educated, the product of a solid middle-class upbringing, and had never before been anywhere *near* a chain saw—didn't make for such juicy copy. Although the low-brow image Pavitt and Poneman created for their stable of bands reaped a lot of ink, a number of the musicians had come to resent the way they were being portrayed—especially Kurt Cobain, who later told biographer Michael Azerrad that it irritated him to no end to be painted as "this stump-dumb rocker dude from Aberdeen who just blindly found his way up to Seattle and this hip label."

"It just felt degrading to be thought of as someone like that," Cobain fumed, "when that was something I was fighting against my whole life."

But the most common point of contention was that Pavitt and Poneman's high-rolling public-relations schemes and frantic release schedule seemed to be funded by money that should have gone toward paying the bands. Despite the flush appearance created by the heaps of press they were receiving, Sub Pop always seemed to be teetering on the brink of bankruptcy. Pavitt and Poneman were writing rubber checks to keep their phones hooked up and were constantly in debt to various bands on their roster, none of whom were too happy about living on corn dogs and ramen noodles while the profit from their records was funneled into releases by other bands.

Compounding the problem was the label's weak distribution. As was typical with indie labels, Sub Pop couldn't hope to compete with the majors who'd begun swooping in to tempt their bands with large advances and massive distribution operations. Pavitt and Poneman tried to resolve the distribution problem, a major sore point with their artists, by entering into negotiations with Columbia for a distribution deal, but no offer ever made it to the table, and the legal fees they poured into the whole fiasco only further drained their coffers. By 1991, the *Rocket* was blabbing about the label's dire financial situation under the headline "Sub Plop," and Pavitt and Poneman themselves were printing up sarcastic T-shirts that bore the slogan, WHAT PART OF "WE HAVE NO MONEY" DON'T YOU UNDERSTAND? A year later, even the devoutly anti-corporate Mudhoney would be rowing their lifeboat furiously away from the sinking Sub Pop ship, to ink a deal with Reprise.

Of all of the defections, the loss of Nirvana—who'd unexpectedly jumped to DGC Records while working on their second album—had been the most crushing blow for Pavitt and Poneman. "When Nirvana left, I cried for a long time," Pavitt said later. "I was in public places, and it was really embarrassing." Thanks to an incident that had taken place in the summer of 1989, though, Nirvana's move to DGC would ultimately prove Sub Pop's rescue from financial ruin.

Not long after Nirvana had released their Sub Pop debut, *Bleach*, the band's towering bassist, Krist Novoselic, had gone over to Pavitt's house late one evening and drunkenly pounded on the door, bellowing that Nirvana wanted a contract—a formality Sub Pop normally eschewed. Pavitt, who'd been next door at a party for the visiting Babes in Toyland, had walked up his drive to find the inebriated Novoselic struggling to rise from a clump of bushes he'd fallen into, a quirk of timing he would later be thankful for, given that he and Poneman might be washing dishes today if he hadn't encountered Novoselic before the bassist stumbled off. At Novoselic's insistence, Pavitt had called Poneman, who stayed up all night drafting a boilerplate contract that Nirvana signed soon afterward. In the end, the document Nirvana had demanded for its own protection would wind up being much more beneficial to Sub Pop.

When Nirvana decided to move to DGC, the label had to buy out the band's Sub Pop contract, for a reported $75,000 and 2 percent of any royalties from Nirvana's next two DGC albums. For the financially strapped Sub Pop, the $75,000 was a relief. As for the 2 percent, it seemed unlikely to amount to much; Pavitt and Poneman were probably more excited that, as part of the deal, the Sub Pop logo would appear on Nirvana's DGC releases.

Little did they know that in the fall, when DGC released Nirvana's *Nevermind* and the roof blew off Seattle, their trifling 2 percent of the take was going to set them up for years.

XOX

By March 1991, an expectant air hung over Seattle. Soundgarden were in the studio beginning work on *Badmotorfinger*, their second album for A&M. Nirvana were in Los Angeles with producer Butch Vig, recording

Nevermind. Singles was moving along, and the release of *Temple of the Dog* was imminent. The city seemed abuzz with promise and possibility.

It was in the midst of this community wide case of spring fever, in mid-March, that Mookie Blaylock began recording their debut album, *Ten*. The band was shooting for a raw, live feel, avoiding studio gimmickry wherever possible, and, with most of the material for the record already written, the sessions at London Bridge, helmed by Rick Parashar, took less than a month.

The recording of *Ten* wasn't without aggravating moments. Jeff did all of his tracks with headphones on and later decided they'd been a hindrance; wanting the bass to sound more aggressive, he had Parashar set him up in the same room as his amp and overdubbed his tracks on half of the songs. Mike, a gut player who was at his best when he had the freedom to noodle all over the fretboard, had the worst time of it: The repeated takes, he later said, began to make him feel like a robot. "I'd get frustrated if I couldn't get the whole thing down," he recalled. "I start thinking about it too much and then it really doesn't work." On a couple of his tracks, the guitarist wound up throwing in the towel, recording multiple leads and splicing the best of them together to create the final version. Comping a few of the leads sped up the sessions, but Mike wasn't happy about the necessity.

Still, by the time they'd finished recording, enthusiasm was high. *Ten* was the best work any of them had ever done, and they knew it.

The album whispered to life with an unlisted interlude that later became known as "Master/Slave"—an ambient piece weaved from sparse percussion, undulating bass, and ghostly strains of keening guitar, with a barely audible Eddie moaning like a madman over the top—before upending listeners' expectations with a brash stylistic shift into "Once," an edgy track built around a frenetic Stone riff and a chorus that mimicked waves crashing against a shore, with a throaty Eddie chronicling his protagonist's descent into madness. "Even Flow" was all upbeat swagger and stomp, unexpectedly juxtaposed with Eddie's fly-on-the-alley-wall view of homelessness. Similarly, "Alive" paired a placid, beautifully constructed melody with a dark tale of deception, loss, and yearning. The propulsive, bass-heavy intro of "Why Go" melded into a sonic wash of serrated rhythm guitar and supercharged wah-wah, Eddie almost viciously growling out his saga of a teenager's fight for independence after her self-centered parents commit her to an institution. "Why

Go" gave way to the bluesy and languid "Black," a stopped-down anthem for the unlucky-in-love and one of *Ten*'s greatest moments.

"Jeremy" wasn't one of the album's most inventive tracks musically—according to Jeff, who authored it, the song almost hadn't made the final cut—but it crackled with electricity once outfitted with haunting cello, new background vocals, and, especially, Eddie's lyrics. The first song that would truly draw the mainstream audience's attention to the band, "Jeremy" was inspired by a newspaper article that had caught the singer's attention in early January. The real Jeremy was Jeremy Wade Delle, a sixteen-year-old loner from Richardson, Texas, who'd taken a gun to school and shot himself dead in front of his horrified English class. Eddie said later that the reason the newspaper account had had such an impact on him was that he'd had a "Jeremy" in his life, too.

"I knew a kid who brought a sawed-off shotgun to class," he recalled shortly after *Ten* was released. "He hid it in the bushes at lunchtime and brought it into Oceanography class and shot up a tank. He didn't kill anybody—they got it away from him. But this was someone I'd had a conflict with about two years earlier. He had eyes like you wouldn't believe. They were just soulless and black, like a shark's."

Coming after "Jeremy," "Oceans"—a take on the parting-is-such-sweet-sorrow theme—was weightless and ethereal, its classical undertones, softly ringing guitars, and soaring vocals imparting the blessed feel of a cool breeze on a blistering day. "Porch," destined as a slam-pit favorite, sandwiched a swirling, dirty blues lead of Mike's between bursts of dizzying guitar and demanding rapid-fire vocals, while "Garden" was meditative and earthy, a quest for clarity in a nightmarish urban world set to tinkling, wind-chime guitar. "Deep" was brutish, its atonal main riff giving way to a deceptively low-key first verse and then accelerating into controlled chaos again, Eddie's tortured screams mirroring every dip and swerve. *Ten* wound down with the fragile, plaintive "Release," Eddie's prayer-in-the-dark to his father, and a reprise of "Master/Slave" that made a stealthy return twenty seconds after the "official" end of the album.

As debuts go, *Ten* was uncommonly intimate, dragging the listener through a dazzling array of emotions. A great deal of the album's power lay in the music itself, the heady interplay between Stone's transcendent tunings and Mike's intricate lead work. But just as much of *Ten*'s high showing on the emotional Richter scale could be laid at Eddie's feet. In later years, the singer would often remark that he found real life to be "much more bizarre than any kind of fiction," and on *Ten,* just as he had in his earlier work with Bad Radio, he'd offered concrete evidence of that belief, building his lyrics around the quirks, tragedies, and spiritual epiphanies of everyday reality. Whether he was expressing empathy for the disenchanted ("Once," "Even Flow," "Deep") or mourning the battered psyche of an abused or neglected child ("Why Go," "Jeremy"), Eddie was clearly a writer who internalized everything he saw. His true gift, though—what would ultimately make his writing so captivating to an entire dysfunctional generation—was his dogged refusal to settle on unadulterated bleakness. At the core of Eddie's songs, no matter how grave their subject matter, some small ray of gritty survivalism or triumph would always be discerned. The natives of Eddie's lyrical universe might be downtrodden or teetering on the brink of insanity, but they would rarely be beyond redemption, or beyond longing for it at very least.

With the *Ten* sessions complete, the band turned their attention to their contributions for the *Singles* soundtrack. On April 11, Jeff dropped by the movie set around lunchtime to hand over a rough tape of potential songs—among them "Breath" and "State of Love and Trust," the two which would ultimately be used—to Cameron Crowe. The director was struck by the change that had taken place in the bassist. "A little over a year after losing Andy Wood, Ament walks with quiet pride," Crowe wrote in his journal. "Like maybe lightning is striking twice."

In the same entry, Crowe noted another change: "Mookie Blaylock is now Pearl Jam."

It had only been a matter of time. The band members had long been aware that as monikers go, Mookie Blaylock wasn't going to fly. There'd been rumblings about potential legal problems, and using the name of an established hoop star was also going to create trouble when it came to trademarking the band's name for merchandising purposes. After brainstorming for a few days, they'd zeroed in on the word "Pearl," one of Jeff's suggestions, and then amended it to Pearl Jam.

Exactly how the name evolved, and what it initially signified to the band, may remain an unsolved mystery forever. There've been numerous interpretations by curious fans over the years, incorporating everything from basketball connotations (Earl "the Pearl" Monroe, and the practice of "jamming," or slam-dunking) to sexual ones ("jam" is a common slang term for semen, and some believe that Pearl Jam was just a more descriptive extension of that). But what does seem clear is that the story the band publicly offered about the origin of its name was an exercise in mythmaking on Eddie's part.

Early on, Eddie began telling reporters that the name Pearl Jam had been inspired by his great grandmother, whose name was Pearl. "We'd kind of been bouncing words around, and 'Pearl' came up," he related in 1991. "And then there was this thing that stems from my strange history. Great Grandpa was an Indian and totally into hallucinogenics and peyote. Great Grandma Pearl used to make this hallucinogenic preserve that there's total stories about. We don't have the recipe, though."

Epic quickly seized on the "Great Grandma Pearl" story, even including footage of Eddie sitting by a campfire and telling the tale in a video press kit they put together to promote the band. As stories go, this one had legs. Reporters loved it, and as implausible as it might have sounded coming from someone else, Eddie had the natural charisma to carry it off. Given the singer's earth-guru leanings and wiser-than-his-years demeanor, it was easy to believe he had some Native American blood in him, and Great Grandma Pearl and her hallucinogenic "jam" quickly became so firmly enmeshed in the band's legend that even today, most fans think it's the truth.

At least *part* of it is, anyway. Eddie did in fact have a great grand-mother named Pearl—her maiden name was Pearl Hazel Howard. But according to Richard Price, a genealogist who traced Eddie's lineage for this book and spoke to a number of the singer's relatives in the process, neither Pearl nor her husband were of Native American descent. Rather, Pearl, who was Scotch-Irish, married a gentleman named Anthony Sorensen, who migrated to the United States from Denmark at the age of sixteen. Sorensen, who was a circus contortionist when he came to America, later made his living as a photo retoucher. He died in an accident at the age of forty-five, and Pearl never remarried after his death.

Pearl's son (and Eddie's great-uncle), Troy Sorensen, seemed puzzled when asked about a Native American in the family. "I don't know where that came from," he mused. Eddie's grandmother Margaret also confirmed that her mother had never married a Native American, but declined further comment, claiming Eddie had asked her not to talk about the family. A third source claims to have heard Eddie's mother, Karen, speak of a distant relative with Cherokee blood, but it seems certain that it was neither Pearl nor, as Eddie claimed, her husband.

It's possible that, like countless leg-pulling rock icons before him, Eddie just wanted to have a little fun with gullible reporters. But he may have indulged in the Great Grandma Pearl tall tale for less complicated reasons. At the time, he'd yet to find an apartment and was living with Kelly and Peggy Curtis,* and Sheri Fineman, then working as a live-in nanny for the Curtises, says the singer told her that he found the band's new name embarrassing and intended to rectify the situation.

"He kept telling me how he was going to have to come up with something, because he just couldn't live with that name," Fineman recalls. "You know, 'This is gonna represent me, I just have to have it be the right thing, because it's me it's representing.' Then next thing I know, there's this story about some aunt or grandma or whatever."

Eddie's concern over the band's image manifested itself again when Jeff created the artwork for *Ten*. Although Eddie wouldn't admit it publicly until years later, the artwork all but gave him hives, as Fineman discovered when she awoke one morning to make coffee and found the distraught singer sitting at the Curtises' dining room table, surrounded by proofs.

"He was showing me the mock-ups and what it was going to look like, and he was just *completely* traumatized by it," says Fineman. "He'd stayed up all night worrying about it—he said he hated it because it was *mauve*. I remember asking him, 'Well, did you say anything to Jeff?' And he said, 'I'm the new guy, I can't do that yet.'"

Eddie would not always be so shy about asserting himself when it came to band decisions. Already, people were beginning to perceive him as the focal point of Pearl Jam, and while that may have meant additional pressure, it also meant additional power.

XØX

"Congratulations," said Beth, calling from California. "You're in *Rolling Stone*."

---

*Eddie has told countless reporters that during this period he was living in a tiny alcove at Pearl Jam's rehearsal room—deprived of kitchen and bathroom facilities and forced to relieve himself in Gatorade bottles in the alley outside—but that appears to have been something of an exaggeration. Several sources place Eddie in a basement guest room at Kelly Curtis's home at the time, and although he sometimes slept at the studio when working late and would spend more nights there after Jerry Cantrell, the normal occupant of the Curtises' guest room, returned home from tour, he usually turned up at the Curtises' in the morning to shower and eat. Curtis has been overheard on at least one occasion commenting wryly about the singer's selective memory with regard to his hospitality. Eddie indulged in similar poormouthing during early interviews when he described girlfriend Beth Liebling's San Diego apartment as "this little run-down shack I was living in on the beach."

Eddie listened as his girlfriend described an item she'd seen in the magazine about the recently released Temple of the Dog album. *Wow*, he thought. *What a trip. My picture's in* Rolling Stone. *Wow.*

Memory took him back to his bedroom in Encinitas, California, the one with the hand-drawn portrait of the Who on the door, faint tracings of which would still be visible years later after it was painted over in preparation for the new owners. He thought about the crate in that room that had held his record collection, and the issue of *Rolling Stone* that always held the place of honor atop that crate. It was a yellowed, crumbly copy, from the days when *Rolling Stone* was still published on newsprint. Pete Townshend had graced the cover.

Chances are, Eddie pushed aside other thoughts of that room—like the day his father had broken the lock on the door, or the fist-sized holes he himself had put in the wall shortly afterward. For now, all that mattered was that he had a little more in common with Pete, and a little less in common with the guy he'd been in Encinitas.

It didn't take him long to find a local market with a copy of the magazine. He stood at the rack, thumbing through the pages until he found the item. *Wow*, he thought again, flushing with pleasure as he stared down at his own likeness. *What a trip.*

As he stood at the counter, digging in his pocket for money to buy the magazine, he couldn't resist sharing his excitement. He motioned conspiratorially to the middle-aged Asian man who was on duty behind the register.

"This is the weirdest thing," Eddie began shyly. "Can I show you something?" Quickly finding the page with the *Temple of the Dog* item, the singer passed the magazine back to the clerk.

"That's *me*," Eddie said proudly, pointing himself out in the photo.

"Oh!" the clerk responded. He glanced up from the magazine to look at Eddie, then reexamined the photo. "Oh!" he said again. Nodding politely, the man flipped back to the magazine's cover and took a quick look at it.

"*Rolling Stone* . . ." he said, still nodding and smiling. "That a bike magazine?"

✕◈✕

In May, Epic began laying the foundation of its marketing plan for *Ten*. Pearl Jam planned to travel to Dorking, England, to mix the album in June, and with the release slated for late August, the label's goal at this point was to build a street buzz that would pump up initial sales and, hopefully, provide incentive for radio and MTV to add the band's first single, "Alive," to their playlists.

The opening salvo of Epic's campaign for *Ten* involved the Coca-Cola Pop Music series, a multimillion-dollar promotional blitzkrieg that had been jointly announced by Coca-Cola and Sony, Epic's parent company, back in March. Beginning on May 13, specially-marked "multipacks" of Coke, Diet Coke, and Sprite began showing up in stores; inside, purchasers found either a free compact disc or a certificate that could be redeemed for one of ten different cassettes. Pearl Jam's "Alive" was featured on *Rock Cassette Volume 1*, which could be had for the certificate plus $1 in postage and handling.

Meanwhile, in what would ultimately be a much more effective move, Epic had pressed a three-song sampler featuring "Alive," "Wash," and the band's cover of "I've Got a Feeling," and, obtaining mailing lists for both the Mother Love Bone and Soundgarden fan clubs, sent the sampler out to members. Press and radio types got a CD version.

It's interesting to note that the artwork Jeff created for the *Alive* EP— the smiling, shaggy-haired stick figure, face upturned and arms reaching for the sky in joyous, triumphant fashion, would come to symbolize the band's message to most of its fans—almost didn't make the cut with Epic. Jeff later recalled a meeting about the artwork during which one Epic staffer told him that the stick figure "just doesn't fit the vibe of the band."

"I love that," fumed the bassist. "Somebody who's listened to our fucking tape three times is telling me what the vibe of our band is. They wanted to change it, and they had all these different ideas for it."

Among those ideas, according to Stone (who, it should be noted, is often given to sarcasm and might have been joking), was that the stick-man be outfitted with spiked wristbands, a motorcycle, and, as the guitarist disgustedly put it, "a Billy Idol snarl mouth."

"I just don't think they're used to having bands come in and say, 'This is how we do things,'" said Jeff, adding that he'd had similar problems when he presented the artwork for *Ten*. "I went in and said, 'This is the album cover, and this is how much money I need to do it,'" the bassist recalled, "and they all just sat there with their mouths open. They didn't know how to respond. They're sitting there with all these photographers' books showing me photographers that could shoot the album cover, and I was like, 'I already have somebody.'" (Seattle local Lance Mercer, who would become Pearl Jam's primary photographer, was the lensman Jeff chose to shoot the band in the all-for-one, one-for-all pose that was used on the *Ten* cover.)

Disagreements with the label over album art, though, were small potatoes compared to another problem Pearl Jam had encountered. It had become apparent that their drummer, Dave Krusen, wasn't going to be able to go the distance.

First of all, Krusen had just become a parent—his son, Micky, had been born just after Pearl Jam began recording *Ten*—and first-time fatherhood, while it might have been joyful, was also extremely stressful. Worse, Krusen had developed an especially nasty alcohol problem. The members of Pearl Jam were far from being teetotalers, but after Andy, substance abuse of any kind was cause for alarm.

Krusen played his last gig with the band on May 25 at Seattle's RKCNDY, when Pearl Jam served as the entertainment at a wrap party for *Singles*. His ex-bandmates have never publically discussed his departure from Pearl Jam in any detail; when Jeff was asked about the situation, his response was "Just go watch *Spinal Tap*." A more typical line of patter is that the drummer "left to deal with personal problems." Krusen himself said as much to Jo-Ann Greene of *Goldmine*, who reported that he'd checked himself into a rehab the day after the RKCNDY gig. The drummer declined comment for this book, but others who were close to Pearl Jam at the time say his exit from the band wasn't voluntary, and one insider claims that Krusen's ouster was precipitated by an extremely serious incident. "He had a *bad* drinking problem, and he beat up his girlfriend and put her in the hospital one night," says the source. "I think that was the end of it for them. He got fired—or he was asked to leave and he left, let's put it that way."

Obviously, they were concerned about their friend, but on a more pragmatic level, this was hardly a time for Pearl Jam to be minus half their rhythm section. Their trip to England to mix *Ten* was right around the corner, they'd booked a run of East Coast shows in July to bracket their appearances in New York City during the annual New Music Seminar, and in early August they planned to shoot a video for "Alive." Quickly, they recruited New Bohemians drummer Matt Chamberlain, whose work they liked and who'd been recommended by mutual friends.

Chamberlain's stint in Pearl Jam would only be temporary—although he didn't know it at the time, he was about to get an offer from NBC to join the *Saturday Night Live* band—but rather than leave Pearl Jam high, dry, and drummerless when he took his new television job, Chamberlain would do the gentlemanly thing and give notice. He would also suggest a candidate for the seat he was vacating, a friend and fellow Texan whose gregarious nature and dislike for arty pretense would quickly endear him to Pearl Jam's fans—and to all but one of his band mates.

X◊X

David Abbruzzese, the second of three boys born to Catherine and Frank Abbruzzese, had been drumming for as long as he could remember. Born in Stanford, Connecticut, on May 17, 1968 ('Taurus with a bad moon rising," he adds, laughing), Dave spent his early childhood listening to Beatles records and surf music, banging along in accompaniment on various household items until, when he was seven, his parents finally broke down and bought him some proper drums.

Inquisitive, with a mischievous spirit, Dave was easily bored—a problem, given the rigidly structured curriculums typical of the U.S. public education system, that would plague him well into his teens. The summer before he was to enter the seventh grade, in preparation for joining the junior high school band in Mesquite, Texas, where his family had relocated, he came home with his newly purchased percussion gear, trundled it all up to his room, spent about four hours teaching himself to read music and fiddling around with his new drums, and then sat back on his bed. "Well this is fucking *easy*," he thought, somewhat deflated.

"I think that's why I got into pot at such an early age," the drummer muses. "I was just *bored*. It was a lot less boring when you were stoned."

After devoting the following year to playing stand-up bass in the junior high orchestra ("I thought it'd be good for my drumming to understand the other instruments."), Dave began his first year in high school, joining the marching band at North Mesquite High. "Marching band," he says, "treated me right." The way he describes it, he and the other drummers could have been the models for Jeff Spicoli and his perpetually wasted cronies in *Fast Times at Ridgemont High*.

"Me and my buddies on the drum line would drive to school together and drink Everclear punch and smoke tons of pot, go to school and strap on our drums and beat the hell out of 'em and make our way through a couple hours of the day, and then go to this girl's house that we knew and either eat acid or smoke more pot. Then we'd go back to school. Marching season was totally rockin'."

Maybe. But the rest of school was intolerable for the drummer. He didn't feel he was learning anything valuable, and his habit of challenging his teachers often got him into trouble. When he was fifteen and in the ninth grade, Dave angered one of his teachers to the extent that he was kicked out of the school band. With no band practices to attend, school lost its only real charm for the drummer, and he had a long talk with his parents. He'd fallen in with a group of older musicians who jammed together around town, and he felt that the experience he was soaking up with them was much more valuable to his chosen career than formal schooling could ever be. Bottom line: He wanted to drop out.

"When I talked to my folks, it just seemed like I could either stay in school and miss all these opportunities to learn about life and music, or I could quit school and seize all these opportunities," Dave recalls. "I knew that if one day when I was twenty-five, I looked back and realized, 'Okay, I fucked up,' then I could always go back to school. And my parents let me take that chance."

By 1991, Dave was living in Dallas, playing in a funk band called Dr. Tongue, and hanging out with an ever-expanding circle of like-minded bohemian friends. On Sundays, with his friend Chris Viamonte, he hosted an hour-long radio program on the Dallas community station KNON, the "Chris and Dave's 'Music We Like' Show."

"It was basically Chris and I sitting in the attic of this beat-up old house, watching people across the street shoot each other, playing music we liked at just *incredibly* loud volumes, and treating people very badly over the phone," says the drummer. "It was a pretty eclectic format. We'd play David Sanborn, a little bit of Brand X, and then we'd play Zeppelin. Or we'd play Stanley Clarke and then we'd play Slayer. It was a lot of fun."

Dave and Matt Chamberlain had often crossed paths in Dallas; the two were the favored session drummers of David Castell, a local producer-engineer, and had formed a mutual respect over the years. In mid-July, while Matt was in New York with Pearl Jam for the New Music Seminar, he phoned Dave to ask if he'd be interested in auditioning for Pearl Jam, explaining that he was considering taking the *Saturday Night Live* job and wanted to be able to suggest someone to replace him.

"He was supposed to send me a tape the next day," Dave remembers, "but I didn't hear from him. During that week, I found a Mother Love Bone CD and the three-song Pearl Jam CD at the radio station. I listened to the Mother Love Bone and thought, 'God, forget it, that's horrible.' It wasn't my trip at all—it was too glossy. So then I put on the Pearl Jam sampler, and I was thinking, 'Eh.' I looked at Chris and said, 'Well, the singer's voice is different, but I don't know if I'd want to be in something like that.' So I kind of put it in the back of my mind."

A week and a half later, Chamberlain called to tell Dave that he'd decided to take the *SNL* job and planned to start right after he and Pearl Jam shot the band's video for "Alive." He put Dave in touch with Pearl Jam, and after talking to Jeff and Eddie—and later to Kelly Curtis, who was offering free plane tickets—Dave decided he might as well jam with the band for a few days and see if anything came of it. If nothing else, it was a trip to Seattle, and he'd never been there before.

XOX

Dave arrived in Seattle on August 3 and took a cab to RKCNDY, where the video for "Alive" was scheduled to be shot that evening. He'd arranged to meet the band at the club, but when he got there, there was no sign of them. Nervous, he watched as Josh Taft, a longtime friend of Stone's who was directing the video, worked on the stage backdrop that would be used in the shoot. Eventually, Mike McCready showed up on his bike, followed shortly by Stone, Jeff, Eddie, and Matt Chamberlain. Everyone was friendly, although Dave remembers getting a rather intense vibe from Eddie when introductions were being made.

"When he first shook my hand, he looked me in the eye *really* hard," says the drummer. "He was kind of nodding his head, just a total checking me out kind of thing. I thought, 'Wow, okay, well whatever *that* is.'"

After a few minutes of conversation, Dave moved to the sidelines; the band members were obviously wrapped up in their shoot and he didn't want to intrude. After borrowing Mike's bicycle to make a beverage run to a deli down the block, he kept to himself, standing against a wall in the rear of the club to watch.

For Pearl Jam, there was a fair amount of tension surrounding this shoot. Reluctant to submit the standard-issue performance clip that purported to be live but was really lip-synched, the band had insisted on recording the *sound* for the video live as well.

"You see so many videos where it's obvious that they aren't playing their instruments; you hear all these background vocals, and pianos and cellos and that sort of stuff," Jeff recalled. "I think more than anything, we just wanted to strip the song bare. We already had the show set up, so it was kind of like, let's shoot this video at the show and make it seem as little like a video shoot as possible."

Unfortunately, this idea had flown like the proverbial lead balloon with the suits at Epic. "We told them, 'We're gonna film a live video,'" Eddie recalled, "and they said, 'Great.' Then we said, 'It's gonna be recorded live, too,' and they said, '*Recorded* live? It has to be the record, or MTV won't play it.'"

A compromise of sorts was reached, wherein Pearl Jam would record the video live before an audience as they wished, and Taft would also shoot some backup footage of the band lip-synching to the *Ten* version of "Alive," just in case the live version didn't cut it. In the end, Pearl Jam's attempt to lip-synch to the album track failed so miserably that nobody would have even considered using that footage. With dead microphones and no sound coming from their amps, their coordination went right out the window.

"They did three live cuts," says Dave, "and then they attempted to lip-synch it. Halfway through, it was just *mayhem*. It was funny as shit."

So, live it was. In addition to a crane-mounted camera that Taft had set up in the balcony at RKCNDY, five or six cameras were employed during "Alive" to film the band from various angles. Taft and his company also shot a lot of hand-held footage during the show to capture the feel of the audience. As was already becoming the norm at Pearl Jam's shows, the area in front of the stage quickly turned into a roiling sea of bodies, with an endless string of overexuberant types clambering onto the stage to dive off into the maw. Only once did the chaos get in the way of the shoot, when Jeff suddenly realized there was no sound coming from his instrument. He found the culprit at the lip of the stage: a fan in the grip of euphoria who'd grabbed his rack of effects pedals and begun pounding on them hard enough to dislodge the plugs.

"I reached down and tapped him on the shoulder," Jeff recalled, "and he looked up and I was standing there right in front of him, like, 'Plug it back in!' He totally freaked out. Finally, he helped me plug it in, and I started playing again. The guy was having such a great time that I didn't want to wreck it for him, but he ended up moving, he was so freaked out."

Taft's video for "Alive" expertly captured the energy that Pearl Jam had wanted it to, and while the live version of the song might have been, as Jeff put it, "inferior," at least it was honest. "It's not the greatest video in the world," Eddie said later, "but it's live, and I can sleep at night because I feel like it's totally representative."

With the shoot out of the way, the band and their new candidate for drummer spent the next few days sizing each other up. Musically, the bond was instantaneous. Personality-wise, Dave seemed a good fit, as well—so much so that the members of Pearl Jam found themselves wondering what the catch was.

"We were kind of like, 'When's he gonna start being an asshole?'" Stone recalled.

"It was really weird," Jeff added. "We played with him for a few days, and we were talking about it—'Well, what do you think?' 'Well, God, it's great!' It was like this guy came up and just kind of fit in. We wanted to argue about it a little bit, but nobody could really argue about it. It was happening."

Dave felt the same way. Although he'd been worried about how his funk-oriented style would fit into a rock band, the others had told him to play as he normally would, and the results had been positive. "It felt comfortable," he said not long afterward. "I kept the groove approach, and it felt good—my style didn't really change at all."

Personally, too, he liked the others, especially Stone. "I thought Stone was just great," Dave remembers. "He and I went down to the Market one day and hung out, just walking around talking about music. I really felt like we bonded a bit."

While the two were at the Public Market that day, they were approached by a homeless man who was selling braided rope bracelets—one for $3 or two for $5. They bought two of them, Dave choosing a black one and Stone opting for army green. A few years later, long after Dave's bracelet had worn thin and fallen off, Stone would finger his own bracelet during a fateful breakfast meeting between the two and remind the drummer of the day they'd bought them. But by then, the memory would be tarnished with bitterness.

Thursday rolled around, and Dave still had no clue whether he'd come close to passing the audition. He was set to leave in two days, and finally, he asked Eddie if the band planned on giving him an answer before he left Seattle. Eddie was noncommittal.

"I think we're gonna check out a couple other guys," the singer replied.

Dejected, Dave returned to his hotel on Thursday night and called his girlfriend in Texas to tell her he was coming home early. "I didn't want to be a part of this band because somebody else *wasn't* the right person," he told her. "I wanted to be part of the band because *I* was the right person."

He phoned Kelly Curtis on Friday morning when he awoke, planning on changing his return flight and going home that day. Kelly said hello and then put Dave on hold. When the manager got back on the line, he had a question.

"The guys are here," Kelly said. "We were wondering how long it would take you to go get your drums and move up?"

Part Two

※◉〜 ‡

Alive

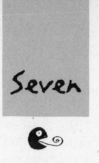

Seven

International Underground Pop Fest: Eddie Gets Religion / Doing What It Takes / This Is Your Life on Toast / Epic Throws a Party: Welcome to the Machine / The Great Lightbulb Caper

As Dave Abbruzzese arrived back in Seattle with drums in tow and began familiarizing himself with his new home and his new band mates, August was giving way to September, the breezes rolling in off the Sound just beginning to hint at the invigorating fall to come. Inspiration seemed to be everywhere that late summer of '91, not only for the members of Pearl Jam, who were gearing up for the release of *Ten* and a lengthy tour, but for any music fan who had an ear to the ground. Something was changing.

On the surface, the mainstream music machine was chugging along as usual, its greedy cogs whirring in answer to a money-making schematic as old as rock & roll itself: You took a look at what your competitors were selling the most of and you quickly produced your own version. The wildly successful Guns n' Roses had been the prototype since the late Eighties, the band every magazine wanted on its cover and every other band envied, and as such the band all the major labels had been busily cloning. By 1991, to watch MTV for any length of time was to be greeted by a parade of GNR knockoffs, one video after another featuring some long-haired Stepford band with angry lyrics, wailing guitars, and a bad-ass caterwauling singer. So what if the clones could never hold a candle to the originals—the kids were buying it, weren't they? This was the way things had always been done in the business. Why mess with a formula that worked?

Beneath the surface, though, in that major-label blind spot where musical rebellions have always taken shape, a sea change was underway. Bands like Jane's Addiction, the Red Hot Chili Peppers, and their peers had begun to confound the industry pundits, transcending what had been thought to be mere college radio appeal and attracting followings within the mainstream. The Lollapalooza festival had made its debut that July, boasting a diverse lineup of modern-rock acts (Jane's Addiction, the Rollins Band, Ice-T, the Butthole Surfers, Siouxsie and the Banshees, Nine Inch Nails, Living Colour) and a carnivalesque atmosphere geared toward exposing concert goers to fringe culture. The brainchild of Jane's Addiction leader Perry Farrell, Lollapalooza hadn't been expected to be a bonanza for promoters, but as it turned out, tickets for the early dates sold so briskly that more shows were added, and the festival would later be noted as one of the few hits in an otherwise dry summer for tours. The unexpected success of Lollapalooza was perhaps the first signal the major labels had of the cultural shake-up on the horizon.

Just like hordes of other music fans that summer, the members of Pearl Jam were disgusted with the homogenized pap being offered up in mass quantity on the airwaves. They were eager to see music infused with some spark of originality again and even more excited about doing some of the infusing themselves. Eddie was especially passionate on the subject. Asked for his take on the state of the musical union, he sounded pained.

"How much worse can it get?" he asked, exasperated. "I mean, come *on*. Virgin Records is trying to promote an animated *cat* right now. I know a guy who's in promotion there, and seventeen years ago he started a club in Boston that still stands. He's like a pioneer. He's always been great at what he does, and now he's promoting a *cartoon*."

The singer couldn't understand it. Why shove the latest prefabricated dance diva down everybody's throats when there were so many other artists out there who really *mattered*? Why smother the unfettered creativity he saw all around him beneath mountains of mindless dreck—or dilute it with marketing and promotion and publicity until all that remained was *product*, something to be consumed, totted up on the communal industry abacus, and then abandoned in favor of the next hot item to roll off the assembly line?

Eddie had always harbored alternative sensibilities to a degree, but lately, he'd really been wearing his politics on his sleeve, as if stamping out the evils of the industry was something he'd suddenly adopted as a personal crusade. Much of this could be attributed to the increased exposure he'd had to the inner workings of the industry; since signing with Sony, he'd developed a keener understanding of how the wheels were greased than perhaps he'd have liked. But, to a certain extent, the singer's heightened anticorporate stance was also a product of hero worship.

Eddie would cringe at that phrase—"I don't have any heroes," he said once. "I have people's work I respect, but I could never put anybody in a hero position."—but whether you called them heroes, role models, or inspirations (the latter being Eddie's preference), there were plenty of people around that he admired. And this early in his career, still forming his identity as an artist, it was only natural that he would emulate them. Some of the singer's strongest influences at the time were right in his backyard, like Stone, "who amazes me with how he writes and plays guitar," and Chris Cornell, for "his ethics." Others were simply traveling in the same circles, like Henry Rollins, whom Eddie would often mention during interviews, or the guys in Jane's Addiction. Eddie had met them recently, when a photographer friend, Chris Cuffaro, let him tag along to Lollapalooza at the King County Fairgrounds. Eddie had wandered around for hours, getting his feet muddy in the pit in front of the stage and then rubbing elbows backstage. Jane's Addiction drummer Stephen Perkins hadn't had any idea who Pearl Jam was when Cuffaro introduced Eddie as "Eddie Vedder from Pearl Jam," but that was okay. It had still been a great day—so much to soak in.

Of all the artists he'd been exposed to lately, though, none had had a greater impact on Eddie than Fugazi. Their effect on the singer had been profound—and it would be lasting.

A quartet hailing from Washington, D.C. and led by Ian MacKaye, formerly of Minor Threat, Fugazi dished out a heavenly noise—edgy rock with a hardcore backbone—and their lyrics were introspective and highly political. To call them a thinking-man's band was an understatement. But the most-talked-about aspect of Fugazi was their refusal to play ball with corporate America in any way. Plenty of underground

bands *claimed* to toe that line and then conveniently forgot their vows
when some major-label A&R man came along waving a fat checkbook.
Fugazi, though, truly walked it like they talked it.

They recorded on their own Dischord label; countless times, Mac-
Kaye had been approached about signing Fugazi to a major label, but suit-
ors always received the same polite "No thanks." They wanted nothing
to do with MTV, and refused to give interviews to all but the tiniest
fanzines, a means not only of shunning the media circus, but also of
protesting the alcohol and cigarette ads that filled the pages of glossy
rock magazines like *Rolling Stone* and *Spin*. (Fugazi was a straight-edge
band, meaning they frowned on tobacco, drugs, and alcohol, among
other things.) They played mostly all-ages shows, so that underage fans
wouldn't be shut out, and they limited the cost of their tickets—and
when possible, their albums—to $5 each, insuring that anybody could
afford them. You couldn't find a more politically correct group of musicians. When it came to ethics, they were unimpeachable.

Fugazi had been making records since 1988, but Eddie had only recently become a fan. Beth had discovered them first, and he'd listened
to her enraptured descriptions until he was finally moved to see what all
the fuss was about. When he learned that Fugazi was playing a show at
the International Underground Pop Festival in Olympia, he and a few
friends had taken the drive. Later, Eddie described the experience as
"holy."

"It was amazing," he recalled. "A show hasn't affected me like that
for years and years. I was just in a daze."

Fugazi played three days later in Seattle, right down the street from
Pearl Jam's rehearsal space, but Eddie sat out the show. "I thought it was
too much to expect for an artist to blow me away again that soon," he
explained reverently. Still, the damage had been done. From that point
on, Eddie was barely able to have a conversation without mentioning
Fugazi, and it couldn't have been mere coincidence that his indie politics suddenly became more hard-line as well.

That might win him brownie points with some in the underground
community—where "starving artist" was a veritable mantra, where musicians wore *lack* of popularity like a badge, and where displaying interest in money, celebrity, or any of the traditional rock star trappings
was a considerable faux pas—but just as often, it would open him up to
charges of hypocrisy. As vocal as Eddie was about his purist intent to
duck the limelight, his actions sometimes seemed to contradict him. It
was a duality that was often revealed during interviews: The Eddie who

saw nobility in the indie ethic and sought to behave in accordance with
punk's strict anticareerist tenets seemed constantly at war with another
Eddie entirely—one who still felt like he was back in San Diego with
his nose pressed up against the forbidding glass of the music industry,
unable to resist a little self-promotion when he thought nobody was
looking.

During one early conversation with this writer, Eddie spoke at length
about how he hated interpreting his lyrics for the media—how it robbed
the fans of the pleasure of their own interpretations. Wanting to respect
his wishes, I'd moved away from that topic, but apparently Eddie had
been hoping I'd push a little harder. When I didn't, and it became clear
that the interview was nearing its end, Eddie made a rather ham-handed
attempt to resurrect the topic himself.

"So," he said casually as we walked along. "Have you thought of any
questions for the guy writing the lyrics?"

"What?" I asked, a little confused.

"Did you have any specific questions," Eddie repeated, "kind of
wanting to talk to the guy writing the songs or whatever?"

During a follow-up conversation a few days later, I dutifully asked
Eddie about his lyrics. As I prompted him with song titles from *Ten*, he
offered richly detailed interpretations of most of the songs, but occasionally he would pause, as if the thought of spilling the beans was a
deeply troubling dilemma.

"Gee," he said when I brought up "Jeremy." "I don't know if I can
tell you."

"Well," I said, "if you feel strongly about it, we'll save it for another
time."

"Well, he's one of those kids, and I mean it's happening all the time,"
Eddie said quickly. "So we might as well just bring it out, because it's
happening."

By the end of the conversation, I had filled most of a tape with Eddie's
"reluctant" interpretations of his lyrics.*

If a journalist ventured too far into nonmusical territory during an in-

*During an appearance by Eddie and Jeff on the syndicated radio program "Rock-
line" in 1993, a fan attempted to nail Eddie on this contradiction, pointing out
interviews in which he'd said he disliked interpreting his lyrics and asking him
why he'd revealed the meaning behind "Alive" in a recent *Rolling Stone* story. Eddie's response: "Okay, sir, you've just won a harmonica. Thank you very much.
Next question."

terview, Eddie was quick to point out that "no one wants to read about all this business crap." Similarly, he could moan for hours about the unwanted distraction presented by the nonartistic aspects of the band's career: "I can't philosophize about the band as an entity, and then the next minute write a brilliant song; that's not how it happens."

But at the same time, Eddie was devoting a great deal of his time to the "business crap" he professed to despise. Sometimes the interest he displayed in the day-to-day running of Pearl Jam, Incorporated, seemed to border on obsession.

"He had to be part of all of it," says Sheri Fineman. "Any kind of press, anyone who called, Eddie would talk to them. He answered every single fan letter that came in. Eddie was hard-core, very serious about it. He'd go down to the office every day to be there and get all the information and really make an effort."

The apparent problem for Eddie was that as much as it was ingrained in him to resent the concept of fame, he also recognized the voice it might afford him. For a natural-born communicator who loved nothing better than disseminating his own ideas and absorbing those of others, the idea that he might someday have the ear of millions had to be incredibly tantalizing. But to admit—even to himself—that he wanted that sort of notoriety was something else. Eddie's intense respect for the strict edicts of the underground would be the source of a conundrum that kept him up on countless nights for years: Where should he draw the line between his ambition and his ideals?

As Stone put it to a roomful of people during a gathering in 1991: "I think Eddie really wants to be famous. But he also has a huge moral dilemma with it."

XOX

Pragmatically speaking, this was the worst possible time for *anyone* in Pearl Jam to be entertaining moral qualms over the prospect of fame; Sony, after all, was currently counting on them to put all their energy toward *achieving* it. Unknowns didn't sell records, and to the major label bigwigs, selling records was the only thing that mattered. Artists might not be contractually bound to share that sentiment, but those who wanted careers with any longevity could hardly ignore it, either. If your first record didn't meet your label's expectations in terms of sales, as Eddie pointed out, "it could be the greatest record, but you don't get to make another. That's very frightening."

Given their unproven status at Sony, the pressure was on Pearl Jam to play the game, and they were prepared to cooperate, at least to an extent. "We were going to do what it took," Dave remembers. But they also knew that if the label was given free reign in marketing and promotional matters, their credibility could be ruined. Whenever they could, they reiterated their philosophies to the label staffers they were working with ("You can't just jump in and fucking plaster every magazine with Pearl Jam ads," Stone recalled pleading at one meeting), and sometimes it seemed they were getting through.

Just as often, though, there were horrifying reminders of what could happen when they weren't vigilant. Only recently, Kelly Curtis had shown the band two of the ads Sony had put together for *Ten*. The first bore the slogan PEARL JAM: BIRTHED FROM THE BELLY OF THE BEAST. The second was even more embarrassing: THIS IS YOUR LIFE ON TOAST, the ad blared.

The band members had quite a giggle over the latter, pointing and laughing until Curtis cleared his throat.

"That's the one it's gonna be," he told them.

"Wait a second," said Eddie. "Are you saying we don't get a choice?"

They might have, Curtis explained, but it was too late for that now—the ad had already been sent to a few magazines.

Oh, well, the band reasoned, live and learn. They could always buy up all the magazines and destroy them, joked Eddie, who was blissfully unaware that the slogan on Sony's next planned ad would advise readers to CULTIVATE THE PEARL.

"We try to get approval on everything," the singer recalled glumly. "It's really hard to do."*

Cheesy ads were only the half of it. For *Ten*, Epic was pulling out all the stops. "Pearl Jam is our life," Epic promotional vice president Larry Douglas crowed to *Billboard*. "We're going to work this record through Christmas, through New Year's, through Easter, and if we have to, through Christmas of next year."

That was all well and good—it was nice, after all, to have your label's support—but in fact, the bulk of that "work" would be done by Pearl Jam. Touring was the most important element of Epic's strategy in breaking the band, and, thankfully, that part of the bargain was one the band

---

*Eventually, Pearl Jam would insist on—and win—the right to final copy approval on Epic's ads for their records, a development no doubt precipitated by their embarrassment over Epic's campaign for *Ten*.

could carry out with a clear conscience. Some of the other things the label expected of them—things that tied in with the tour—were a lot less palatable. They were furnished, for example, with long lists of radio stations and record stores, each of which Epic expected the band members to phone personally. It was a sort of scripted "just to say hi" deal. You called the number, introduced yourself, pointed out that Pearl Jam would soon be coming through (insert name of town), and then, with as much casual dignity as you could muster worked in some sort of plug for *Ten*.

In-store appearances were booked along the tour route, uncomfortable shows at record stores where you were lucky if anybody showed up, and even if they did, the vibe was practically guaranteed to be mercenary. How could you maintain some semblance of artistic integrity, strumming away under a big gaudy Pearl Jam banner with crates of your record placed enticingly nearby and cash registers *ka-chinging* in the background?

Every day, there seemed to be another miserable photo shoot, and, for some reason, most photographers wanted the band to pose in an alley.

"It was like, 'What kind of band do we come off as?'" Dave recalls. "Every time, they'd say, 'I found this perfect spot,' and we'd go to the *sleaziest* fucking alley. One photographer crammed us into a doorway, and three feet to the left of us, hanging in a window, was a condom with the receptacle end filled and knotted off. Then she moved us to another part of the alley, and there was a guy peering from behind this dumpster while she was taking pictures. You know, 'Excuse us, homeless people, while we take pictures of ourselves.' It was like, 'I can't *believe* this.'"

And of course, there were interviews, interviews, and more interviews. Five years from now, the news that Pearl Jam was releasing a new album would have the phones in Epic's publicity department ringing off the hook with reporters begging for interviews. At this point, though, Epic was doing the begging, the label's publicists dialing up anyone who could conceivably give the band some ink or airtime and, when they were lucky enough to get a live body on the phone, launching into an age-old dance:

Publicist: "Hi, this is so-and-so from Epic. I sent you a copy of Pearl Jam's debut album, and I'm wondering if you've listened to it yet."

Critic: "Uh, let's see, Pearl Jam . . . Ah, you know, the name rings a bell, but gee, I get so many records in the mail . . . I'm sure it's somewhere in my stack, but I haven't gotten to it yet."

Publicist: "Well, let me tell you a little bit about the band . . ."

And so it went. Most of the time, the publicist struck out royally, never hearing anything from the reporter after the standard brush-off ("I'll give you a call if we decide to review it."). But sometimes a reporter's curiosity was piqued enough to listen to the record, and sometimes that reporter liked—or hated—the record enough to review it. Sometimes, a publicist hit pay dirt and got a journalist to commit to a feature on the band. This rarely happened with new artists—few magazines liked to devote precious column space to unknowns—but in Pearl Jam's case, the sell wasn't as hard. Given the tragic element that Andrew Wood's death lent to the band's history, Epic's publicists were armed with a natural hook to feed to reporters.

Of course, they were also armed with something else. In this business of publicity, where charming the ladies and gentlemen of the press was the ultimate goal, Epic knew they had a powder keg in Eddie.

✗✪✗

In September 1991, when *Rolling Stone* sent me to Seattle to interview Pearl Jam for the first time, I got on the plane with a huge chip on my shoulder.

I hadn't wanted the assignment—or *any* assignment for that matter. A month prior, I'd finished the last in a series of articles on Guns n' Roses that had monopolized my time for nearly a year and a half, and I was grappling with a nasty case of burnout. My editor had been dangling assignments under my nose like smelling salts, but I'd been stalling. Finally, he brought up Pearl Jam, a story I'd pitched during a lull between Guns n' Roses research trips. He also made it clear that my grace period for regrouping was over whether I liked it or not. I took the assignment—albeit with gritted teeth—and booked a one-day stay in Seattle, the general idea being to sleepwalk through the interview process and get it over with as quickly as I could.

Before I left for Seattle, Michael Goldstone had advised me that the key to a great Pearl Jam story was to spend as much time with Eddie as possible, but when I met the singer, I wasn't sure why. My first meeting with the band took place at the Crocodile Cafe, and through a round of drinks and a few games of pool, I watched Eddie. It wasn't as if he exuded star quality; he was unimposing—frankly, something of a shrimp—dressed in a shabby brown jacket and knee-length fatigues, your average surf-punk. He seemed friendly enough, but nothing distinguished him from anyone else in the room. I failed to see what all the fuss was about.

My first glimpse of the famed Vedder mystique came a few hours later when the band invited me to join them at a rehearsal. We walked over to the Galleria Potatohead, and as I sat on a battered couch, taking notes and listening to them tune up, Eddie walked over. With a shy smile, he handed me a slim, antique-looking book of verse entitled *The Eloping Angels*. Then he walked away.

Trying to be polite, I began flipping through the book, which brought Eddie back over. "You don't have to read it now if you're taking notes," he said. "I just thought you might like to look at it."

He then launched into a detailed analysis of the story's plot, which involved Faust and Mephistopheles switching clothes with a couple of angels so that they could sneak into Heaven and the angels could visit Earth. Eddie clearly related to the story's central themes of longing and alienation. (The book would inspire a collaboration between Eddie and Dave on the following night, "Angel," a song Pearl Jam would release as a fan club single in 1993.)

As he talked, I noted the quality of his speaking voice. Eddie, I realized, had been blessed with one of the most melodious voices I'd ever heard. He chose his words carefully. They were poetic and evocative, and the way he formed them, together with the strategic pauses and half smiles he employed, lent an odd formality to his manner even when he lapsed into slang. He came off like a courtly old gentleman stuck in the body of a twentysomething. He was going to captivate hundreds of interviewers. It would have been a pleasure to listen to him no matter what he had to say.

After the rehearsal, Eddie offered me a tour of the building. He led me upstairs to the art gallery and walked around the floor, solemnly pointing out different sculptures.

I'd had countless musicians try to impress me with how intellectual they were, and I assumed this was what Eddie was up to, trotting out the eighteenth century poetry and hitting me over the head with his appreciation for art. But something about his manner gave me pause. I just couldn't be absolutely certain whether he was "on" or whether this was real. More telling, he was so charming that I *wanted* to believe it was real.

Over dinner that night, I did my formal interview with the band, covering the standard topics for *Rolling Stone*'s new artist profiles. Eddie didn't have much to say during the interview; as he had earlier in the day, he let Stone and Jeff answer most of the questions. But when Jeff brought up the cover story I'd just done on Guns n' Roses and began pumping me for inside information on the band's mercurial leader, Axl Rose, Eddie's interest perked up. Jeff and the others indicated that they thought Axl was overly spoiled by success—that his fussing about the pressures of fame was gross. Eddie, though, championed Axl in the discussion.

The interview over, we stopped on the sidewalk outside the restaurant to say our good-byes. Eddie started off with the others, but as I stood waiting for a cab back to my hotel, he changed his mind.

"You feel like going somewhere and talking a little more?" he asked casually. The invitation surprised me, but later I would learn that this was standard operating procedure. Whether he was unwilling to compete with his band mates for attention or he just felt more comfortable outside group settings, Eddie was usually subdued during full-band interviews, but he would invariably pull reporters aside for a one-on-one chat later.

He suggested we go to Seattle Center, a sprawling park and former World's Fair site that is home to the Space Needle, one of the city's best-known landmarks. As we walked through the park, he pointed out the Mural Amphitheater, where Pearl Jam had just performed an outdoor show.

"What a great vibe," he began. "I mean, for me to look out and see, like, three thousand people, and communicate with them...." He paused. "Well, you just went on the road with Axl Rose, you probably think this is silly."

No, I told him, I didn't.

"You know," he went on, "I gotta say that when we were talking about Axl tonight, and they were coming out with, 'Well, he can quit if he wants to'—while they were going one way, I was going the other. It's frightening. There's just things that as a normal person, you don't think you could deal with."

Eddie seemed obsessed with the Faustian overtones of rock & roll celebrity. He'd already begun to get letters from fans who'd heard the "Alive" sampler, and because of his lyrics, they seemed to think he had the answers to all of their problems. He tried to respond to every letter, he said, but who was *he* to play advice columnist to hordes of kids from dysfunctional families? How much was he expected to give? The pressure was wearing on him.

Not only that, but the folks at Sony were hell-bent on turning him into the P. T. Barnum of the alternative set, and he wanted no part of the hype factory. He'd had his first real brush with it a week earlier, at a party Epic threw for the band after their Mural show.

"It just seriously freaked me out," Eddie said of the party. "We'd just played this amazing show, and it was *real*. Then to go into this *disco*, with Pearl Jam posters everywhere and people shaking your hand— 'Hey, this is Barney from Oshkosh, every time you see your record in Oshkosh, Barney's the guy who put it there.' You know, and I tried to talk to them, and they're not prepared for that—they're ready for 'Hi, howya doin', it's great to meet you and sign this and let's take a picture, see ya.' I'm getting my hair pulled, I'm getting dragged here and there, and my friends were kind of laughing at me from the corner. I was like, 'Dude, *fuck* you, this isn't funny. To me it *wasn't* funny. It wasn't what the music was about.

"I just want to hang onto who I am," he went on. "I want to grow, but I want to grow in a natural sense, even with all this other stuff around. There's obviously the other route—'Hey-ho, materialism here I come, now I'm livin' the good life.' But I want to be the other way. I just think everyone's sick of this other crap."

In some ways, Eddie was no different than thousands of others his age, people who were expressing disenchantment with the soulless consumer culture they'd grown up in. An entire generation, shell-shocked by information overload, repulsed by the greed and hypocrisy they'd been force-fed for years by corporate America, seemed to be yearning for something tangible, something real. This was a new counterculture in the making, a network of people who were finding their inspiration in— and basing their identities on—the rejection of anything that smacked even remotely of yuppie materialism. You could compare this generation to the one that came of age in the Sixties, but these kids—who would be saddled a few years later with the condescending moniker of Generation X—were different. They had an ingrained cynicism, a hardness, that the Flower Power set had never displayed. They wanted to get back to the garden, just like their hippie parents had. But what do you do if your parents have swapped their tie-dye for suits and ties and *destroyed* the garden?

"Look what we've done with this place," Eddie said, jumping off our bench and waving an arm toward the perimeter of Seattle Center. "Look at these weird fucking buildings, and the freeways, and . . . look at a place like New York! It's a freak-out. Why is *that* the American dream? It's perverse. I mean, your goals should be so much more connected to the earth and the sky and family, yet this is the way we live."

"You know," he added softly, "when you're in the desert, there's no other lights around, and you can't *believe* the amount of stars. We've sent mechanisms out there, billions of dollars' worth, and they haven't found anything. They've found different colors of sand, and rings and gases, but they haven't found a sign of real life. Nobody's shown me anything to make me feel secure in what happens afterwards. All I really believe in is this fucking moment, like *right now*. It's all I believe in."

Just before midnight, we began making our way out of the park. As we passed the Space Needle, Eddie suggested that we check and see if the observation deck was still open. It was, so we paid our $4.50 and rode to the top. The deck was deserted. We walked out to the rail and gazed out at the lights of Seattle below.

We'd been standing silently for a few moments when I noticed that Eddie was toying with two of the horizontal cables that formed a safety barrier around the deck. Suddenly, he pulled them apart and wedged his head through. Then he asked a question with distinctly ominous overtones.

"Isn't it true that if your head fits through, your whole body will?"

"Don't even think about it," I told him.

He pointed at a row of lights about ten feet from where we stood, on a steel support beam beneath which fifty-six stories of empty space yawned. "I was just thinking of getting some of those light bulbs," he said. "It would be the *ultimate* souvenir."

After some panicky cajoling, the singer relaxed his stance, but he seemed reluctant to abandon his goal entirely.

"Wow," he said softly, taking in the unobstructed view, his head still lodged stockade-style between the cables. "This is *so* awesome."

Fifteen minutes later, as we walked away from the Space Needle, Eddie looked back over his shoulder at the structure.

"I'm totally bummed right now," he said. "That would've been *such* a thrill.

"It would've been such a great example of what we're all about," he went on. "Exactly what I'd want to say to somebody. Just that life is, like, *so* much to live, and we don't know how long we're gonna be here. Actually, that's what our whole album is about. It wasn't a conscious thing, but it just turned out that way. Everybody in the band was going through this kind of rebirth, and it went from the burdens of being alive to appreciating being alive."

Jeff had said as much earlier in the day. "I know that everything that led up to this, all that stuff that was totally painful at the time, happened for a reason," he'd said. "I haven't really had a lot of faith in any sort of God or anything in a long time. It's always just been, 'Well, yeah, if it exists, I'll know it when I die.' But somebody's definitely been making sure everything's okay. Somebody's looking out for us. 'Cause there's no other way to explain this."

In their early interviews, the members of Pearl Jam often put this kind of mystical spin on things, painting a picture of five individuals who'd reached crisis points in their lives and then magically come together as if it had been predestined. The band's collective joie de vivre was infectious, perhaps more than any of them realized. The "rebirth" angle would be heavily played out in all of their early press, nearly every article written about Pearl Jam during the media blitz for *Ten* describing them as having "sprung from the ashes of Mother Love Bone." This would prompt some wags to accuse Stone and Jeff of playing up the triumph-over-tragedy angle for their own gain, but those who were close to them at the time insist that that wasn't the case. "Stone and Jeff really felt that way," says Sheri Fineman. "It *was* a rebirth for them to get into another band. I don't think they ever tried to use [Andy's death] to their advantage."

Whether or not the members of Pearl Jam counted on it, all this talk of "rebirth" was going to have a most desirable effect. Youth culture was in a serious state of flux at the time. Mainstream music fans, by then bored with the endless stream of Guns n' Roses clones that had commandeered MTV, were sniffing around for something new on which to base their identities—in effect, seeking the catalyst for their *own* rebirth. This was a generation faced with AIDS, global warming, drive-by shootings, and all manner of other evils. The Wingers, Warrants, and Poisons of the world—those tireless proponents of Seventies arena-rock glitz, with their silly costumes, sexist traditions and insipid lyrics—no longer spoke for them. Life in the Nineties was serious business, not a frat party. The kids needed some new heroes.

With their carpe diem vibe, and with "Alive," a song that seemed tailor-made as a reclamation for troubled slackers, Pearl Jam was going to step into that early Nineties void and fill it—if not by offering instant answers, then at the very least by expressing the same concerns. Here was a band that seemed a refutation of the *Headbanger's Ball* ethic on every point, their spiritual, earthy vision and live-for-the-moment philosophy a blessed respite from the dime-store nihilism that had been so prevalent.

Here was a band you could really believe in.

How could you *not* be dazzled by a fellow like Eddie Vedder, some-one who spoke with such evangelical zeal of things like the earth and the sky, someone who seemed so intent on breathing inspiration back into every tired soul he came across? How could anyone not recognize, in this self-effacing urchin with the searching eyes and feverish passion for life, the stuff that messiahs were made of?

XOX

Back in New York, a week after my interview with Pearl Jam, I got a package in the mail from Seattle. I read the accompanying note:

Miss Neely:

I've currently a vision of your face, and you're smiling. Hope my picture correlates with your reality.

Now . . . a present for you. It's exactly 1:01 A.M., Wednesday, September 25th. We leave at 6:00 A.M. for Canada and the begin-ning of tour. I collected this for you with courage 71 minutes ago. Wanted so badly for you to have it as a symbol. I've got one . . . you've got one . . . bonded & alive. Again, may this be a symbol.

Love, Eddie

I looked into the box. Nestled inside was a grime-encrusted lightbulb from the Space Needle.

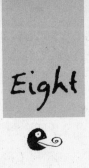

Eight

Van Tour '91 / Fast Times at the Airport Marriott / The Lost "Jeremy" Video / Spinal Tap's Last Stand / *Nevermind*

Onstage at Harpo's, a club in Victoria, British Columbia, four members of Pearl Jam gawked openly at the fifth, who had just unscrewed the heavy steel base of his microphone stand and—*whaaaaaaang!*—shot-putted it over the heads of the crowd.

Just like that, casually as you please. Eddie was now grinning broadly, watching people scramble away from the back bar, where the twelve-pound disc had crashed loudly into a wall. Nobody was hit, but the patrons who'd been standing nearby weren't taking any chances. *Jesus*, their faces seemed to say. *Better take cover in case he goes off again.*

It had been a long time since Stone and Jeff had allowed a disinterested audience to get under their skin; they'd played to enough of those crowds with Green River and Mother Love Bone to learn how to feed off their *own* energy onstage. As Jeff put it, "If the crowd loves it, that can take it to the next level, but ultimately, it doesn't matter."

For Eddie, though, audience participation was mandatory, what made a show worth playing. He couldn't bear it when all attention in the room wasn't focused on the stage. "I'll see people standing on the outskirts, kind of chatting," he explained, "and know that the next day, those people are gonna say, 'Oh, it was' *amazing*,' when they didn't even *see*—it they weren't even involved. I'm gonna do anything I can to get them going."

Within the span of Pearl Jam's last few shows, the withdrawn, spotlight-shy singer Stone and Jeff had recruited a year ago had been replaced by another Eddie entirely—a whirling dervish with veins standing out on his forehead who joked about having an "ammunition roadie," who could wield a mike stand like a lethal shepherd's crook, or scale a lighting rig or balcony in the space of seconds to dangle like a monkey and taunt the crowd. Chris Cornell was the obvious influence here; he'd been doing this kind of thing for years. But Eddie was taking it to new extremes, sometimes leaving his band mates to wonder if perhaps he wasn't taking it *too* far. Just a week ago, before they'd left Seattle for this tour, the subject had come up between Pearl Jam's road manager, Eric Johnson, and Dave.

"Eric," Dave had said, "Eddie scares me."

"I bet," said Johnson.

"Something's gonna happen," the drummer went on. "We're doing forty shows—it's the law of averages! He's gonna take one of us out with the bottom of a mike stand or kill himself falling off a light scaffold. Somebody's gonna get conked."

"Don't worry," Eric replied, laughing. "We'll just duct tape him to a chair or something."

However wary the others might be of Eddie's increasing volatility, they also recognized what a shame it would be if they had to put a straitjacket on their singer's daredevil alter ego. You couldn't help but be charmed by such a childlike lack of inhibition; Andy had had the same gift, and it was part of what had made him so special. Besides, with Eddie out front harnessing all of the crowd's energy and funneling it back through the band, their shows had become so deliciously charged that the risk of getting clubbed on the head with a mike stand almost seemed an acceptable one. Kelly Curtis had also noticed the change.

"I don't know what to say to you guys anymore," the normally low-key manager had told them after their last Seattle show. "This was like a religious experience."

"It's just fucking amazing," Dave said at the time, of the surreal electricity that had begun to permeate the band's shows. "Have you ever had the dream where everything was perfect, and then you woke up? That's what it's like after a show. I open my eyes in the dressing room and realize I'm not on stage anymore, and I don't remember how I got offstage. I don't remember standing up, I don't remember the last downbeat of the last song—all I remember is having cold chills from the second song to the end of the set. The last show we played, I thought I was gonna faint—I felt like, 'Oh, I can't handle this.'"

The energy level was about to go up a notch, too. Back at the hotel after the Harpo's gig, word came in that the Chili Peppers had invited them to open on an upcoming tour. Between now and mid-October, Pearl Jam would continue their van tour as planned, working their way through Oregon, California, Arizona, Texas, Georgia, and North Carolina. On October 16 they would join the Peppers and the Smashing Pumpkins in Madison, Wisconsin, for a two-and-a-half-month trip that would take them from the Midwest to the East Coast, down through the South, and back to the West Coast in December. They'd have January to rest up before heading to England for the start of a European tour in February, and after Europe they would crisscross the United States again. The year ahead of them was going to be exhausting. It was fortunate that they loved what they were doing.

Most of it, anyway.

※◈※

The first major decision in any label's marketing plan for a new artist is which segment of the music-buying population the company will focus its promotional muscle on. Pearl Jam, the folks at Epic had determined, were likely to go over well with both the hard rock–heavy metal and college radio–alternative markets. The latter was probably more in line with Pearl Jam's low-key aesthetic, but it was also the least accommodating to new artists. Hard rock, on the other hand, was currently booming—and notoriously welcoming to newcomers. With that in mind, Epic was going for the metal market with both barrels, and in addition to showering metal-friendly reporters and radio stations with promo CDs, the label had set up a dizzying schedule for Pearl Jam in Los Angeles the first week of October, when *Ten* would arrive in stores.

First on the agenda was an appearance on MTV's *Headbanger's Ball*, the late-night gabfest hosted by the channel's fashionably tattooed, long-haired veejay, Riki Rachtman. Eddie hadn't been exactly eager to do the show—*Headbanger's Ball* was the domain of old-school metallers, and Pearl Jam were better suited for *120 Minutes*, MTV's alternative program—but Epic's arguments had won him over: If Pearl Jam wanted any play for the "Alive" video they'd just submitted to the channel, it would probably be a good idea to cooperate. So Eddie and Mike toughed it out, slouching on the show's ragged sofa and fielding Rachtman's questions. They were gracious throughout, although Eddie (who casually scrawled FUGAZI on his bicep with black Magic Marker during the show) did joke at one point that he felt like "somebody on Carson, plugging a movie."

On October 1, Pearl Jam played the Cathouse, Rachtman's nightclub and a longtime haunt for the city's spandexed faithful; the band's performance netted a rave review in the *Los Angeles Times*, writer Steve Hochman comparing them to the Who—an occurrence that no doubt left Eddie pleased—and describing the show as a "celebration of the death of nihilism." On the next night, there was a reception arranged by Epic at a posh restaurant, followed by a second gig, this time at the Troubador, a metal dive with scaled-down gymnasium decor. The venue was crawling with buzz killers—suits were everywhere, and Epic's publicity staff had thoughtfully festooned the Troub's balcony railings with huge Pearl Jam posters before the show—but the stilted Industry Event vibe dissipated as soon as the lights went down, and Pearl Jam won over yet another jaded L.A. crowd. Among them, a *Hollywood Reporter* scribe who was wowed by Eddie's high-wire act, but apparently not enough to note the proper spelling of his name ("And when Vender climbed the lighting columns and sang from the ceiling, the crowd nearly erupted," read the review), and Guns n' Roses bassist and transplanted Seattleite Duff McKagan, who turned up backstage after the set. Kelly and Peggy Curtis and most of the band spent the rest of the evening at McKagan's house, shooting pool and getting an eyeful of life at the top. It wasn't quite what they'd expected.

McKagan was drinking heavily at the time, and on this evening he was near the stumbling point, going on and on about the solo album he'd just made and previewing it—over and over and over—for his guests. Hangers-on drifted from room to room, and it appeared that McKagan barely knew most of them. He seemed lonely in a way, and his huge house, with its platinum-album-lined walls and kitchen overflowing with empty beer cans, was oddly devoid of warmth. The others had known McKagan long enough to feel comfortable, but Dave wandered around for a few minutes, pronounced the scene depressing, and called himself a cab. He waited for the car outside, explaining to a slightly hurt-looking McKagan that, yes, he did know the taxi would take about half an hour to arrive, but he wanted to enjoy the night air.

Compared to what awaited Pearl Jam the next day, the gathering at McKagan's was a tea party.

Epic had arranged for the band to perform at Foundations Forum '91, a convention organized by the hard rock–heavy metal P.R. firm Concrete Marketing. It wasn't exactly the hippest of gigs—the conference, held at the Los Angeles Airport Marriott hotel, would be jam-packed with aspiring poodleheads, there to play showcases, shop their demos, and talk up A&R staffers from the major labels. But it would also be heavily attended by press and radio types from across the country, which made it an opportune place for Pearl Jam to play. When the booking had first been discussed, it hadn't sounded as if it would be all that excruciating. Hard-rock convention? Sure, no sweat. They *were* a hard-rock band, technically, even if they had little in common with some of the other groups that would be appearing. It sounded like it might be something of a schmoozefest, but at this point a little networking would help get the word out about *Ten*. Besides, Soundgarden and Alice in Chains were going, so how bad could it be?

Mike and Dave walked through the main doors of the hotel on the first day of the convention, took a look at the scene unfolding before them, and stopped dead in their tracks. Their expressions were identical.

Oh, gross. Get me out of here.

If ever there were such a thing as Heavy Metal Hell, this was it. Swaggering, bare-chested metal dudes with poofy, Aqua-Netted hair prowled the corridors like deranged sideshow barkers, pressing their tapes and postcards and buttons and bumper stickers into the hands of anyone within spitting distance. Elevator doors sprang open every few minutes, vomiting boisterous groups of Slash wannabes into the already teeming lobby. The hotel bar was overflowing by eleven in the morning; Lemmy Kilmeister of Mötörhead was holding court there, along with Jason Bonham, son of the late John "Bonzo" Bonham and bearer of the Led Zeppelin genetic torch. Both were surrounded by admirers, many of whom were female and displaying what appeared to be store-bought cleavage. Gaudy booths lined every conceivable inch of wall space, plastered with glossy posters and staffed by miniskirted girlfriends or harrassed-looking label employees. One enterprising young man had set up a stand to peddle custom-made rock logo panties: YOUR BAND NAME HERE.

Uh-huh.

This would have been Pearl Jam's audience when they performed at the hotel later in the evening, but at the eleventh hour they were spared

by tight scheduling. The band was slated to play after the Concrete
Foundation Awards Ceremony, a $200-a-seat benefit for the T. J. Martell
Foundation, a music-industry AIDS and cancer research charity. Unfortunately, the awards show—a painful-to-watch jumble of missed cues,
technical glitches, and no-show recipients—ran well over its planned
length, which would have put Pearl Jam on stage at around two A.M. On
any other night this wouldn't have been a problem, but they had a video
shoot scheduled bright and early the following morning. After some de-
liberation, they canceled their set—although Stone, Jeff, Eddie, and
Mike did join Chris Cornell and Matt Cameron during the ceremony for
a brief Temple of the Dog reunion on "Hunger Strike." Bailing on a gig at
the last minute was a no-no, but they'd promised Chris Cuffaro they
would be available at seven A.M. This was the young photographer's first
attempt to direct a video, and it was important to him. It was equally
important to Eddie, who'd convinced Cuffaro to tackle it in the first
place.

Later, Eddie would probably wish he'd left well enough alone. In the
end, Cuffaro's video would stand as just one more glaring reminder to
the singer of the intrusive influence that commercial concerns had begun to have on Pearl Jam's creative decisions.

XOX

Eddie had first met Chris Cuffaro during another convention, when
Pearl Jam had been in New York in July for the New Music Seminar. Cuffaro, a Mother Love Bone fan, had been anxious to photograph Stone
and Jeff's new band, and Julie Farman, a publicist at Epic, had arranged
for him to meet Pearl Jam after a Seminar-sponsored performance at the
Marriott Marquis hotel. He and Eddie had hit it off that night, and later,
during a trip to Los Angeles, Eddie had introduced him to Beth. "Eddie
had moved to Seattle and Beth hadn't," Cuffaro recalls. "Beth was still
in L.A. working at Virgin Records and stuff, so we used to do lots of
things together." After sojourns to Lollapalooza together and, later, to a
midnight Fugazi show in the Mojave Desert, Cuffaro had become close
to the couple, and the last time he'd seen them, during a visit to Seattle
just after Beth had moved there, the idea that he should direct Pearl
Jam's next video had taken root.

"I took them out to dinner and we were having a really good time,
and Eddie said 'You know, you should do a video,'" says Cuffaro. "I was
bitching and complaining about how I should've been directing, and he

said, 'I bet you can do it.' So the next day, I said, 'You're right, I can do it, but if I'm gonna do it, I want to do it with you guys.'"

Eddie had talked to the other members of Pearl Jam about having Cuffaro direct their next video, and they'd been enthusiastic. The folks at Epic, on the other hand, freaked out.

The way Epic saw it, music videos were one of the most vital sales tools any band had in its arsenal, and Epic certainly wasn't the only label to harbor that belief. It was common knowledge within the industry that getting a video played on MTV could mean the difference between an album's languishing in the bins or breaking wide open, and since the channel was so notoriously picky in its selection process, most labels treated video making like a science, a process with set parameters that shouldn't be deviated from. Pearl Jam had already come up against this attitude to a small degree—during the making of the "Alive" performance clip, when Epic had balked at their idea of recording the music live as well—but in that battle, Epic had eventually come around. This time, they would never waver in their disapproval.

From the start, the label treated Cuffaro's video like a bad toothache, something that would hopefully go away if they ignored it long enough. Perhaps because Eddie was gung ho on the project and they wanted to humor him, Epic agreed to give Cuffaro permission to use any song from *Ten* that he liked. But they also informed Cuffaro that they wouldn't pay for the video, and when he told them he'd chosen "Jeremy," their reaction was lukewarm at best. They'd already earmarked "Even Flow" as Pearl Jam's second single.

"They said, 'We're not gonna use that as a single, no way,'" Cuffaro recalls. "'We'll give you permission because Eddie wants to, but we have no desire to use "Jeremy" as a single.'"

Confident that with the band's support he didn't need Epic's approval, Cuffaro decided to fund the project himself. To raise the money, he took out a loan and sold all of his furniture and half his guitar collection. Meanwhile, he and Eddie began brainstorming over the phone to put together a treatment. "I told him I really thought the images should be subtle, not too literal," Cuffaro says, "and he liked what I was coming up with. The band really didn't have any say in it—it seemed like they really didn't care."

Through all of this, Cuffaro had been operating on instinct and the feel of the song; Eddie had never told him the story behind "Jeremy," or that it was based on a real-life tragedy. When the singer finally did reveal all, he did so in a typically fanciful manner.

Perry Farrell had announced that he was breaking up Jane's Addiction after a Hawaiian concert in late September, and Cuffaro had flown Beth out to see the band's final show. When she arrived in Hawaii, she handed Cuffaro a small box, telling him it was a gift from Eddie. Inside was the clipping Eddie had torn out of the newspaper about the real Jeremy, the boy from Richardson, Texas, who'd shot himself in front of his English class.

"All of a sudden," remembers Cuffaro, "I knew what the song was about."

The shoot went extremely well. Cuffaro had rented a warehouse on Pico Boulevard, and he and his crew—all of whom had agreed to work for next to nothing—had already spent a day filming the young actor who would portray Jeremy in the clip. Dave had the first call on the morning of Pearl Jam's shoot, and he arrived raring to go. "He was really pumped, which made me happy," says Cuffaro. "You always wonder if the band even cares. Stone was good friends with Josh Taft, and Josh was doing all their videos; it was the same thing with [photographer] Lance Mercer. You know, they have their guys, and you're crossing the line. But it was magical."

Cuffaro had rigged a revolving platform at the center of the set, and one by one, the members of Pearl Jam climbed onto it to lip-synch or play air guitar as a crew member, lying on his back, spun the giant turntable by hand. Eddie, as usual, had something special planned. He emerged from the dressing room when it was his turn, and a few of the crew members glanced at each other, puzzled. The singer had wrapped black gaffer's tape around his bicep, mourning-style.

"Everybody was like, 'Why does he have black tape on his arm?'" Cuffaro recalls. "Nobody understood what the tape was for. He wore that for Jeremy, for the real kid."

Eddie did about ten takes, arms crossed in front of him, shadows dancing across his contorted features as the platform spun slowly into and out of the light. You'd never know from watching Cuffaro's footage that he'd been lip-synching; the performance was that emotional. After the final take, everyone on the set burst into spontaneous applause. "The crew was just blown away," says Cuffaro. "I swear to God, it was so powerful. He was just brilliant in it. In all my years of shooting, I've never come across anyone like him."

Cuffaro had to beg, borrow, and steal to get the first rough edit of the video together, and to save money, he did all of the postproduction himself. All told, it took him six months to finish the project, but it was worth it. The completed video was an arty masterpiece, ghostly images of the boy intercut with performance footage of the band, simple in structure but rich in shadowy, chilling nuance. It fit the song perfectly.

"And then," recalls Cuffaro, "they canned it."

In 1992, while Cuffaro was still trying to get a straight answer from Epic on the status of his "Jeremy" video, Epic released "Jeremy" as a single, contrary to what they'd told Cuffaro about having no plans to do so. And not long afterward, a different video for "Jeremy"—shot by a director named Mark Pellington—started showing up on MTV.

If you wanted to stack the deck in your favor when it came to getting a video played on MTV, you couldn't do much better than Mark Pellington. Right after his graduation from the University of Virginia in 1984, the young Baltimore native had begun a long and illustrious association with MTV, joining the channel's On-Air Promotions department. The groundbreaking promotional spots Pellington created for MTV were so much a part of the channel's feel that he would later be credited with helping to define the so-called "MTV look." (Pellington also directed videos for artists including Public Enemy, Alice in Chains, INXS, PM Dawn, and U2, and helped design the set for U2's Zoo TV tour. Later in the decade he would lend his talent to commercials, directing ads for Reebok, Converse, and Mountain Dew, as well as those ubiquitous "Got Milk?" spots.)

Pellington's big-budget "Jeremy" video, shot in London with the Epic seal of approval, employed many of the techniques he'd made popular with his MTV promotional spots, incorporating rapid-fire editing and the juxtaposition of found images, sound, and text with film sequences to create a collagelike effect. Like Cuffaro, Pellington had hired a young actor to portray Jeremy, and some of the stock imagery was similar as well—blackboards, guns—but when it came to the band, Pellington focused almost exclusively on Eddie. The others, in fact, were barely seen in the final cut, which was heavy on close-ups of the singer, his features contorted as he dramatically lip-synched the song. A much more MTV-friendly production than Cuffaro's mini art-house film, Pellington's "Jeremy" video would quickly find its way into heavy rotation on the channel, helping to catapult Pearl Jam to fame and winning numerous awards in the process. Cuffaro's version would live on in bootleg form, a curiosity passed from fan to fan. Most who saw it would say they preferred it to Pellington's.

Eddie was enthusiastic during the remake of the video—he stuck to Pellington like glue on the set, and the two were often spotted with their heads together, laughing and trading ideas—but his public stance on Pellington's "Jeremy" clip was decidedly less spirited. When a crew from MTV Europe interviewed Eddie and Stone during a break in the shoot, the singer seemed wooden. His demeanor as he sat down on a staircase to face the whirring MTV cameras was distinctly glum, his sole comment about the shoot an indictment of videos in general.

"Before music videos first came out, you'd listen to a song with head-phones on, sitting in a beanbag chair with your eyes closed, and you'd come up with your own visions, these things that came from within," Eddie told the MTV crew. "Then all of a sudden, sometimes even the very first time you heard a song, it was with these visual images at-tached, and it robbed you of any form of self-expression."

He stared down morosely at his shoes, leaving Stone to answer the rest of the questions. Later, when Eddie spoke of Pellington's video dur-ing interviews and award acceptance speeches, his comments would be similarly unenthusiastic, as if he were embarrassed to have participated in the project and wanted to disassociate himself from it.

Chris Cuffaro has seen Eddie many times in the years since, but Ed-die has never offered him a reason why his "Jeremy" video was shelved in favor of Pellington's, and Cuffaro has never pressed the issue. Why put Eddie on the spot, force him to admit aloud what they both already knew?

"It's all business now," the photographer says with a sigh. "That's the sad part about it. Those were great times, and I had a blast. But it's just not the same."

"It took me a while to get over it," Cuffaro adds. "No matter how hard they'll sit there and deny it, it's like, '*You're* the one who's changed, not *me*.' But you know, my life's going on just fine without them, and it will continue to go on. I'd like Eddie's help here or there— I'd like some things to do, or whatever. But I won't hold my breath. He's got his own agenda."

XOX

Tomorrow, Pearl Jam would finally make their escape from Los Angeles, traveling on to Phoenix, where a whopping audience of seven would watch them tear up the stage at a club called the Mason Jar. But that was tomorrow. Tonight, they were capping off their heavy-metal Hell Week in the most appropriate manner possible, with an appearance at *RIP* magazine's fifth anniversary bash.

The evening would be memorable if a little chaotic. Pearl Jam's thirty-five-minute set had gone off well, but there'd been a radio station camped upstairs waiting to interview them afterward, and then Eddie, joyously crowd surfing during Soundgarden's set, had been grabbed in a headlock and shoved out the back door of the theater by an overzealous security guard. He'd barely made it back in time for the Temple of the Dog reunion scheduled next in the running order. (From the stage during the Temple set, Eddie got his revenge on the guard who'd ejected him, waiting until he drew close enough and then "accidentally" lobbing a big wad of spit onto the back of his head.)

Alice in Chains had also performed at the party, and Metallica were rumored to be making a surprise appearance as well. (They never showed.) But the real draw of the evening, for the four thousand-plus crowd of inebriated fashion victims who were packed onto the floor of the Hollywood Palladium, and even more so for the musicians on the bill, was a set by the legendary Spinal Tap.

To a generation of musicians who'd grown up fantasizing about being rock stars—and then *become* rock stars, only to find themselves free-falling into the chasm between myth and reality—the members of Spinal Tap, the dim-witted fictional metal band whose trials and tribulations director Rob Reiner chronicled in his 1984 mock-rockumentary *This Is Spinal Tap*, were no less than supreme beings. Reiner's satire, starring Harry Shearer, Christopher Guest, and Michael McKean as the band's irrepressible Derek Smalls, Nigel Tufnel, and David St. Hubbins, so closely mimicked the real rock & roll lifestyle that the film had quickly become a tour bus staple. You couldn't be a touring musician and *not* relate to the series of ridiculous mishaps that plagued Spinal Tap on their way up to—and back down from—the top. Nigel, Derek, and David had always been celluloid flag bearers for everything about rock & roll that was silly, politically incorrect, fun for the sake of being fun. And tonight at the Palladium, they were here in the flesh.

On the right side of the dance floor, about twenty feet away from the Palladium's stage, Mike and Dave stood awaiting the appearance of their idols. There were other Seattle musicians, the guys from Alice in Chains and Soundgarden, milling around as well, but they were more subdued. Pearl Jam's guitarist and drummer, on the other hand, were beside themselves, practically jumping up and down. "I can't wait," Mike kept saying. "This is gonna be so cool." Every now and then one of them would sarcastically thrust a forefinger and pinkie into the air in the classic heavy-metal devil horns salute and bellow, *"Rock and ROLLLLL!,"* setting off a new round of high, excited laughter.

Spinal Tap would be the talk of the town for days afterward, those who'd witnessed their performance describing it in minute detail to friends who'd been unlucky enough to miss it. With hindsight, though, the most significant occurrence that evening wasn't the spectacle of Nigel, David, and Derek plowing through Tap classics like "Big Bottom" or "Break Like the Wind." Rather, it was something that happened before they ever took the stage.

During the set change, about midway through the charged twenty-minute interlude when everyone had been waiting for Spinal Tap to appear, the last strains of Guns n' Roses or Metallica or Faith No More or whatever band it was the deejay had been playing had faded out, and there'd been a brief lull, the hall filling with the noise of the rowdy crowd.

Then the opening chords of Nirvana's "Smells Like Teen Spirit" had come booming over the club's P.A., and for a single, frozen moment in time, the electricity coursing through the Palladium was palpable.

It was that striking, the sight of L.A.'s metal youth perking up their ears en masse, moving in time to a song they recognized as theirs and *only* theirs—and you couldn't ask for stronger symbolism. They'd come here tonight to pay tribute to a band that was a walking parody of every arena-rock cliché in the book—to them, Spinal Tap embodied every sexist lyric that had ever been written, every TV set that had ever been heaved out a hotel room window, every pair of ruby-red spandex jeans that had ever been tugged over a posterior one size too large for their cut. These were the time-honored rituals that had been set in place by their parents' musical heroes, and, in a sense, they'd come to the Palladium to honor them. But at that moment, singing along with Kurt Cobain— "Here we are now, entertain us . . ."—what they were really doing was bidding those rituals farewell.

It was October 6, 1991, and Nirvana's *Nevermind*, the album that would later be credited with sparking the alternative explosion on the horizon—or blamed for it, depending on who you were talking to—had been in stores for twelve days. From the beginning, it had been selling more briskly than anyone at Geffen had ever expected. Early demos had been floating around for nearly a year prior to the album's release, resulting in a strong street buzz on the band; that aside, *Nevermind* was simply a great record, a spine-chilling twelve-track battle shriek that was uncannily right for its time. In two weeks, the album would be certified gold. Within a month, after MTV put the band's pep-rally-from-hell video for "Teen Spirit" into Buzz Bin rotation, it would jump into the Top Forty.

In a way, the dawn of Nirvanamania would be for twentysomethings the same sort of generational snapshot that Woodstock had been for their parents, fans able to remember with crystal clarity where they'd been and what they'd been doing the first time they heard "Teen Spirit." Just as another Seattle son, Jimi Hendrix, had taken a hatchet to a dated tradition with his gnarled, blistering version of "The Star Spangled Banner," so was Nirvana hammering in the coffin nails on a musical era that had overstayed its welcome.

Seemingly overnight, the rules had all changed. And as was always the case when pop culture was busy ushering in a new regime, either you played by the rules, or you were out of the game.

Nine

On the Road with the Chili Peppers / Kurt Cobain, Alternative Watchdog / Don't Shoot Me, I'm Only the Drummer

Opening a three-act bill isn't exactly a cushy gig; usually it entails playing half-empty halls, to audiences who are impatiently awaiting the headliner. Thanks to a combination of luck and careful planning, though, word of mouth on Pearl Jam was so strong by the time they hit the road with the Chili Peppers and Smashing Pumpkins that they were able to sidestep opening-band syndrome completely.

For starters, Nirvana's *Nevermind*, still blowing out of stores, had focused even more media attention on the Seattle music scene, and Pearl Jam was among a number of bands benefiting from the increased interest. Critics and deejays who might otherwise have let *Ten* get lost in the shuffle now had a reason not to. The album was getting regular write-ups, and metal and college radio stations were adding "Alive" to their playlists. On top of that, Epic's thorough promotional groundwork and Pearl Jam's heavy press schedule were beginning to bear fruit. The label's mass-mailing of the "Alive" sampler to Mother Love Bone and Soundgarden fan club members had set in place a street buzz, and the dozens of newspaper and magazine interviews the band had done during their van tour all seemed to be hitting the newsstands at once.

These elements converged right about the time the Chili Peppers tour started, and as a result Pearl Jam enjoyed a much more receptive audience during their opening set than would normally have been the case for a new band. As the tour progressed, in fact, the turnout for Pearl Jam began to rival that of the Peppers, which probably left the Smashing Pumpkins—in effect sandwiched between *two* hot headliners—cursing the day they'd signed on for the trip.

"The crowd on that tour was insane," Dave recalls. "I mean, they were still there to see the Peppers, but when we played, it was crazy. We'd play for thirty minutes, and it was like the Smashing Pumpkins had to earn their forty-five minutes, and the Peppers even had to earn theirs. By the end of that tour, it was almost like they were our audience in a lot of respects."

Getting the fans to the venues early enough to see their set had been the only real hurdle Pearl Jam needed to jump on this tour. Already, they were developing a reputation as one of the most dynamic live acts around, and if fans—no matter how jaded or impassive—showed up, it rarely took long for the band to draw them in. In a live setting, their enthusiasm was infectious.

"It was quite funny to see that," says Chris Cuffaro. "I got tickets for friends in New York when they played there with the Peppers, and they all went, 'Oh, okaaaaay, we'll go.' They came out the next night saying, 'Oh my God, I haven't seen anything that good since I saw *Zeppelin*.' Pearl Jam just converted people—it was like religion, people walking in going, 'No way,' and walking out going, 'I believe!' You could see it on people's faces."

Nowhere else in the set was that sense of magic as pronounced as it was when Pearl Jam played "Alive." Ultimately, when it was released as a single and the accompanying video was picked up by MTV, "Jeremy" would be the track from *Ten* that broke Pearl Jam wide open, but "Alive" was the song the fans most strongly identified with, the one that cemented their emotional connection with the band. During that number in Pearl Jam's set, you could usually scan the crowd and spot dozens of fans in tears, caught up in the song's self-affirming chorus. Eventually this spectacle would border on the absurd, so many fans experiencing "rebirths" at Pearl Jam concerts that the first few rows resembled tent revivals. Adding to the phenomenon, Pearl Jam's defacto mascot, the primitive, shaggy-haired stick figure Jeff had drawn for the *Alive* EP cover, also took on a life of its own during the tour.

The fans weren't the first to recognize the drawing's powerful symbolism. Two weeks after he'd joined the band, Dave had had the logo—these days fondly known to Pearl Jam followers as the Stickman—tattooed on his bicep to commemorate an emotional milestone. For the first time in his life, the drummer had a sense of peace about who he was and where he was going, and one day in the midst of this natural high, he'd come across Jeff's original artwork for the *Alive* cover at the Curtis Management offices.

"I saw the drawing," he said later, "this symbol of everything that I [was feeling], and it just blew me away. I didn't want to take out my book and write, 'Wow, I feel great, I feel alive, I feel totally secure.' I wanted to make it permanent. I wanted to remember that second of my life for the rest of my life."

When they first began to see the occasional fan sporting a Stickman tattoo, the band members were touched. The charm quickly wore off, though—especially for Dave, whose once-unique tattoo was now turning up everywhere he looked. Soon it seemed as if at least one fan at every aftershow meet-and-greet was shyly approaching the band and raising a shirtsleeve or a pants leg to reveal the inevitable logo. Worse, fewer and fewer of the tattooed disciples seemed to be submitting to the needle for anything but fashion's sake—they were merely declaring allegiance to a favorite band, the way you'd slap a trendy sticker on your backpack or pin a button to your jacket.

"There were always kids coming up and showing me their tattoos," Dave recalls. "At first, I thought, 'Wow, that's kind of cool.' But it got to where I'd ask them, 'What does that mean to you?' and they'd say, 'Pearl Jam rules, *dude*.' Or girls would say, 'Eddie's so cute!' It was just a nightmare."

The Stickman phenomenon was one of the first real clues Pearl Jam had of the magnitude of their impending fame, and although the fans' enthusiasm was gratifying, it was accompanied by a growing sense that the band members—and not their music—were the primary object of all that adulation. For another band, a realization like that wouldn't be cause for concern; it might even warrant popping a few champagne corks. But for Pearl Jam, already fighting off a reputation as the bastard sons of Seattle—a community where phrases like *rock star* and *celebrity* had always been uttered with a sneer—it just meant one more thing to live down. It also meant one more thing that was likely to freak Eddie out, and that list had been growing longer by the day.

Little more than a year ago, he'd been a virtual nobody, and now he was the man everyone wanted to meet. In and of itself, that wasn't a problem; Eddie liked talking to people. Rather, it was the *kind* of conversations he found himself having. Sometimes, he felt like he was in small-talk hell, drowning in the inane, sycophantic chitchat that was typical backstage at shows. Other times, it was the opposite end of the conversational spectrum, complete strangers who approached him with stories so heartwrenching and personal that he wished he could spend his entire evening listening and felt guilty when he couldn't. A prime example was an encounter he had with a fan after a show in New York.

Eddie, sweaty and tired, had been picking his way through the crowd when a teenage boy drew him into a bear hug and wouldn't let go. As they embraced, Eddie felt something bulky between his chest and the boy's; he noticed after they pulled apart that the fan was wearing a leather pouch on a thong around his neck.

"I just need to tell you that this meant so much," the boy said excitedly. He began pouring his heart out, telling Eddie that a friend of his, who'd died recently from a heroin overdose, would have loved the *Temple of the Dog* record and would've really been into Pearl Jam as well.

"My friend was here tonight," the fan said meaningfully.

Eddie, touched, turned his eyes heavenward. "Yeah," the singer said, smiling, "I think he was."

"No," said the boy, holding up the pouch around his neck, "I mean, he was *here*. His remains are in *here*."

How on earth were you supposed to respond to something like *that*?

✕◇✕

The more the evidence mounted that Pearl Jam was on the fast track to fame, the more vocal Eddie became about not wanting any part of the hype. During stops along the tour, he confided in one reporter after another his fears that the band's snowballing celebrity would dilute the power of the music.

"I'd like to keep this thing really small for a while," he said. "I want to play clubs for a long time, and I don't want to be opening for a big act. There's an energy happening when you're face-to-face—there's something happening there that's really intense. It would be unfair to the music to play it in a different arena."

As sincere as the singer was about wanting to protect the music, it was apparent that the *concept* of celebrity was as troublesome to him as anything else—that he worried about how it might cause him to be perceived. During a conversation with this reporter for a *Rolling Stone* piece, he'd hinted rather broadly that the finished article would probably be "about me, fighting to stay small"—a bit of spin-doctoring that was probably much more transparent than he'd have liked. Eddie might have been wary of Pearl Jam's growing fame, but at the same time, he clearly wanted the world to know how hard he was struggling to push it away.

Most of the public accepted Eddie's reluctant-messiah proclamations at face value; to some, in fact, it was his presence and his actions alone that allowed Pearl Jam to disinherit Stone and Jeff's Mother Love Bone–era reputation as commercialists with arena-rock ambitions. You couldn't talk to Eddie without being taken by his passion, and he'd quickly cultivated friendships with the Seattle-scene old guard, seeking them out at their gigs to let them know how much they'd inspired him, sometimes sending them the elaborately decorated notes that were one of his trademarks. "The first time I ever met Eddie was at a show in Seattle," Kim Warnick of the Fastbacks told *City Revolt*. "Obviously I had heard of Pearl Jam. They were getting popular, but I didn't know he was the singer yet. So he introduced himself as Eddie Vedder and I said, 'Oh yeah, you're that guy—I've heard about you.' A couple of days later him and [Beth] sent me this glittery thing that said WE LOVE THE FASTBACKS."

Eddie had even managed to charm the members of Mudhoney, who never seemed to be able to mention Pearl Jam without an accompanying smirk. Chris Cuffaro says the seeds for the public reconciliation between the two bands that would take place a few years down the line were planted when, hanging out with Eddie one day, he invited the singer along to a photo shoot he was doing at Mudhoney guitarist Steve Turner's house.

"No way, I don't want to go there," said a stricken Eddie, well aware of the bad blood between Mudhoney and Stone and Jeff.

"Just shut up and get in the car," said Cuffaro.

Eddie caved in, and when they arrived at Turner's house, Cuffaro made introductions all around—"Hey guys, this is Eddie"—but neglected to mention Eddie's affiliation, an oversight that allowed the musicians to meet on neutral turf. After they'd spent the afternoon talking music and philosophy with Eddie, Turner and Dan Peters, Mudhoney's drummer, pulled Cuffaro aside.

"Who is this guy again?" Cuffaro recalls them asking.

"Eddie?" asked Cuffaro. He paused for a moment, wanting to drop the bomb as casually as he could. "He's the lead singer for Pearl Jam."

"No way," said Turner.

"God," said Peters, sounding slightly bewildered. "He's really cool."

A few hours later, the whole group was enjoying a raucous dinner, trading phone numbers and making plans to get together again. "All of a sudden they were all lovey-dovey, buddies and pals," says Cuffaro, laughing.

But others—especially those who'd never met Eddie—weren't so quick to forgive the past. No matter what the singer did or said to drive home the image of Pearl Jam as a humble garage band that had been swept up in a tornado and transported to an evil, corporate Oz, some within the insular Seattle scene wrote it all off as a lot of hooey, carping that Pearl Jam were mere opportunists, hair-band pretenders to the suddenly lucrative alternative throne. And leading the pack was Kurt Cobain.

XOX

At the time, Cobain was fighting off his own critics. He'd become something of a pariah among the underground cognoscenti in the wake of *Nevermind*'s success, a favorite target for disillusioned purple-hairs and snotty fanzine correspondents who now saw Nirvana as corporate turncoats. Given his own position as the human rope in an indie-mainstream tug-of-war, Cobain had perhaps a better understanding than anyone else of the pressure Pearl Jam was under. He was the last person they'd have expected to add to it.

But whether it was good old-fashioned competitiveness or the need to find a scapegoat for his own diminished indie credibility, Cobain had it in for Pearl Jam big time. Not only did he dislike their music, he seemed to loathe *them*, complaining that they were hypocrites, the worst kind of sellouts. As a close friend of Mudhoney's Mark Arm, Cobain's primary beef with Pearl Jam was Jeff Ament. He'd resented the bassist ever since the Green River split, and had described him to Nirvana biographer Michael Azerrad as a "careerist—a person who will kiss ass to make sure his band gets popular so he can become rich." In that respect, Cobain was no different than any of the other Sub Pop bluebloods who'd been badmouthing Jeff for years. What made Cobain different was his visibility: Whereas previously he might have batted around a few insults over beers in someone's Seattle living room, he was now hurling zingers in the presence of reporters.

"I felt proud to be a part of the Seattle scene when we came there out of Aberdeen," Cobain had seethed to a *Chicago Tribune* writer in late October. "But now there's a corporate tag on the Seattle scene, and I find it offensive to be lumped in with bands like Pearl Jam . . . They were never part of the underground."

Critics, always eager to be of service when it came to stirring up a rock & roll feud, got wind of comments like this and egged Cobain on in their own interviews, facilitating a one-man smear campaign that would continue well into the following year. During a *Musician* interview, Cobain griped that Pearl Jam seemed to mention Nirvana in every interview they did. "I would love to be erased from my association with that band," he snarled, after denouncing Pearl Jam as "the ones responsible for this corporate, alternative, and cock-rock fusion." A few months down the road, he would also share his views with *Rolling Stone*'s readership: "I do feel a duty to warn the kids about false music that's claiming to be underground or alternative. They're just jumping on the alternative bandwagon."

From the beginning, Pearl Jam tried to laugh off Cobain's sour commentary—at one point, Epic even printed one of his choicest quotes on a joke promotional T-shirt—but for more reasons than one, getting dissed by the reigning king of Seattle was bad news. For starters, what Cobain said *mattered*. He might not hold the punkest of the punk in his thrall any longer, but in the eyes of thousands upon thousands of fans who'd had their first taste of so-called "alternative" music when they'd bought *Nevermind*—fans who'd glommed on to Nirvana by way of Aerosmith or Mötley Crüe—Kurt Cobain was the arbiter of alterna-cool, punk personified. To these fans, any utterance of Cobain's was received as if it had been brought down from Mount Sinai, and to have him jabbering "Thou shalt not honor Pearl Jam" in interview after interview was simply bad P.R. That aside, Cobain's incessant mudslinging hurt Pearl Jam on a personal level.

"You try your hardest not to be affected by that," Jeff admitted later, "but it bothers you. Whether it's Kurt Cobain or whoever, when people say shit about you without knowing you, it stings."

When people asked Eddie about Cobain's remarks, he usually tried to downplay the issue. "Lord knows, I've got so much more important stuff on my mind," he told a *Washington Post* reporter who dangled the bait. But at least once he slipped up and exposed his true feelings on the matter, in the bargain offering a rare glimpse of his shrewdness when it came to passive-aggressive battle maneuvers. "In many ways, I feel sorry for Kurt Cobain," Eddie purred to a reporter for *Raw*. "How frustrating can it be, having as much money to do whatever you want to do, you know? How's he going to sing punk rock songs?"

If Eddie knew how to hit back where it was guaranteed to hurt Cobain the most, it was only because he had the same Achilles heel. Deep down, he respected Cobain deeply, and the Nirvana leader's scorn wounded him perhaps even more than it had his band mates. Cobain's public flogging of Pearl Jam was just one more contributing factor to Eddie's growing fears about his own credibility.

Already, there were signs that Eddie's sensitivity about his image was becoming an issue within the band. He'd made a stink about traveling in a tour bus—it was unseemly for Pearl Jam to have a bus so soon, when so many punk bands had slugged it out in vans for years—and not even his band mates' gear escaped his scrutiny. During one early interview, Eddie had looked pleased as Jeff explained that on their tour Pearl Jam wanted to play "as many all-ages shows as we can, in smaller places." But when Jeff began bragging that his huge wall of bass speakers would probably require their own tour bus, Eddie cut him off.

"We're kind of a dichotomy between simplicity and total complexity," the singer said sarcastically.

"I like it simple," Jeff stammered defensively. "There's just a lot of it."

Dave's drum kit was also large and flashy enough to be a thorn in Eddie's side—"Eddie complained a lot, like, 'He's using too many cymbals'" remembers Chris Cuffaro—but that was the least of the drummer's sins. "I never sensed that Dave fit in," says Cuffaro. "In a weird kind of way, Dave was too normal for the band. All Dave wanted to do was have fun. He wasn't so uptight and hung up on every little thing—he was just like, 'Hey, I wanna play *drums*, I like being in a band.'"

Dave didn't give a flip about the punk rule book Eddie seemed to be carrying around in his head. To him, Pearl Jam's success wasn't anything to be embarrassed about, it was something to celebrate. In a few years—after Nirvana and Pearl Jam's breakthroughs kick started the industry clone factory again and music was overrun with political correctness, false modesty, and fame ducking—Dave's attitude would be seen as a welcome relief from a tedious overabundance of shoegazing. But at the time, in a climate where it had suddenly become distinctly *un*cool to be a celebrity, his unabashed happiness about Pearl Jam's soaring notoriety made him conspicuous. He might not have been the only member of Pearl Jam who was enjoying their ascent to hot-band status, but he *was* the only one who was *visibly* enjoying it. And that, he says, was a no-no, especially around Eddie.

"All of a sudden here was all this success, but nobody could say anything about it because they were afraid of Eddie's reaction," recalls the drummer. "No one could say anything about how we'd just played in front of seven thousand people and it was amazing, because if Eddie wasn't in the mood to hear it, he'd be all pissed off and his reply would be 'We need to get back in a van and go play clubs.' And nobody *wanted* to do that. Yeah, sure, it sounds romantic, but it was *difficult*, so why should we do that if we don't have to? I thought that was stupid."

The differences between Dave and Eddie were just one more extension of the turf war between the DIY and corporate factions of music that had been raging since the Seventies—the same punk vs. rock pissing match that had divided the Seattle community; the same rift, marked by bickering over who was *really* alternative and who was just posing, that was developing between bands like Nirvana and Pearl Jam and would soon begin to fragment their audiences.

In some ways, Eddie and Dave were very much alike. Both warm and personable, they were the two members of Pearl Jam it was easiest to have a rambling conversation with; they were also the two with the most spiritual, earthy outlooks on day-to-day life. Professionally, too, they had similarities—both were extremely ambitious.

But when it came to handling life in the public eye, their styles clashed dramatically. Where Eddie could be cunning, appreciating the value of mystique and often keeping his cards close to this chest, Dave tended to be a blurter, guileless and eager to share whatever was on his mind. While Eddie claimed he was uncomfortable doing interviews, Dave loved the exchange and would even wheedle for more questions if a reporter stopped asking them before he'd talked himself out. Eddie would hem and haw his way around the how-does-it-feel-to-be-so-popular question, often answering with a treatise on the folly of celebrity. Dave would respond to the same question with a wide-open laugh and a thumbs-up, as if to say, "Are you crazy—who *wouldn't* like all this?"

Even with such vastly different ideas about what it meant to be in a popular band, the two might have been able to peacefully coexist. But from the beginning, there had been other factors that exacerbated the tension between them.

For one thing, Dave was highly skeptical about Eddie's public persona; he believed the singer was much more calculating and image conscious than he let on, and that Eddie's humble-stumblebum manner was an affectation. In a nutshell, Dave viewed Eddie the same way environmentalist Linda views traffic engineer Steve in Cameron Crowe's *Singles*. As Linda tells Steve when they first meet: "I think that, A, you have an act, and that, B, *not* having an act is your act."

Perhaps unwisely, Dave never bothered to hide his suspicions about what he called "Eddie's shtick" from Eddie himself. Rather, he made a habit of calling Eddie on it any time he thought he'd caught the singer in a disengenuous moment. As one example, Dave says that during the first interview he and Eddie sat for together, Eddie "talked about his Great Grandma Pearl, and all this stuff which I *knew* to be made up." Dave waited until the reporters were out of earshot and then turned to Eddie.

"Man, why'd you say all that stuff?" he asked.

Dave says Eddie stared at him hard for just an instant, then shrugged the question off: "Aw, I was just fuckin' with 'em."

Not only did Dave make it obvious to Eddie that he thought Eddie was a little too interested in mythmaking for someone who professed to abhor celebrity; the drummer also shared with others his suspicions that Eddie, contrary to what he would have everyone believe, was actively courting fame. According to one source, Dave wasn't exactly discreet about his belief that Beth, by then living in Seattle and working as an assistant for Kelly Curtis, was playing picky-choosy with interview requests and filtering the best of them to her boyfriend.

"Beth took care of all the publicity stuff—all of it went through her," says the source. "One of the things Dave talked about the first time we had a conversation was how frustrated he was about Beth, and how she was screening the calls. Eddie would find out about stuff that the rest of the guys might not find out about until later."

Whether or not that bit of watercooler gossip ever got back to Eddie, it had to be irksome for the singer to have one of his own band mates constantly peering over his shoulder and insinuating that he was a hypocrite. And, apparently, Eddie had had reservations about Dave from the beginning. According to Sheri Fineman, he found the drummer's happy-go-lucky manner irritating. "When Dave first came up, Eddie just didn't know if he was going to be able to deal with him," Fineman recalls, "because, as he put it, Dave kept high-fiving him and asking him how he was doing all the time."

Another obvious sore point, she says, was that Dave, who was having trouble breaking off a relationship in Texas, started seeing a Curtis Management staffer before the split with his old girlfriend was a done deal. Fineman believes Eddie found that off-putting, a breach of his own views about relationships ("In Eddie's mind, you meet someone, you stay with them forever, and everyone lives happily ever after.") and also of the antimacho, antisexist sensibility that was so much a part of the politically correct alternative code. She adds that Beth's influence almost certainly fueled that particular fire. In an observation shared by other sources, Fineman notes that the friction between Eddie and Dave grew more pronounced after Beth moved to Seattle.

"Beth was obviously the one who wore the pants in the family, and she's very, very dogmatic in her [feminist] views," says Fineman. "She has a very big ax to grind when it comes to that stuff. She really hated Alice in Chains, because they were a typical rock band and did drugs, but worst of all, they had *chicks*—there were girls there. That was just disgusting to her, and that was *not* gonna happen with the Pearl Jam guys. Thus the rift with Dave and Eddie. That really was a big part of it. Because once they were on tour, Dave was always picking up on some girl. I don't think he was sleeping around; he's just a huge flirt. We used to make fun of him, because it was hilarious. But Beth was really offended. She judged Dave very harshly for that."

Whether it was caused by the number of cymbals Dave used, his overt skepticism about Eddie's image, or the perception that he'd violated the alternative antiwomanizing code, Eddie's discontent with the drummer was obvious by the time Pearl Jam started opening for the Chili Peppers. It showed in his behind-the-scenes inquiries about possible replacements—Chris Cuffaro says that not long after Jane's Addiction broke up, Eddie asked him if he thought Stephen Perkins would be interested in drumming for Pearl Jam—and often spilled over into the band's shows. On some nights, Eddie even threw things at the drummer, in full view of the audience. Dave says the latter most often took place when he disobeyed marching orders.

"There was a fill that he wanted in 'Release,' and if I didn't play it, he'd get pissed and throw something, or turn around and give me this 'you suck' look," remembers the drummer. "I believe part of that was just him pumping himself up, but it was really a pain in the ass. I felt like, 'Okay—you're my friend, you hate me, what's the deal here?' If I tried to talk to him about it, he'd just be, 'No, man, I don't want to talk about it.'"

The cold shoulder he was getting was bad enough, but for Dave, not being able to hash it out was even worse. In Milwaukee, he finally blew a gasket.

"We'd played this horrible show, and everybody was totally disconnected," the drummer recalls. "I felt like I was on stage with a bunch of people going through the motions, yet at the same time doing interviews about how great it was to be in a band, and the love and respect and brotherhood, all this stuff that I didn't feel was going on at *all*."

After Pearl Jam's set, Dave went to the bus and grabbed up a few of his belongings. Jeff's bass tech, George Webb, saw the drummer stomping off the bus and asked him what was wrong.

"Man," Dave spat, "I want to play music with my *friends*."

He stalked off into the night, not sure where he was headed, and then the thirty-degree Milwaukee wind started whipping through the wringing-wet shorts he was still wearing from the stage. Once reality set in— "It's wintertime, I have forty bucks in my pocket, and this big bag of clothes, where the fuck am I going?"—he went back into the venue and told Eric Johnson he wanted to talk to the others.

"Eric gathered everybody up," he recalls, "and they came into our dressing room and I said, 'Look, this is the way I'm feeling.' And all of a sudden it turned into the four of them against me—'You're always asking me how I'm doing, fuck, man, you asked me that this morning, why do you need to ask me that again tonight?' And then Eddie went off; he was pissed because he didn't feel like I was representing the band the way he wanted the band to be represented. You know, I had no right doing this or that, or hanging out with people I met at shows, or whatever. I just sat there going, Jesus *Christ*."

Fineman says the chilly vibe Dave was getting from the others was simply the result of mismatched perceptions about what it meant to be in a band, and the different ways the members of Pearl Jam had of coping when problems arose. "When Stone was upset, he'd crawl inside himself. Jeff would logically analyze the problem and try to make it okay. Mike would just go drink, and that would be that. And Dave would want to sit down and say, 'Okay, we had a bad show, and we're gonna work this out because we're a team,' but it didn't ever happen. They were never a band that was always hanging out together. It was just a business arrangement."

That had never been how Dave perceived his role in the band, but it seems clear that, at that point at least, the others viewed him as little more than a paid sideman. Whether he'd missed the signals they'd been sending or just chosen to ignore them, the signals had been prevalent. There'd been Stone's awkward reaction when the drummer got his Stickman tattoo—"You know that's for *life*, don't you?"—and Jeff's non-committal, half-joking response when Dave had asked about his future in the band: "Well, you're in for the *tour*." There was Eddie's frustrating standoffishness, and the lethargic attitude Epic and the band had displayed about revising Pearl Jam's press materials. All of the bios and photos still featured Krusen's name, and when Dave had asked when the press handouts would be updated, the others had told him to lighten up, as if it mattered too much to him that his name wasn't included. (It's possible he was just weary of guiding reporters through the spelling obstacle course that was his last name. "Abbruzzese" was such a mouthful that half the staff at Curtis Management couldn't even pronounce it. Shortly after he arrived in Seattle, in fact, he'd picked up the nickname "Ockus," an abbreviated version of a comically mangled pronunciation attempt by staffer Krisha Augerot that had come out "Ab-bruise-ee-ockus.")

In a few years, Dave would find himself thinking back to this time, ticking off the signs on his fingers and wishing he'd paid closer attention to them. For now, though, he put his concerns on the back burner. Things were happening so fast for Pearl Jam that all any of them could really do was hang on for the ride.

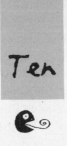

Ten

Home for the Holidays / London Calling / Attack of the Killer Stage Divers / Mike and Dave Do Amsterdam

The Chili Peppers tour passed in a blur, the members of Pearl Jam barely able to assimilate their experiences in each town along the tour route before they rolled into the next one.

Years from now, they would only be able to connect some of their memories to the cities that had birthed them: New York, where they'd played at CBGB to a few hundred hand-picked fans and then taken their act uptown to the Roseland Ballroom, thrilling a frenzied mob of thousands, among them John F. Kennedy, Jr., and Sean Lennon. San Francisco, where Nirvana had replaced the Smashing Pumpkins on the bill for a New Year's Eve show and, in a disappointing development for the gossip columnists, Pearl Jam and Nirvana made it through the night without any harsh words or fisticuffs breaking out. (Kurt Cobain had bared his teeth and growled at Dave when he passed the drummer in a corridor, but the other two members of Nirvana had been cordial, even after Pearl Jam played a teasing few bars of "Smells Like Teen Spirit" and Stone told the audience, "Just remember, *we* played it first."*

Other experiences would become orphaned in their minds, vivid snapshots in time with no geographical parents. What city had they been in the night nobody could find Stone and they started the set without him, only to have him turn up onstage breathless and red faced and admit he'd been in the basement playing chess with the Chili Peppers' sound man? Where had they been the night Mike got plastered on Chartreuse and Dave caught him peeing in the hotel flower bed, in full view of a startled desk clerk who was watching through the window? Or the time Mike and Stone went shopping together and bought those ridiculous-looking male purses, which they'd worn for a while and then quietly abandoned after the jokes got irritating? Many of their favorite war stories would be fuzzy around the edges by the time they attempted to tell them. Call it an occupational hazard, the result of too many towns traversed in too little time.

Pearl Jam spent the majority of January 1992 back home in Seattle, playing a few local shows and logging some time at London Bridge with Rick Parashar to rerecord "Breath" and "State of Love and Trust" for the upcoming *Singles* soundtrack. While they were in the studio, they recorded a new, rawer version of "Even Flow," Epic's second planned single from *Ten*. (Aside from limited promotional copies, most of the U.S. "Even Flow" singles shipped by Epic would feature the album version. The newly recorded alternate version would be used as the soundtrack for an upcoming video and would also be released on CD-single and 12-inch white vinyl in the United Kingdom.) During these sessions the band also cut "Alone" (later to turn up on a CD-single release of "Go" from their second album, *Vs.*) and "Yellow Ledbetter" and "Dirty Frank," both of which would turn up on B-sides and become fan favorites.

"Yellow Ledbetter," a leftover from the *Ten* sessions that was crafted

---

*In a 1995 biography on Kurt Cobain, writer Christopher Sanford quoted two anonymous sources who claimed to have witnessed a brawl between Cobain and Eddie backstage, culminating in Eddie's being kneed in the groin by Cobain and Cobain throwing a "wild punch" and staggering into a buffet table. None of the sources interviewed for this book who were present on the night in question recalled any such incident taking place, and the members of Pearl Jam have never spoken of such an incident in any of their conversations with this reporter.

around some beautifully Hendrixian noodling of Mike's, would spark more intense argument than any other song in Pearl Jam's oeuvre when it came to just exactly what the lyrics were. Even today, Internet-savvy fans who populate alt.music.pearl-jam, a Usenet newsgroup devoted to the band, can usually be trusted to break into feverish debate about the song once a month or so.

Throughout the band's career, Eddie would display a certain caginess about revealing his lyrics—although Pearl Jam's album artwork would usually feature lyrics written in the singer's own hand, they rarely appeared in their entirety—so in and of itself, debate over the lyrics wasn't unusual. Listening to the newest Pearl Jam record and figuring out what the "missing" lyrics were would become a favorite pastime of the fans over the years, and usually some consensus could be reached. What made "Yellow Ledbetter" such an enigma, aside from its curious title, was that Eddie's *vocals* were virtually indecipherable, too. Only a few phrases were even remotely understandable, and the rest sounded as if Eddie had sung them through a mouthful of pudding. Worse, there didn't seem to be an obvious storyline to provide context; when fans tried to transcribe what they were hearing, the lyrics made no sense. In 1993, when Epic included "Yellow Ledbetter" on a Japanese CD-single of "Daughter," from *Vs.*, and the package included a lyric booklet, pulses would quicken, but even the purportedly *official* lyrics were nonsensical—seemingly disjointed lines concerning a letter, a porch, people who "don't wave," and something about "a box or the bag."

There would be countless interpretations of "Yellow Ledbetter" batted around over the years, and Pearl Jam's fan organization, the Ten Club, would regularly receive pleading letters from fans who wanted the "real" lyrics. In fact, there never were any real lyrics. Eddie had simply improvised them during the one-take session, singing whatever phrases happened to pop into his head.* The song's odd title was a joke, in honor of a Chicago friend of Eddie's named Tim Ledbetter.

"Dirty Frank," written during the Chili Peppers tour, would be much less a headache for fans to interpret. Bearing a heavy Peppers influence in both its funk feel and its uncharacteristically jocular lyrics, the song tells the tale of "Dirty Frank Dahmer," a cannibalistic tour bus driver

---

*In concert, Eddie has outfitted "Yellow Ledbetter" with countless different sets of lyrics over the years, further thwarting fans' attempts to sniff out the elusive "real" meaning of the song.

who prowls concert venues across the nation looking for fans to eat, all the while driving drunk and transporting a terrified band who mostly hide under their bunks. Mike McCready meets a grisly fate at the end of the tale ("My God, he's been ate!") and fans howled over it, especially after they learned that it had been inspired by one of Pearl Jam's *real* bus drivers, a fellow named Frank who wasn't by any means a cannibal but who'd been just off center enough to set the band's imaginations awhir.

"We were convinced he was a serial killer," Mike joked to writer Jeff Gilbert. "We would find piles of empty beer cans under his driver's seat after a whole night's drive, and it was like, 'Oh, man, I'm glad we're still alive.'"

By January, *Ten* had jumped from *Billboard*'s Heatseekers chart—the portion of the magazine devoted to tracking promising "baby" bands—into the all-important Top 200 Albums chart, where it began moving steadily upward. Prodded by the band's growing sales, MTV put the "Alive" video, previously relegated to the odd late-night showing on *Headbanger's Ball* or *120 Minutes*, into Buzz Bin rotation, a coveted slot that meant repeated, prime-time airings. Not wanting to lose the momentum, Epic began preparing for the release of the "Even Flow" single. On January 31, on their way to England for the start of their European tour, Pearl Jam stopped in Los Angeles to shoot a video for the song with director Rocky Schenck, who'd previously made Alice in Chains' "Man in the Box" clip.

Schenck's take on "Even Flow" would find its way into the "reject" vault much in the same way that Chris Cuffaro's "Jeremy" clip would later in the year—but for opposite reasons. Schenck's offense would be creating a video that was *too* high-concept.

For reasons known only to him, Schenck had been inspired by "Even Flow"—a song about homelessness—to film Pearl Jam frolicking at the zoo. He'd arranged a nighttime shoot at an old, closed facility, brought in all manner of wildlife ("He had monkeys, and a fucking panther, and wolves—it was just *awful*," recalls Dave), and set up his lights among the cages and in the trees. Along with the animal footage, Pearl Jam were filmed, individually and as a band, standing on the side of a cliff and air jamming. The shoot took hours, and as it wore on, the band members became more and more convinced that the video was going to be a groaner.

Schenck's video would ultimately be replaced with a raw performance clip, culled from footage shot during a January 17 show at Seattle's Moore Theater. Josh Taft was filming that night not in his capacity as a director but as a friend of Stone's. (At one point during the show, Eddie had even stopped the proceedings, clearly of the opinion that Taft's presence was intrusive. "This is not a TV studio, *Josh*," he'd yelled indignantly, in an interlude that Taft left in his final cut but that MTV snipped out of most versions it aired. "Turn those lights out, it's a fuck-ing *rock* concert!") But in the end, Taft's presence at the Moore show, and the fact that he'd shot sufficient footage to cobble into an interesting video, was a lucky break. Otherwise, with Epic hot to service MTV with an "Even Flow" clip and Schenck's ridiculous zoo extravaganza already completed, Pearl Jam would have had little choice but to go with it, and they unanimously despised it when they saw the final edit.

Schenck's nightmarish "Even Flow" shoot was a colossal waste of time and money, but one member of Pearl Jam came away from it with more than just a crappy video to worry about. In an early sign of the se-rious carpal tunnel syndrome that would plague Dave throughout Pearl Jam's next few tours, Schenck's grueling takes and retakes during the shoot had wreaked havoc with the drummer's wrists, especially the right one. At the end of the night Dave was taken to the emergency room, where the doctor who checked him out advised him that putting further strain on his wrists—for example, the kind of strain caused by vigorous, nightly drumming on an extensive, tightly scheduled tour—would cause permanent damage. Dave spoke to Kelly Curtis about the problem, and Curtis, according to the drummer, simply gave him a choice: do the tour or lose the gig.

Europe beckoned. When Pearl Jam got on the plane the following morning, Dave—his right wrist outfitted with a clunky splint into which he could just wedge a drumstick—was with them.

XOX

Pearl Jam's arrival in Europe was much more hotly anticipated than any-one in their organization had expected when the trip was booked. Al-though *Ten* wouldn't see release in Britain until February 24, it had been available there on import, and when the U.K. "Alive" single had been released in four different formats on January 28, it had begun selling at an astonishing rate. (By the end of the month the single would be firmly lodged in the U.K. Top 20.) Features touting Pearl Jam as the next hot Seattle band had been appearing in the U.K. music press before they ever set foot on British soil, and by the time they did, interest in them was ravenous.

What this meant was that virtually all of the band's shows in Europe, booked at tiny four to nine hundred capacity venues that were far too small to meet the fan demand, would be packed, sweaty, and chaotic. Pearl Jam got a little breathing room during a single gig—an unannounced, unadvertised warm-up show on February 3 at the Esplanade club in Southend, England—but it was their "official" European debut on the following night, at the Borderline club in London, that set the tone for the rest of the tour.

Perhaps unaware that they were priming a pump that had already started to gush, Epic had earmarked the show as Pearl Jam's coming-out party for London's music tastemakers, filling the guest list with all of the writers, radio staffers, and industry movers they'd been able to rope in. The Borderline was tiny, a three-hundred capacity room in the basement of a Mexican restaurant called Break for the Border, and the industry turnout alone had been enough to fill it. This was great news in the eyes of Epic's publicity department, but the enormous crowd of "regular" people who thronged outside the club in sleety, sub-zero weather on show night, only to be denied entry, didn't see it that way. By the time Pearl Jam's set started, the street outside the Borderline was blocked with fans who'd been turned away at the door, most of them kicking up a bitter, resentful ruckus. The band members were furious when they learned what was going on, and Eddie and Dave stood outside for hours after the show, signing autographs and passing out CDs to try and make amends. (This apparently escaped the notice of Fleet Street's finest, who were being wined and dined by Epic inside the warm club. Although many of the reviews were glowing, the show sparked scathing commentary in a few British papers the following week, critics carping that Pearl Jam had a lousy attitude toward their fans. *Nirvana*, the reporters sniffed, wouldn't have shut out *their* fans in favor of the industry elite.)

During their next show, at the KoolKat club in Stockholm, Sweden, the band was beset by sound problems; everything plugged in was feeding back, and Jeff was visibly aggravated during the early part of the set. Two songs in, he admonished sound man Brett Eliason to "get rid of that feedback, it's fucking ridiculous." Later, Jeff complained about the drum mix, coopting Eddie's microphone to ask heatedly if Eliason could take some low end out of the kick drum, which was also "fucking ridiculous." (Eddie, perhaps as a gentle reminder to Jeff that a roomful of Swedes were watching him pout, informed the audience that in English, "take some low end out of the kick drum means 'We love you.'")

The band fared better at the Club Alaska in Oslo, Norway, although stage divers turned the show into such a zoo that a writer covering it for *Melody Maker* likened it to "rush hour at the New York Stock Exchange, as choreographed by Caligula." (The same writer lost his photographer in the maw; when he found him after Pearl Jam's set, the lensman had footprints all over the back of his T-shirt.) As he would on nearly every date of the tour when the venue's architecture provided a serviceable jumping-off point, Eddie used the long instrumental jam toward the end of "Porch" as a soundtrack for a daredevil run, tossing his microphone into a ceiling vent, where it stuck, and using the trailing cord to hoist himself up into the rafters. After finding a foothold, he peered out over the sea of faces fifteen feet below him, quipped, "The audiences aren't this good in Seattle," and did a graceful free fall into the outstretched arms of the audience.

The tour rolled on through Copenhagen, Paris, Amsterdam, Madrid, Milan, and Winterhur, Switzerland—a February 19 gig where the stage was so microscopic the crew couldn't even load in, and Pearl Jam had to do an off-the-cuff acoustic set—before swinging back through Britain at the end of the month. At each stop, the shows seemed to grow more intense, the crowds completely losing themselves in Pearl Jam's heady sound and ferocious stage presence.

Before Dave had joined the band, Matt Chamberlain had warned him that touring with Pearl Jam was "like fighting Mike Tyson every night," and you couldn't watch the band take over a stage without viewing Chamberlain's analogy as apt. Jeff, in particular, often stumbled off the stage after a set looking as if he'd gone up against a prize-fighter— shoulders sagging, feet dragging, his face leaden with exhaustion, as if one more minute would have seen him down for the count. The athletic bassist spent so much time leaping around the stage that he'd taken to wearing elastic bandages on his calves to prevent them from ballooning up during the shows. Ace bandages were getting Dave through the sets, too; the drummer would wrap his inflamed right wrist in one before going on, positioning a drumstick inside and then duct taping the whole mess together so that when his hand started going numb, as the grueling pace of the shows inevitably caused it to, he wouldn't lose his stick.

Mike's style was as unpredictable as his personality, contemplative one moment and manic the next. In his customary spot at the right lip of the stage, the guitarist would be soloing away, seemingly in his own world, and then suddenly, as if propelled by a giant, unseen hand, he'd launch into a calisthenics routine, somersaulting, leaping high into the air, or breaking into a run and darting around among his band mates. He was also big on guitar trashing, demolishing a seemingly endless supply of his favored Stratocasters during the shows, tossing them high in the air at set's end and leaving them to land with a satisfying crunch, or using the more time-honored method of simply bashing them against the stage. Sometimes, he'd take one by the neck and, unexpectedly advancing on Dave, use the guitar's body to attack the drum kit, sending cymbals crashing to the floor like misshapen brass bowling pins and the drummer into a protective, terrified crouch, arms shielding his head. "Mike gets this look in his eye," his tech, Jeff Ousley, once said of his charge, "and you know something's about to happen."

Stone was a tad more subtle. Although he would often get carried away and break into a weird, skipping trot or a funkified take on the classic Chuck Berry duckwalk, he was usually content to let the riffs and the reckless antics of his band mates do the talking. (Well, *most* of the talking. Early on, concert audiences got accustomed to the guitarist's unintentionally funny habit of mouthing the chords as he played them, which gave rise to all manner of horrific facial expressions and often made it seem as if he were talking to himself during gigs.)

Most remarkable about Pearl Jam was that despite the high level of onstage gymnastics, they were decidedly *un*sloppy in a musical sense, playing with a finesse that some far more seasoned performers found it difficult to master even standing stock-still. Rarely did they turn in an inferior performance that couldn't be blamed on venue acoustics or technical problems, and even their long, impromptu jams—prime time at the hot dog stand during your typical rock show—could transfix crowds, emerging like fully structured songs. No matter how expert the production on their records over the years, Pearl Jam would always be a band best experienced live. As Eddie put it, "The album is like visiting an animal in a zoo, and the live show is seeing in it its natural surroundings." It would always be impossible to capture in a sterile studio environment the combination of explosive energy and superlative musicianship Pearl Jam dished out in concert.

During the European tour, with the band often playing on postage-stamp-sized stages, that combination sometimes proved a little *too* cathartic for the fans in attendance, growing numbers of whom seemed to view their ticket stubs as a license either to clamber up on stage and attempt to hang out there, joining in with the band's antics, or to dive back into the crowd. These rambunctious show-offs were making it increasingly difficult for Pearl Jam to get through a set without some sort of fracas breaking out. In-house security staffs were rarely trained properly when it came to dealing with moshers and stage divers and would either let them have the run of the place—generally a bad idea—or approach the task too enthusiastically, roughly grabbing fans and tossing them away from the stage as if they were crash-test dummies. Pearl Jam's crew were good at maintaining order without bullying anyone in the process, but there were so few of them that dealing with equipment snafus *and* overzealous fans was often more than they could handle. Sometimes one victorious breach of security was all it took to set off a rowdy chain reaction, the stage becoming overrun with emboldened, giddy fans in a matter of minutes, as it had during a February 17 show at the Sorpasso, in Milan.

"That was totally over the top," Stone later said of the gig. "People were balancing on speakers, just wobbling back and forth. What goes through your mind is, 'Let's get this over with.'"

To have your concentration broken by the sight of a dangerously teetering P.A. stack with a kid hanging off of it—or to trace the foreign squeal coming out of your guitar to a fan who was stomping all over your wah-wah pedal—those moments were nerve-wracking enough. But the band members also stressed out over the safety risk the stage divers represented to the rest of the crowd, always aware of the possibility that someone could be injured. Sometimes, fans did appear to be getting hurt, and Eddie, who usually had the best view of the carnage, began to lose patience with the trendy acrobats who were ruining the party for everybody else. At nearly every stop on the tour, he took a few moments early in the set to remind fans to look out for their neighbors; by the time the band finished their second pass through England, with a February 28 show at the six hundred capacity University of London Union, the gentle admonishments he'd been issuing had taken on a much angrier tone. Four songs into the U.L.U. Show, after a rafter-rattling version of "Alone"—an as-yet-unreleased song dating back to Stone, Jeff, and Mike's earliest demos that the band had rerecorded during their sessions for the *Singles* soundtrack, later to turn up as a B-side—Eddie turned the full force of his irritation on the relentless stage divers who'd been having a field day from the moment the band played their first note.

"Hold on one second," he began, pointing at the most recent offender and gathering steam. "See your boots there, those big shiny metal buckles? Those are people's *heads*, they're not casaba melons." Even as the singer spoke, another wave of buffoons was washing up over the barricade, and a few had already made it onto the stage and were preparing to fling themselves into the melee. That they were so oblivious to his words enraged Eddie further. "You guys may think you look like Jesus Christ when you lie down on top of the crowd like that," he observed, pointing out a few crowd surfers who were making aimless excursions across the mosh pit, clubbing other audience members in the head with their steel-toed combat boots in the process, "but I swear, when I see you smashing people's heads, all I want to do is crucify you." (Eddie's outraged lecture probably lost a little of its punch in the eyes of the audience after the stunt he pulled five songs later during his customary spot in "Porch." Swinging Tarzan-style on the curtains that lined the hall until he reached a balcony opposite the stage, the singer paused for effect and then plummeted off the ledge into the crowd, who managed to catch him without collapsing under his weight.)

After a month in Europe, the band members were exhausted. They'd barely had a day off, and even when they had, there'd still been interviews on the agenda, thanks to the dizzying press schedule set up by Epic. Eddie was equipped with an excuse to sit the interviews out if he wanted—the strain of the tour was beginning to show in his vocals, and he needed to preserve his pipes for the most important business at hand—and often he simply declined to show up at the appointed time. But the others didn't have that luxury, and some days they would spend six hours at a stretch entertaining one reporter after another. They were getting so tired of answering the same questions that they sometimes improvised new, ridiculous answers on the spot, just to entertain themselves.

One interview, toward the end of the tour, gave rise to a surreal evening that later became one of Dave and Mike's most recounted adventures. Before the band's March 2 show in Den Haag, Holland, Epic had arranged for the two to meet with a pair of fanzine writers who were covering the show. After Pearl Jam's set, when it was determined that Eddie's voice was blown out and that the following night's show in Nijmegen would have to be cancelled, the band and crew decided to travel on to the hotel in Utrecht, where Pearl Jam were playing on the fourth. Mike and Dave, however, seized on the glorious opportunity presented by a day off in nearby Amsterdam—just think, all those hash bars!—and decided to stay over in Den Haag for the night, so they could take a train to Amsterdam first thing in the morning. In need of a place to sleep and someone who could point them in the direction of the train station, they took the two female fanzine writers up on an invitation to "crash at our place." Unfamiliar with Holland's population of squatters and probably picturing themselves sacking out on a cozy couch in someone's warm living room, the drummer and guitarist were slightly taken aback when, as they left the venue, one of the fanzine writers mumbled something that sounded like "We'll have to stop at a friend's and get you a bed."

"We just looked at each other, like, 'Uh . . . oooookay,' " recalls Dave. "So here we are, walking the streets of Den Haag at two in the morning, and all of a sudden the girls start screaming up to this window: 'Hooten grooten hooten grooten.' Me and Mike were like, 'What the *fuck*?' Then a light comes on in the window, and a guy sticks his head out. We're standing there going, 'What the hell is this all about?' "

They waited there for a few minutes, until some more activity drew their attention and they looked up to see the inhabitants of the house struggling to push a mattress through the window opening. It landed at their feet with a heavy thud. Mike and Dave looked at each other.

"Far *out*," said Dave.

The mattress was followed by a rain of sheets, pillowcases, and pillows, all of which were retrieved by the fanzine writers. Dave took one end of the mattress, Mike took the other, and the happy little caravan moved on—and on, and on. They walked for what seemed like *hours*. The farther they walked, the heavier the mattress got, and both Mike and Dave were out of breath. This wasn't the sort of after-gig activity they were used to. They were also getting hungry.

"Is there any place open?" Dave asked as they trudged along.

Mike, still huffing and puffing along in the front, said, "Yeah, let's put this mattress down and then get something to eat." The guitarist stopped short, a bemused expression on his face.

"I don't think those exact words have ever come out of my mouth before," the others heard him mutter under his breath.

The ordeal continued. It took them forever to get to their destination, and the two girls kept up an annoying, flirtatious chatter the whole way. By the time Dave and Mike had lugged the mattress up a flight of stairs and settled it on the floor of "our place"—which turned out to be a seedy, cavernous flophouse—they were exhausted to the point of delirium, thinking longingly of the hotel rooms they'd waived. Around four in the morning, just as they were beginning to lose consciousness, Mike rolled over and issued one last, weary comment on the whole fiasco.

"I can't believe I'm sleeping with the Ockus."

XOX

After a day of sight-seeing in Amsterdam—most of which Mike and Dave spent in a hash-induced haze, trying to ditch their starry-eyed fanzine buddies, who'd tagged along uninvited ("We finally ducked into a building when they weren't looking," says Dave)—the band turned their attention back to the business of dodging stage divers, wrapping up their stop in Holland with shows in Utrecht, Eindhoven, and, most notably, Rotterdam, where Mike secured his place in the Bootleg Video Hall of Fame. The guitarist, who'd had one too many beers, slipped into the wings somewhere around the mid-set mark and shucked his clothes; when he came casually strolling back out for a solo, wearing only his shoes, socks, and Strat, the others were so caught up in the show that they didn't immediately notice. Their reactions when they did were not only priceless, but also captured by a camcorder-wielding audience member who wasted no time in making apparently hundreds of copies. The bootlegged video featuring the incident—Stone doubled over in helpless laughter, and a stunned Eddie doing a double take and yelping, *"Jesus!"*—is today a hotly traded fan favorite.

By mid-March, the members of Pearl Jam felt like they'd been through a war, but it was almost over. After five German shows, including a stop in Berlin where they debuted their cover of Neil Young's "Rockin' in the Free World," and a date in the Beatles' old haunt, Hamburg, where they respectfully capped their set with the Fab Four's "I've Got a Feeling," the band headed home in high spirits.

When they visited Europe again in June, their return to America would not be as jubilant.

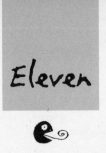

Eleven

Unplugged / We're Gold-So What? / Live from New York / Shannen Doherty, Grunge Chick / Showdown at Gas Works Park / Meltdown in Denmark

After their last show in Germany, Pearl Jam flew straight to New York to play an eight-song set for *MTV Unplugged*.

The idea of taping a live acoustic show that would be aired to an audience of millions was intimidating enough for the band—as Stone put it, "An acoustic show is really sort of a naked, exposed way of playing your songs, because you can't hide behind distortion"—and it didn't help to calm any nerves that with their own gear being transported back to Seattle from Europe, they were going to have to do the show on rented equipment. Even worse, when the already jittery band members showed up for the taping, the basses Jeff had requested from the rental company weren't there, and the acoustic guitar Mike was to play had such a high string action that it would be nearly impossible for him to play any decent leads. Stone had asked for a Chet Atkins steel-string guitar only to find a run-of-the-mill classical model waiting for him instead.

At the eleventh hour the band members made a few quick phone calls and scoured up some serviceable replacements, and despite their trepidation, the taping went extremely well, Pearl Jam working their way through pared-down versions of "Alive," "Even Flow," "Black," "Porch," and "Jeremy" from *Ten*, as well as "State of Love and Trust," and their cover of Neil Young's "Rocking in the Free World." Eddie amused himself during the long jam in "Porch" by standing up and surfing in place on the teetery-looking barstool he'd been perched on, scrawling the words *Pro Choice* on his arm in Magic Marker, and eventually falling off the stool backward, much to the delight of the studio crowd. "We actually went out there and had a fun, energized show," Stone remarked later, adding that when the episode aired in May, it "gave people a different perception of the band."

Of course, to a large extent, that had already begun to happen. In the relatively sheltered environment of Kaufman Astoria Studios in Queens, where the show was taped, America looked much the same to Pearl Jam as it had when they'd left for Europe. But when they hit the U.S. concert trail a week later with a string of dates in the Midwest, the leap they'd taken in popularity while they'd been overseas became apparent to them. "When we got to Ohio, like the seventh or eighth show," Jeff recalled, "there were three or four hundred people outside by our bus, and I walked out and they all started *screaming*. I was like, 'What the fuck's going on, man?' That was a freak-out."

Nirvana's *Nevermind* had passed the three million sales mark back in February, and releases by other Seattle bands, including *Ten*, had begun to follow it up the charts. *Time* magazine was now plugging the "Puget Sound" as the "Hottest in Rock," and Pearl Jam, as purveyors of that sound, had suddenly become a *very* hot property. True to form, the band members' reaction was low-key. When they learned that *Ten* had gone gold, Dave was the lone celebrant.

"We were at a restaurant and Jeff said, 'Oh, the record went gold a couple days ago,'" the drummer remembers. "It was just in passing— 'Oh, by the way.' And nobody even really reacted *at all*. I just kind of bit my tongue, went back to the hotel and went straight up to Eric [Johnson]'s room. 'Hey, man, the record went gold, whooo!' I would always go up to Eric's room and celebrate with him, smoke pot and jump around and go, 'Kick ass, whoooo!' Because if I did it around the band, I'd get looked at like, 'What's your problem?' "

Dave wasn't the only one feeling as if his every move was being scrutinized. Eddie was beginning to learn that anything he said in public could have serious ramifications. During a March 27 show at the Marquette University Alumni Hall, in Milwaukee (opened, interestingly, by the Smashing Pumpkins, who'd topped Pearl Jam on the bill only a few months prior during the Chili Peppers tour), Eddie had apologized to the crowd for the presence of metal folding chairs on the floor, pointing out that Pearl Jam didn't like playing venues with floor seating and urging the stage divers to be careful so that no one got hurt. Backstage, the promoter and a troop of Epic executives heard this and nearly went into apoplexy. This kind of patter was practically an invitation for thousands of fans to uproot their chairs in deference to Eddie's wishes, and when he got offstage, he got a lecture on the psychology of crowds—and on the fine print in rock & roll insurance policies.

"I found out that by simply apologizing to the audience for the presence of chairs, the band's insurance for the gig immediately becomes void," he said later, annoyed.

The band's burgeoning fame did have its perks—none of them were denying that. Suddenly, musicians they'd admired for years were clamoring to meet *them*, and though the celebrity attention was something of a mindblower, as rock fans they were tickled pink by all the opportunities they were getting to rub elbows with their idols. In Chicago, the night after the Milwaukee chair-scare, all of U2 except Bono turned up at the Cabaret Metro to see their show, and the band members happily snapped pictures of themselves with Edge when he made his way backstage. Mike even got in a little quality time with the U2 guitarist, after Edge noticed the Muddy Waters T-shirt Mike was wearing and mentioned that blues great Albert King was playing in town. Later that evening Mike was grooving to King's set at a joint called Blues, Etcetera, in the company of Edge and Christina Petro, the belly dancer on U2's Zoo TV tour. (A few nights later in Toronto, Mike's birthday was cause for another "celebrity" visit. The whole band was in stitches after Eddie introduced "Henry Rollins," and resident sillyhead Eric Johnson, dressed like the influential punk veteran—with a huge smiley face drawn on his back in answer to Rollins's oft-seen "Search and Destroy" tattoo of a blazing sun—bounded out on stage to lead the crowd in a rousing "Happy Birthday to You.")

On April 11, Pearl Jam were allowed to tread the boards on one of the most hallowed stages in mainstream pop culture, performing "Alive" and "Porch" on NBC's *Saturday Night Live*. The invitation might not be as hip or prestigious as it had been in the show's Seventies heyday, but it was one the publicity department at Epic had worked hard to wrangle—an audience of twenty-five million television viewers was nothing to sneeze at—and for the band members, who'd grown up watching the antics of the original "Not Ready for Prime Time Players," just the *idea* of playing *Saturday Night Live* was cool. ("Me and a buddy went in one of the rooms and got loaded in honor of John Belushi," Mike said later.)

As he would often do during the band's television appearances, Eddie took the *SNL* gig as an opportunity to do some political lobbying, altering one of his brown military-surplus T-shirts with black electrician's tape. On the front, he affixed a crude coat hanger symbolizing the pro-choice movement; on the back, he addressed the upcoming presidential elections, with the message NO BUSH '92. The coat hanger got airtime, but at the end of Pearl Jam's performance when Eddie turned his back to the camera and pulled his jacket down to reveal his anti-Bush slogan, he was foiled by the quick reflexes of the cameraman, who pulled back on the shot before the message could be broadcast to the television audience.

Elsewhere, the band took the *SNL* appearance less seriously. The show was being hosted by actress Sharon Stone, at the time still basking in the limelight for her notorious pantyless interrogation scene in *Basic Instinct*, and the producers used Pearl Jam in a running gag that played up her sex goddess status, cameras repeatedly panning to reveal the band members leering, goggle-eyed, at the actress. This was something they'd never have done in real life—in Pearl Jam's circles, undressing a strange woman with your eyes was a major political faux pas—but it was all in good fun.

"Skully [Tim "Skully" Quinlan, Stone's guitar tech] got her blouse after the sketch where she had to take off her clothes," Mike deadpanned later. "We took turns smelling it."

XOX

If the *Saturday Night Live* appearance was typical of the kind of doors Pearl Jam's rising-star status was opening for them, there were other doors the band members were finding it increasingly difficult to keep shut—namely, the ones that protected them from the prying eyes and clutching hands of the public. As the band's first American headlining tour progressed, Eddie was clearly having trouble dealing with the increased demands on his time and his inability to get a quiet moment to himself.

"The thing about Eddie was, he couldn't say no," says Chris Cuffaro. "Maybe now he can, but back then, he couldn't, and it made it harder on him." Typical was a scene the photographer witnessed when he visited Eddie at a show the band played in Ventura, California, on May 12. Cuffaro and a friend arrived at the gig and found Eddie sitting on Pearl Jam's bus, looking stressed. When Cuffaro asked what was wrong, Eddie shook his head. "I'm just getting really tired," he said.

"So we sat down and started talking," Cuffaro remembers, "and he's giving us this story about people constantly asking him for everything— how everybody's his best friend, everybody wants this and that. He's like, 'I can only give so much.' And I'm like, 'Eddie, you just gotta learn to say no.'"

Cuffaro's words were still hanging in the air when the door of the bus was thrown open and a teenage girl with an armload of T-shirts clambered up the steps, planting herself in front of Eddie.

"Eddie," she said excitedly, "I just want to say that I think you're the greatest. I drove down here from San Luis Obispo so I could give you these T-shirts."

"Oh—thanks," said Eddie, not unkindly but not smiling either, as if to hint to the girl that the bus was off-limits and she shouldn't be there uninvited.

"I wanted to give you these shirts, but . . . uh . . . I don't have any tickets. Can you give me tickets for the show?" the girl asked.

"I really can't," Eddie replied awkwardly. "You know, I can get in trouble, 'cause my road manager—"

"But I came here all the way from San Luis Obispo," the girl whined.

"It took her five minutes," Cuffaro recalls, "and the next thing you know, Eddie was saying, 'Okay, give me your name and I'll put you on the list.' She walked out, and we just looked at each other like, 'Okay.'"

Dealing with the expectations of the typical fan was the least of it. As Eddie's profile had increased, so had his stock as a potential Celebrity Date. Once word got out that there were new fish in the Cute Rocker pool, fashion models had begun turning up at Pearl Jam's shows in major cities, their delicate nostrils twitching with the scent of Lead Singer blood. Hanging out and comparing notes with the famous musicians who were coming around was one thing, but Eddie had little interest in playing celebrity footsie with a cavalcade of haughty mannequins. Beth, too, harbored a fair amount of contempt for the snooty fashion set. At one show, Beth came clattering into a backstage hallway with an isn't-this-icky expression on her face and issued an alert ("Models! Models are coming!") just moments before an unsuspecting Naomi Campbell and Kate Moss came strolling around the corner and poked their heads into the dressing room.

Shannen Doherty got a much more public—and much more humiliating—rejection. When the bratty *Beverly Hills 90210* starlet tried to get her hooks in Eddie a few days before Pearl Jam's Ventura show, all she netted for her trouble was an embarrassing replay of the incident by Eddie in a fanzine called the *I Hate Brenda Newsletter*, devoted to covering the spoiled escapades of both Doherty and her television character and published, unfortunately for Doherty, by friends of Beth's.

The Doherty episode began when Pearl Jam played Iguana's, a club in Tijuana, and Eddie decided to revisit his old stomping grounds and stay at the La Valencia hotel, across the border in San Diego. While he was checking in—under the pseudonym Ruben Kincaid, a means of avoiding any hassles—an old friend who was still working at the La Valencia as a valet warned Eddie that Doherty, who'd been staying at the hotel while she filmed a TV movie, was hot on his trail.

"He goes, 'Let me tell you, this person has been trying to figure out when you were going to stay here, and she's been fucking with everyone at the hotel,'" Eddie told the folks at *I Hate Brenda*. "I heard she was really rude to a lot of people. . . . They have a concierge at the hotel, and they said she came up to him and said, 'I heard this band is playing in Mexico, and I want tickets and I want passes. Make it happen.'"

Doherty had also, according to a newspaper gossip item reprinted in the zine, phoned the hotel's front desk after Eddie checked in. "Can you tell me what room he's staying in?" she reportedly wheedled. "He's a friend of mine and we're supposed to party together tomorrow night." When the desk clerk informed her that Eddie wasn't taking calls, the self-assured Doherty was said to have insisted, "Oh, he'll take mine." She was wrong.

"And then she was calling our office," Eddie went on. "[Beth] just happened to be at our management office and was there the day that Shannen's office called, and wanted to know if I had a girlfriend and wanted pictures and all this shit."

Asked about this later by a reporter for *Us* magazine, Doherty claimed she'd only been scouting out potential dates for the MTV Awards, an event some four months away. "I was trying to figure out who I should take," she said. "So I guess my publicist called his publicist, and it turns out that he's been with the same girl for, like, seven years, which I think is great. It was dropped, and that was the end of it."

When *Us* pressed on, telling the actress what Eddie had said about her alleged behavior at the La Valencia, Doherty bristled. "I don't think so!" she fumed. "Did he really say that? That's pretty tacky. . . . I didn't try to call up his room or anything. Even if I did, it would make me a very normal girl. The sad part is that he felt like he had to lie and pump up his ego by saying that I did that. I just think he should have been flattered that I even wanted to meet with him at the MTV Awards, and left it at that.

"My crush," the actress huffed dramatically, "is now over."

Eddie was surely devastated to hear the news.

⁂

By May, "grunge" and "the Seattle Scene" had moved to the top of every mainstream critic's pet-phrases list, and the Seattle bands were getting fed up with their role as the latest media darlings. Pearl Jam's interviews all took on a similar tone around this time, as they began trying to distance themselves from the furor.

"There's so much hype you could choke on it," Stone told the *Los Angeles Times* just before Pearl Jam's Tijuana gig. "I wish people would forget that we come from Seattle. It'd be nice if they thought we came from Cleveland or some place like that."

More and more reporters were approaching the Seattle bands as if they were indistinguishable human jukeboxes, as if the so-called "Seattle Sound" were a generic, identical product being sold under half a dozen different brand names. But as much as the members of Pearl Jam had come to resent the media's typecasting-by-geography, they never lost sight of the fact that, as residents of rock's city du jour, they'd also been able to avoid paying an awful lot of dues. "I'm sure some kids bought our album after reading stories about that 'scene' business," Stone remarked. "So I guess the hype has helped us in that respect."

With that in mind, and with a window of opportunity beckoning between the end of their U.S. tour and a run of European festival dates in June, Pearl Jam had decided to share some of their good fortune with the community that had birthed them, in the form of a free Memorial Day concert at Seattle's Gas Works Park. Eddie, who'd recently done a public service spot for Rock the Vote, also seized on the event as the perfect occasion for a voter registration drive, and the band had jumped through all manner of bureaucratic hoops to make the concert a reality, submitting requests for permits to officials ranging from the police to the Seattle Parks Department. Kelly Curtis had brought in his old partner Ken Deans at Mark Allen Productions to handle support services for the concert, addressing issues such as first aid, parking, security, and sanitation. By May, the band had put five months' worth of planning into the event.

"We had people who knew what they were doing," Eddie recalled. "This wasn't a fly-by-night thing. We had people who were organized. We had all the permits."

"Had" being the key word. When the powers-that-be had issued the permits, they'd expected a turnout of around five thousand fans. But calls had been coming in from fans all over the United States who wanted to attend, and as show day approached, the audience was being estimated at between twenty and thirty thousand. With the city's police force already occupied by the holiday weekend, the thought of such a large gathering sent officials into a panic. Three days before the concert, the Parks Department pulled the plug, citing crowd-control issues.

Pearl Jam considered moving the show to the Gorge, an outdoor amphitheater in George, Washington, over an hour's drive from Seattle, but completely reorganizing the show in a different location would have been a nightmare on such short notice. Seattle officials then suggested a compromise, offering permits for a daytime concert on May 27, after the Memorial Day weekend crowds had thinned. But by that time, Pearl Jam would be on their way to Europe. And even if that date had been convenient for Pearl Jam, it fell on a weekday, making it problematic for much of their audience.

"I'm not sure if Mayor Rice had planned to sign excuse notices to every kid in town," Eddie said acidly at the press conference the band held to announce the show's cancellation, "but in case he didn't notice, Wednesday is a school day for a lot of our fans. We're not going to get into a pissing match with the city, but I think they'll find that a lot of people are going to be up in arms about this."

Because of their touring commitments, Pearl Jam had no choice but to put the concert off until September, when they returned home from playing Europe and Lollapalooza. Eddie found this an outrage, going so far as to suggest that Seattle's heave-ho was a deliberate attempt to thwart the band's voter registration efforts. He worked himself into a lather at the band's press conference, doling out with relish his view of the city as an evil bureaucracy hell-bent on repressing the band and their fans.

"Get your bodies into the trenches and empower yourselves," he urged, grim faced, as the cameras whirred. "You have to do this. Silence equals death." As would often be the case when Eddie pitted himself against a powerful foe, his soapboxing carried a hint of martyrdom that some found off-putting. It never occurred to the singer that his use of an AIDS activism slogan to protest a cancelled rock show might be inappropriate, or, to some ears, insulting. To Eddie, this wasn't about a scrapped gig. This was about us-against-them, a dynamic that would characterize nearly every public battle of the singer's career. As Pearl Jam's power had increased, so had the frequency with which Eddie found himself wearing the privileged shoes of "them," a fact of celebrity life that ran counter to the singer's populist ideals. Perhaps for that reason, whenever he had the chance to play David opposite a perceived Goliath, he would unfailingly pick up a bullhorn along with his slingshot. No matter how powerful or wealthy he would become, Eddie would always display a genius for putting himself in the role of underdog, a trait that sometimes left skeptical critics sharpening their claws but would always endear him to Pearl Jam's followers.

Wanting to offer something for disappointed fans to do on the day the concert was to have been held, the band erected a skateboard ramp and a stage on private property owned by a friend in Renton, ordered a few kegs, and recruited two local bands, Seaweed and 7 Year Bitch, to play.* On the appointed day, Pearl Jam showed up at Gas Works Park to intercept fans who hadn't heard of the cancellation and point them in the direction of the party in Renton. Eddie, flanked by a pair of reporters from England's *Melody Maker*, wandered around the park addressing small knots of fans—signing autographs, posing for pictures, and, whenever he could, wedging in a word or two for the cause. "How come one hundred thousand red, white, and blue frat boys get to sink Bud and beat up on each other, and we can't hold a peaceful rock concert?" he asked one group of fans.

"Thanks for being vocal," he told another group. "That's the thing—it *is* changing. There is gonna be a show. And even if it wasn't our show, I'm really happy about it. Hopefully it'll open up, where if anybody

---

*According to erroneous legend passed along from fan to fan, Eddie paid for this last-minute Renton party entirely from his own pocket. In fact, the party was funded with the $1,800 Pearl Jam had set aside for a liability insurance policy on the skateboard ramp they planned to erect at the site of the now-cancelled free show.

wants to do this they can go through the legal channels, as they should be able to, and push it through."

Eddie carried his freedom flag throughout the afternoon, with the *Melody Maker* team, known to their readers as the Stud Brothers, capturing the scene for posterity. If they'd been disappointed to learn that the concert they'd flown over to cover had been canceled, they weren't any longer. Here was all the story they needed, this plucky ragamuffin in the brown corduroy jacket who was feeding them one delicious, highly printable quote after another. Was this guy for *real*?

A few of those on hand were clearly skeptical, viewing the singer's politicizing as so much grandstanding. "He's beyond Bono," one spectator muttered to the Stud Brothers as he watched Eddie espousing his views to a large group of fans. Eddie ducked this comparison when the writers repeated it to him. "No, I don't wanna be Bono," he told them. "I don't want to be a leader, I don't want to be a politician." But, he added, "if people call on me, I'll be there."

In the story they filed, the Stud Brothers would later describe Eddie as an "all-singing, all-dancing hybrid of John the Baptist and Robert Kennedy," clearly impressed by the singer's social consciousness even if they didn't entirely buy his claim that he didn't want to be defined by it. For someone who didn't want to be a leader, he certainly seemed comfortable working the crowd he'd drawn—a lot more comfortable than his band mates were.

Through all of this, the other members of Pearl Jam had been scattered around the park, greeting a few fans here and there but clearly approaching the day in a more relaxed manner than their singer. At some point, Dave looked up from the spot where he was sitting on the grass and saw what appeared to be a small army approaching.

"I was about a hundred yards away," the drummer recalls, "just laughing, enjoying the day. There were a couple of kids with Pearl Jam shirts on, and they smiled and I smiled, and everything was cool. And then over this hill comes Eddie and like forty fucking people." He laughs at the memory. "All the people in front of him were walking backwards, and it was just this big *thing*. We're just sitting there, and here comes, you know, 'Ta, ta-taaaaaaa!' It was like, holy *shit*."

Dave raised a hand in greeting as the throng approached. Eddie glanced at his band mate briefly, then turned back to his gaggle of fans and reporters, not even bothering to acknowledge the drummer's presence. He and his disciples marched on by, his impassioned speech— "Some 'Seattle Scene' bands can't even *play* here . . ."—occasionally audible above the commotion as stray followers bee-lined across the grass from all directions, attaching themselves to the pack.

※◇※

Two weeks later, Pearl Jam were in Holland playing to a crowd of sixty thousand—the largest audience of their career to date—at the annual Pink Pop Festival. The experience was humbling. When a Dutch television reporter pulled Eddie aside after the gig, he still looked shaken, like he was about to throw up.

"How do you feel?" the reporter wanted to know.

"I don't know," said Eddie. "How *should* I feel?"

When his interviewer observed that he looked "mixed up," Eddie dug into the breast pocket of his jacket. He'd elected himself Pearl Jam's resident documentarian some time ago and was rarely seen without his Super-8 or a still camera. Since the band's earliest shows he'd made a habit of snapping a few pictures of each audience before he left the stage. He kept them in a scrapbook in chronological order—hundreds of photos, each freezing in time the sweaty, adoring faces of sated fans.

"Look at these," he said, producing three of the Polaroids he'd shot earlier in the day and arranging them side-by-side to reveal a panoramic view of the Pink Pop crowd. "Here's why I feel the way I do." Although he didn't fail to slip in his standard disclaimer about the size of the venue—"We're used to playing small clubs, and we want to go back to playing small clubs."—the singer was obviously moved.

Within the band, the vibe was a little less warm and fuzzy. Pearl Jam had been touring for almost eight solid months now, and, perhaps inevitably, they were beginning to get on each other's nerves.

Eddie's moodiness was a pain—it was becoming more and more difficult to predict what would set him off, and sometimes the others felt as if they were walking on eggshells. Mike's drinking had stopped being amusing and become a concern, occasionally affecting his playing and resulting in a number of weird public displays. What *was* it about 'Cready, they wondered, that always made him want to drop his pants when he got drunk? Stone, an avid and impressionable reader, had an annoying tendency to analyze everything—including his band mates' behavior—using whatever book he'd just read as a blueprint. He was also a virtual black hole when it came to his personal belongings; he lost *everything*, and hardly a week went by without a panicky search for some misplaced object. Jeff kept burning smelly incense on the bus, which inflamed Dave's allergies and also his sense of justice. He wasn't allowed to smoke cigarettes on the bus, he griped; how come Jeff's choking clouds of patchouli were permissible? Dave, meanwhile was still unapologetically enjoying the limelight—posing for too many pictures, chatting up too many reporters, signing endorsement deals with drum manufacturers—all of which embarrassed Eddie and contributed to a simmering, unspoken tension between the two.

Compounding the general sense of weirdness within the band was the fact that reporters, aware of Pearl Jam's lightning transition from playing clubs to stadiums, seemed to be placing bets on when they'd self-destruct. Nearly every writer they spoke to during their second visit to Europe prodded them to comment on the stress they must be under, a trend that, Dave says, only served to encourage them to dwell on the negative.

"Everybody was saying, 'Oh, the pressure must be *awful*,'" the drummer recalls. "But what kind of pressure is it to play music and make money? I don't think anyone ever felt any pressure until people started *asking* us about the pressure. There was like this *expectation* of it. So any time anybody would have a hard time, they would immediately blame it on, 'Whooo, the *pressure*.'"

Whether or not it was exacerbated by copy-hungry journalists, by the time Pearl Jam rolled into Milan on June 17 there was definitely a sense that the band members were operating on thin emotional tethers, and halfway through their Milan set, when Eddie saw the inevitable head-busting crowd surfers mobilizing down front—during the languid "Black," no less—the press finally got the spectacle they'd been begging for.

"Hey, you fuckers!" Eddie yelled. "Why don't you stop that?" A hopeful swan diver tried to climb on stage and Eddie gave him a dirty look and a backward push with his microphone stand. The fracas in front of the stage continued. Eddie sang a few more bars of "Black" and then, exasperated, hopped into the photo pit, waving his arms at the troublemakers. Seething, unable to get their attention, the singer spat at them. One of them spat back.

"Come on, spit on me," Eddie yelled. "I don't give a fuck!" A member of the venue security team stepped in and tried to pull Eddie back onto the stage, and the enraged singer wheeled around, shoving the man away. He turned back to the rowdies. "You guys are *hurting* people," he pleaded. They ignored him.

As his band mates finished the song, a fan down front hollered out to

Eddie, wanting to know what his problem was. Eddie repeated that people were getting hurt, and he didn't want to watch it. Then someone loudly grumbled about a refund.

"What?" Eddie blustered. "You want your money back? Go *get* your money back! We'll give it to you *twice* back!"

At this point, many of the fans near the front of the stage started looking confused. "We love you, Eddie!" someone called plaintively.

"I love you, too," the singer responded. "Just don't hurt anybody. I want to be your friend. I want all of us to be friends." He shook a few hands and patted a few backs. "Is everyone okay now?" he asked, to rising cheers. "We just want you to stay alive."

Behind him, his relieved band mates kicked into "Alive," and the rest of the Milan show passed without incident. But Eddie had crossed a dangerous line, and they all knew it. In the past, no matter how angry he'd been, he'd always dealt with the band's more ill-mannered fans in a respectful, if reproachful, manner. This time, he'd displayed obvious contempt—and it hadn't been just the targeted rabble-rousers who'd felt the sting.

The tour only got worse from that point.

At Stockholm's Melody Club on June 25, Pearl Jam turned in one of the most enjoyable sets they'd ever done. Factoring in a stint by Eddie and Mike on acoustic Police ("Driven to Tears") and Hunters and Collectors ("Throw Your Arms Around Me") covers, they played for nearly three hours. It was the kind of show, Eddie said later, that felt like they'd "really shared something with the audience."

Then they returned to their dressing room and discovered just how *much* they'd shared.

"Hey," said Dave, looking around. "I think my bag's missing."

"Don't worry," someone said. "Just be cool, you'll find it."

But then *everyone* was frantically looking around the room; *everyone* was missing something. Clothes, books, the souvenirs they'd been collecting on the road—someone had broken in while they were on stage and pulled off a world-class memorabilia heist. To Eddie's horror, among the missing items were two composition books he'd been carrying around, one in which he'd kept personal scribblings and the other containing all of the lyrics he'd written since the band's *last* trip to Europe. The journals would never be recovered.* It was a devastating loss,

---

*A fan claims to have seen copies of the notebook pages being sold in 1996 by street vendors in New York's East Village. Asking price: $50 per page.

a violation of the band's good will that Eddie equated to "a rape situation." Three months later, the singer would still be seething.

"[The notebooks are] no big deal to anyone else," he said, "but they mean a fucking lot to me, man. It was real personal shit, you know? And someone walks in while we're playing and steals 'em. Some fucking *asshole* just walks in and steals them. . . . You're on the stage, you know, and you think you're giving everything you've got—but there's always someone who wants more. And if you can't give it, they'll just fucking *take* it."

Emotionally, Pearl Jam's second European tour ended for them that night, as they stood in their Stockholm dressing room numbly sifting through the remainder of their personal belongings. Officially, it ended the next day, after Eddie lost it during the band's set at Denmark's Roskilde Festival.

Once again, a stage diver was the catalyst. This time, though, the focus of Eddie's wrath wasn't the fan but, rather, the Roskilde security goons who set about turning the kid into lunch meat after he made his successful dive.

"There's like thirty feet separating the stage and the crowd," Eddie recalled, "and that was something I had a problem with. But despite this insane fucking distance, this one guy actually manages to get onto the stage. It's just amazing. Incredible. The fact that he can get through that amount of security. I mean, that guy wins. That guy gets the prize. And to top it all, he does this amazing dive off the stage. Hey! Give him *another* prize. He deserves it. But what he actually gets is a pretty solid fucking beating. He jumps off the stage and, like, six guys—six overzealous guys who've probably been watching too much American football— they jump on him and they've got him in a headlock and they're pounding on him. It's a bad fucking scene. I mean, these guys are really *pounding* him."

Eddie, incensed, jumped into the fray at that point. The guards, mistaking Eddie for an audience member, started pounding on Eddie as well. Eric Johnson—by now an unruffled veteran when it came to fishing Eddie out of concert crowds, his protectiveness over his charge always carried out in an efficient, good-natured manner—had been watching agitatedly from the lip of the stage; now he stripped his shirt off and waded in to help Eddie, and in the confusing melee of flying fists that ensued, a wild swing of Johnson's just missed a female audience member. Eddie, taking note of this, promptly hauled off on *Johnson*. By the time the tour manager—aided by the audience and hampered at every turn by the Roskilde thugs—had pulled Eddie out of the tangle and back onto the stage, the singer was livid. He addressed the audience, Dave pounding out a plodding, thunderous snare beat behind him.

"I hate to cause trouble," Eddie said between deep breaths, "but then again, I'm just sick of these big fucking places where we feel so far away." He pointed at the row of security guards lining the stage. "And maybe if some of you guys would even pay attention to what bands are playing . . . maybe we should distribute pictures of Nirvana, so you can see what they look like and won't beat the fuck out of 'em.

"You guys probably know what *Extreme* looks like," he sneered in closing, a comment on the commercial-metal leanings of another act on the bill. Coming from Eddie, this catty, unprofessional attempt to simultaneously insult the guards and elevate his own "cool" quotient at the expense of another band was uncharacteristic, at least in a public setting. He'd clearly had enough.

"That's it," he spat disgustedly as Pearl Jam filed off the stage. "Let's go home."

With eager fans still awaiting the band in Finland, Norway, London, France, and Belgium, that was easier said than done. The band members, realizing for the first time how close they were to losing control, spent the afternoon following the Roskilde incident debating the pros and cons of cancelling the remaining seven dates. Scrapping a tour was never a move to be made lightly. There were the fans to consider—nobody wanted to disappoint them. The crew members were depending on this tour to feed their families. There would be the record company to deal with, not to mention the promoters, who would be livid, calling for blood.

At the same time, would the band even survive the tour if they carried on? They were physically and spiritually exhausted, going through the motions on stage, losing touch with everything that had made the band important to them. And what about Eddie? He'd clearly snapped during the Roskilde set—what would happen *next* time? To put Eddie in front of seventy thousand people again in such a volatile emotional state, not knowing what he might do or how the crowd might react, would be flirting with a riot situation. Either that, or he'd do one bad show too many and just walk away from the whole circus for good, and where would *that* leave them?

Eddie's fragility was the deciding factor. For insurance purposes—so that the band wouldn't be liable to promoters for the cost of the canceled dates—a doctor was called in to examine the singer and confirm that he was indeed physically unable to continue. When the physician arrived, Eddie did not disappoint.

"I realize that this guy wants to write down that I'm fucking crazy," Eddie recalled, "So I thought, '*I'll* give you crazy.' And I start walking around the room, really freaking out. Gibbering. Kicking stuff over. Ranting and raving. I mean, really giving him something to fucking diagnose. As far as he was concerned, there was no question about it. I'd flipped. I was fucking crazy, man. I was gone."

Wearily, under a cloud of defeat, Pearl Jam returned home. Reports of the aborted tour began filtering back to the States almost immediately, complete with speculation that the band had broken up. Epic released a terse statement on the canceled dates, citing "physical exhaustion" and assuring the public that the band was still intact and just needed a rest.

A few days after the band got back to Seattle, Sheri Fineman stopped by Eddie's house to drop off a note and was shocked at the changes she saw in him. The singer barely spoke—just mumbled a distracted greeting as he let her in, then shambled back to the corner of the living room where he'd been sitting, head down, lost in his thoughts.

He sat there, silent and dull eyed, until Fineman left. She didn't know what had happened in Europe, but it must have been bad. Fineman thought about the spirited, enthusiastic young singer she'd met a little less than two years ago, comparing him to the broken, confused figure she'd just encountered inside.

She suppressed a shudder as she closed the door behind her.

Twelve

Lollapalooza '92: Don't Hate Me Because I'm Grunge / All Apologies at the MTV Awards / The *Singles* Premiere: Spills, Thrills, and a Last-Minute Save by Brendan O'Brien / "Drop in the Park"—Enter Ticketmaster

After a few weeks of badly needed recuperation from the European debacle, the band members were feeling up to snuff again; even Eddie snapped out of his funk once he'd had time to regroup. Rested as they were, though, the kickoff of Lollapalooza '92 was hardly encouraging.

The bus that rolled up to the curb to collect the band on departure day was a garish embarrassment, boasting flashing neon lights, airbrushed desert murals on the sides, and—the most groan-inducing touch of all—the words HOTEL CALIFORNIA topping off the whole tacky mess in loopy, ornate script. Not exactly your hip conveyance of choice. And on opening day, at the Shoreline Amphitheater in Mountain View, California, Pearl Jam's set was fraught with technical problems. "It was the worst show we ever played, and I was really embarrassed," Mike grumbled. "If it's going bad, you know it, and it sucks. It's like going to the dentist. I just couldn't wait to get off stage."

This year, Lollapalooza was being perceived differently than it had been in 1991. What had been counterculture a year ago was now the mainstream, and artists like Pearl Jam, Soundgarden, and the Chili Peppers, viewed as fringe, college radio acts back when the '92 tour was booked, were now beginning to dominate the *Billboard* charts. A festival that had been considered a shaky business proposition the first time around was now known as a rock & roll cash cow, and the tour's organizers were fending off the inevitable charges that they'd sold out.

"There's nothing revolutionary about playing for big commercialistic rock promoters for damn near forty bucks a ticket," said former Dead Kennedys leader Jello Biafra, who was on hand at the opening '92 show to hang out with his friends in Ministry. "There are some interesting organizations allowed to set up booths. That, at least, is a start, for these suburban kids who are used to simply marching down to the cattle hall, staring at the icon onstage, and then going home. But it's still Vegas with a flannel face."

Soundgarden's Kim Thayil had a similar take, clearly annoyed that the tour was being sold as something radical, a means for mainstream kids to, as he put it, "affirm their alternativeness"—when in fact nothing that could really be considered alternative was taking place. "This whole tour is entertainment for the leisure class—there's no pretending about that," Thayil pointed out. "All it is, is a guilt release for the establishment's kids. I'm tired of the lie that alternative music somehow offers something that's anticorporate."

Eddie, still trying to convince himself that Pearl Jam's audience was predominately made up of punkers, had been skittish about how it would look for Pearl Jam to cater to such an overwhelmingly mainstream, middle-class audience. "Eddie was saying, 'Well, we have our crowd, some skaters and stuff like that,'" Mike recalled. "He was worried about mass appeal." The singer had also been concerned about the pressure to live up to expectations created by last year's Lollapalooza ("I have to admit, there was probably a little bit of skepticism after seeing the first one," he said. "Nothing's ever as cool as the first thing.") and Pearl Jam's opening-day set certainly hadn't been reassuring to him on that front. Afterward, he'd gone back to the band's hotel to sulk, only to be waylaid in the lobby by a group of Hebrew students. At first, he'd been irritated by the intrusion.

"Aw, c'mon, why aren't you at the fucking show?" he said, trying to brush past them. "Don't bug me here."

But the students had persisted, even inviting Eddie and Beth to come to a class with them. The singer had declined, signed a few autographs, and turned to leave. But then he'd changed his mind—and later he would credit the experience with lightening his mood.

"I didn't feel obligated to do it," he said the next day, laughing, "but then I was walking away, thinking, 'Man, I bet I could throw a serious monkey wrench into that prayer meeting if I showed up in the back.' So me and Beth did. They were talking about religious philosophy. And I was so glad I was there. It was pretty cool."

By the time Eddie and Beth got back to the hotel, he'd been able to put the substandard show in perspective—and by the following day, the whole band had relaxed. "The coolest part was realizing that it didn't fucking *matter*," Eddie said, "because there was so much to do. You realize, 'Okay, so the bass guitar went out on two songs,' or, 'They couldn't hear my vocals—big fucking *deal*.' It's so much bigger than just individual bands."

Ultimately, after the opening dates were behind them, the media had gone home, and the cynics on board had relaxed a bit, it was the camaraderie among the bands on the bill that made Lollapalooza a blessing in disguise for Pearl Jam—the antithesis of their mind-numbing, stressful European tour and as such the perfect antidote. With Soundgarden and the Chili Peppers along, there was a comfortable, familial air to the proceedings. The billing was low-pressure; because of their almost unknown status back when the tour had been organized, Pearl Jam had been given the second slot of the afternoon, following openers Lush. This not only left most of the crowd-pleasing burden on the shoulders of the nighttime acts, Ministry and the headlining Peppers, but also meant that the members of Pearl Jam were free by early evening to relax and spend their time as they wished. They enjoyed themselves tremendously for the rest of the tour, hanging out with the other musicians and bonding with the carnies from the Jim Rose Circus Sideshow, a group of fellow Seattleites whose not-for-the-squeamish extravaganza—featuring all manner of dangerous and stomach-turning stunts—would become the tour's most-talked-about attraction. "Jim Rose is amazing. . . . He's a full-on freak," a bemused Stone said of the ringleader. "I've never seen anyone open a can of tunafish with his *finger* before."

According to Sheri Fineman, along for the trip in her capacity as a massage therapist ("Mostly it was to keep Eddie together, because he was stressed out and losing it."), once Lollapalooza was in full swing, the band members were happier than she would ever see them again, displaying a sense of humor about their celebrity status that they'd never before managed.

"In Miami, the bus driver got stuck in a traffic jam leaving the gig, and we were sitting there for a long time," Fineman recalls. "Mike and Dave and Stone were sitting up in the front, going, 'Don't they know who we *are*?' and 'Hey, we'll just buy this road, we'll just buy all these cars.' Mike's going, 'We'll throw money out the window, man, just get out of our way.' And it was great! It was the healthiest, funniest thing— they were making fun of themselves, happy about who they were."

It was a mood that would prevail for the duration of the tour. In Cleveland, when a sudden rainstorm turned the backstage area into an oozing swamp, Eddie and Chris Cornell joyously wallowed around in the mud and, pleased with the anonymity granted by their dirt-caked faces, went out onto the festival field to wallow around some more with the fans, who had no idea who they were. (Elsewhere that day, a similar identity ruse was taking place, Jim Rose and his circus cronies having figured out how to stop the fans who were pelting their bus with mud balls. One of them had fashioned a joke face mask from a magazine photo of Eddie, and every time a new onslaught of mud started, he'd hold the mask up to the window, eliciting cries of apology from the contrite mud throwers outside—"Eddie, we didn't know it was you!"—and hoots of laughter from the sideshow crew inside.)

After the ice was broken, the shenanigans came nonstop. The bands gathered nightly in hotel bars, on one occasion wresting the equipment away from a hapless salsa band and clearing the lounge of its normal paying customers with the ensuing ruckus. A member of Ministry, upon learning that a decibel meter had been set up in one city to keep the bands' sound levels in check, found the gadget and surreptitiously disabled it, becoming hero for a day. When Mike fell and broke his leg midway through the tour, Jim Rose became the hero, hot-writing one of the golf carts that were on hand for the use of the festival crew and helpfully squiring Mike around in it—and in the process sparking a cart-stealing craze that annoyed the tour organizers to no end. After the other artists saw Rose and Mike tooling around, they *all* started hijacking the carts, stranding the crew members who needed them to quickly get around the sprawling Lollapalooza grounds. Eventually, the powers-that-be posted notices in the catering tents threatening $50 fines for golf-cart thieves, and most of the artists reacquainted themselves with the drudgery of wandering around on foot.

Eddie got a little *too* fond of wandering, a habit that drove Eric Johnson crazy and resulted in a scare a week into the tour. Somewhere in Wyoming, on the way to the St. Louis show, the hellish "Hotel California" chariot broke down and Pearl Jam had to wait for a replacement bus. Exhausted, they'd finally settled in on the new bus and bunked down for the rest of the drive to Missouri—only to be abruptly awakened a few hours later. Dave opened his eyes to find a worried-looking bus driver leaning over him, shining a flashlight into his face.

"Six!" the driver standing over Dave bawled to his partner. "We got six!"

"Seven," said the other driver, passing his light from Mike's bunk to Stone's. "And here's eight! We got eight!"

The band members were all sitting up in their bunks now, wondering what the confusion was about.

"Shit," said one of the drivers. "We got eight, there's supposed to be nine. Who's missing?"

The musicians and crew members aboard blinked at each other. The band had a longstanding rule about getting off the bus during middle-of-the-night stops, when everybody else was asleep and the driver was off doing his own thing. If you did, you left something in the driver's seat, so that when he returned he'd know you weren't still asleep in your bunk. Eddie, apparently, had meandered into the night at the last truck stop—about 150 miles back—without leaving anything behind to signal the drivers.

"Who's this Eddie Vedder?" one of the drivers asked when it was determined who was missing. "Is he important?"

Dave and his drum tech, Jimmy Shoaf, Jr., looked at each other.

"Nah," they answered in unison, straight-faced. "Not really."

The crisis was over nearly as soon as it began. Eddie hitched a ride with a trucker while the bus drivers, alerted to his whereabouts via CB radio, waited for him on the shoulder. But the singer would be the object of a number of panicky searches before the tour was over, and at least once, on August 14 in Fairfax, Virginia, he cut it so close that the band actually took the stage with Chris Cornell on vocals. Eddie made a heroic, show-stopping entrance midway through "Even Flow," pushing his way through the crowd at the front of the stage—his clothes in tatters from the struggle—and breathlessly explaining to the audience that he'd been stuck in traffic.

By the time Lollapalooza '92 was drawing to a close, Seattle Mania was at its peak, the Mark Pellington–directed "Jeremy" video was in heavy rotation on MTV, and Pearl Jam had the distinction of having played on three of *Billboard*'s top twenty albums. *Ten* had climbed to No. 2 in late August. The soundtrack for Cameron Crowe's *Singles*, featuring tracks by Pearl Jam, Mother Love Bone, Alive in Chains, Soundgarden, Mudhoney, and Screaming Trees and released by an impatient Epic well before the film saw the light of day, was hovering in the high teens. *Temple of the Dog*, which had sold less than a hundred thousand copies after its initial release in 1991, had been reissued by A&M in June to capitalize on the resurgence of interest, and thanks in part to an old video for "Hunger Strike," shot in 1991 at Seattle's Discovery Park and featuring members of Pearl Jam, the album was now at No. 8 and had gone platinum. MTV had studiously ignored the clip when it was originally submitted, but now they were playing it constantly.

The *Temple of the Dog* collaborators agreed that it would have been senseless to block the rerelease on principle—"It would be silly to make a record and then not want anyone to know; I have too many friends who make albums and wish people were listening," said Chris Cornell—and on the final Lollapalooza date, not wanting to disappoint fans who'd bought the album and were clamoring for a live reunion, Cornell and Matt Cameron would join Pearl Jam to play "Hunger Strike" and "Reach Down." But the way the reissued *Temple* was being hyped by the label, the press, and MTV, with an emphasis on Pearl Jam's involvement, was a sore point for everyone involved.

"The whole thing was kind of embarrassing," Cornell recalled. "It was hard for everyone. I think the guys in Pearl Jam were already realizing that they no longer held the reins over who they were. It was funny, because it went from being 'the Chris Cornell solo album' to being 'the Pearl Jam project.' That was the strange and almost humorous aspect of it. It was still the same songs, the same mixes, the same packaging—it hadn't changed at all. Just everybody else changed."

PolyGram, meanwhile, was gearing up to snag its own piece of the Pearl Jam pie, with the rerelease of Mother Love Bone's *Apple* and *Shine*—along with an alternate version of "Capricorn Sister" and the previously unreleased "Lady Godiva Blues"—on a two-CD set titled *Mother Love Bone*. This, too, Pearl Jam saw as annoyingly exploitative. "If the band had its druthers, they might not want it out," said Kelly Curtis. "The guys are well beyond Mother Love Bone, and that band doesn't exist anymore. Pearl Jam won't be performing any Mother Love Bone songs."

Before long, the members of Pearl Jam would be frantically back-pedaling, trying to turn down the intensity of the hype storm they'd been caught in and regain some control over their lives and their credibility. For now, though, it was understood that Epic expected them to play out the winning hand they'd been dealt—to adhere to established industry promotional practices, accept the hype as a good thing, and, to put it crudely, milk their sudden success for all it was worth. The band members resented this, especially Eddie, who viewed the hype—much of it rooted in Epic's promotional zeal—as a primary source of the criticism being heaped on Pearl Jam by people like Kurt Cobain. "I can relate to people having animosity or suspicion," he said at the time. "If I was them, I'd probably be knocking the band, too. If people only know the band from what they've read in the press or the way the record company was trying to sell us—especially in Europe, where they had all these 'Seattle Sound' stickers that they put on the record, which is stuff we don't have any control over—then I might have said pretty much the same."

A year would pass before Pearl Jam felt they'd amassed enough power to buck the system. And when they did buck the system, they would do it in a major way. But in the meantime, common sense dictated that they save their battles, following the promotional course Epic charted for them wherever they could so that the label would be more forgiving in cases where they balked. Eddie agreed with his band mates on that point, but, as he went out of his way to prove in early September, that didn't mean he had to like it.

Sandwiched between the September 8 Lollapalooza date in Phoenix and the tour's final three-night run at Irvine Meadows in Los Angeles was a pair of star-studded industry back-patting affairs where, Pearl Jam's advisors had urged, it would be advantageous for them to be seen. The first of these was the 1992 MTV Video Music Awards ceremony, held on September 9 at UCLA's Pauley Pavilion in Los Angeles and hosted by *Saturday Night Live* comic Dana Carvey.

Pearl Jam had been nominated in the Best Alternative Video category for "Alive," as well as being tapped to perform during the televised portion of the event. Although the rehearsals were somewhat chaotic, most of the band members were looking forward to the show, which would also feature performances by fellow nominees Nirvana and the Red Hot Chili Peppers. But Eddie, whether he was intimidated by the presence of faithful detractor Kurt Cobain or just nervous about performing before such a large gathering of highly respected luminaries, arrived at the

Pauley Pavilion wearing his resentment for the whole affair on his sleeve. He seemed determined from the start to out-punk everyone else on the bill.

The band's plan to perform the Dead Boys' "Sonic Reducer"—a song they'd covered for the first time during their set in Phoenix the day before—would have dovetailed nicely with that goal, but ultimately all it did was send the first sparks flying in a night that would be fraught with tension for most everyone involved. Not long after Pearl Jam's sound check, Kelly Curtis nervously gathered the band members outside the auditorium. MTV's producers, he informed them, had given "Sonic Reducer" a vehement thumbs-down, insisting that they play "Jeremy," their current video hit.

"Well, fuck *them*," said Eddie. "Let's just do it anyway."

"Maybe we shouldn't play at all," someone else suggested.

Curtis, muttering expletives under his breath, went off to have another talk with the producers while Pearl Jam stood in a bereft huddle, weighing their options. Unbeknownst to them, the members of Nirvana were in their trailer wrestling with the same dilemma, the MTV brass having vetoed "Rape Me," a track from Nirvana's forthcoming *In Utero* album, and demanded that they perform either "Lithium" or "Smells Like Teen Spirit," their own hits. As it turned out, Nirvana would give in to the pressure, and so would Pearl Jam.

"MTV wielded a lot of power," says Dave. "I don't remember who finally talked us into it, but all of a sudden, we were doing 'Jeremy,' Eddie was pissed, and everybody was frustrated."

Pearl Jam did play "Sonic Reducer" that night, but only during a commercial break, when the television cameras weren't trained on them. Right up until the band launched into "Jeremy," the MTV bigwigs were placing bets on whether they would toe the line, and Carvey had obviously been warned that there might be a mutiny afoot: When he introduced the band, it was with a relieved, "They're not quitters, ladies and gentlemen: Pearl Jam."

The band's televised performance of "Jeremy" turned out to be one of the most talked-about segments of the broadcast, stunning both the viewing audience and the newspaper critics who reviewed it the next day. Pearl Jam were at their energetic best, but most of the critics focused their accolades on Eddie; typical was a review in the *Seattle Times*, which described his performance as "dramatic" and "anguished."

Anguished, for sure. To those who knew Eddie, what stood out the most was how *terrified* he looked; what read as passion that night was just as likely his frustration over the "Sonic Reducer" flap combined with an especially bad case of the jitters. His entire body trembled violently as he led the band through the song, and his two-fisted grasp on the microphone seemed desperate, as if he were relying on the mike stand for support. The look in his eyes was animal-in-a-trap tortured, and at the song's end, he let out a deranged, bloodcurdling scream, flinging his microphone to the stage floor and dropping into a crouch, his unkempt hair falling into his face and obscuring it. Just before the cameras cut away, Eddie retrieved his mike and added one plaintive line: "I don't need . . . I don't need no mom and dad." Most viewers probably thought this was an improvised addition to the neglected-child theme of "Jeremy." In fact, the line was a lyric from "Sonic Reducer," Eddie's way of thumbing his nose at the priggish MTV brass and the only public statement he would make on the earlier standoff.

Apparently, he was saving his bile for the after-show festivities. Not long after Pearl Jam performed, MTV reporter John Norris cornered Eddie and Dave for an interview, and Eddie's comments were so withering that by the end of the conversation the flustered Norris probably wished he hadn't bothered. Before Norris started the interview, Eddie was cheerful, laughing about Nirvana's Krist Novoselic, who—in one of the funniest awards-show moments ever televised—had exuberantly tossed his bass into the air during his band's set only to miss catching it and have it conk him in the head on the way back down. But as soon as Norris began asking questions, Eddie's demeanor changed dramatically.

"How you doing, guys?" Norris asked.

"We're great," said Dave.

Eddie, red faced and wearing the kind of too-wide smile that means "I'm fake smiling and I want you to know it," suddenly had sarcasm coming off him in waves.

"I'm *brilliant*, John," he said in a caustic tone that matched his fraudulent smile. "I get *so* excited at these events."

"I don't know if you've been to many awards shows in the past, but people say this one is different," Norris said. "Any impressions?"

"It's *big*," said Dave, trying to be cooperative.

"This is the only one we've been to, so it could be different but we wouldn't know," Eddie said in a curt monotone, exchanging his fake smile for an expression of bored, let's-get-this-over-with politeness. "But we expect them to all be like this in the future."

Norris tried another tack. "Did you guys have one or two nominations tonight?" he asked.

"Just one," said Eddie, looking down at his shoes.

"Well," said Norris, "'Jeremy' didn't quite make the cut. I think it was released a little too late this year, but hopefully it'll be up next year, 'cause it's a great video and it'll be in contention—'"

Eddie began shaking his head and making dismissive motions with his hands. "It doesn't *matter*, John," he said, clearly agitated. "It doesn't *matter*." Norris asked Eddie to clarify.

"There's no way to *judge* these things," said Eddie. "There really isn't a way to judge these things. Hopefully, you make a good piece of art, and the fact that you show it, that's something to be said. I mean, that's like winning. Then people can see it. That's all that counts."

Dave stood by silently, his expression vascillating between amusement and embarrassment; at one point he actually rolled his eyes, as if to say, "Here he goes again." By the time Eddie finished his lecture, Norris was looking for the first road out of Dodge. "Well, as far as I'm concerned, these are some of the best new artists of 1992," the reporter said briskly, moving on to a clip of Nirvana as quickly and professionally as he could. The segment was unflattering. For all of his impassioned rhetoric, Eddie came across as humorless and strident; to some, he looked like he was trying too hard to appear unimpressed.

The night was far from over. All evening, industry gossips had been practically rubbing their hands together every time Eddie and Kurt Cobain were in the same room. Cobain and his wife, Hole vocalist Courtney Love, were loaded for bear that night—earlier, a not-so-friendly conversation between Kurt, Courtney, and Axl Rose had nearly erupted into a brawl between members of Guns n' Roses and Nirvana—and given Kurt's scathing remarks about Pearl Jam in the press, the assumption was that Eddie was going to be next in line at the whipping post.

The bloodthirsty mob would go home disappointed. Toward the end of the show, as Eddie stood backstage watching Eric Clapton's emotional performance of "Tears in Heaven," Love appeared and drew Eddie into an embrace, leading him in a slow dance. After a few moments—as everyone in the vicinity looked on, anticipating another mini drama—Cobain walked over and cut in. He looked directly into Eddie's eyes.

"I want you to know that I think you're a respectable human," Kurt later recalled telling the startled singer. "I still think your band sucks, but after watching you perform, I realize that you're a person who has some passion."

"Alive" didn't win any awards that night—Nirvana walked away with the honors, taking home statuettes for "Smells Like Teen Spirit" in the Best Alternative Video and Best New Artist categories. But as victories go, this one meant far more to Eddie than a tacky MTV trophy ever could. He was so moved by Cobain's unexpected offering of the olive branch that later, when reporters prodded him for the details, he refused to give up the goods.

"It's personal," he would tell them when they asked. "End of story."

※◇※

On September 10, the night after the Video Music Awards, Pearl Jam showed up at the Park Plaza hotel ballroom in Los Angeles for an invitation-only party celebrating the premiere of *Singles*, the highlights from which would air a week later as an MTV special called "MTV's 'Singles' Scene." By now, what Cameron Crowe had called his "very small, very personal" movie was being perceived as one of the summer's biggest potential box office hits, but—much to the chagrin of everyone involved, including Crowe—for all the wrong reasons.

Crowe's intent with the film had never been to exploit the Seattle bands appearing in it, but rather, to pay tribute to the artists he'd enjoyed seeing in the city's clubs, most of whom had been largely unknown in 1991 when *Singles* was written. Before the so-called "Seattle Sound" broke into the mainstream, in fact, Warner Bros. had had so little faith in the movie's box office potential that the studio had stalled for months, refusing to give Crowe a firm release date. Now, with the Epic soundtrack climbing the charts and Seattle basking in the spotlight, Warner Bros. jumped on what it saw as the movie's best marketing hook, seeking to play up its Seattle location and Matt Dillon-as-rocker subplot in promotional efforts. As Crowe wrote in *Rolling Stone*, "The hometown music that helped inspire the script is now our best ally in getting the movie released."

Although Crowe was mostly diplomatic in his public statements about his behind-the-scenes wrangling with Warner Bros., the young director was horrified by the studio's insistence on selling the film as a grunge musical, embarrassed that *Singles* "might be perceived as jumping on the [Seattle] bandwagon," when in fact, he pointed out, he'd been "one of the first guys out there with a hammer building the bandwagon." At one point, Warner Bros. had even suggested to Crowe that the movie's title be changed to *Come As You Are*, after the Nirvana song of the same name. No matter that Nirvana appeared neither in the film nor on the soundtrack. (Crowe later said that he'd intended to include a Nirvana song, but "the bigger they got, the more complicated the negotiations became.")

Like the other real-life Seattleites Crowe had sprinkled through the movie—among them Tad Doyle, Chris Cornell, and Sub Pop's Bruce Pavitt in cameos, and Soundgarden and Alice in Chains in performance scenes—Eddie, Stone, and Jeff had little more than bit parts. As members of Citizen Dick, the fictional band led by Matt Dillon's character, Cliff Poncier, they first appear in a rehearsal room segment, Eddie behind the drums, Stone noodling on a guitar, and Jeff complaining to Poncier that his vehicle needs to be moved. (Backstage at Lollapalooza the day after the premiere, Jeff would be teased mercilessly about his rather stiff acting, the other artists on the tour following him around all day and intoning, "Hey Cliff—while we're young?" in the same stilted way he'd delivered one of his lines in the film. "Acting was really uncomfortable," he said at the time. "I felt like I really didn't pull it off, and I knew then that it came off as bad as I thought.")

Another scene finds the three comically engrossed in a TV nature show about bees, their eyes glued to the screen and an enrapt Eddie shushing his band mates, while Janet Livermore, played by Bridget Fonda, asks rocker boyfriend Cliff if he thinks her breasts are too small. ("Sometimes," he says with a smirk.) They rack up the most screen time in a scene filmed at Seattle's OK Hotel (the "Java Stop" in the movie) where they're shown poring over a newspaper review of their band. When they begin reading the review aloud and the ego-driven Poncier warns them that he doesn't want to hear anything negative, they're forced to read him only the last line, which praises their skill as a backup band. Eddie delivers his most substantial piece of dialogue—his character attempts to placate Dillon's by telling him, "a compliment for us, is a compliment for you"—with convincing earnestness; when *Singles* hit the theaters, many moviegoers would be unable to hear it over the delighted screams of the teenage Pearl Jam fans in the audience.

Which, of course, was exactly what Warner Bros. was banking on—and what had prompted the studio, in an unthinkably humiliating development for Crowe, to inform him back in July that *Singles* would not be released in theaters unless Pearl Jam agreed to promote it on MTV. Crowe knew how this was going to fly with Pearl Jam—Eddie had already told him that "if anyone at Warner Bros. made too much of the Seattle scene, I would go buy a gun"—but unless the director wanted his movie to rot in the can, all he could do was try and meet the studio's demands. So, he said later, "I went hat in hand and begged them to do the show.

"It's so vivid," Crowe recalled, "just the way my stomach ached begging those guys—who were friends of mine and who had been struggling six months earlier and were now the biggest band in the world. They eventually said yes, and we got the movie released. But it was painful."

As was the MTV special—at least for the producers. After the chaos of the MTV Video Music Awards the night before, Pearl Jam had had their fill of glitzy showbiz affairs, and the only reason they bothered to show up for the *Singles* premiere party at all was because they'd promised Crowe. When they did show up, most of them wasted no time getting sloshed, especially Eddie, who by all accounts was feeling no pain well before Pearl Jam ever took the stage. The singer had walked in with a gang of surfer friends, a couple cases of beer, and mischievous intent written all over his face; he'd then holed up in Pearl Jam's dressing room, taking greedy pulls from a bottle of vodka until he was, in the words of one backstage observer, "just stupid, drunk as hell"—a mumbling, unruly mess.

"The whole reason Eddie got so drunk was because he was frustrated," says Dave. "Initially, we were told that this was going to be a small, intimate party for Cameron, and then we get there and there's all these MTV cameras everywhere and it's this *huge* MTV production. We weren't ready for that, and it just got a little out of hand."

Eddie wasn't the only one who shook things up at the televised party—Soundgarden's Ben Shepherd also caught some flak, for brawling with what one witness described as "an annoying, motorized fan"—but Eddie was the one whose antics got the most press the next day. During Alice in Chains' performance, he instigated a slam-dancing epidemic in the mostly industry crowd, and when Pearl Jam took the stage, the real fireworks started. In a slurred, droning voice evoking the onstage ramblings of another celebrated rock & roll boozer—the late Jim Morrison, with whom Eddie would soon be compared alarmingly often—Eddie dedicated the Who's "Baba O'Riley" to "Cameron Crowe, because he's got *greeeat* taste in *muuuuusic*," officially kicking off such a rowdy, unpredictable display that the only way MTV commentator Chris Connelly could manage to sum it up afterward was "We try to keep it clean here, folks—we don't always succeed." (The profanity would be edited out of the broadcast, leaving the television audience to wonder what Connelly was talking about.)

During the first verse of "Baba O'Riley," something in the wings caught Eddie's eyes and, pointing and yelling, he lurched over and darted through the curtain; after getting into a shoving match with a security guard standing on the other side, he got tangled in the curtain, gave it a vicious yank, and sent both it and the frame that supported it toppling to the floor. Elsewhere during the set, with his band mates in various degrees of amusement behind him, the singer—looking disheveled in the bright yellow flowered Hawaiian shirt he was wearing over a long-sleeved pullover, one cuff of which hung floppily off his wrist because he'd put his hand through the wrong hole—baited the L.A. fire marshalls with a string of expletives; made repeated crowd surfing forays into the melee on the floor; swung his microphone by its cord like a lasso and nearly hit himself in the head; tripped over his abandoned microphone stand nearly every time he walked by it; and so completely butchered "State of Love and Trust," mumbling some of the lyrics and replacing others with four-letter substitutes, that all the MTV producers could do was groan in horror. (When the broadcast aired, more than a few viewers would groan as well, over an apropos—but widely misunderstood—improv at the song's start, Eddie growling out the first line of Mudhoney's "Overblown," a scathing take on Seattle's media-darling status that also appeared on the *Singles* soundtrack. The reference, which would have escaped many viewers to begin with, was further obscured by Eddie's inebriated state, the lyric "Everybody loves us, everybody loves our town," abbreviated by Eddie into "Everybody loves us . . . everybody loves us!" Some Mudhoney-illiterate television viewers would cringe at this, wrongly thinking they were seeing a bastardized version of the infamous Sally Field Oscar-acceptance speech.)

During the set-closing cover of Neil Young's "Rockin' in the Free World," Jerry Cantrell of Alice in Chains, Chris Cornell and Ben Shepherd of Soundgarden, and Ministry's Al Jourgensen clambered onto the stage; in one of the comic highlights of MTV's broadcast of the party, Dave was seen as the credits rolled, frantically fleeing his drum stool as an evil-looking Jourgensen loomed behind him, clearly out to do some damage. The drummer barely made his escape before Jourgensen sent the whole kit crashing to the floor.

MTV had no problem editing most of Pearl Jam's set for broadcast purposes, but "State of Love and Trust" was a glaring exception. Eddie had laced the song with so much profanity that it was virtually un-airable, and the show's producers were aghast when they saw the footage. This was the only song in Pearl Jam's set from the *Singles* soundtrack, the one that MTV most needed for the broadcast. It was al-most as if Eddie had deliberately set out to sabotage the "hit."

Days before the program was to air, MTV put in a frantic call to staffers at Epic, who in turn called Brendan O'Brien, already tapped to produce Pearl Jam's next album. In a last-minute scramble, O'Brien painstakingly overdubbed the unusable portions of the band's live per-formance of "State of Love and Trust" from the party with Eddie's vocals from the *Singles* soundtrack version, using studio wizardry to doctor and sweeten the mangled MTV video footage until it was suitable for broadcast. A comparison of the soundtrack cut with the performance aired by MTV bears witness to O'Brien's seamless handiwork, Eddie's "live" vocals from the broadcast note-for-note identical to the *Singles* version of the song in several places. Thanks to clever editing—close-ups were lifted out of the videotape and replaced with distant shots whenever it would have been apparent that the words Eddie was mouthing didn't match the audio—the television audience was never the wiser, and Eddie's reputation as rock's most articulate stumbling drunk was cemented.

✖◈✖

On the afternoon of the final Lollapalooza date, Eddie sat down with writer Steve Hochman of the *Los Angeles Times*. In an effort largely spearheaded by Eddie, Pearl Jam had decided at the outset of the tour to consent to fewer interviews, a means of combating their overexposure in the media. But as would always be the case with the band's press em-bargoes, writers for the publications considered important within the industry usually managed to sidestep the no-interviews edict. The *Los Angeles Times* was one of those publications.

Hochman's piece would be the blueprint for virtually every inter-view Eddie did in the next few years. Primarily, the singer bemoaned his fame; included was a scene the writer witnessed outside Pearl Jam's trailer, with a female fan begging for Eddie's attention and Eddie cutting her off with a terse "Not now—just leave me alone. I'm sorry."

"I can't stand the little girls," Eddie told Hochman once they were safe inside. "I just can't deal with that. They see you on TV and they

Eddie, not quite two, with his future adoptive father, Peter Mueller. On the road to Houston. Galveston, Texas, Fall 1966. *Courtesy Peter Jerome Mueller.*

Eddie poses in front of the apartment shared by his mother and his new father, a few months before the birth of the sister he won't know he has until he's seventeen. Houston, Texas, Winter 1966. *Courtesy Peter Jerome Mueller.*

Eddie, just after his third birth-day. Houston, Texas, April, 1967. *Courtesy Peter Jerome Mueller.*

Eddie, dressed up for Halloween. Evanston, Illinois, 1968. *Courtesy Peter Jerome Mueller.*

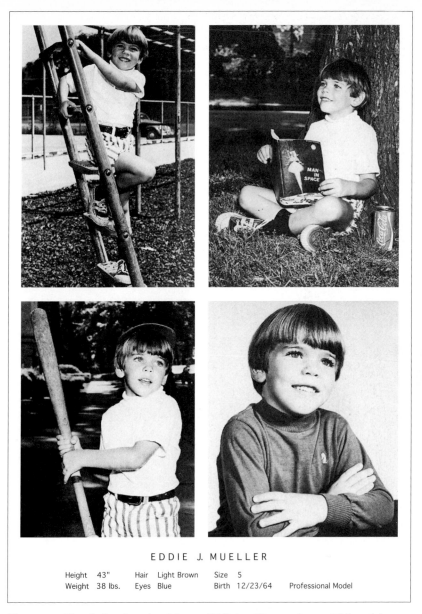

 EDDIE J. MUELLER

Height	43"	Hair	Light Brown	Size	5
Weight	38 lbs.	Eyes	Blue	Birth	12/23/64	Professional Model

Five years old and already a showbiz pro. Eddie's calling-card as a child model. Evanston, Illinois, Summer 1970. *Courtesy Peter Jerome Mueller.*

Offering a toothy grin for a school photo, age eleven. Encinitas, California, 1976. *Courtesy Peter Jerome Mueller.*

Eddie (far left, in wet suit) just after he began surfing, with his grandmother, Inez Mueller, his brothers, and his adoptive father. Cardiff Beach, California, Christmas 1975. *Courtesy Peter Jerome Mueller.*

Posing with his mother, father, and brothers. Encinitas, California, Fall 1977. *Courtesy Peter Jerome Mueller.*

Eddie and Karen, a year before the family split. Encinitas, California, 1979. *Courtesy Peter Jerome Mueller.*

Eddie at age seventeen, with his high school girlfriend, Liz Gumble. Encinitas, California, Spring 1982. *Courtesy Peter Jerome Mueller.*

From left: Jeff and Stone during an early Mother Love Bone club show, Seattle. *Private collection.*

Love Rock awaits you. The late Andrew Wood, on stage in Seattle. *Private collection.*

Pre-gig shenanigans during the 1991 tour. Stone and Eric Johnson share a tender moment while Jeff (left) provides accompaniment. *Private collection.*

Riot "Grrrls." Eddie (left) and Pearl Jam's merchandise man, John Schilling, decked out as Smashing Pumpkins groupies during the 1991 tour. Eddie has "Billy I'm Yours" scrawled on his midriff. *Private collection.*

Pearl Jam clowning on the roof of their Stockholm hotel during the band's first European tour, February, 1992. *Jana Mistenius.*

Jeff, signing autographs—and modeling one of his ever-present hats—during the 1992 European tour. *Jana Mistenius.*

Eddie lets loose onstage
in Stockholm. June, 1992.
Jana Mistenius.

Stone shows off a typically horrific mid-solo facial expression, onstage in Europe, 1992. *Jana Mistenius.*

Mike onstage, fingers ablur. Finsbury Park, London, June, 1992. *Maria Möllberg.*

Abbruzzese with Mike Myers, following a show at the Limelight in New York City, April, 1992. *Private collection.*

Backstage at the Cabaret Metro, Chicago, 1992. From left: Mike, U2 guitarist Edge, Dave, Jeff. *Private collection.*

Eddie (note the wig) with future wife Beth Liebling, "Drop in the Park" free concert, Magnuson Park, Seattle, September, 1992. *Private collection.*

Blondes have more fun. A newly-bleached Gossard, Magnuson Park, September, 1992. *Private collection*.

McCready and Abruzzese in drag, preparing for a guest appearance with Lush at the final Lollapalooza show. Los Angeles, 1992. *Private collection.*

Kelly Curtis, 1992. *Private collection.*

January 14, 1995: A pensive Eddie, with Gloria Steinem and members of L7, during a press conference on the day of the Voters For Choice benefit concert, Washington, D.C. *Jonathan A. Cohen.*

think weird things and they just want to . . . to touch you or something really gross. I've had a girlfriend for eight years and so I'm totally focused. I have no interest in any of them." Hochman went on to note that Eddie seemed "confused and overwhelmed" about the number of teens who identified so heavily with his songs. "I guess when we were writing the songs, I had no idea that so many people would relate," Eddie said. "It's really depressing—and enlightening at the same time—to think that, Jesus Christ, we've got a lot of problems here. A lot of problems with parenting, in general."

This was the real meat of the matter—what the fans who'd been listening to the dramatic slices of dysfunctional life on *Ten* were most curious about. Was Eddie, as his songs made it seem, just like them? Had he had it as tough as they had, growing up?

Eddie hinted to Hochman that he had indeed had it as rough as any of his fans, but as he would always do in interviews, the singer refused to offer many details about his background when Hochman pressed for them. "I don't really like talking about it," he said. "It'll get back [to my parents] and it'll affect them. I probably should do it to get back at them, but it's not my way to approach things. I'd just rather not deal with it at all. I think that probably at least one of my parents is pretty upset about my songs. Sometimes he probably can't escape from my face in certain places. I'm sure he's had his MTV removed."

※◇※

In mid-October, the day Hochman's piece appeared in the Sunday *Los Angeles Times*, a prominent West Coast attorney read it with interest and not a little sadness. He reacted much in the same way he had when he'd bought Pearl Jam's album, *Ten*. He sat down and poured his heart into a letter.

> Dear Eddie:
>
> First, don't feel like you have to respond. Second, get something straight: if we could get MTV, we would be first on the list. We all love your music and videos. They don't bring cable out this far now.
>
> As to the truth, I live with it. It's so wonderful to see you make it magic. . . .

The attorney, who'd built his practice on the representation of fathers in divorce cases—"so that their families don't have to suffer what ours did," he often said—labored long over his letter, struggling to express his feelings about events that still haunted him and, from what he could tell, still troubled Eddie as well. But after it was finished, he could never quite bring himself to mail it. The things he wanted to tell Eddie—things he'd never had a chance to say in the heat of the moment—were crucial. But, he reasoned, no matter what he said at this point as a means of reaching out, Eddie would probably just think he was trying to jump on the gravy train.

The man sought healing for his broken family. So he kept the letter, just as he'd kept the one he wrote after reading the lyrics for *Ten*, just as he would keep the ones he wrote in later years. His unsent letters would continue to stack up in a drawer as he followed Eddie's career through the newspapers, the same way millions of other Pearl Jam fans did, and waited for a day when he might be able to talk to his son.

✕◈✕

"I can't believe we did it! We're like a fucking rash on Seattle that they never thought they'd catch!"

On September 20, 1992, Eddie stood onstage at Seattle's Magnuson Park, addressing the thirty thousand some-odd fans who'd turned up for "Drop in the Park," the rescheduled free concert authorities had scuttled back in May. The singer, sporting the batting helmet he'd been wearing everywhere lately (and a blond wig beneath it that purported to be a disguise but actually did little to hide his identity), was jubilant over the band's finally keeping its promise to Seattle. And from the sound of the cheers, so was Seattle.

The weather wasn't cooperating; everyone had been hoping for the kind of day Seattle old-timers describe with a nonchalant "The mountain's out,"* but it had rained the night before, and dawn had broken grumpy and gray. Still, what the *Seattle Times* would later call Pearl Jam's "loud, gritty, throbbing thanks to the city that spawned them" was a rousing success. Fans had begun arriving at eleven in the morning to hear early sets by Cypress Hill and Seaweed; Jim Rose was in fine circus-

---

*Local code for "clear and sunny," meaning that the peak of Mt. Rainier is visible on the horizon.

barker form as emcee; one of Mike's personal heroes, writer Robert Anton Wilson, had accepted the band's invitation to give a political address; and several musician friends showed up to lend either their talent or their support, among them Ministry's Bill Rieflin, who sat in on drums for a song or two, and Krist Novoselic and Dave Grohl of Nirvana, whose presence as spectators, the omnipresent MTV would note, "[laid to rest] any remaining ill feelings between the two bands."

The icing on the cake was the news that Rock the Vote registered nearly twenty-five hundred voters at the concert, a record for a single event and a turnout that left Eddie, still itching to see George Bush booted out of the White House, thrilled. He was characteristically provocative as he gave MTV reporters a tour of the site, summoning his much-loved us-vs.-them theme to send a message of empowerment to the band's fans.

"It's interesting how difficult they make it [to register to vote] in some cities, especially college towns," he pointed out. "I've learned all this stuff about how they don't make it that convenient . . . and what that says to me is that they really do consider the youth voting crowd a strong public." Eddie delivered this last with a sudden, radiant smile, clearly delighted with the idea of America's youth pulling a fast one on the stodgy powers-that-be.

The Seattle papers unanimously applauded Pearl Jam for their efforts on the following Monday, noting how trouble free the festivities had been, playing up the hometown-boys-make-good angle, and offering the free concert as proof that Pearl Jam hadn't forgotten their roots. In the words of *Seattle Times* writer Vanessa Ho: "They're darlings of MTV, music-magazine pinups, movie stars even. Some were wondering: Did they get a little too big for Seattle? The answer [yesterday] was a resounding 'No.'" View Ridge resident Linda Furness, whose home overlooked Magnuson Park, wrote a letter that was published in Tuesday's edition of the *Times*, congratulating the band and their fans for their exemplary behavior and in the process taking a neat jab at city officials for their panic attack back in May. "While I was not fond of the 'music' I overheard," Furness wrote, "I must assume that if Elvis-the-Pelvis, Little Richard and James Dean did not completely ruin my generation, then this generation will probably survive Pearl Jam."

"Drop in the Park" was a significant turning point in the band's relationship with its hometown, bonding Pearl Jam with the residents of Seattle in a way the band members had never expected. Whereas local musicians had previously been crawling out of the woodwork to accuse them of careerism or bandwagon jumping, after the concert, Pearl Jam began to be perceived quite differently. They might be bigger than white bread, everyone reasoned, but, as *Rocket* editor Charles Cross later put it, "For a group to want to do a free show to give something back to the fans really was a very classy thing. . . . They gained points for that."

Unfortunately, "Drop in the Park" marked another turning point for Pearl Jam as well—a grim milestone that wouldn't come to light until a few years later and certainly not one that would warrant any celebration.

When they'd begun planning the rescheduled concert, city officials had informed Pearl Jam that although the show was free, they needed to distribute tickets for security reasons, to limit the size of the crowd. The band had asked Ticketmaster—the venerable ticketing agent used by the majority of promoters in the country—to distribute the tickets, only to come away fuming when the corporation refused to do the honors for less than a $1.50 service charge per ticket. Nobody begrudged Ticketmaster its right to fair compensation, but in the eyes of Pearl Jam, this was hardly fair. The idea of shelling out $45,000 to Ticketmaster—an amount equal to well over a third of what it had cost Pearl Jam to stage the entire concert—so that fans wouldn't have to pay anything for their "free" tickets, was ridiculous. Ultimately, the band sidestepped Ticketmaster, making their own arrangements to have the tickets printed and enlisting the help of local radio stations to direct fans to a distribution site at the Seattle Center Coliseum.

The disagreement was one small setback in an otherwise smoothly orchestrated event, but the ill will it created between Ticketmaster and Pearl Jam would have lasting reverberations. Within a year, the two entities would be embroiled in a second skirmish, and by 1994, the acrimony between Pearl Jam and Ticketmaster would explode into the fiercest public war of the band's career—a feud so bloody and no-holds-barred that the fallout would overshadow the music and, ultimately, drive a wedge between the band and its fans. Pearl Jam didn't know it yet, but they'd just tweaked the nose of the most formidable opponent they would ever face. In a few years, when they challenged Ticketmaster in earnest, the ensuing battle would nearly destroy them.

Thirteen

A Very Wary Christmas / Channeling Mr. Mojo Risin' / Dave Braves
the AMAs / Setting Up Shop at the Site

At the end of September, Pearl Jam finally got a chance to step off the treadmill, the band members, the crew, and Kelly Curtis treating themselves to a working vacation in Hawaii. There, they played a few shows and shot another video with Josh Taft—a grainy, black-and-white postcard for the *Ten* track "Oceans," featuring the band scampering on the beach, that would be released only in Europe. But mostly, they spent the time communing with nature, taking stock and trying to put the last year in perspective.

Between October and February, when they would begin rehearsals for their second album, they would make a few public appearances together as a band, but for the most part the members of Pearl Jam scattered during this period, seeing to personal relationships they'd neglected during the past several months and grappling individually with the odd emptiness that, they would learn, always accompanied the end of a lengthy tour. Throughout their career, no matter how rigorous the tour or how anxious they were to get home, they would always dread it just a little—the feeling of jumping off a fast-moving train and onto the back of a tortoise; the stifling, dusty panic of being deposited on your doorstep and realizing, suddenly, that you don't know how you're going to spend your days. But, as they did when they returned home in October 1992, they would usually keep busy enough to burn the blues off quickly.

Jeff took off for Montana, where he would soon buy a parcel of land and build a house. Stone poured his excess energy into a side project, recording an album, *Shame*, with Brad, a band featuring Luv Co. alumnus Shawn Smith on vocals and drummer Regan Hagar, formerly of Malfunkshun.* Dave, who'd finally begun to equate Seattle with "home," set about exploring the city's offerings and looking for a permanent residence, something he hadn't previously had a chance to do. A romance also blossomed between Dave and Sheri Fineman around this time. Still living in the basement room at Kelly Curtis's that had earlier been occupied by Jerry Cantrell and, later, by Eddie, the drummer had turned to Fineman, who was still nannying for the Curtises, as a defacto Seattle tour guide. The more time the two spent together, the closer they became. Before long, they would be sharing an address.

Mike and Eddie decided to accept one of the countless invitations that were pouring in, traveling to New York in mid-October to perform a fiery version of "Masters of War" at a Bob Dylan tribute concert at Madison Square Garden. In typical we're-not-worthy form, Eddie joked to reporters that he and Mike were only there because they'd "volunteered as roadies," either unaware of or unwilling to accept the symbolic torch that was being passed. A *Newsday* reporter recounting the event on the following day would opine that Pearl Jam was "as important to music today as Dylan was" back in the Sixties—and when the reclusive Dylan and a hand-picked crew of high-wattage friends retired to Tommy Makem's Irish Pub after the concert, Eddie and Mike were heartily urged to go along. But even surrounded by rock royals like Eric Clapton, George Harrison, Ron Wood, Tom Petty, Neil Young, and Joe Crocker, trading jokes and singing traditional Irish tunes until sunrise, Eddie

---

*Initially, Shame was to be the name of the band, not the album. But a third party surfaced, waving legal papers and insisting that his band had prior claim to the Shame moniker. So Stone and crew coolly elected to call their band Brad—the first name of their litigious friend—and their album *Shame*, neither of which the guy could legally oppose.

couldn't seem to admit to himself that he'd arrived, that he'd passed all the tests, that this was a pantheon to which he'd been deigned worthy of inclusion. These people were legends. What was *he* doing here?

Mostly, he was learning—how to survive, how to stay off the mile-long casualty list generated by a business that churned out overnight superstars like a toy company produces plastic action figures, each boasting a flashier gimmick than last year's model. Pearl Jam would devote much of 1993 to what amounted to a crash course in rock & roll longevity, a series of guest appearances and tours with rock elders who'd beat the system, the ones who'd managed to emerge from the idol mill with their sanity and their integrity intact, going on to enjoy viable, decades-long careers.

They chose their teachers well. On November 1 in Mountain View, California, they began a long and fruitful friendship with Neil Young, appearing at the Bridge School Benefit, a charity concert staged annually by Young to raise money for the high-tech school for the handicapped that his sons attended. They rang in the New Year opening for Keith Richards and his band, the Ex-Pensive Winos, at New York's Academy Theater, an evening that had Mike walking on air. And as the presenter list for the eighth annual Rock & Roll Hall of Fame dinner was finalized toward the end of 1992, some of the most powerful individuals in the music industry made it clear whose historical lead *they* were betting on Eddie to follow, inviting him to appear at the celebration and induct the Doors.

True to form, Eddie downplayed the event later, describing it as "no big deal" and saying that he'd only been chosen because his vocal register was similar to the late Jim Morrison's. He did, however, cram for the appearance during his and Beth's drive from Seattle to Los Angeles, immersing himself in Morrison's unique vocal inflections to the extent that when he took the stage with the surviving Doors at the Century Plaza Hotel on January 12, 1993, his performances of "Roadhouse Blues," "Break on Through," and "Light My Fire," sent chills running down jaded spines all over the room. Eddie flubbed a few lyrics, and he came in early on a few choruses. But at certain moments—when he shrieked, "Try to run . . . try to hide . . . *break on through to the other side*," or wailed out the last emphatic, "try to set the night on . . . *FIRE!*" in "Light My Fire"—his vocals were uncannily like Morrison's, and the industry tastemakers noticed. Soon afterward, the Vedder-is-the-new-Morrison theories would begin turning up in the press. The comparisons would only intensify later, after Eddie took to carrying a bottle of wine around with him on stage, and began looking bloated and unhealthy.

If the comparisons between Eddie and Morrison were mostly superficial, the mark of a music industry and media staffed largely by ex-hippies who stubbornly insisted on viewing every young, up-and-coming talent as a knockoff of some hallowed Sixties fossil, the two *were* very much alike on other, deeper levels, the kind that usually went unremarked upon by pundits focusing on their physical and aural similarities. Writing about Morrison in the foreword of the Doors biography *No One Here Gets Out Alive*, author and former Morrison confidant Danny Sugerman could easily have been referring to Eddie:

> Rock and roll has always attracted a lot of misfits with identity problems, but Morrison took being an outsider one step further. He said, in effect, "That's okay, we like it here. It hurts and it's hell, but it's also a helluva lot more *real* than the trip I see you on." He pointed his finger at the parents, teachers, and the other authority figures around the land. He did not make vague references. Angered by the fraud, he did not imply—he blatantly, furiously accused. . . . He communicated with emotion, rage, grace, and wisdom. He offered very little in the way of compromise.

More than a taste for the grape or a powerfully throaty tenor, it was this rage-against-the-machine outlook that Eddie had in common with Morrison, a hunger for truth and a hatred for hypocrisy that both strove to communicate to their audiences even when it meant angering them in the process. Like Morrison, Eddie felt deceived by life even as he went out of his way to celebrate it; like Morrison, he seemed to value experience and action over materialism. Most notably, like Morrison, he abhorred the plastic machinations of the industry icon factory even as he clearly benefitted from them. Both men were haunted by the same internal conflict, longing to be respected as artists rather than pinup gods, yet driven almost compulsively to seek out the mass audiences that their mutual love of pushing the public's buttons demanded.

They both needed their fame as desperately as they hated it.

It was a paradox that was ultimately believed to have killed Jim Morrison. And by January, it had begun to wreak serious havoc on Eddie, as illustrated by a humiliating experience he suffered at the Hollywood Palladium.

Just over a week after he fronted the Doors at the Hall of Fame dinner, Eddie made a solo appearance at a benefit concert staged by Rock for Choice, a charity organized by the members of L7 to mobilize rock fans against the powerful fundamentalist groups who were terrorizing women's clinics and chipping away at *Roe* v. *Wade*. The appearance was especially important to Eddie, a longtime champion of the Choice movement for philosophical reasons and, as he'd indicated in an essay he wrote for *Spin* the past November, personal ones as well. "Ten years old. That's the age my child would have been,"* Eddie wrote. "And I would not be here in Glasgow. I wouldn't be in this band or traveling. And I wouldn't have seen the liberal ways in which other countries we have visited deal with this issue. I wouldn't have been asked to write this piece. The fact that I've been through it on all levels is the only reason I accepted. Perhaps I'll have a child in the future, when I can provide properly. Who knows. But as individuals in this 'free' country, we must have the right to choose when that time is right."

In fact, Eddie's vehement pro-choice stance was rooted in experience much more wrenching than he'd hinted at in *Spin*—the issue had not only affected him personally; it had also, in the days before abortion was legal, touched the life of his mother, Karen. Throughout his career, he would tirelessly use his star power to support pro-choice efforts. "These are things I've witnessed, things I've documented in my soul, and it's always good to speak for groups that aren't being heard," he later said of his appearance at the January benefit. In the same conversation, he mentioned that such events were the only real reason he valued his celebrity status. Fame was almost worth its dehumanizing side effects, he said, as long as it meant he was "able to say so much, and have so many people's ears to the wall."

But at the Rock for Choice benefit, Eddie's celebrity status reared up and bit his message in the ass. Even worse, it happened in front of the one person present whose respect he coveted the most. Exene Cervenka, formerly of the seminal Los Angeles punk band X and one of Eddie's longtime personal heroes, was emceeing the show. For the most part, each new performer or speaker introduced by Exene had been received respectfully and attentively by the Palladium audience. But when Cervenka introduced Eddie and he walked out with his guitar, pan-

---

*Given the timing, many fans have mistakenly assumed that the mother of the child referred to by Eddie in the *Spin* piece was his high-school girlfriend, Liz Gumble. Although neither Vedder nor Gumble would talk about it, sources say the potential mother was not Gumble.

demonium struck. The air was rent with hooting, hollering, and the ear-splitting, high-pitched screams of teenage Pearl Jam fans, and the atmosphere, steeped only moments earlier in the political significance of the event, suddenly took on the mindless, frenzied air of a Sixties teen-show taping.

Eddie was mortified. Years ago, he'd gone to an X show in Chicago and stood in the very front row, and during a break between songs, Exene had given him her Miller beer to hold. He'd never even taken a sip— he'd just held it, as reverentially and carefully as someone else might hold a Fabergé egg, and stood motionless, in awe of this furious, dazzling woman whose songs inspired him more than anything he'd ever heard.

Now, at the Palladium, his punk goddess was exiting the stage with both hands clapped over her ears and a disgusted expression that looked, Eddie would say later, "like she'd just sucked on a lemon." He wanted to thank her, to shake her hand, something. But all he could do was look after her, helpless and cringing, as the deafening adulation of his fans obliterated both his pride and his apology.

"I'm sorry," he mouthed to Exene's back as she fled the stage. "It's not my fault."

XOX

Dave drove to rehearsal in his brand-new black Infiniti. He was pleased with his purchase; he'd scouted around until he found a car with all the features he wanted and haggled the salesman down to a figure well below the sticker price.

The drummer was one of the last in the band to take the new-car plunge. Jeff had bought a Grand Cherokee, loaded. Stone got himself a Volvo station wagon with every option imaginable: Not long ago, Dave had watched, amused, as the guitarist piled a bunch of friends into the wagon outside a club, eager to chauffeur them around. "And look," Stone had told them excitedly. "The seats warm up!"

Dave didn't mention the Infiniti to the others when he got to Galleria Potatohead. He'd never in his life imagined that he would own a car as nice as this, and he was fairly bursting with pride. But he wanted to be cool about it, so he'd decided to wait until after rehearsal to show them.

A few hours later, they all gathered their coats and climbed the stairs that led out of the basement. Dave fingered his shiny new keys, anticipating the unveiling. Outside, he led the others to his new wheels.

"Check it out," he said, beaming. "What do you think?"

The others stood in a huddle, silent.

"Huh," Jeff said finally.

"Well." said Stone. "That's *rock*."

Nobody got in, nobody wanted to see the interior or peek under the hood. Eddie, who'd parted with some of his *Ten* royalties to pay off the same beat-up truck he'd been driving when he first arrived in Seattle, stood with his arms crossed, eyes flickering distastefully over the Infiniti's shiny black paint job and bright chrome wheels.

Whatever, Dave thought. He sat in his new car as they walked away, absentmindedly jiggling the keys that hung from the ignition with one aimless finger. He sat there for a long time after the others had gone home.

※◇※

In late January, Dave got stuck holding the acceptance-speech bag at the twentieth annual American Music Awards.

Eddie hadn't wanted to have anything to do with the ceremony, and Stone and Mike were busy, so Jeff and Dave had volunteered, bringing Eric Johnson along for company. Dave went shopping with an Epic staffer to find a jacket for the occasion, and Jeff even had a suit specially made.

"Everything was cool," Dave remembers. "We got all dudded up in our little outfits, and like an hour before the cars came to pick us up, Eric and I got really stoned. If we won anything, my whole plan was to get up on stage and say, 'Ladies and gentlemen, Jeff Ament,' and then stand back. You know, 'Jeff will handle it.'"

It might have worked beautifully. But fifteen minutes before the driver showed up, Dave and Eric got a call from Jeff, who claimed to have food poisoning and said he would not be attending.

Stoned and completely unprepared, Dave was in a state of panic by the time he and Eric got to the ceremony and found their seats; he prayed Pearl Jam wouldn't win in any of the categories for which they'd been nominated. In desperation, he turned to Eric. Pearl Jam's tour manager was known far and wide for his lack of inhibition—he was the kind of guy who should have had "Watch me, I'm about to do something silly" tattooed on his forehead. Eric was always drawing attention to himself with some goofy comedy routine or other. He'd be the perfect foil in a situation like this.

"Man," Dave said to Eric, "if we win, I'll give you fifty bucks to go up there with me. Fifty bucks. Come on, you *have* to."

Johnson agreed, and Dave relaxed a bit.

"I thought, 'This'll be cool,' " Dave recalls. "You know, Eric, who gets up on stage in a bra and *humps* people." But a few minutes later, when Pearl Jam was announced the winner for Favorite New Pop/Rock Artist, Johnson's legendary cool failed him.

"We got up there," says Dave, laughing, "and I looked over at Eric just in time to see his beet-red face, sweat just *dripping* off his forehead. He was *totally* frozen."

Petrified, Dave stumbled through an acceptance speech. "Wow," he told the crowd. "This is the first time I've ever done this—this is pretty heavy." He let out a haggard rush of air. "I want to keep it short . . . I want to thank everyone at Epic and Sony, and . . . I wish the rest of the band were here. . . ." He shot a glance at Eric, who looked as if he might keel over any second. "I actually paid Eric Johnson, our tour manager, to come up and stand here with me, 'cause I was kinda nervous," Dave went on. Eric grinned stiffly at his side. "But just . . . thanks everybody. Thanks."

Later, when Pearl Jam won the Favorite New Artist, Heavy Metal/ Hard Rock category, Dave was on his own, one trip to the podium having been enough to last Eric a lifetime. Members of Firehouse, a lite-metal band whose videos were heavy on big hair, scantily clad models, and pyrotechnics, were presenting the award. Dave had previously met the drummer, and, relieved to see a familiar face as he made his second unbearably long trek across the auditorium's stage, he gave the Firehouse drummer a quick hug when he reached the podium. "Man, am I glad to see you," he whispered. "I'm nervous as shit."

Dave faced the audience, clutching Pearl Jam's statuette. "Well, now I can make up for what I didn't say last time," he began. Then he looked into the front row, where a line of superstars—among them Michael Jackson, Diana Ross, and Gladys Knight—sat watching him like a jury.

"Whoa," he said, flustered. He tried to coax from memory the list of record company executives he'd forgotten when he accepted the first award, but it was not use. "Kelly Curtis and Michael Goldstone are up there somewhere," he finished lamely, waving a hand toward the balcony. "Thanks to them, too. And thanks to everyone else. Thanks." The drummer returned to his seat, relieved that the nightmare was over and that he'd gotten through it without too much grief.

Or so he thought. Back in Seattle the week after the broadcast, word came in that the top brass at Epic were furious. In mentioning Michael Goldstone and failing to thank anyone else at Epic, Dave had apparently committed a serious breach of unwritten awards-show etiquette, which mandated that record company executives be showered with gratitude in ranking order—first the president, then the vice president, and so on. Dave stood listening in disbelief as Kelly Curtis explained this to him. Then he went ballistic.

"Listen," he shouted, "you tell those fucking people that when they call me at home and say hello, I'll remember who they are!"

Dave thought that was the end of it, but he still had one flogging left to go. A few months later on the tour bus, somebody brought up the American Music Awards. They joked about it a little, but then Eddie piped up from the corner.

"That was the most embarrassing moment of my life," he said.

"What?" said Dave.

"You embarrassed the shit out of me when you did that," Eddie repeated.

Dave just stood there, ineffectively gulping air like a trout tossed into a boat. *How the fuck am I supposed to please this guy?* he wondered.

※◈※

In March, Pearl Jam traveled to San Rafael, California, where, at the Site, a recording compound perched high in the hills outside San Francisco, they would record their second album, *Vs.*, with producer Brendan O'Brien.

The band's home for the next two months was a facility geared toward providing a relaxing, cozy recording environment for rock stars accustomed to creature comforts. There was a chef on call, a golf course not far away, and a basketball court off the main building where Pearl Jam would spend countless hours shooting "hoops for bucks"—games of Horse where they all ponied up $5 to be collected by the victor. Most of the band members felt comfortable at the Site. Dave described the studio, with its magnificent view of lush green forest, as "paradise." Eddie, naturally, hated it, condemning it as the kind of place "old rockers" went to make "dinner music."

From the beginning, the band members and O'Brien had agreed that the bulk of the writing should take place in the studio, to facilitate the

seat-of-the-pants experimentation and loose jamming that often made
Pearl Jam's live shows so dazzling. To that end, they'd deliberately held
to a minimum of tinkering during their Seattle rehearsals, the goal being
to arrive at the Site armed with only the germs of ideas and allow the finished songs to emerge organically. At O'Brien's suggestion they also
agreed to mix down every track completely before moving on to the
next, an unusual practice that, according to Mike, "kept us focused, kept
the basic tracks more live, and kept us working."

On the first day, O'Brien had the band set up in a semicircle around
the drums, planning to let them limber up for a week or so before he began the actual recording. But they'd barely begun jamming on the ideas
they'd brought in before the producer was scurrying around the room,
excitedly setting up mikes. Soon afterward, O'Brien gave up all pretense
of letting the band rehearse and moved Dave into a separate, tiled room
to isolate the drums. Clearly, this was a band ready to make a record.

Rising in the early afternoons and usually recording until six or
seven in the evening when they would break for dinner, Pearl Jam cut
three tracks—"Go," "Blood," and "Rats,"—before a week was out, the
loose vibe of the sessions nurturing their intuitive need to stretch their
legs and, at times, resulting in songs that changed radically between in-
ception and completion. "Go," for example, had begun life as an
acoustic riff of Dave's, and when he'd first played it for the others in
Seattle, nobody seemed very interested. But once he'd played it for them
in amplified form on Stone's rig, the others seized on it, and it emerged
as a much harder track, Eddie spitting out rapid-fire lyrics over a propulsive bass-and-drums foundation and Stone, playing through an old
rotating Leslie cabinet, infusing the chorus with a sirenlike counter-
melody. On the second take, Mike expertly nailed an off-the-cuff,
CryBaby–laden solo so intricate that attempting to recreate it on stage
would always be frustrating for him.

O'Brien allowed them to roam, keeping the tape rolling to capture
the count-offs, rough endings, squeals of feedback, and dislocated, experimental riffing that would give the record its comfortable, spontaneous feel. He also encouraged them to experiment with role switching,
which resulted in moments like the burst of choppy, wah-informed soloing after the second chorus of "Rats." The solo was believed by many to
be Mike's handiwork, but it was actually rhythm-ace Stone's, and his
funk leanings served the lurching, slinky feel of the track well.

Typically, Eddie would sit around with a notebook while the band jammed, jotting down the spare lines and phrases he would eventually weave into songs. The lyrics he penned for the initial three tracks reveal much about his state of mind at the time. "Blood"—set to a meaty, descending riff laced with squalling funk wah-wah right out of the "Theme from *Shaft*"—was an injured rant about media exploitation, Eddie enjoying some wordplay at the expense of the three well-known rock magazines ("spin me round . . . roll me over . . . fucking circus"). In one striking example of his inventiveness with the language, he used his own name as a device to blur the line between passive and active voice ("paint Ed big . . . turn Ed into one of his enemies"), slamming home with one deft stroke of the pen both the (active) evil intent of his perceived media antagonists and the (passive) victimization he felt as a result. On "Rats," an ironic commentary on the sleazier side of human nature, he ran down a litany of despicable rodent behavioral traits, purportedly as a means of distinguishing humans from their four-legged brethren, and then punctuated it with the assertion "Rats, they don't compare," pointing up plainly that he believed they did. "Go" appeared to address feelings of dependence and insecurity, the protagonist begging, "Please don't go out on me," as if anticipating the loss of someone he relied on. Some fans, focusing on these lines, would view the song as a comment on a failing relationship; others imagined the narrator to be extending a hand to a friend pondering suicide. As a mark of Eddie's gift for presenting personal observations so obliquely that they lent themselves to numerous interpretations, few would ever guess at the initial inspiration for the song. "He told me it was about his truck," says Dave.

Pearl Jam recorded one more track before they hit a snag. The explosive "Leash," a longtime staple of the live set, was Eddie's declaration of solidarity with Dysfunctional Nation ("I am lost, I'm no guide, but I'm by your side"), playing on the same themes of parental repression that had fueled "Why Go" from *Ten*. Many of the lyrics Eddie had in his head for the album dealt with similar issues, and as he laid down his vocals for "Leash" he was apparently struck by the incongruity of plumbing those themes in such an upscale, comfort-oriented setting. "He felt the studio was a little too nice to really write some of these heavy lyrics that he'd been thinking about," recalled Kevin Scott, one of the engineers who worked on the album.

Just after he finished his vocals for "Leash," Eddie disappeared in his truck for a few days, seeking the privacy and change of setting that would allow him to immerse himself in the subject matter of his songs.

It was a pattern he would repeat throughout the sessions, and it inconvenienced his band mates—becuase they'd agreed to complete mixdowns of each song before moving on to the next, the others were often left twiddling their thumbs until Eddie showed up to do his vocals for any given track. But eventually they adjusted, coming to view the singer's unpredictable comings and goings as a necessary element of his creative process. And, gradually, the songs emerged.

"Glorified G" was a sarcastic antigun thesis, pitting a countrified main riff against a sprawling melange of upright bass, Grand Funk–style power chords, and lyrics Eddie claimed to have transcribed verbatim from a heated conversation that ensued after Jeff blurted out during a rehearsal that Dave had just bought a gun. ("I think it's fair to say that Eddie was pretty outraged," the drummer said later.) "W.M.A." had evolved in a similar manner. Crafted around a tribal tom-tom drum loop and a stuttering bass line that imparted an atmosphere of urban panic, the song was a statement on police racism, inspired by an incident Eddie witnessed between the police and a black vagrant outside the band's rehearsal space. "Daughter" was a low-key breather from the harder-edged material, a relaxed, black-porch acoustic number enlivened by cymbal taps and tambourine, Eddie using broad angry-child brush-strokes to mine the familiar parents-are-jerks territory of "Leash."

On "Dissident," "Elderly Woman Behind the Counter in a Small Town,"* and "Indifference," the band kept their amps turned down, to captivating effect. All three songs resonated with Eddie's plain-stories-about-plain-people sensibility, and "Elderly Woman" and "Indifference," in particular, would supply the finished record with two of its most starkly powerful moments. "Elderly Woman," written by Eddie on acoustic guitar (he also played on the track), was quietly emotional, weaving wistful metaphors ("cannot find a candle of thought to light your name") and shopworn, threadbare imagery into a Faulknerian portrait of stagnant small-town life. "Indifference," which would close the album, was a velvety meditation on integrity in the face of adversity, drenched in the languid, break-out-the-bong moodiness of classic Pink Floyd.

On first listen, "Animal," the pounding track from which Stone lifted

---

*The wordy title was a joke of Eddie's, a play on Pearl Jam's history of one-word song titles.

the album's initial title of *Five Against One*,* seemed to be written from the viewpoint of a gang-rape victim, veins in Eddie's forehead audibly standing out as he screamed, "Torture from you to me . . . abducted from the street." His artwork in the CD booklet appeared to support this interpretation, the word "torture" written out as "torch her."

But as was typical with Eddie's lyrics, the song could be interpreted in another manner entirely, one that few fans seemed to pick up on but that was championed by more than a few insiders in the Pearl Jam camp. To anyone who knew about the tugs-of-war that had taken place between Eddie, and his antieverything punk ethic, and the others, who were generally less rigid when it came to toeing the industry line on business decisions, it wasn't at all difficult to perceive "Animal" as Eddie's take on the interpersonal dynamic of the band, with the "five" in the five-against-one lyric representing the other four members of the Pearl Jam and Kelly Curtis, and the "one" being Eddie himself. In an interview with Cameron Crowe, who was on hand during the *Vs.* sessions doing reporting for a *Rolling Stone* story, Stone hinted that such a reading of the song would not be off the mark.

"That title represented a lot of the struggles that you go through trying to make a record," said the guitarist. "Your own independence— your own soul—versus everybody else's. In this band, the art of compromise is almost as important as the art of individual expression. You might have five great artists in the band, but if they can't compromise and work together, you don't have a great band. It might mean something completely different to Eddie, but when I heard that lyric, it made a lot of sense to me."

If Eddie felt outnumbered in Pearl Jam—that he'd been "abducted from the street," dragged kicking and screaming into a situation where he alone resented the constant focus on publicity and record sales—it certainly wasn't for lack of trying on the part of his band mates. By now, weary of the tension that permeated the band when Eddie was unhappy, the others had begun to defer to his judgment more and more often. Even Stone, who'd founded the band, written most of the songs, and who was named in the corporate documents as the president of Pearl

---

*A month before the release, the band would decide to change the title to *Vs.*, resulting in some copies from the first pressing surfacing with only the band name on the spine.

Jam, Incorporated, had recognized the folly of butting heads with the one band member who was truly indispensable in the eyes of the public.

That Eddie might become unhappy enough with the trappings of fame to leave the band was a threat that the others were always conscious of, whether or not it was intentional on Eddie's part. Crowe witnessed an exchange between Eddie and Jeff that was indicative of the subtle psychological leverage the singer had over the others. Speaking of the friction in the band, Jeff said hopefully, "There's going to be a point where it'll revert back to the way that it was. . . . We'll get back to actually being five guys who want to work it out together." Eddie replied that he would "really like that"—and then mused a few minutes later that if things in the band didn't work out, he could always sell solo tapes out of his house.

Moments like this served as a constant reminder to the others that their hold on success was tenuous, dependent on the whims of a man who clearly did not need them as much as they needed him. By virtue of his raw star power, Eddie was the member of Pearl Jam who was destined to bear most of the pressure that came along with being in the public eye. But because of that pressure—his negative reaction to it, and the fear of his band mates that he would succumb to it—he was also the member of Pearl Jam who was destined to hold all the cards. It was an old game, one that had been played out in every band that had ever risen to success. And the name of the game was Keep the Star Happy.

"I remember an article somebody in Seattle wrote, I think it was in the *Rocket*," Dave recalls. "And it basically said everything that we wanted to say to Eddie, but never did. Which was, 'Why the hell are you whining about this—if you don't like it, just quit.' It really spelled it out, hit the nail right on the head. And all of us read it. We were like, 'Ooooh.' You know, 'Should we show this to him?' and '*I'm* not gonna show it to him.' So it came down to Eric and I, we gave it to him. We just said, 'Hey, man, here's this thing.' He read it and didn't say anything about it, and that was that. There was some resentment about the fact that he was bitching about everything—everybody thought it was silly. But nobody would say anything. It was always, 'Let Eddie be Eddie, as long as he's here to sing.' Which was something Stone said a long time ago."

In the coming months, "letting Eddie be Eddie" would require a lot more from his band mates than tolerance for his I-hate-fame dissertations. It would also mean humoring his paranoid behavioral quirks, more than a few of which had emerged of late. The singer had taken to disguising himself with a series of gruesome rubber monster masks*— apparently he was unaware that they drew more attention to him than they deflected—and in June, when the band played a few warm-up shows for their upcoming European dates opening for Neil Young and U2, there would be an alarming incident in the dressing room, the other band members discovering a tape recorder that Eddie had "accidentally" left running in a gym bag. An Epic publicist claimed at the time that when the others realized their conversations were being surreptitiously recorded it nearly broke up the band, but according to Dave, the publicist was exaggerating. "It was kind of joked about," he says. "There was a week of time where everybody would make little comments in passing, like 'We could be being recorded now, maybe we should talk out in the hall.' I don't think it surprised anyone. Everyone was more like, 'Whatever, another weird thing.'"

Keeping Eddie happy would also mean giving him a larger share of Pearl Jam's publishing, although it's unclear whether Eddie himself requested the change or whether Stone initiated it as a peace offering. While it isn't uncommon for the chief lyricist in a band to enjoy a bigger piece of the publishing pie—from a strictly legal standpoint, Eddie would probably be entitled to 50 percent—it was a departure for Pearl Jam. Previously, they'd split the publishing proceeds equally, each receiving 20 percent. But in the van driving back to Seattle after the Missoula and Spokane warm-up shows, Stone announced that, effective with *Vs.*, Eddie would be taking a 36 percent cut while everyone else received a 16 percent share. When Dave questioned the change—he claims he was the only one who did—he recalls Stone saying that it was justified "because Eddie has to deal with more shit." Eddie, listening to music on his headphones, did not participate in the discussion.

If Jeff, Stone, and Mike knew where their bread was buttered and had made their peace with the idea of Eddie being, as Stone would put it a few years later, "the man," Dave had a severe case of not being able to see the forest for the trees. Whether it was out of naiveté, stubbornness,

---

*In June, Eddie insisted on wearing one of his masks during a photo shoot for Cameron Crowe's *Rolling Stone* cover story. When the magazine's photo editor, Jodi Peckman, requested that he remove it, Eddie did—and then changed tactics, looking down or turning away from the camera every time photographer Mark Seliger got a shot lined up. The magazine wound up without a single usable frame; in every decent shot of his band mates, Eddie was either masked or playing possum. The magazine had to create a composite from several different shots for the October 28, 1993, cover, on which Eddie was seen frowning down at his feet.

or just garden-variety competitiveness, the drummer was unable to accept the reality that the others had already begun to adjust to, and of all the cracks that had formed in Pearl Jam's foundation, the biggest fault line ran between Eddie and Dave. More than any of his band mates, Dave resented the constant tiptoeing around Eddie and the scarcity of communication it caused in the band, and by the time *Vs.* was recorded, the drummer's frustration was frequently manifesting itself in fits of temper.* His band mates tried to make light of the situation—Dave was seen scowling so often that the running joke was that he had only one eyebrow—but in fact, his resistance to the power shift that had taken place in Pearl Jam was beginning to make life difficult for the others, who were going out of their way to keep Eddie on an even keel. What had already become glaringly apparent to Stone, Jeff, and Mike—that no member of Pearl Jam was irreplaceable except Eddie—never seemed to occur to Dave, and it was an oversight that would ultimately cost him. His disappointment over the result of his talk with Cameron Crowe during the *Vs.* sessions was typical of his naiveté with regard to the realities of the time-honored drummer–lead singer pecking order, as well as the media's long tradition of upholding it.

"I talked to Cameron very frankly about my relationship with Eddie and the band," the drummer recalls, "and really just kind of bared it all. Cameron was aware of the dynamic of the band—the fact that that was how things worked, and that it disturbed me, and that no one else in the band ever made any effort to change it.

"When the article came out," he remembers, "I was heartbroken. No one else gave a shit, but I just thought, 'Man, this has nothing to do with this band.' You know, Eddie always talked about how he was terrified that someone would use the band's name for their own cause, but that always blew me away, because that's what *he* was doing. All he ever did in interviews was promote himself."

Maybe. But if Crowe's *Rolling Stone* piece was, as the drummer puts it, "The Eddie Vedder Story with a few quotes from Eddie's band thrown

---

*The beginning of one such outburst was memorialized on *Vs.*, at the end of "Rearviewmirror." O'Brien pushed Dave mercilessly on the track, repeatedly interrupting takes and telling the drummer he needed more from him. After he finally made it through an entire take to O'Brien's satisfaction, Dave stood up and angrily flung his sticks against the studio wall. (The sticks can be heard clattering against the tiled wall at the song's end.) He then put his fist through the snare drum, picked it up, stomped outside with it, and threw it off the side of a cliff.

in," it surely had as much to do with Crowe's instincts as a writer. In his story, Crowe did make use of some of what the drummer had told him, exploring the contrast between Dave and his band mates with respect to their mismatched feelings about success. But otherwise, he did what any celebrity journalist would have done, and gave his readers what they wanted—namely, the skinny on Pearl Jam's mysterious, tortured lead singer. In fact, given Crowe's comments within the narrative of the piece, he printed much less of the skinny than he'd have liked to, because Eddie wouldn't give up the goods.

In order to flush out some detail on Eddie's past, Crowe had to sit through an awful lot of what he described as "perfect sound bites for populist mythmaking," and his story reflected that, hitting all the usual touchstones in Eddie's interview repertoire: Eddie hated fame, fashion models, opulence, seeing his own face in magazines, and playing arenas when he could be playing clubs; he respected Ian MacKaye and Henry Rollins, and "would do anything to be around music. You don't even have to pay me." Eventually, Eddie did offer some revelations about his childhood, disclosing that "Alive" had been autobiographical and recounting his discovery, in adolescence, of the secrets his parents had kept from him while he was growing up. The story made for dramatic reading, just as it made for a powerful song. But as much of a coup as it was for Crowe, he claimed that he'd only scratched the surface. "For all his open-wound honesty," he wrote, "there are many mysteries that Vedder still clings to. When confronted with questions about his childhood, Vedder becomes vague."

This was Eddie's special genius. Always, he revealed just enough about himself to pique curiosity, but never enough to sate it. Always, he hinted at a horrific upbringing, but he rarely went into any more detail about his family than he'd given Crowe: "I'm thankful that they've given me a lifetime's worth of material to write about."

The details of Eddie's shadowy past, he always intimated, were in his songs, right there for anyone willing to look for them. And so always, the curious—reporters seeking answers, fans seeking a glimpse of the man behind the mask—returned to the songs, puzzling over them and sifting for clues. On every Pearl Jam album, there would be at least one that added a few more pieces to the puzzle—a song that Eddie put more heart into than the others or singled out in his conversations with reporters as being especially important to him.

On *Vs.*, that song was "Rearviewmirror." Cameron Crowe grasped its importance enough to open his story with it, and he described it as being "about suicide." It's uncertain whether that was his inference or Eddie's synopsis, but more specifically, the song would seem to be about *outrunning* suicide, or a situation that might have warranted it. Framed as a companion to the *Vs.* track "Daughter," whose main character is repressed by a parent and "holds the hand that holds her down," "Rearviewmirror" invoked imagery of an adolescent "forced to endure what I could not forgive," a struggle with a stronger opponent that left him wounded spiritually more than physically. "Daughter" carried the repeating phrase, "the shades go down," an allusion to dark family secrets unfolding out of the neighbors' sight. On "Rearviewmirror," the secrets have been brought to light and no longer bind. "Finally," Eddie sings, "the shades are raised."

Introducing "Rearviewmirror" during a concert in London just a few months after it was recorded, Eddie advised fans to "listen to this song in a car really fast, driving away from someone you hate." As always, he was dropping clues—dangling the keys to his past, his own secrets.

And, as always, all the fans could do was wonder. They all knew what the song meant to them. But what they really wanted to know was, what did it mean to Eddie?

Part Three

✵ ◎ ∾ ╫

Blood

Fourteen

Class of '61 / My Two Dads and Sister Parish: The Shades Go Down /
Eddie Mueller, Child Model / The Vagabonds /
Friend of the Family

In 1958, six years before Eddie Vedder entered the world as Edward Louis Severson III, the tangle of long-buried family secrets he would publicly unravel in his first hit song had already begun to form.

Karen Lee Vedder, a pretty freshman attending Niles Township High School in Skokie, Illinois, was fifteen years old when she first met Peter Jerome Mueller, the neighbor and classmate who would eventually adopt and raise her firstborn son. Karen lived with her mother, Margaret, on a quiet residential street just off Oakton Park. Peter and his parents, Inez and Jerome Mueller, lived a few blocks away on Kenton Avenue, at the other side of the park.

Peter, the oldest of two children, had enjoyed a comfortable, stable upbringing. Jerome Mueller, a gifted athlete who had played for the St. Louis Cardinals and the Chicago Cubs, had, following a tenure in the military, gone on to make his living as an attorney. Jerome had provided well for his family, and he and his wife, Inez, would enjoy a close, loving relationship until his death in 1975. Both of the elder Muellers were poets—Inez's work would win awards after her death—and they prized education above all else, working hard to instill a love of literature in their children. The Mueller home was always well stocked with books, their dinner conversation spiced with literary references. By the time Peter reached high school it seemed a forgone conclusion that he would either study medicine or follow in Jerome's footsteps and pursue a career in law.

Karen's future did not seem so readily mapped out for her. The second of six children born to Margaret and Ivan Vedder, Karen had grown up in a strict Baptist household, the peace of which was often disrupted by the twin blights of alcoholism and abuse. Karen's mother was, in the words of one neighbor, "a saint"—a big-hearted, deeply religious woman whose steadiness and loving nature made her the backbone of her entire clan. But Karen's father was said to have been cut from coarser cloth.

In 1938, when twenty-year-old Margaret Sorensen married handsome, brown-eyed Ivan Vedder, she already knew all about hardship. Her father had died young, leaving her mother, Pearl, financially unprepared to care for Margaret and her four siblings. Anthony Sorensen's death might have resulted in his children being parceled off to live with various relatives had it not been for Pearl's determination to keep her family together. Following her husband's death she had moved her children from their comfortable apartment in Rogers Park, Illinois into a smaller, more affordable place in Skokie that was heated by a coal stove, and she'd worked her fingers to the bone to feed her family, entrusting the care of the younger children to her eldest son, Troy, while she worked long days as a domestic. Pearl's steely resolve to keep her family afloat and her children feeling secure even in the toughest of times was a lesson that came in handy for her oldest daughter.

If Margaret Sorensen brought into her marriage to Ivan Vedder a gritty, love-conquers-all sensibility instilled in her by her mother, Ivan brought into the marriage the old scars of childhood abandonment by his father, and throughout the marriage he would either be numbing those old hurts with alcohol or exorcising them in outbursts directed toward his wife and children. Money was as short as Ivan's temper. Working as a salesman, he brought home between $90 and $110 per week depending upon the hours he worked, and toward the end of the marriage he was apparently more interested in squandering money in the bars than he was in earning it to feed his children. Marge squared her shoulders and took care of business, applying for the job at Montgomery Ward she would keep until she reached retirement age. On October 11, 1959, Ivan walked out on his family, leaving Marge with a house full of kids to support, the payments on a $408.80 loan she'd cosigned with him six months earlier, and just enough dignity to file for divorce on grounds of desertion after the requisite year had passed. "I was a good wife," Margaret said in her April 1961 complaint. Ivan, she said simply, had treated her "very poorly."

Throughout high school, Karen Vedder told Peter Mueller much about her family. Privacy for courting teenagers was a commodity in those days; Skokie was a tight-knit, conservative, church-oriented town, and police seemed to take glee in questioning hand-holding, necking couples. But Karen and Peter made do. He would sneak through the windows of houses where she was babysitting, or they would take long, aimless walks, often winding up at Oakton Park or Searle Park, where they spent hours talking in the shelter of a green gazebo. During these innocent meetings in the summers of 1958 and 1959 as they talked of their hopes for the future, a closeness formed between the two. There was a vulnerability about Karen that tugged at the heart, and Peter was smitten with her from the beginning. A few times during their talks they flirted with the notion of marriage, and had it not been for Peter's college plans, the idea might have taken root. But by the summer before their sophomore year, the two seemed destined for separate futures. And late that summer of 1959, Peter was supplanted in Karen's affections by a formidable rival.

Eighteen-year-old Edward Louis Severson, Jr., was the sort of enigmatic, darkly handsome man-about-town that dependable, academic types like Peter Mueller have never been able to compete with. "Ed was a cut above," says Mueller with genuine admiration. "He was just a sparkler, everything I felt I wasn't." The Seversons lived on Latrobe Avenue, just north of Main Street and a few blocks west of the Chicago & Northwestern rail line that bisected Skokie and Morton Grove. They were a prosperous family—Edward, Sr., was a highly successful real-estate broker—and around town, their eldest son was known as a charismatic force to be reckoned with. Striking a commanding presence at 5'11", with wavy dark hair and dark eyes, Ed had a sophistication that belied his age. A year ahead of Karen and Peter at Niles Township, he'd played football for the school and been popular in his class, and he tooled around Skokie in a two-tone green '57 Pontiac remembered by one envious classmate as "a beast." Though of high intelligence, Ed was not academically inclined. Just as his son would do twenty-three years later, he dropped out of high school during his senior year to pursue his dreams as a musician.

By 1960, working professionally in Chicago nightclubs, Ed looked to have a promising career awaiting him. Years later during an interview, still feeling the sting of never having gotten to know his biological father, Eddie would bitterly describe Ed Severson as a "broken-down old lounge act," but Mueller, expressing regret that Eddie never had a chance to see his father perform, says otherwise. "Ed was hardly a lounge act," he says of his former rival. "Ed was a *masterful* musician. He was wonderful. In addition to being an accomplished singer and organist, he was a songwriter, and he just enraptured everybody." Later, before his career was cut short by a debilitating illness, Ed would be living in Hollywood, taking singing classes with Ethel Merman and rubbing shoulders with Carol Burnett and Jimmy Durante.

Only one thing seemed to hang like a cloud over Ed Severson: His mother had died when he was still very young, and he'd always felt deprived by the loss. Ed's father had remarried and gone on to have three daughters with his second wife, Lorraine, and Ed was said to have had an uneasy relationship with his stepmother. To friends, he complained that Lorraine favored her daughters, but it's likely that no matter how caring or well-meaning Lorraine had been to her stepson, she'd never have been able to compete with the perfect mental image he carried around of his mother. To have lost his mother before he'd ever really had a chance to know her created in Ed Severson an open wound that would never fully heal, much in the same way his own death, years later, would haunt Eddie. And as would also be the case with Eddie, by the time Ed reached adolescence, the hurt had manifested itself in rage.

XOX

Peter Mueller had been out of touch with Karen Vedder for over a year and a half by the time their graduation from Niles Township loomed. Friends had passed along snippets of gossip about his old girlfriend that made it clear she was off limits—Karen and Ed had been seen making out in Ed's Pontiac; Karen had come to class sporting a diamond engagement ring—and besides, he had plenty to keep him occupied. By spring, he'd been recommended for an opening at King's Point Merchant Marine Academy in the fall, and he only needed to pass an eye exam before it was official.

But that June, Mueller recalls, Karen began seeking him out when she and Ed fought, complaining of Ed's quick rages and showing him bruises she claimed Ed had caused. The first of these meetings took place the night before their graduation. They sat beneath a tree in Oakton Park, talking until three in the morning about the doubts Karen was having about her fiancé. Before they said good-night, they made plans to go out after the graduation ceremony. But the following morning, when Jerome Mueller found out his son had spent the previous evening with another man's intended, he hit the ceiling and announced that he was boycotting Peter's graduation. Later that night when Peter accepted his diploma, the achievement felt hollow, and, depressed, he sat out his planned date with Karen. She and Ed reconciled that night.

Peter went on with his summer, taking a job as a stockboy at Sun Drugs in Morton Grove, working weekends as a crossing guard for the Skokie Police Department, and looking forward to his enrollment in King's Point. But a month later, on Fourth of July weekend, a distraught Karen found him playing basketball in front of his house and again asked if they could talk. She and Ed had had another fight, and she showed Peter bruises on her legs and on her shoulder. Not wanting to be seen in Oakton Park, they decided to take the North Shore (a now-defunct rail line) into Milwaukee and talk on the train. For Peter, the trip was nerve-wracking. He had no money in his pocket, they got lost in a seedy part of Milwaukee looking for a park he remembered, and when they found their way back to the train station they were hassled by the police, who wondered what two teenagers were doing there at four in the morning. Peter flashed his crossing guard badge and told them he worked for the police in Skokie, and the officers let them go on their way. But the worst was yet to come.

In Skokie, Karen and Peter got off at the Dempster Street station and began making their way toward the east end of town, where Karen was staying at the home of a friend. Not wanting to be seen together—Karen was still engaged—they were taking a convoluted route, walking mostly on side streets. Unfortunately, they were forced to walk a few blocks on Main Street to navigate around the golf course of the Evanston Country Club. And, unbeknownst to them, as they walked east on Main their progress was being observed by the one person in the world whose attention they most wanted to avoid.

Karen and Peter had been off Main Street and walking along a side street for a few minutes when they rounded a corner and saw Ed Severson's Pontiac, its front grille glittering evilly in the moonlight. Behind the wheel sat a glowering Ed. "He had his shirt off—you know, this bronze body," remembers Mueller, "and he was hell-bent for *leather.*" Peter, wearing a dorky madras shirt and loafers, quickly sized up his rival and wished he could be anywhere else.

Ed came out of the car swinging and swearing, Peter began jabbing, and the battle for Karen Vedder was officially on. Ed landed two solid rights on Peter's left eye and then pulled a surprise move, yanking Peter's shirt over his head and trying to force him down to the ground. The two wrestled briefly, and Peter got out of the tangle, letting fly with a couple of satisfying left hooks and then quickly pinning Ed's arms. Just then, Peter heard a car door slam. He glanced over his shoulder and there was Karen, sitting primly in the Pontiac's front passenger seat.

Obviously, a victor had been named.

Ed stalked off to the car. Peter followed him, holding the driver's side door so that Ed couldn't close it. "If you ever hit her again, I'll kill you," he warned.

"Sailor boy," said Ed, "if I catch you with her again, *you're* dead."

It was July 1961, and a decade would pass before the two men met again. Neither of them could have predicted, as they stood scowling at each other under a street lamp that night, the strange course their relationship would take in the coming years. The next time Peter Mueller and Ed Severson came together, they would not be fighting over a woman. Rather, they would be bonding over a son.

XOX

Karen and Ed were married on March 24, 1962, in Chicago, and moved shortly to Denver, where Ed got a nightclub engagement.

Almost immediately, things went sour. In October, Peter began receiving letters from Karen at King's Point in which she described her unhappiness with the marriage. "Her first letter to me was about Ed having affairs, hitting her again, reverting to the old patterns," Mueller recalls. "I wrote her back and gave her all the hints I could think of on how to make a man happy. It was none of my business, but I told her what I thought she should do. She answered and said that she'd tried all that, and that it hadn't worked."

In December, when Peter traveled to Skokie for Christmas leave, Karen was already there, having left Ed and moved back in with her mother. She and Peter spent a long night talking in her uncle Ken's car, Karen pouring out her troubles and telling Peter she was considering a divorce. They kissed, and Peter recalls Karen falling asleep with her head in his lap as he stroked her hair. Later, Peter had a heart-to-heart talk with his mother, wondering what he should do. Karen, he says, sought advice from her mother as well. It's uncertain what Inez Mueller told her son or what Marge Vedder told her daughter, but it's staggering to think what might be different today had either mother not given exactly the advice that she did.

Peter was back at King's Point when Karen decided to give her marriage to Ed Severson one more chance, and he doesn't recall exactly when the reconciliation took place. But counting backward from the birthdate of a certain well-known rocker; it's a safe assumption that Ed Severson was back in the picture by the spring of 1964. On December 23 of that year—almost nine months to the day after Karen and Ed's second wedding anniversary—Edward Louis Severson III came squalling into the world at Swedish Covenant Hospital in Chicago.

In keeping with the reclusive behavior for which he would be known some thirty years later, he was born breach.

XXX

Eddie was four months old when his mother gave up on her marriage to Ed Severson. Living in the Chicago suburb of Evanston, where Ed had taken a job with the Seabord Finance Company, Karen and Ed had undergone counseling through the Edgewater Baptist Church in an attempt to overcome their problems, but it hadn't helped, and Karen had begun to worry that Ed's violent outbursts would eventually extend to Eddie.

Karen filed for divorce on April 29, 1965, alleging that Ed had struck her "with great force and violence" during separate incidents in March and April. She asked for custody of Eddie in her complaint, citing Ed as an unfit father because of his "uncontrollable temperament, bad habits and abusive manner."

In October, just before she was to make a court appearance related to the divorce, Karen went to Peter Mueller's father, Jerome, for legal advice. A few weeks later, she sent him a note, thanking him for taking the time to talk with her and expressing relief over the finalization of the divorce. "I should have gone through with it two years ago when I came home from Denver," she wrote, "but of course, then I wouldn't have my son."

By now, Karen and Peter had renewed their old ties. "I was truly in love with Karen," he recalls. "I would meet pretty girls, but I saw nothing in them. Even when this German beer company in New York had a 'Miss whatever' that they sent around for promotion, and she came to King's Point. She was gorgeous, and everybody was trying to get close to her. But not me."

During Peter's Christmas leave in Skokie, he proposed, and Karen accepted. But in February, during Peter's next break from the Academy, Karen returned his ring. "She said, 'Well, I want to see other guys, I want to be sure it's right,'" he remembers. They'd spent their first night together, and it had been awkward—both of them knew something wasn't right. "Karen later characterized us as 'oil and water,'" Peter recalls. "We didn't mix. And there was a lot of truth to that. Something about us was attractive to each other. There was a fundamental passion. But there was a cerebral chasm." It was a dynamic they would have been wise to pay attention to but that both would soon find themselves denying again, Karen out of a need to build a secure home for her son, and Peter for his own reasons. "He could not risk losing this one wonderful girl," Inez Mueller recalled later. "He thought he would never meet another like her."

After Karen broke off their engagement, Peter tried to return to routine. He graduated from King's Point in June and then moved to Houston, where he'd been commissioned as a naval officer. Karen, working as a waitress, began dating a fellow named Tom, one of her coworkers at the restaurant.

In May, she discovered she was pregnant.

The child's father, she recalled later, said that he would marry her, and "moved to another state to find a job and a new home for us." But by August, he was nowhere to be found, and Karen was terrified. She went to an obstetrician and told him of her dilemma. The doctor told her he knew someone who could help her and wrote down a name and address. Abortion was still illegal, and he warned Karen that if she told anyone of the referral, he would deny it. Karen went as far as visiting the address the doctor had given her, but it was in a seedy part of town, and she lost her nerve. She drove around the block, crying and wondering what to do, and finally decided to proceed with the pregnancy. She told no one. "My divorce had already been a black mark on my name and my family's name," she remembered. "I felt my family couldn't handle my being single and pregnant."

So it was that in September 1966, when Peter Mueller returned to the Chicago area to look up some old friends, he finally got his girl.

※◈※

Mueller recalls being "hugely shocked" the night he learned about Karen's pregnancy. They'd already been out a few times before Karen confided in him, during a late-night talk at her mother's home in Skokie. By this time, the pregnancy had progressed to the point where abortion would not have been an option even if Karen decided to risk the shady doctor she'd been referred to. But according to Peter, she was also afraid that if she carried the child to term, Ed Severson would find out about it and make trouble. "She didn't want there to be any connection between that child and her, for fear of losing Eddie to Ed," Mueller remembers. "She was concerned that Ed could criticize her as a bad mother, and try to take Eddie away from her custody."

Peter listened, and offered a solution. "I told her I had friends in Houston, and that we could go there and give the baby up for adoption," he says. Karen agreed, and the two began making plans for a hasty departure. Just before they left for Houston, Karen told her mother of the pregnancy. Peter remembers Marge Vedder trying to talk them out of leaving, offering to help Karen find another solution. Karen swore Marge to secrecy, insisting that having the baby in Houston and giving it up for adoption would be best for everyone involved.

In October, Peter and Karen left Skokie in Peter's black M.G. convertible. Eddie, not quite two years old, sat quietly between them, one tiny hand clutching the gear-shift knob.

※◈※

Two days into the drive, the us-against-the-world feel of the journey began to work its magic. Karen and Peter had not discussed marriage before they left. "We decided, simply, that I would help her out, no strings," says Peter. But back in Skokie, Karen had mentioned being upset when she saw Inez Mueller wearing the ring she'd given back to Peter when she broke their engagement. And unbeknownst to Karen, he'd retrieved the ring and brought it along.

"I told her halfway down that I had brought her diamond ring," Peter recalls, "and just before we got to Houston to meet my friends, she asked me to stop the car. She said, 'Peter, can I wear the ring, so we can tell everybody we're married? And can we tell everybody that Eddie's our son?'"

"We're embarking on this big adventure," remembers Mueller, "and all of a sudden, these feelings of protection are building up in me. I'm responsible for this little group here. And I was becoming *very* fond of that little boy. We were already perceived as husband, wife, and child everywhere we were on the trip to that point. And it felt real good. Primarily because Eddie was such a good little guy. He was just wonderful.

"So I agreed," he says. "And from that point on, everybody thought Eddie was my son. How I did that with my friends, I don't know. But I did."

X◊X

Karen and Peter were married on November 5, 1966, by a justice of the peace in Columbus, Texas. There were no witnesses to the ceremony. Afterward, the two threw their own rice, showering themselves with handfuls from a box Peter had stashed in the car. They'd left Eddie with friends so that they could spend a honeymoon weekend in San Antonio, but they hadn't been able to reveal to anyone the true nature of the trip. All of their acquaintances in Houston believed they were already married and that Eddie was Peter's son—that they were, in Karen's words, "a wonderful, cute young family from up North," with another baby on the way.

As they waited for Karen to deliver, they moved into a two-bedroom apartment on Park Place, in a nice complex with a swimming pool. Peter was often away at sea, so Karen passed the time familiarizing herself with her new home and enjoying the company of her son. She and Eddie began attending a local Baptist church, where she made a few new friends. Eddie charmed all of them, telling everyone he met that "my daddy went bye-bye on a boat." He apparently had no memories of Ed Severson, who'd moved out of his life at such an early age, and when Peter, the only father he'd ever known, went to sea, Eddie missed him. Chattering away to Karen in the mornings, "reading" to her from his storybooks, he would always interrupt his narrative when he came to a page in one of the books that Peter had repaired with Scotch tape. Daddy, he would say importantly, had fixed this for him.

In the afternoons, while Eddie was napping, Karen would read or write letters. Inez and Jerome Mueller, having learned of Peter and Karen's marriage after the fact, had written Karen a letter beginning "Dear daughter Karen," and it clearly meant a lot to her. In early December, she penned a thoughtful reply, writing delightedly of Eddie's emerging personality—he was "such a ham," and she loved to watch

him "perform"—and going on to describe at length his affection for Peter. The letter was optimistic, brimming with idyllic imagery and hope
for a promising future, and a casual reader would have found nothing in
it to distinguish it from any other letter written by a new bride. Its
poignance lay in what it did not contain. There was no mention of the
baby Karen was nurturing inside her—there couldn't be—and to read
the letter with that omission in mind is to gain heartbreaking insight
into how it must have felt for her to write it.

By the time she wrote to the Muellers, Karen wanted to keep the
child she was carrying. Just after their arrival in Houston, she and Peter
had found an adopting family and completed all the legal paperwork,
Peter signing as the baby's father. But now, she was having second
thoughts. According to Peter, it was in late December or early January, a
few weeks after her letter to his parents, that Karen asked him if they
could keep the baby.

In a 1993 book, *Stories of Adoption: Loss and Reunion*, Peter was
portrayed as something of a villain with regard to the adoption. If author
Eric Blau's paraphrasing of her words is accurate, Karen told Blau that
she gave the child up because "her husband did not want to raise two
children by other men," and she felt that "she had no other choices."
While Karen may indeed have perceived it that way, Peter's recollection
puts the circumstances of the adoption in a slightly different light. According to Peter, he and Karen were not yet married when they signed
the adoption papers, and she never indicated to him that she wanted to
keep the baby until after their marriage, by which time Karen's due date
was nearing and the adoption process was already well underway. Before they met with the lawyer for the adopting family and signed the
relinquishment papers, Peter remembers, he and Karen had discussed
their plans for the future, including their marriage. He was concerned
about his ability to support a family while pursuing a medical degree,
and recalls asking Karen if she would be willing to go to work to help
support them while he went to school. Karen, he says, agreed, and because the idea of keeping the baby never came up during those earlier
discussions, her later suggestion that they keep the child came out of left
field, and he was completely unprepared for it. He wasn't confident that
they could support two children while he was in medical school, he was
uncertain about the legality of reversing the adoption process, and he
had emotional reservations about his ability to raise the in utero child as
his own. In the end, he says, he told Karen he just didn't see how he
could manage it. Even today, Mueller clearly finds his memory of that

conversation upsetting. There is a long pause when he's asked about it, and when he speaks, his tone is contemplative.

"I don't want to say, 'She's wrong that I was insensitive,'" he says finally. "But we'd already committed to it. I had no idea what our rights were, having signed the contract. We weren't visited by a social worker. We had no court appearance to make, and there was nobody to tell us our rights.

"I tried to be as kind as I could," he goes on, "but it was too much for me—it was too much for me to even imagine. I was twenty-three years old. I was already living this fabrication with regard to Eddie, and I could *handle* that. I was ready to be Eddie's stepfather the year before. That was part of the deal when I proposed to Karen, and as far as that went, I was fulfilling my dream. That was a challenge I took on with relish. But with regard to the other child—to fabricate about this other man that interrupted my engagement to her? This *creep* that got her pregnant and then took off?" He pauses. "There wasn't anything I couldn't accomplish," he says. "That was my attitude. But I had been wounded enough that that wasn't in my capacity. That, I just couldn't imagine my heart was big enough to handle."

Karen delivered the child in January 1967, and she later told Blau that it was "an awful experience. I had no counseling at all. They discharged me from the hospital, and that was the end." Six weeks later, Karen and Eddie walked out to get the mail, and as they returned to the apartment, Karen flipped through the envelopes. Tucked among the letters and bills was a notice from the health department: *Has your baby daughter had her shots yet?*

"That's when she became very real to me," Karen recalled. "Once I realized the baby was a girl and she was my daughter, I fell apart. I remember that I started crying, and when I got back into the apartment, I threw myself across the counter and just sobbed and sobbed." Peter was livid; he remembers phoning the hospital and upbraiding them for sending the notice. But the damage had already been done. Karen knew she had a daughter, and she would pine for her for the next eighteen years. Her grief would play a large part in the slow death of her marriage to Peter, and looking back, he, too, seems to recognize their departure from Houston as a turning point.

"Those months were very, very difficult," says Mueller. "I was young and dumb, but strong. Those were tough days—they were very tough days. And yet, there was a cohesiveness in adversity. During the Houston days, we were the keepers of that secret, and that opportunity for a second chance, for us and for Eddie. I think Karen and I were the closest in those four or five months. It didn't last very long. When we moved from Houston to Chicago, it ended, that cohesiveness and that bond. Because it was behind us, and now we had to forge on with our lives."

XOX

By the fall of 1968, the Muellers had returned to Illinois and were living at 825 Forest Avenue in Evanston. They'd lived in Champaign for a few months while Peter took a stab at medical school, but that dream had been short-lived. Even with Karen waitressing to help out, the rigors of medical school weren't compatible with supporting a family, and by October, Peter had switched gears and enrolled at the Loyola School of Law, which would enable him to attend night classes and work full-time during the day. He took out a $10,000 student loan to cover his tuition, and he and Karen settled into a routine, Peter taking a full-time day job as a buyer for the U.S. Gypsum Corporation and Karen working part-time at a local pub, Chances 'R,' on nights when he didn't have classes and could stay home with Eddie.

For the first time in their marriage, they were living in the same general area as Ed Severson, and Ed's proximity sparked the idea of Peter's legally adopting Eddie. Ed was having medical problems; he'd been diagnosed with multiple sclerosis, and while they'd been living in Houston, he'd been out of touch. According to Peter, he and Karen were both worried about the prospect of Ed's reentering the picture, for different reasons.

"Karen believed Ed was gay,"* Mueller says. "I didn't know. Later, when I got to know him, he always had a girlfriend with him. But she told me about this gay boyfriend he had, an so on . . . and that was a concern she had. I don't think she felt hatred for him because of it, but she feared its potential impact on Eddie. She was negative about him—she felt that if he decided to become reinvolved, it would be uncomfortable for her, and it would be difficult for Eddie because he knew himself to be Eddie Mueller.

"Karen pursued the adoption," he goes on, "but I acquiesced with enthusiasm, because I wasn't sure how I could interface with Ed. I had already assumed an identity in Houston as Eddie's father, and that was a concern to me. 'How is Ed going to respond to this?' I mean, my only memory of Ed at that point was a fistfight. And I was dealing with feelings of insecurity about being Eddie's father, and how I could be his father if Ed were actively involved. From a selfish standpoint, that was a small part of it. But the primary reasons given to me by Karen were the issue of homosexuality, and the issue of Ed's multiple sclerosis. I think all of that combined, and she didn't feel comfortable about him becoming an active parent in Eddie's life. My father was available to [handle the adoption] free of charge, and we just thought it was best."

That spring, just after they'd returned to Illinois, Jerome Mueller had contacted Ed and asked him if he would agree to Eddie's being adopted by Peter. "I never really had a chance to talk to Ed then, which I tried to make up for when I talked to him about it later," says Peter. "But my dad told me he was completely cooperative." In June, Ed signed the consent form, relinquishing his parental rights over Eddie, and that fall, Peter and Karen stood before a Chicago judge to finalize the adoption.

Eddie was with them during the brief court appearance, but he would not remember it. He would grow up completely unaware of what had transpired during the first four years of his life.

XQX

Even as a toddler, Eddie drew admirers like flies. He was an especially adorable child, with a halo of sun-streaked brown hair, eyelashes long as your arm, and an enthusiastic, loving nature that could melt the iciest of hearts. "He would literally stop people in the street," Peter remembers. "They'd just stop and say, 'Gosh, what a beautiful child.'" Back in Houston, Peter and Karen had taken a two-year-old Eddie with them to watch Muhammed Ali train at the Astrodome for his fight with Cleveland Williams, and Ali had spotted Eddie immediately, walking over to the rope and asking for Eddie to be lifted up to him. Later, a similar incident would occur when they took Eddie to see Ben Vereen. "We were way up at the top, because we didn't have great seats," Peter recalls. "Ben Vereen came running out into the audience and saw Eddie, and he went right up to Eddie and picked him up and hugged him. Karen and I were just breathless. Everywhere we went, Eddie would get that form of attention."

It was this irresistibility to complete strangers that landed Eddie his

---

*In a 1983 court deposition, Karen confirmed that "for a period of time" she had believed Severson was bisexual, but said "I don't recall" when asked if she had thought so at the time of Eddie's adoption.

first showbiz experience, at the ripe age of five. It started one day when he was visiting his grandmother Marge at her Montgomery Ward job. A coworker spied Margaret's angelic young grandson and promptly drafted him to pose for the store's catalog. "Somebody didn't show up for modeling," Eddie recalled in 1991, "and they needed a kid. So they put me in a suit and took pictures, and all of a sudden I was in a couple of little commercials. It was pretty much a trip."

It was also the beginning of a successful career as a child model that would last a number of years. After he appeared in the Montgomery Ward catalog, a local agent, Shirley Hamilton, took notice and began booking Eddie to do catalogs for Marshall Fields and other stores. "Shirley was ecstatic with him," Peter recalls. "He was just a very docile, clever, and loving little boy. He was very successful in modeling because he was smaller, yet he was a year ahead of the competition in his maturation."

Armed with a photo composite announcing him to potential employers as "Eddie J. Mueller, Professional Model," Eddie began going out for auditions and quickly moved into television work. Between 1969 and 1971, he was, according to what Hamilton told his parents, the leading child model in Chicago, appearing in a Hallmark Christmas commercial and an ad for Big Wheels, among others. Eddie was a far cry from the archetypal bratty child star. He went about the job in a well-mannered way, with a plucky confidence about his abilities. After his Uncle Johnny accompanied him to the second day of cuts on an audition for a television spot advertising Chuckles candy, for example, he returned home and matter-of-factly informed his parents, "I think they're going to want me to do that commercial." Sure enough, it was Eddie who was later seen on TV pushing a toy shopping cart through a check-out stand, offering a toothy grin as he purchased his Chuckles. He'd beat out five hundred other young hopefuls for the job.

If he was mostly nonchalant about his modeling, Eddie wasn't too young to recognize its perks. Mueller still laughs about the day Eddie charmed his way onto the Bozo the Clown show. At the time, the show was a huge hit in Chicago, and everybody wanted to get their children on it. "You had to sign your kids up before they were *born*," remembers Peter. None of this waiting-list business for Eddie. He'd taken notice of the show one day while shooting a commercial next door to the Bozo studio, and, interested, walked over to investigate. The producers took one look and put him on the program.

The same year Eddie started modeling, his younger brother Jason was born in July. Peter was then in his second year of law school, still taking night classes. He'd left U.S. Gypsum and moved into a job as assistant dean of the Loyola School of Business, and between Jason's birth in 1969 and the summer of the following year, he'd moved into the top of his law class. Karen and the kids, he remembers, were "100 percent supportive," helping him through endless hours of studying, and at the end of his second year, he was offered a scholarship for the third. With money so tight, it would have helped. But as it turned out, he wouldn't be able to accept it.

During the summer and into the fall of 1970, Karen was still working nights at Chances 'R,' and one night, according to Peter, she didn't come home. It was a clear signal to Peter. "Our marriage was dissolving," he recalls. "I was working so hard and going to school and everything else, and she loved me, but she wanted more attention."

Drastic measures were in order. After a heart-to-heart talk, Karen and Peter decided they needed a break from the rat race, and Peter took $350 of the money he'd borrowed for his second-year tuition and bought a used red van. Over a three week period beginning in late September, he transformed the van into a camper, adding insulation and paneling, cutting up one of Karen's rugs to line the floor, and outfitting it with a hammock for Eddie and Jason to sleep in. In mid-October, Peter delivered the final touch, painting THE VAGABONDS on the van's side. Then he dropped his scholarship—and the Muellers dropped out.

For the next three months, the family wandered through the South, primarily Florida. They cooked meals of brown rice and hot dogs on a propane camping stove, and lived three or four days out of the week on beaches, where they could shower. Not long after arriving in Florida, they discovered the amazing resources provided by real-estate shows. "They'd let you keep your car in a parking lot, and then they would take you to different inland areas where they were trying to sell property," Mueller remembers. "We really got treated like kings when we did that, and we ate very well. It was free housing, free food, free hotels, baths, everything else. We did that about five times. One time, we actually ended up at the future site of Disney World as one of the tours we took for property that was going to be valuable some day. Of course we had no money to buy property. But that's the way we lived."

Eddie took an immediate liking to the road and adopted a whole new persona for the occasion, informing Peter and Karen that henceforth he would be known as "Jack." His parents complied—not that they had a choice. If anybody made the mistake of calling Eddie by his given name, he wouldn't answer. "Jack" stayed around for about two weeks. By the time the Muellers returned to Illinois, Eddie would be Eddie again.

As always, Eddie drew strangers to him. In Fort Lauderdale, the Muellers camped inland at a county park, and Eddie struck up a friendship with a distinguished-looking man named Miller. Miller had a bad heart—doctors, he told Karen and Peter, had given him only a year to live—and walked in the park every day. He took a shine to Eddie instantly and would always look for him when he arrived at the park for his walk.

At a campground in the Everglades, Eddie caught the attention of a gypsy. "She was either a gypsy, or some type of performing fortune teller," Peter remembers, "and she wanted to hypnotize him. I don't know what the reason was, but I had read enough to know that it could be damaging if it wasn't done professionally, and Karen agreed with me. So we refused."

Before the woman went on her way, she took Eddie's chin in her hands and looked into his eyes. Then she drew back and turned to Karen and Peter.

"This boy is going to be famous," she told them.

※◈※

Back in Illinois after their getaway camping trip, the Muellers tackled their next adventure when Karen heard of the need for house parents at a group home sponsored by the Lake Bluff–Chicago Homes for Children. With Peter still in school and working full-time—in April, he'd been hired as a clerk for a Cook County judge—most of the day-to-day management responsibility would be Karen's, but as she told family and friends in a Christmas letter that year, they needed the extra money, and she saw it as a challenge and a good opportunity. The job provided a furnished home and salaries as well as financial support for their wards; in return, they needed only to provide a loving, stable environment for six boys who were orphaned or from otherwise broken homes. Karen and Peter moved in as house parents of the home on Chicago Avenue—then the only boys' home in the organization—in May 1971, when Eddie was six. The first few months were fairly rough.

"I went from being the older of two brothers at this point, to all of a sudden being in the same household with, like, fourteen-year-old black kids and Irish kids who'd lost their parents somehow, or whose parents couldn't take care of 'em," Eddie recalled in 1991. "It was just bad, the mental states of all these kids—any kid is pretty much a nightmare at about fourteen or fifteen, and to have like six or seven strange kids, it's pretty intense." The former house parents, according to Peter, hadn't been up to the job, and when he and Karen took over, the general atmosphere was one of "terrible unruliness." Peter recalls Eddie as being "part of the glue that brought these kids into the new regime comfortably." Eddie was still modeling, and his commercials became a point of pride for the other boys in the home.

"We were having some problems," Mueller remembers. "We had some real heart-rending kids who moved in with us, kids who had been badly abused. From time to time we would have a problem with the police. But all of a sudden Eddie's ads started coming on TV, and all these older boys would gather around to watch. It was exciting for them because he was their group home brother. Eddie was nonchalant about it, as if it were just standard stuff. But from that point on, even though they ranged in age from nine to twenty and Eddie was only six, Eddie was kind of the leader of the pack."

Between Eddie's unifying influence and the contacts Peter and Karen had with local officials—the judge Peter worked for had influence in the juvenile system, and one of their former classmates at Niles Township was a psychologist working with the Evanston police—the Muellers, recalls Peter, "turned the group home around. It was the most notorious one in the system, but we turned it around to the point where it was a model home." Years later, Eddie would speak fondly of his foster brothers and of their influence. "That's when I cracked open my first Motown records," he said in 1991. "My foster brothers had Sly and the Family Stone, and the Jackson Five, all these things. I'd love to see those guys. They were huge influences. I think about them all the time."

In April 1972, about a year after they took over the group home, Karen and Peter had another son, Chris. Two months later, Peter graduated from law school and started a job with Kirkland & Ellis, a firm in Chicago. Between the new baby and the new job, he and Karen decided it was high time they became homeowners, and Inez and Jerome Mueller loaned them the money for the downpayment on a house in Morton Grove. By summer, they were settled in.

It was just a few months later, in October, that Ed Severson reentered their lives.

XXX

Karen and Peter had already discussed telling Eddie the truth about Ed when the time was right. It was, says Peter, "in the plan to have Eddie and Ed know one another." At the same time, they worried that telling Eddie when he was too young might cause him to feel, by virtue of his adoption, that he was less important to Peter than his younger brothers. "We didn't want to spoil anything for Eddie," Peter remembers. "We wanted to give him as normal an upbringing as possible, without any feelings of being less than number one."

Still, Ed missed his son, and neither Peter nor Karen wanted to deprive him of the right to see Eddie. "Ed and Karen had spoken," Peter recalls. "He sounded very friendly, and he wanted to meet me. She asked me if it would be all right to have him over for dinner some night, and I said, 'absolutely.'"

Peter doesn't recall how Ed knew, when he came calling that October, that he wasn't to spill the beans; he says only that when Ed did come to visit, it was clear that he knew what the boundaries were. "Karen must have told him we didn't want Eddie to know he wasn't my son," Mueller surmises. "I don't know how it was done, but he must have known. I think Ed and Karen talked after he signed the adoption papers, and he was okay with that."

Before that first dinner, Mueller says, neither he nor Karen "were in the position to commit to any particular concept that involved Ed—we weren't that close yet." It's uncertain whether Karen's concerns about Ed's bisexuality were in play at the time. "I don't remember discussing that with her in connection with that dinner," says Peter. But in any case, he adds with a laugh, "Ed managed that marvelously by showing up with a girlfriend." The dinner, a means of testing the water, could have gone either way, but as it turned out, it did much to ease any trepidation that Karen or Peter might have had about Ed's involvement, and paved the way for a friendship between the three, particularly between Peter and Ed, that would remain intact until Ed's death.

"I really enjoyed meeting [him]," Peter recalls, "and it was amazing, because we were all relaxed." After that first visit, there seemed to be an unspoken understanding between Karen, Ed, and Peter that they were laying important groundwork for the future. "In our image of what it would be like someday when we explained to Eddie the truth, Ed was an integral part of it. And establishing contact with him and inviting him to our home, I felt, was the beginning of a progression of events that might make it much nicer, because Ed would already be part of our lives."

Ed visited twice while the Muellers were living in Morton Grove. One of those visits gave rise to an incident that was insignificant for Eddie at the time, but that would haunt him years later, after he knew the truth about Ed.

"I remember him being really cool," Eddie said later, "but he was like a friend of the family, you know? This guy comes over, and we're hanging out, talking in the living room with my mom. And I'm like seven years old—I ain't gonna stick around for this. So I'm outside playing football or something.

"The house had these stone steps, and he had crutches," Eddie recalled. "And he fell, like really hard. I remember looking up and seeing the whole thing, and it was really an embarrassing situation. At the time, I was just, you know, trying to ignore the guy with the crutches. But now, I always think about what must have been going on with his *pride* at that point. It really pisses me off that it was a fucking secret. It really bothers me that they didn't tell me, at least before he died. Maybe I could've hung out with him for a day or something."

That, Peter says with not a little regret, was part of the plan—a goal he and Karen were moving steadily toward before unforeseen circumstances got in the way. "When Ed came to that first dinner at our home, he still seemed vibrant," he recalls. "We weren't thinking about his demise then. There was another person I knew who was dying of MS, but he was much older than Ed. He was in his fifties, and he was still going to work every day. Ed was maybe thirty-one. So we thought we were looking at twenty years down the road, at least."

Mueller pauses. "Karen and I both had good intentions," he says finally. "But we didn't count on death or divorce."

Fifteen

Trouble in Paradise / ToughLove / Tug-o-War / Mom Spills the
Beans: The Making of a Dysfunctional Messiah

In the mid-Seventies, the Muellers relocated to California,
spending a year in the Los Angeles suburb of Hacienda Heights,
where Karen and Peter's youngest son, Michael, was born in 1974, and
then moving to Encinitas, where they would remain until Eddie's final
year of high school.

At age nine, Eddie was cheerful and well-adjusted, active in school
athletics—though usually the smallest boy on the team and not especially gifted, Mueller says Eddie's "indomitable spirit" never failed to
impress his coaches—and extremely precocious. In a letter Peter wrote
to his mother in the spring of 1974, while he was in California studying
for the bar and the rest of the family was still back in Illinois preparing
for the move to Hacienda Heights, he described his adopted son with
something close to awe.

> Eddie—a prodigal son of the first order—with rare beauty for a
> boy, unbelievable ability to adjust and dominate, keen (proven)
> intelligence and rare charm—sets the stage for the personality

of our little family. At his conference, Eddie's science teacher told Karen she has to pinch herself to believe she is talking to a nine-year-old boy and not a young man. His letters to me reflect abilities far beyond his age and experience. He is a child who combines all that I have ever admired in another person.

Ed Severson, now living in California, remained in close touch with the family. Back in Morton Grove, Severson had surprised Peter by becoming Peter's first legal client, retaining him to draw up a partnership agreement for a business venture. Since then, the two men had become friends. During the Muellers' first few years in California, Severson visited often. By now, Ed's multiple sclerosis had begun to take its toll.

"It was very poignant when Ed would come over," Mueller recalls. "He'd pick up his hands as he came in the door in his wheelchair, and Eddie would come up to him. Ed's hands were shaky, and he would lift his hands up off the wheelchair and reach out to Eddie's face. His hands would be shaking until they came to Eddie's face, and then they'd stop. He'd hold Eddie's face in both hands and just look into Eddie's eyes— they'd stare at each other for this pregnant ten or twenty seconds, and it was out of this world. Karen and I would stand there at a distance and just kind of look at each other. There was nothing that would convince me that I was doing what was appropriate during those moments."

Karen and Peter were still conscious that they needed to be preparing for the day when they would tell Eddie the truth about Ed, and according to Peter, they came very close to actually having Ed move in with the family, which would have enabled them to look after Ed's health and would also have given Eddie more time to get to know him. Unfortunately, their plans were scotched by the tension that had crept into their marriage.

By the time the family moved to Encinitas, Peter had become an accomplished lawyer. In 1977, he bought a practice from a local attorney, and after a year in business his income rocketed to $150,000. For the first time in Peter and Karen's marriage, money wasn't a problem, and the Muellers enjoyed a standard of living they'd never before been able to manage. During their first few years in Encinitas, Karen wrote chatty letters to her mother-in-law, enthusing about the area and the family's new, more comfortable lifestyle. The letters were filled with the minutiae of the Muellers' day-to-day lives—the boys' soccer games, Karen's exercise regimen, the new Bible church they'd been attending, various purchases and home decorating projects—and brought to mind a contented household bustling with activity, with Karen holding down the fort, the classic Supermom.

In fact, Karen was becoming increasingly unhappy. Still haunted by the daughter she had given up for adoption, badly in need of an identity other than that of wife and mother, she was frequently depressed, finding it more and more difficult to maintain a cheerful facade.

"When I look back on it," Karen later told writer Eric Blau, "it was as if I was two different people: the perfect mom to my sons, submissive, obedient wife to my husband, and a shame-based woman living a lie. Because of the lying, my true feelings were never expressed. . . . Through the years, my grief would get so overbearing that I would cry out to my husband and let him know how hard this was on me. He wasn't very understanding, and I'm not sure he knew how to be. I would have fantasies about my daughter. . . . When I would go to school functions, I would always look at the grade my daughter would be in. I'd look at the outfits, look at the hairdos, and wonder how my daughter was being cared for."

By late 1977, when Eddie was in eighth grade, Ed Severson's visits had stopped. His health had begun to deteriorate, and he was living in a Los Angeles rest home, Long Wood Sanitarium. Most of the time, he was confined to bed. Ed's surroundings left much to be desired, and at the time, Karen and Peter were contemplating a move into a larger home. Peter says he suggested to Karen that they have Ed move into the new house with them, where he could receive in-home care by a nurse.

"The house had a separate wing where Ed could have lived," Peter recalls. "It was a magnificent place. It was six acres and four thousand square feet; it had a swimming pool, and a gorgeous three-hundred-degree view of the entire city. And of course my idealized attitude was, I could just see them [Eddie and Ed] being together, and then Karen and I telling Eddie, 'That's really your father.'

"She was originally open to that," he remembers. "We had agreed in principle to bring Ed into that house, and we opened escrow—I put a down payment on it. I don't know if Ed was the primary reason or a supporting reason for our excitement about buying this mini mansion. But he certainly was a cause, and I was all for it."

Early one evening, though, just before they were set to close escrow on the new house, Karen and Peter had a disagreement that culminated in a decision to back out of the deal.

"This was really before the devastating end of our marriage, but they were not good years," Peter recalls. "Karen was having more and more happy times away from me, so we were going through some struggles. And I'm sure that the aspect of having two men in one house about whom she had unpleasant feelings was too much for her. We had a difficult argument, and she made the remark, 'Wouldn't it be something if I caught you and my ex-husband in bed together?' So the homosexuality issue had continued for her. I had completely [forgotten about it]—he was so helpless and so sweet. He and I were distant perhaps in space, but we were close in heart. She obviously had a lot of insecurity about our relationship, otherwise she wouldn't have said something like that. But as soon as I heard that, I said, 'Whoa, I can't do this.' There were her feelings about Ed, and also my concern, even without Ed, of bringing Karen across North County. Her friends were so important to her that I felt it would be traumatic for her to move that far away from them. So we decided to opt out of the house."

Peter made it a personal project to find Ed a more comfortable place to live. When Sonya Mitchell, the aunt of one of Ed's old high school friends, offered to take care of Ed in her Orange County home, it seemed like the perfect solution. But Ed required more care than the elderly woman could manage, and the arrangement didn't work out. Three months later, Ed was taken by ambulance from Mitchell's home back to Long Wood. Shortly afterward, while on a business trip to Los Angeles, Peter stopped by to see how Ed was doing. It was during this visit that he and Ed had the only real heart-to-heart talk they'd ever had about Eddie.

"I just dropped in on him," Peter recalls. "And he was so happy to see me, because as you can imagine, his life was pretty routine at that point. I asked him if he needed anything, and he asked me to get some items for him—a toothbrush and some other things. So I went to a little shopping center across the street and got the things he wanted, and came back.

"We just had a few minutes to talk," he goes on. "I thanked him for trusting me. Because for me, it was just remarkable that I had gone from being his adversary to helping raise his child, with his blessing. And what a beautiful child, you know?

"I told him that I was very proud, that I felt honored, to be Eddie's father. And that he could always be sure that I was going to treat Eddie like every other son of mine—that there would be no discrimination of any sort. Ed made some joke about that, almost as if to say, 'You can be tougher on him,' or something. And I had little tears in my eyes, and I think he might've made a little fun of that, too. But pretty soon he had tears in *his* eyes, so I reached out and held his hands. And he cried, and I cried. It was a very touching time.

"I left that meeting with a sense of, 'I've gotta do something,'" Peter says. "You know, 'This can't be where he ends up.'" Not long after that, Peter got in touch with Ed's father, who located a place for Ed at a convalescent home in Northbrook, Illinois.

Karen and Peter, meanwhile, had found another house they liked, a modern two-story in a well-tended neighborhood, situated at the end of a cul-de-sac at 458 Zarina Lane in Encinitas. But if they thought the new, larger home would act as a salve on their problems, they were wrong. It was in this home, on Zarina, that everything would come falling apart.

※◇※

Publicly, Eddie has said little about his parents' divorce, but it's clear from what he has said that he holds Peter entirely to blame. The way Eddie tells it, the family made sacrifices for years to put Peter through law school, and then Peter abandoned them just when the going got good.

"I made a little bit of money [modeling]," the singer said bitterly in 1991, "and that went towards my dad going to law school; my mom was waitressing to help put him through law school. And then as soon as he became this lawyer who had any money whatsoever, it was about six months of good times, and he bailed on everybody."

Peter doesn't remember it that way. In fact, he says, he tried everything he could think of to save his marriage. By August 1979, when he and Karen separated for the first time, they had already been in therapy for a year trying to work out their problems. According to Peter, even after their separation, he continued to push for a reconciliation.

"I tried for a year to save [the marriage]," he recalls. "I was living in a condo in La Costa, and I would bring over to the house ham and turkey dinners that I'd made over at the condo and surprise them. We'd all sit down to eat, and I remember one time, Mike looked around and kind of said what everybody was feeling—except Karen, perhaps. Which was 'The whole family's together again.' I can remember him saying that, and it was music to my ears, because I was trying so hard to save this marriage."

In November 1979, Peter arranged for a two-week European trip, and asked Karen to come away with him so that they could try to work out their differences. Karen agreed. The two departed from Chicago so they could attend the wedding of Karen's brother on the way to Europe, and

while in the Chicago area, they stopped to see Ed Severson at his convalescent home in Northbrook. It would be the last time Peter saw Ed in
person.

When they walked in, Ed was entertaining the nurses with tapes of
his old performances. During their brief visit, the two told Ed that they
were reconciling, news that Peter says pleased him. "He was encouraging us to save our marriage. We were always open about those types of
things."

Ed's surroundings were much nicer in the new convalescent home,
but his condition had worsened drastically. "He was terribly debilitated
at that point," says Peter. "He was obviously close to death, and we did
know that. I remember leaving there feeling that I had done everything I
could do at that point."

As Karen and Peter got up to leave that day, Karen leaned over to give
Ed a kiss good-bye. Clearly, the kiss reignited some fond memories.

"Wow," said Ed, winking at Peter. "She's still got the fire."

※◇※

Two weeks in Europe, concluding with a leisurely train trip from the
Italian Riviera to Greece, may have worked like a tonic on Peter and
Karen's marriage—according to Peter, Karen insisted during the trip that
he move back in again when they got home—but within a few months of
their living together again, the tonic began to seem more like snake oil.

"There would be these peaks and valleys, and then things would
calm down," Peter recalls. "Emotionally, Karen was extremely labile. I
mean, things were done that were just beyond my comprehension."

As the relationship went from bad to worse, there were a number of
what Peter refers to as "rip-roaring evenings"—the kind where anything
could happen, and often did. On one occasion, Peter says, he and the
boys looked all over the house for Karen before finally finding her hud-
dled in a closet, sobbing. Another time, there was a scene after Karen
had the family dog, Chewbacca, euthanized.

"The dog was part shepherd and part coyote, and it was chewing
through everything," says Peter. "Karen wanted to have the dog brought
to the pound, and I said, 'The only way I'll agree to that is if they won't
put the dog to sleep.' And without my knowledge, she did it. When I
found out, I called, but it was too late. They had already put the dog to
sleep."

When Peter confronted Karen about the dog, her response was telling: "How could you be so caring about a damn dog," he recalls her saying, "when my daughter is somewhere in Texas?"

Again and again, in Karen and Peter's discussions with their therapist, the daughter Karen had given up in 1967 had surfaced as a troublesome issue. "There was a lot of pain and insecurity arising from that adoption that our doctor felt it was important for Karen to have closure on," says Peter. In February 1980, desperate to do anything that might bring some peace to his marriage, Peter took the therapist's advice and started a search, working through a Texas attorney named Dermot Rigg.

Within a week, Rigg phoned Peter and Karen. He'd located the girl.

As she was still a minor, the attorney refused to divulge her name. But, he told Peter, he'd elicited a promise from the adoptive family that the girl would be told who her birth parents were when she turned eighteen. Rigg said he was also somewhat shocked to learn who the girl's adoptive parents were.

"Peter, I've tried a lot of cases, and I've handled a lot of stress," Mueller says Rigg told him, "but when the butler answered the phone and I learned who [the family was], I've never been more surprised. She is quite possibly the richest little girl in Houston."

Karen, receiving the news she had waited thirteen years to hear, was apparently less than overwhelmed.

"It sounds, Karen, like you're actually disappointed that we found her well off," Rigg is said to have commented. "It sounds like you wanted us to find her *not* well off, so you could bring her home."

Karen would finally meet her daughter, Gina, in 1986, when Gina was nineteen. As is often the case when birth mothers meet their lost offspring, the reunion would be bittersweet; Karen reportedly told writer Eric Blau that she found it less than ideal. Gina would stay in touch with all of the Mueller boys, though—including Eddie, who thanked her ("Sister Parish") in the liner notes of *Ten*.

But all of this was still years away. If Karen was touched by Peter's efforts to reunite her with her daughter, it wasn't evident to Peter, and just a few weeks after Rigg phoned with the news that Gina had been located, Peter decided that he'd done everything he could to make Karen happy, with the exception of leaving her alone.

For Peter's birthday that year, Eddie had given him a copy of the Kenny Rogers album *The Gambler*, featuring the song that was a radio hit at the time: "*You gotta know when to hold 'em / know when to fold* 'em. . . ." Whether the gift of that particular song held any significance for Eddie is unknown, but it did hold some significance for Peter.

In March 1980, he decided to fold 'em.

✖◆✖

As his parents' marriage crumbled around him, Eddie, age fifteen, was finishing his sophomore year at San Dieguito High School, where he had already begun to make a name for himself as a talented thespian. During his years at San Dieguito, he would appear in a number of productions, first as a chorus player (*Little Mary Sunshine*), and then almost always in lead roles (*Adam and Eve, Bye Bye Birdie, Outward Bound, Butterflies Are Free, The World of Carl Sandburg*). Asked what they remember most about Eddie, those who knew him in high school almost unanimously name his acting skills first. In his senior year, in fact, Eddie would be voted "Most Talented."

Though most of his old acquaintances say they were surprised to learn that Eddie chose music as a career, none of them appear surprised to have seen him become so successful at it. He is remembered as being very driven.

"My sisters and I always knew that Eddie would be famous," says Kerryanne Donohue, who lived across the street from the Muellers on Zarina Lane and was close to Eddie and his brothers during those years. "But we thought he was going to be an actor. We always went to see him in plays." Donohue remembers that Eddie talked often about wanting to be a successful actor, adding that she never hears the song "On Broadway" without thinking of him, because he treated it like a personal mantra, playing it constantly.

By 1980, music had become at least as important to Eddie as his acting; time and again, the singer has said that music was his primary refuge from the family drama that whirled around him during his last few years in high school. He'd begun dabbling in garage bands—neighbors often saw him sitting out on his bedroom balcony playing the guitar his parents had given him as a birthday present—and his growing record collection, remembered by friends as a "wall of records," was precious enough to him that it was strictly off-limits to his younger brothers.

"It was a big deal not to touch his records," says Scott Caesar, a former friend of Eddie's younger brother Jason. "He would go crazy, chase me and Jason all over the house. He loved his records—you didn't play with those."

For the most part, Eddie carried on like a normal teenage boy, right down to a growing interest in girls. Kerryanne Donohue, who imparts the tidbit that it was Eddie who gave her her first kiss, says, "He was real popular in high school. A lot of girls liked him, and in fact [my] mom would go out on dates, and he would bring his girlfriends over here to make out on the couch." As typical as his behavior was for a boy his age, though, Eddie was clearly unhappy about the discord wracking his parents' relationship. The subject, says Donohue, was a touchy one for him.

"I knew about it," she recalls, "but he didn't want to talk about it, so I didn't push. We just kept everything on the surface; it was kind of an avoidance thing. He'd ride his skateboard around the circle for hours, and I'd just listen to him, and he'd talk. He was a deep person—he tried to analyze *everything*. He was always looking for answers to things, and it seemed like he could never find them."

Donohue began seeing less of Eddie after Karen and Peter separated for the second time and Peter moved out, primarily because Eddie was older and had begun to spend more time with his high school friends, but also, apparently, because Karen disapproved of her sons keeping company with the Donohue girls.

"Peter had handled a case for me and was a good friend, but Karen didn't like me so much," says Sharon Donohue, Kerryanne's mother. "I never did know what her problem was."

In the winter of 1980, when Eddie was a few months into his junior year at San Dieguito and his sixteenth birthday loomed, Peter reevaluated his resolve to call the marriage quits for good and made one final attempt to reconcile with Karen. As a surprise for her and the boys, he purchased six round-trip tickets to Hawaii. "I was hoping she'd say, 'Sure, come along,' and we'd try another reunion," he recalls.

Instead, Karen announced that she wasn't going if Peter was.

Peter stayed behind while Karen, the boys, and Karen's mother, Marge—who used the ticket Peter had hoped to use himself—flew to Hawaii. As it turned out, Peter would not spend the time alone. Just before the family left for Hawaii, he'd met an attractive young woman at his apartment complex, and after he knew that he wouldn't be part of the Hawaiian getaway, he decided to take his new friend to San Francisco. The relationship didn't go anywhere, but Peter says the San Francisco fling finally helped him to feel more comfortable about dating other women.

Eddie, though, was clearly resentful of Peter's fledgling attempts to build a new life for himself without Karen. That same year, with Christmas around the corner, Peter stopped by the Zarina house one day to pick up some Christmas ornaments so that he could trim a tree at his condo. Eddie was livid when he found Peter bringing the ornaments down from the attic.

"He really spewed out his mind to me," Peter remembers. "That was the first time he'd ever talked to me like that."

In January 1981, just a few weeks after the incident between Peter and Eddie at Christmas, there was another unfortunate milestone: Ed Severson finally succumbed to his illness, dying at the age of forty in the Illinois nursing home where Karen and Peter had last visited him.

Peter claims Karen was so reluctant to see him at that point that it felt like an honor just to give her a ride to the airport. Karen went to the funeral by herself.

Eddie would never have the father-and-son talk with Ed that Karen and Peter had envisioned. But Peter's last communication with Ed, a month before Ed's death, did concern Eddie, and it resulted in a bit of symmetry more striking than either Peter or Ed ever could have predicted. Eddie's sixteenth birthday was approaching, and Peter had phoned Ed to suggest that they go in jointly on a gift. Karen had told them what Eddie wanted.

During the brief conversation, the two men had made plans to buy Eddie his first microphone.

✕◈✕

In the spring and summer of 1981, the opening salvos began in Karen and Peter's divorce, a dissolution so messy and drawn out that one San Diego judge would later tell Peter it was the worst divorce case he had ever seen. Before it was all over, Eddie would be dragged right into the middle of the fray.

Outwardly, Eddie was still plugging along, going about the business of being a high school junior. He had a new job as a stockboy at Long's Drugs, and a new girlfriend, Liz Gumble, whom he'd met when the two were cast together in a play. But by now, there were signs that the constant bickering between his parents was taking its toll on Eddie emotionally. Although he was still active in drama at San Dieguito—his drama teacher, Clayton Liggett, would in fact become one of Eddie's closest confidants*—his grades had begun to fall, and he'd started to miss classes. For Peter, who had college dreams for his "prodigal son," the changes were reason for alarm.

"I am very concerned about Eddie," Peter wrote to Karen in March 1981. "Why wasn't I consulted re Eddie's job? Why in hell is he working when his grades need improving? How does he expect to go to a good college unless he shines his last two years in high school, what colleges look at most for admissions?" In a second letter to Karen around that time, Peter was even more insistent that action be taken to bring Eddie's grades out of their slump: "I ask that we meet as soon as possible to discuss Eddie's extracurricular activities and promote whatever the counselors and doctors prescribe. . . . I believe that he must: 1. Discontinue outside jobs indefinitely; 2. Curtail band activities; 3. Meet with me and his counselors to see what he must do to cure his second year of poor performance."

In the letter, Peter also suggested that he and Eddie go into counseling together to work on their relationship, which he was convinced Karen was trying to sabotage. "I believe from what I've seen and heard that you are encouraging Eddie not to see me," he wrote. "Since I haven't seen or spoken with him for five months, I suspect the problem is severe."

After talking with Eddie's counselors, Peter bought the English, biology, and geometry books used by San Dieguito, so that he could help Eddie study the subjects he was falling behind in. He also—in a crowning touch that was almost certainly horrifying from Eddie's viewpoint—got permission to attend some of Eddie's classes. Apparently, Eddie managed to reverse his fate just before Peter actually tagged along to school with him and cost him his cool forever in the eyes of his classmates.

"He basically told me, 'Dad, I don't want you around,'" says Peter, laughing. "Don't blame you, kid. I probably scared him to death. It was too ambitious, and it didn't work out. But he was my first son, and I didn't want him to fail."

By now, Karen and Peter's attorneys were trading correspondence

*Eddie would dedicate "Long Road," a 1995 single released by Pearl Jam, to Liggett after Liggett's death.

fast and furious, with a focus on predictable grievances: Karen alleged that Peter wasn't paying enough in child and spousal support, and Peter contended that Karen was interfering with his visitation of the boys. As the hostility between the two escalated, Eddie and his brothers were apparently witness to a number of nasty verbal and physical exchanges between their mother and father, who now found it difficult to be in the same place at the same time without lashing out at one another.

Letters and court documents paint a grim portrait of Eddie's family life during those months. In March, as part of a divorce declaration, Karen asked for an order keeping Peter away from the Zarina house, citing an incident in which she alleged he'd broken the lock on the door, gone into her bedroom, removed a framed photograph from the wall and smashed it to pieces, leaving her "nervous, upset, hysterical and frightened." In August, via a letter from Peter's attorney to Karen's, Peter claimed Karen had attacked him when he dropped by the Zarina house to deliver child support: "Mrs. Mueller berated her husband in front of the children, commented on his financial abilities in a voice loud enough for the entire neighborhood to hear, and used vulgar and obscene language. . . . Mrs. Mueller then physically attacked her husband which resulted in medical treatment and analysis. . . ."

In late September, Karen's attorney filed a contempt of court claim against Peter, alleging that he was $1,900 in arrears on his support payments for the previous three months. Just after an October 8 hearing on the matter (during which the judge found Peter not in contempt, declaring that he in fact owed Karen less than $100) Karen and Peter met at an Escondido restaurant in an attempt to talk civilly about their case.

Despite all the legal wrangling, both had begun taking steps to put their lives together again, and during the meeting, they discussed their plans for the future and how those plans would affect the boys. Peter was in the midst of a new relationship. In June, he'd met a lovely, dark-haired computer engineer named Rose, whom he would marry the following February and who would make an immediate connection with the boys. Karen, meanwhile, had spent a few weeks with her mother in Skokie during August and renewed ties with some of her old acquaintances. The trip had been good for her, and now, she told Peter she'd decided to move back to Illinois. "Because of the circumstances," she said later, "I felt it was in the best interest of the children and me to get out of the state."

If Peter received this news less than enthusiastically, his reaction paled in comparison to Eddie's. Then a month into his senior year at San

Dieguito, Eddie was getting ready to open in a play when Karen dropped the bomb, and he was devastated by the news. "He enjoyed his intact family," Peter recalls. "He liked San Diego, and he didn't want there to be a Chicago involvement. It was very inconvenient for him."

In a later court deposition, Karen was tight-lipped about Eddie's reaction to the planned move, saying only that when she talked to him about it, Eddie told her that "he definitely wouldn't go with me." Asked pointedly whether Eddie was upset about the idea of leaving San Diego, Karen seemed defensive, responding, "We were all upset . . . we were all reacting to the situation."

Some much more strongly than others, if a serious physical confrontation that occurred between Karen and Eddie that October was any indication. Just after the meeting with Peter during which Karen announced her intent to leave San Diego, one of Eddie's younger brothers reported to Peter that Eddie and Karen had gotten into a fight in the Zarina hallway, Eddie wrestling Karen to the floor, choking her and only letting her up when she began gasping for breath. Karen later confirmed that an incident took place, but denied that the argument had anything to do with the move. Eddie would not talk about the confrontation at all.

Whether or not the fight with his mother was a manifestation of it, Eddie was clearly distraught about Karen's intent to leave California. He'd been so upset when he confided in Clayton Liggett about the move that a concerned Liggett had mentioned it to Peter, and Eddie's school records from the same period plainly reflect a disruption, showing several conferences with counselors and a number of unexplained absences that Karen had to meet with school officials to clear. For the next two months, Eddie remained adamant that he wanted to stay in San Diego when Karen returned to Illinois. In December, with the move right around the corner, Karen and Peter had a telephone conversation about the matter, the details of which are still in dispute.

According to Peter, Karen made an outright threat that she was going to tell Eddie he was adopted if Eddie insisted on remaining in San Diego.

"She told me, 'Pete, if Eddie decides to stay with you, I'm going to tell him he's adopted,'" Peter remembers. "I said, 'I don't think that would be healthy for Eddie,' and she said, 'Fuck you.'"

Karen, in a later court deposition, claimed that Peter's recollection of the conversation was inaccurate. According to Karen, she and Peter had been arguing, Peter had told her, "I bet that just to keep Eddie [from staying in] California, you'll tell him that he's adopted," and she had responded with a flip, "Yes, I probably would." She added that Peter should have known she wasn't serious when she made the comment—that "knowing me as a mother," Peter should have realized that there was no way she would tell Eddie something that important in anger.

In fact, Peter took the possibility of Karen's telling Eddie that he was adopted—especially in the midst of the emotional turmoil Eddie was already experiencing—very seriously. Immediately, he sought professional advice.

"I talked to two doctors and a priest," Peter recalls, "And all three of them told me, 'He shouldn't know now, it's too late, you made the mistake earlier, you should've told him earlier.' They said, 'Don't put it on him until he's in his twenties.'" Worried, Peter marched down to the courthouse and got a restraining order preventing either parent from discussing the adoption with Eddie.

Karen obeyed the order. In January 1982, when she and Eddie's brothers left for Illinois, Peter moved back in to the Zarina house and Eddie remained behind with him, still unaware that Peter was not his natural father. By the time the original restraining order expired, Peter was relaxed enough about the situation that he did not pursue a new one.

"I thought it was over," he says.

XOX

In interviews, Eddie has never even hinted that he lived with Peter after his mother and brothers returned to Illinois. He has always spoken of that time as if the entire family left San Diego while he remained in California by himself to finish high school, often claiming that the reason he didn't graduate was because it was such a struggle for him to support himself.*

"I had to explain to my teachers why I wasn't keeping up," Eddie told Robert Hilburn of the *Los Angeles Times* in 1994. "I'd fall asleep and things in class, and they'd lecture me about the reality of their classroom.

"I said one day, 'You want to see my reality?' I opened up my back-

---

*Although he did finish out his senior year at San Dieguito, Eddie was two credits short of graduation. Later, he would obtain a GED.

pack to where you usually keep your pencils. That's where I kept my bills . . . electric bills, rent. . . . That was my reality."

Eddie was living under Peter's roof during his senior year at San Dieguito and was, at least technically, in Peter's care. Also living in the Zarina home at the time was Fred Perkins, a friend and business acquaintance of Peter's who'd moved in with Eddie and Peter to share expenses.

Perhaps Eddie omits the time he spent living with Peter from his history because of his well-documented anger toward his father; perhaps he tells reporters he was on his own at that point because he *felt* like he was. It's possible that the truth about what transpired during those seven months in the Zarina house will never be entirely known, not because that time went unchronicled but, rather, because it was a time so complicated and fraught with changes for everyone involved that none of them could possibly have viewed it with any objectivity. Even fifteen years after the fact, separate accounts of those events are so obviously rooted in individual perception that it's necessary to hack through a dense thicket of pain, guilt, fear, and spite to arrive at some understanding of what actually occurred. And, though in Eddie's case the emotional fallout would be greatly heightened by the revelation of long-kept secrets surrounding his birth, what really emerges after all the thorns have been cut away is a story all too common for someone his age—a drama that was more than anything else a product of the time and social climate it played out in.

"I think the Seventies and Eighties were a really weird time for parenting, especially in the middle class," Eddie once told writer Steve Hochman. "Was that the 'Me Generation' or something? Parents were looking for their things, which means a lot of kids got left behind."

He clearly felt that he'd been one of those kids, describing the parenting he received as "inconsistent, and then nonexistent."

"I should be sending Pete Townshend cards for Father's Day," he remarked. "His records—that was more parenting than I got, just relating and having an outlet."

That's an accusation Peter Mueller still has some difficulty accepting. If Eddie was craving more attention from him during that time, Peter says, he never saw it. To the contrary, he recalls, Eddie seemed comfortable with their routine, and appeared to like the privacy and independence their living situation afforded him.

"Rose had her own condominium, and we had just been married,"

Peter remembers, "so I would sleep most of the nights over at Rose's place. I would get up early in the morning and drive to the house, get Eddie, and drive him to school. And then after work I'd go home, and be there when Eddie got home from work, which was often late. I didn't do that every day, but at least three out of five days every week. And then I'd drive back, and spend the night with Rose. I had a divided requirement. I was a new husband for this beautiful woman, and at the same time, I was the resource person and father for this young man who was very independent.

"He was *very* independent. He was working at Long's Drugs and going to school and acting. I noticed in him a desire for privacy, and I wanted to honor that."

Apparently, Eddie pretty much did as he pleased during those first few months, with minimal supervision from Peter. That all changed, though, when Peter began to perceive that Eddie was out of control. By late February, Fred Perkins had approached Peter and suggested that Eddie needed more discipline, telling him that Eddie was smoking pot regularly and even growing it in his bedroom. According to a later account by Perkins, Peter was slow to take action.

"On several occasions I spoke to Mr. Mueller as a friend to be more strict with his son," Perkins wrote in a later court declaration. "On each occasion we spoke about the subject, Mr. Mueller responded that he felt it would take time and [that] Eddie needed special consideration because of the stresses he had experienced during the break-up of the family."

But soon Rose, too, was expressing concern about Eddie. And in March, he was suspended from school twice, once for marijuana use and a second time for what San Dieguito assistant principal Roy Risner referred to as "physically attacking his girlfriend on the school campus." After Peter had to go to San Dieguito and meet with Risner to have Eddie reinstated, he went from neutral into overdrive on the parental gearshift, and seized on Eddie's marijuana use with a vengeance.

It's possible that, like many teenagers of divorced parents who are pushed too soon into adult responsibility and come to view pot the same way their elders viewed an after-dinner martini—a relief from the stresses of day-to-day life—Eddie was using the drug as an escape from his problems. But Peter, like many parents, now saw the drug as the cause rather than the result of those problems.

At the time, programs like ToughLove—a support group for parents of troubled teenagers founded by a pair of Pennsylvania family therapists in 1979—were becoming increasingly popular in the United States, no surprise in an era when the divorce rate was at its highest point since the Fifties, and newly single boomer parents all over the country were struggling to handle their unruly, emotionally troubled kids. Always quick to seek professional help in times of crisis, in late March Peter consulted a psychologist about the possibility of getting Eddie into therapy. Around the same time, he also spoke with Robert Bell, a business acquaintance whom he'd learned was the president and founder of Parent Alert, a ToughLove-type program that specialized in teenage drug use.

Bell told Peter about the measures Parent Alert suggested for such situations—among them strict enforcement of a "no drug" policy and regular room inspections. Peter decided the program was worth a try and began employing some of those strategies with Eddie. He disposed of a bong he found in Eddie's room and also insisted that Eddie remove the lock from his bedroom door.

According to Peter, Eddie had made a habit of entertaining his girl-friend, Liz, behind the locked door. Peter disapproved. "I was trying to cautiously bring him back to some form of responsibility with regard to this type of activity," says Peter. "I said, 'Eddie, you gotta get that lock off your door. That isn't appropriate, I'll give you your privacy as long as you maintain some form of responsibility.'"*

On the morning of April 8, 1982, just after Eddie's brothers arrived in San Diego from Illinois to spend their Easter vacation, Peter says he again found Eddie and Liz behind the locked door. Feeling as if he'd given Eddie fair warning, he broke the lock and forced his way into the room.

Presumably after a heated verbal exchange, Eddie and Liz stormed out of the house. When the two returned, Peter was downstairs in the kitchen making pancakes for Eddie's brothers. Shortly after they came back, he heard loud banging coming from upstairs and went to investigate. Eddie, he claims, had punched a hole in his bedroom door, and was in the bathroom running cold water on his hands.

Following is Peter's recollection of what happened next.

*Addressing an audience during a March 1994 concert in Murfreesboro, Tennessee, Eddie was obviously drawing from his own adolescence. "We all need our fuckin' privacy," he said from the stage. "Do you ever wonder why your mom and dad don't let you have a lock on your door? I still suffer from that. I need a lock on my fuckin' door. What the fuck is a door for if you can't have a lock on it? Tell your mom and dad I said hi . . . then fight for your rights as kids."

"I grabbed him around the back and said, 'That's it—you're out.' I started walking with him down the stairs, and he broke loose and went down the stairs. He caught himself at the bottom step on his hands, so he didn't hurt himself. He held on to the railing between the living room and the entry hall, and I went behind him to pick him up and pull him away from that railing and walk him out the front door. He was very powerful. He was only about 135 pounds, but it was all I could do to try and control him without hurting him."

At that point, Peter says, he put Eddie in a headlock, wrestled him to the floor, and lay on top of him. "I said, 'Eddie, I want you to calm down, and I want you to leave until you can come back and obey.' And he said, 'All right, Liz is all upset, it's okay now, I'll do what you want, let me up.' So I did.

"After I let him up, at the front door, I put my hands on his shoulders and said to him, 'You're not gonna remember much about this, but I never want you to forget I love you.' And boy, he just let loose with this *volley* of invectives. That was hard to hear. I said, 'That's permitted, you can talk to me that way, but when I tell you to do something, you need to listen and obey, otherwise you're not welcome here.' "

Eddie and Liz reacted by going straight to a nearby sheriff's substation and reporting the incident.

Later that afternoon, Peter was outside doing some work in the yard when two squad cars pulled up. He told the officers that the fight with Eddie had been part of a ToughLove confrontation, and that Eddie was welcome to come back home if he agreed to "listen and obey." The officers backed off, logging the incident as "settled, no report or action." In fact, says Peter, one of the deputies reached out and shook his hand, commending him for being "a father who cares."

Peter never seems to tell this story without adding the saccharine kicker about the cop shaking his hand. It's as if, fifteen years later, he still feels a little guilty about the altercation and needs to reassure himself that, in demanding that Eddie leave until he agreed to follow the house rules, he was doing the right thing.

Whatever the experts—or Eddie—would say, Peter claims he and Eddie were on much better terms after Eddie had some time to cool off. Rose, who always got along well with Eddie, found him later that evening and had a long talk with him, after which he agreed to come home. He complained of a stiff neck that night and would visit a chiropractor later in the week for treatment. Peter and Rose say they urged him to see an orthopedic surgeon in case his neck was seriously injured, but he refused. According to Peter, there was a noticeable improvement in Eddie's attitude after the confrontation—so much so that he decided to buy Eddie a car, a blue 1968 Mustang that Eddie promptly christened with a Talking Heads bumper sticker. Eddie accepted the car gratefully. But within a few months he would make it crystal clear that all was not forgiven.

In early June, after school let out in Illinois, Eddie's brothers again returned to San Diego, this time for a month-long visit. Eddie was home that day and very anxious to see them; Rose says she'll never forget the sight of him running down the stairs when they arrived and sweeping the youngest, Mike, into an off-the-ground bear hug. "It made me want to cry," she recalls. "He just missed his brothers so much."

Eddie's brothers apparently felt the same way. Within a week, Chris began asking Peter if he could move back to California.

Chris had already spoken to Karen in Illinois about wanting to live with his dad, and she'd told him to wait until a later date to make that decision. But she apparently had no intention of consenting. When Peter called her that June to discuss Chris's request, she told him in no uncertain terms that if he moved for a change of custody, she would oppose it.

By the second week of July, with Chris still firm that he wanted to move to California, Peter relied on habit and called in a professional for advice, taking Chris to a psychologist for an evaluation.

"Mr. Mueller indicated that his son had voiced his preference to live with his father," Dr. William Dess noted in the report on his July 12 meeting with Chris, "and Mr. Mueller desired assistance in determining whether this was indeed his son's preference, or whether his son was merely struggling with loyalty issues between his father and mother."

Dess met conjointly with Chris, Peter, and Rose and then conducted separate interviews with both Rose and Chris. If what ten-year-old Chris told the psychologist during their session was accurate, Karen was in a panic about the prospect of the custody change—and was apparently not beyond manipulating her son with guilt in an effort to thwart it.

"Chris was very clear in verbalizing his desire to live with his father," wrote Dess, "despite what he claimed were phone conversations with his mother putting pressure on him to live with her. He reported rather sensitively and with some grasp of his mother's pain how she allegedly indicated to him, 'I can't live without you' and 'He's [father] taken my house and now he's trying to take my children.'

"He seemed to care for his mother very much," Dess went on, "believes that both his mother and father love him, and was able to engage in some analysis regarding the pros and cons of leaving his mother and coming to live with his father . . . and was rather unwavering in his desire to come live with his father. On the other hand, he did not wish to hurt his mother and seemed concerned about what her reaction might be about his decision. . . ."

XOX

From a sworn declaration by Fred Perkins, February 3, 1983:

> During July, 1982 I observed that Edward's behavior had reverted to anger and hostility. Shortly thereafter, I learned that the Petitioner, Karen Vedder, was in California.

XOX

From a *Rolling Stone* interview with Eddie, October 1993:

> She came out with the specific purpose to tell me that this guy wasn't my father. I remember at the time I was like, 'I know he's not my father, he's a fucking asshole.' And she said, 'Oh, Eddie, he's really not your father.' At first I was pretty happy about it, then she told me who my real father was.
>
> . . . There was a piano in the room, and I remember really wishing I knew how to play a happy song. I was happy for about a minute, and then I came down. I had to deal with the fact that he was dead. My real father was not on this earth. I had to deal with the anger of not being told sooner, not being told while he was alive.
>
> I was a big secret.

XOX

From a 1983 court deposition given by Karen Vedder, during which she was asked what she told Eddie when she revealed to him that he was adopted:

> I just explained to him the whole circumstances of his father's and my love and marriage and relationship and his birth and

everything leading up to [Peter's] and my marriage, and he was
upset that his stepfather had not been more understanding of
everything that went on than he was.

※◇※

It's uncertain why Karen chose the precise moment she did to reveal to
Eddie that Peter was not his natural father. What is known is that,
shortly after Peter filed for custody of Chris, Karen arrived unexpectedly
in San Diego; that she helped Eddie move out of the Zarina house
during a weekend when Peter, Rose, and Eddie's brothers were vaca-
tioning in Big Bear; and that with her assistance, Eddie moved into
the home of Richard and Susan Muir, mutual friends of Karen and
Peter's with whom Eddie would live for the next six months. Whether
Karen told Eddie he was adopted before he moved out of Peter's home
or after he moved out is still a matter of dispute between Karen and
Peter.

Peter and Rose still believe that Karen told Eddie about his adoption
prior to his moving out of the Zarina house—that Karen's news, coming
at a time when Eddie and Peter were already experiencing tension, was
in fact the catalyst for Eddie's leaving. The two cite a conversation they
say Chris had with Rose during the vacation at Big Bear, indicating that
he knew Eddie was adopted.

"During a July weekend in Big Bear, California, the weekend that
Eddie left the Encinitas home, my stepson, Christopher, spoke to me
privately about adoption," Rose said in a later court declaration. "The
conversation occurred just after Christopher had spent approximately
two and one half (2½) days with his mother and brother, Eddie, at another home in Encinitas, California, after his mother had driven to California from Chicago shortly after my husband filed a change of custody
request concerning Christopher.

"Paraphrasing Christopher's questions, he asked whether parents
sometimes do not tell their children they are adopted until they are
teenagers, especially when one of the child's natural parents has died.
When we returned to Encinitas to find Eddie had left the home, I expressed my concern to my husband about the coincidence."

Karen, on the other hand, has always maintained that Chris couldn't
have known Eddie was adopted at that point. Though she admitted in a
1983 court deposition that she had made the trip to California that July
specifically to tell Eddie about his adoption, she claimed she hadn't re-

vealed the secret to Eddie until "after he had moved out of Peter's house and he came to me confused and upset about the way his father was treating him."

As for *why* Karen chose that particular moment in time to tell Eddie that he was adopted, Peter believes she had a very deliberate purpose. "She wanted to break up the relationship between Eddie and me," he says, "because it was putting her at risk with regard to Chris."

It's uncertain how Karen would respond to that allegation, but what can't be questioned is that after his mother told Eddie he was adopted, she did enlist him in her battle against Peter for custody of Chris—and in a manner that was practically guaranteed to sever any bond that was left between Eddie and Peter.

On August 16, Karen filed in opposition to the custody change, citing in a host of reasons why Chris should remain with her in Illinois. Most of Karen's declaration was fairly standard family court fare, describing how well Chris had adapted to life in Skokie and alleging that "except during periods of discipline or when we have disagreements, Christopher had not at any time while we were in Skokie, Illinois, indicated that he wanted to live with his father." Elsewhere in the document, she questioned Peter's fitness as a parent, alleging that when the boys visited him in Encinitas they were "left alone much of the time and there was no adult supervision," and that "they eat junk food . . . seldom if ever are substantial meals prepared."

The strongest accusations in Karen's declaration concerned Peter's alleged treatment of Eddie. "It is of great concern to me that because of the Respondent's tantrums and his violent temper that he is going to find it difficult to cope with Christopher who is 10 years of age," Karen stated. "During the time that Edward, our oldest son, stayed with the Respondent in the Encinitas residence, the Respondent was seldom home in that he spent most of his time at his girlfriend's residence. Eddie found himself at home most of the time. . . .

"It is also of great concern to me that the Respondent's behavior towards Eddie as demonstrated during the period of time that Eddie lived with him will sometime in the future also be demonstrated towards Christopher whenever the Respondent cannot cope with situations. Attached to this response is the Declaration of our son, Eddie Mueller. I ask that his Declaration be made part of this responsive declaration, herein incorporated by reference and made part of this response."

XOX

Eddie's declaration—which was included along with Karen's in the filing and would within four months find itself at the center of an entirely separate court action—made Karen's look like a Hallmark card.

In the declaration, seventeen-year-old Eddie stated that Peter was seldom home, and that after Easter Peter had told him he had to budget and had then stopped giving him money for expenses at all, requiring him to support himself entirely from his part-time salary from Long's Drugs. He claimed that Peter seldom ate at home and rarely bought groceries; that Peter seldom talked with him; and that he was constantly reprimanded by Peter and made to feel that everything he said and did was wrong.

More disturbing was Eddie's account of the Easter confrontation between him and Peter four months earlier.

Contrary to Peter's version of the incident, Eddie alleged that during the altercation Peter had hit him and punched him, pushed him down the stairs, and then grabbed him and thrown him onto the cement on the front patio. He claimed that after he visited a chiropractor for his stiff neck, Peter became angry about it and "told me not to see a doctor anymore."

By the time he moved out of the Zarina house, Eddie stated, he was unable to sleep because of the fear he had developed of his father. "I was so nervous and fearful that during that time I contemplated committing suicide," he wrote. "I never said that to anyone, but I submit to the court that on several occasions I thought this would be the only way to handle it."

In a closing paragraph that Peter describes as "the real reason [Eddie's declaration] was written," Eddie said that he hoped Peter's alleged behavior would be taken into consideration before any of his brothers were allowed to live with Peter on a full-time basis.

Peter was shocked when he received a copy of the filing. It was not, he says, written by the Eddie he knew. "This was the product of an agenda," he says. "It was written by a child who was heavily, at least at the time, dependent upon drugs. . . . And it was postured in a way that would be most damaging to my request to have Chris come and live with both of us."

Peter characterizes Eddie's claims as half-truths and exaggerations. For example, he says, while it's true that Eddie's paychecks from Long's Drug did help with food and household expenses, Eddie was never in a position where he had to support himself entirely with his own money. As for Eddie's version of the Easter confrontation, Peter says he never once struck or punched his son, nor did he throw him down the stairs or onto the concrete patio outside.

"*He* never claimed I did until he wrote this declaration," Peter notes. "I mean, he signed the declaration in August, but the incident occurred in April." Eddie's claim that Peter got angry with him after he saw the chiropractor, Peter says, was similarly skewed. "That's just not *true*," he says. "I told him, 'I don't want you to see a chiropractor, Eddie—if you've got an injury to your neck, we want you to see an orthopedic surgeon.' And *he* didn't want to do that. That makes me look *terrible*."

Convinced that Eddie's declaration was a product of heavy coaching on the part of Karen and her attorneys, Peter began rounding up witnesses who could corroborate his side of the story. Within a few months, he'd produced a raft of documentation countering Eddie's claims of abuse, much of it focusing on Eddie's alleged drug use and out-of-control behavior.

San Dieguito assistant principal Roy Risner supplied a letter describing Eddie's attitude as "one of the most hostile that I have witnessed in my twenty years in education," claiming that Eddie was "often under the influence of marijuana" and opining that Eddie was a "disturbed young man who needs counseling and guidance." Another of Eddie's counselors provided a letter about Peter's visits to San Dieguito during Eddie's junior and senior years, describing Peter as being "sincerely interested in Eddie's welfare, his education, and in his future." Roland Fleck, the psychologist Peter had consulted just prior to the Easter confrontation, confirmed Peter's meeting with him about Eddie, stating that Peter's primary concerns had been Eddie's "destructive outbursts of anger," his "problems with drug usage," and his "problems in school including a recent suspension for marijuana usage."

Fred Perkins also wrote a declaration, describing the living situation at 458 Zarina from his point of view and offering his take on Eddie's emotional state.

"Rather than suicidal," he wrote, "I believe that Eddie displayed anger, disobedience and open hostility, to which his father responded often too leniently and slowly to my liking, when he responded at all." Of the Easter 1982 incident between Eddie and Peter, Perkins stated that he saw no bruises on Eddie afterward, adding that Eddie appeared to be on good terms with both Peter and Rose the same evening. In summary, he asserted that Eddie's declaration, "if not completely false and untrue," presented "a completely exaggerated and distorted picture of the relationship that I observed between father and son and stepmother and stepson during the four and one half months I observed that relationship."

Rose, too, gave a declaration stating that she had not observed any bruises following the Easter incident and recalling that she and Peter had advised Eddie to see an orthopedic surgeon for his stiff neck, adding that she had observed what she believed to be "Eddie's positive response to our concern and the guidelines that his father and I had established for living together."

Rose made it clear that she believed Karen's telling Eddie he was adopted was responsible for the anger he harbored toward Peter. "I . . . believe that Eddie has been told that he is not his father's natural son," Rose wrote. "If this is the case, I believe it essential that we all know the truth so that parenting can resume without secrets and feelings of guilt and doubt among us all."

By the time all of these statements were taken, the possibility that Eddie's declaration might prevent Peter from gaining custody of Chris was no longer even an issue. "I later withdrew the petition for Chris," Peter recalls, "because the doctor told me that his younger brother, Mike, would be at risk if he lost his best friend back in Chicago."

Eddie's declaration would never be considered in the matter regardless. Armed with the documents and statements he'd collected chronicling Eddie's alleged drug abuse and emotional problems, Peter convinced Karen's attorneys that Eddie was not credible enough to be believed—that they'd made a serious legal misstep to have incorporated his declaration into their filing. Eventually, he would sue them for malicious prosecution and abuse of process, alleging in the suit that Eddie's declaration was a result of their "direction, influence, suggestion and prompting with the ulterior motive to discourage [Peter] from further attempts to pursue custody of [Chris]."

The suit would end in a settlement, but well before that, Peter obtained an agreement from Karen and her attorneys to withdraw Eddie's declaration. In March 1983, a judge made it official, ordering the document sealed and expunged from the record.

✖◈✖

"Eddie was very upset when this was sealed," Peter says, fingering a copy of Eddie's declaration during a visit to his San Diego law office. "It was his way of speaking out against me."

Peter mentions this almost as an aside; it's as if he makes no connection at all between the Eddie he knew then—an angry, emotionally troubled teenager whose attempt to "speak out against" his father was deemed invalid by the grown-ups—and the Eddie known by millions today, an angry young man whose stock in trade is an uncanny ability to empathize with the emotionally muzzled child. Time and again, and more evocatively than any other writer of his generation, Eddie has pitted adolescents against authority figures who either shut them out or shut them up, almost always to tragic result.

As Peter has revisited his own family's tragedy, reading aloud from Eddie's 1982 declaration and itemizing his son's old accusations against him, he has been responding to each of Eddie's statements with a qualifier. "That's half true," he will say, or "I think that's a mischaracterization."

When he gets to the portion of the document in which Eddie states that he felt constantly reprimanded and contemplated suicide, Peter appears ready to launch into another round of defensive commentary. He is brought up short, though, by a simple question. Isn't it possible that, even if Peter didn't perceive those particular statements to be true, Eddie did?

Peter is silent for a moment before answering. "If he felt that way, he didn't express it, you know? He never told me.

"I don't know what Eddie really felt," he goes on. "I mean, we were constantly asking Eddie, Rose and I, to come and see Dr. Dess, and he refused. We knew he was going through trials. . . . I wanted guidance with regard to the drugs, I wanted guidance from Dess with regard to the adoption, I wanted these things to be brought out. But I never observed him to be suicidal. I observed him to be quite the opposite, to be very productive, and to be satisfied with me constantly. Probably more disturbing to me than the issue of suicide was the fact that he characterized me as being indifferent to him. That probably hurt a lot more."

If Peter was not indifferent to his son, he does appear to have been so caught up in discrediting Eddie's declaration, clearing his own name, and exacting retribution from Karen and her attorneys that he never really considered how his actions would be experienced by Eddie. Even if Eddie's declaration *was* filled with misstatements, exaggerations, and half-truths, how must it have been for Eddie to watch his father work the system against him as if he were just another legal opponent, rounding up a cavalcade of witnesses to attest that Eddie was a fuckup and did not deserve to be believed; that the only possible explanation for Eddie's version of the truth was that he'd been stoned when he offered it; that Eddie's thoughts and feelings were simply invalid, and should be given no credence whatsoever? It's telling that when Eddie talks about Peter in interviews today, he usually limits his description to a few well-chosen epithets. But he almost always mentions that his father was a lawyer.

Peter seems to recognize that while his legal expertise put him at an advantage in his court battles with Karen, his willingness to ply that savvy on his ex-wife was hardly conducive to healing the family's wounds. "I was unable at the time, in the passion of the events, to separate my lawyer skills from my fatherly responsibility," he says. "And I filed lawsuits. Those lawsuits were what a good lawyer would have filed, but they were lawsuits that a good father would have told the lawyer to forget about."

Yet, the one lawsuit Peter says he doesn't regret filing—the malicious prosecution suit against Karen and her attorneys, which he says finally "cauterized" the litigation between him and Karen—is the one that likely did the most damage to his relationship with Eddie, not only because of Eddie's direct involvement via the sealed declaration, but also because the proceedings were an ordeal for Karen, something she surely did not hide from Eddie. Peter represented himself in the suit and even cross-examined Karen during her deposition, the transcript of which makes for a distinctly uneasy reading experience.

"She was very frightened, obviously, and annoyed that I was taking her deposition," Peter recalls. "But that deposition was the only time I could ever find out from Karen on a demand basis . . . what she had told Eddie [about his adoption]."

Peter never did get a chance to talk to Eddie about his adoption. Although he blames that largely on Karen, saying that Eddie's negative opinions of him are primarily the result of a longtime "campaign of brainwashing" on Karen's part, his own actions following Eddie's move out of the Zarina house could hardly have helped his case.

During the time when Eddie was living with Richard and Susan Muir, he was virtually in hiding from Peter, refusing to talk to him at all and trying to keep his whereabouts a secret. Peter, who says he was frantic because Eddie had taken his Mustang with him when he moved out—the car was still insured in Peter's name and needed to be reinsured—went to a local deputy and had him arrange a meeting between him and Eddie.

"He called Eddie in, and Eddie and I sat down, and I explained what I needed the car for," Peter recalls. "Eddie said he would think about it."

Five months passed with no word from Eddie. In December, Fred Perkins happened to see Eddie's Mustang in Richard Muir's driveway and reported it to Peter.

"Rich and I had been friends for years," says Peter. "I was shocked to find out that Eddie was living with Richard and Richard hadn't told me. I called a judge who was a friend of ours, and when I called the judge, his secretary said, 'Oh, yeah, your son's living with Richard.' I said, 'Oh, god, how do you know? Why don't I know?' So the judge sat down with Rose, Richard, and me, and I said, 'Richard, the only thing I'm concerned about is that car. I need to have it insured.'"

About a week after this meeting, Peter repossessed the Mustang. Despite his insistence that he simply wanted to reinsure it, he never did, nor did he ever return it to Eddie. Asked why, Peter says that by that point, he was in a financial bind and could not afford a new policy on the car. He claims he attempted to sell it, but that it had frame damage and could not be repaired. Eventually, it wound up on the junk heap.

Peter insists that he did not repossess Eddie's car "because I wanted to do him wrong," but that's clearly how Eddie saw it. As late as 1994, he was still making thinly veiled references to Peter's taking his car away. "I resented everybody around me who drove up in a car that someone provided for them . . . [with] insurance that someone provided for them," he told Robert Hilburn of the *Los Angeles Times*. "I'd be underneath some shelf putting price tags on tomato soup and I'd watch them come in. . . . Obnoxious with their prom outfits on, buying condoms and being loud about it. . . . Maybe I would have been doing that too, if the circumstances were different. . . . Maybe that would have made me more forgiving, but I wasn't very forgiving at all. Everything was just such a fucking struggle. . . ."

Eddie moved out of Richard Muir's house around the same time that Peter took the Mustang back. As Peter recalls it, during the meeting with a judge over the return of the Mustang, Richard Muir had requested that Eddie move out, telling Peter that he couldn't handle Eddie anymore. Muir, reached by phone at his office in San Diego, said this was not true. When asked for details, he declined to say more.

Rose helped Eddie move out of the Muirs' that December. He stored his things temporarily in the Zarina garage and then moved into an apartment, which was clearly a financial stretch for him. Rose kept tabs on Eddie as best she could, sneaking him groceries and honoring his request that she not tell Peter where he was. He lasted only a few months there.

Peter had very little contact with Eddie after that point. He claims

Eddie decided to "try out living with me again" that spring, but that Eddie only stayed a few nights before "something developed for him in Chicago" and he returned to Illinois to live with Karen. Despite the fact that he had been out of touch with his son for months by that point, the only thing Peter seems to remember about the time Eddie spent with him that spring is that when Eddie returned to Illinois, he took with him a microcassette recorder belonging to Peter. Peter says he made repeated attempts to get in touch with Eddie and ask him to return the recorder, but that Eddie would not respond. Just as he had done when he wanted the Mustang back, Peter enlisted the cops.

"I called a juvenile officer in Skokie, and he called Eddie, and Eddie sent it back," Peter recalls. "He sent a little tape with it. And on the tape he told me he was sorry he had taken it, that he was just interested in the way it worked. I felt remorse at that point that I had involved the sheriff. But it was crucial for my work."

X◈X

Eddie would stay in Illinois for only a few years, and he spent that time getting his life—and his goals—in order. While waiting tables at Don's Fishmarket, a seafood restaurant in Skokie, he hit if off with Beth Liebling, an employee at a neighboring eatery with whom he would form the strongest and most stable relationship of his life. He enrolled in drama classes—and also obtained his GED—at Oakton Community College. Meanwhile, he continued to pursue his interest in music. In the spring of 1984, he took a job as a bassist in a wedding band called Chariot, playing about ten gigs' worth of Styx and Journey covers in order to earn enough money for him and Beth to return to San Diego.

"He was a guitar player, so I had to buy him a bass and give him $50 to buy clothes," the band's leader, Bill Applehans, later told the *Chicago Tribune*. "Every check I gave him . . . maybe $800 total, I think he saved. It was his ticket out of town. He was a quiet, clean-cut kid who wanted to go to L.A. and become Pete Townshend. He didn't play that good and he was barely there as a background singer. But he was really workable, really willing to learn and practice."

By late 1984, Eddie was back in California, working double shifts to support himself and bouncing from one band to another in an attempt to find his niche. Six years later, exorcising the demons of his adolescence on a home four-track in accompaniment to a demo supplied by Jeff Ament and Stone Gossard, he finally did.

Peter has not spoken to Eddie since 1983. Around Christmastime in 1985, he says, one of his sons gave him a photo of Eddie and his brothers. According to Rose, the photo was a peace offering from Eddie. Peter isn't sure about that, but he likes to think that it's true. He keeps the photo on his office desk in San Diego.

Peter still remembers the day he bought a copy of *Ten* and read the lyrics to "Alive," Eddie's account of the day Karen told him the truth about Peter and Ed.

"There's a shopping mall called North County Fair," he recalls, "and they have one of the big chains where they sell rock music discs. I walked in there and got the album, and as they were ringing it up on the cash register, I was nervously opening it to read the lyrics.

"I was just *trembling* with excitement," he goes on. "I mean, this was a hallmark moment. Then I started reading the lyrics. And my heart just sank as I saw the lyrics to 'Alive.' I just stood there transfixed, reading this. People were wondering, I'm sure, why I was stopping the traffic. But it was almost like an out-of-body experience, standing there and seeing his feelings about me."

That night, Peter wrote to Eddie, enclosing a poem he'd composed as an answer to "Alive." It was the first attempt Peter had ever made to communicate with Eddie about his adoption, and about Ed.

Eddie would never see the poem. As Peter would do with all of the other letters he wrote to Eddie over the years, he stopped short of mailing it, afraid that after all the time that had passed, Eddie would only think he was trying to "ride the wave" of his son's fame.

He has done a little surfing over the years on an involuntary basis, usually winding up in the undertow. Eddie's comments about Peter in interviews have never been flattering. But he displays a surprisingly philosophical attitude about the way his son has portrayed him.

"Well," he says, "I'm hurt by it, but on the other hand, I have a different perspective. And my hope is that maybe some day, there'll be an opportunity for a meeting between us that will give him a chance to get all his anger out, and at the same time, provide me with a chance to clarify some of the things that he may want to talk about."

The rift between Eddie and Peter has been problematic for Eddie's brothers, who are still in touch and on good terms with Peter, but who also, apparently struggle with a sense of divided loyalty. "Eddie will come on television at our home, and they won't watch it in the same room with us," says Peter. "They go into a different room . . . they can't accept Eddie and me in the same room."

After Pearl Jam's rise to fame, Eddie's relationship with his mother would also go through a few rough patches, due to Eddie's perception that Karen was a little too interested in basking in the Pearl Jam spotlight. "Once the band got going," Eddie later told *Spin*, Karen's identity "became that of being my mom, and she forgot that she was special for everything she had achieved on her own."

Karen's biggest gaffe on this front was a promotional campaign she did for Chicago's Q101 FM in 1993, around the time *Vs.* was released. A frequent listener of the station, Karen had phoned Q101 and introduced herself the morning after the 1992 MTV Awards, when she heard one of the Q101 jocks opine that Eddie had been stoned at the show. "Eddie wasn't stoned," she told listeners during an on-air interview that morning, "Eddie's just weird. That's just Eddie."

Following the brief interview, Karen took to calling Q101 with updates or corrections on their Pearl Jam reporting, and developed a rapport with one of the deejays there. "Eddie's mom would call Carla and just say, 'Hi, what's going on,' recalls Bill Gamble, then the station's program director. "It was just this basic deejay/listener thing that was going on." When Q101 came up with the idea of having Karen do promotional spots for a Pearl Jam weekend they'd planned to coincide with the release of *Vs.*, Gamble says, Karen was eager to participate.

"She thought it was great," Gamble recalls. "She got a great kick out of it. She drove down, we put her in a production studio, we talked for a while, recorded some things, and put them on the air. 'Hi, this is Karen Vedder, Eddie's mom, call now to win a copy of *Vs.*, and qualify to see my son Eddie and the band in Seattle.' She recorded a few one liners for us, we had a cup of coffee and a few laughs, and that was it. There was no in-depth interview. But it came back to us via Eddie's record label that he was not pleased. Not even a *tiny* bit pleased. He was furious that his mom would get on the air."

"Obviously, this caused a huge rift between us," Eddie said of his relationship with Karen following that episode. "At the time, I felt like there was ego involved on her side. Like, 'Why would you do this? Why is this important to your personal makeup?' And I think we've gotten through some of that, we're dealing with that. We're in a cool-down period. She just wants everything to be back to normal. I'd love to simplify things. It just seems like it's getting more complicated every day."

In the past fifteen years, Peter and Karen have both made revealing career choices, their personal goals—much like their son's songs—very obviously shaped by the events that shattered their family. Karen, after going back to school and earning a master's degree, ran a home for single mothers; in recent years, she has been a tireless proponent of open adoption. In March 1997, when the open records advocacy group Bastard Nation held a public-awareness rally at the Oscars to celebrate the nomination of the British film *Secrets and Lies*, Karen was among the members there handing out flyers, and turned up in a few newscasts on the event. Peter, meanwhile, has made his living as a divorce attorney, representing only fathers. In yet another unsent letter to Eddie, he once explained that he set up his practice that way "not out of anger, or from a grudge, but to help them do it better than I did . . . so that their families don't have to suffer what ours did." He's seen some nasty cases in his day.

"This kind of thing happens in families all the time," Peter says. "It's just that in our case, Eddie became an international star."

Part Four

✳ ◎ ᥎ ⌗

Around the Bend

Sixteen

Fun with Papa Neil / Roman Holiday / Mike Does Dublin / The Shoe Show / Spit Happens: Brawl on the Bayou / I Passed Out on the Drum Riser, and All I Got Was This Lousy T-Shirt / Ticketmaster Plays Scrooge / Flu Year's Eve / My Generation / Trouble in Italy

With *Vs.* in the can, Pearl Jam took off for Europe, where they'd been booked to open a series of late June/early July 1993 shows for Neil Young and U2. The Neil Young outing, which took the band to Norway, Sweden, and Finland, only served to reinforce Pearl Jam's affection for the so-called Godfather of Grunge.

"We needed to see that," Stone remarked later. "The whole 'getting huge' thing is a pretty strange phenomenon. . . . It was good to see some low-key veterans go up there and totally rock and have a good time with each other."

Eddie felt the same way, by this point having added Young to his growing list of father figures. "I'm happy to have an adult in my life who leads by example," he said of Young. "I've had some crazy adults in my life, and it's about time I got one who inspires me."

The U2 shows, unfortunately, were distinctly *un*inspiring—four sold-out stadium gigs in Verona and Rome, Italy, that were by all accounts a miserable experience for the band. "That week was a nightmare," Dave remembers. "*Everybody* was on edge."

In the early days of their career, U2 had devoted just as much energy as Pearl Jam to avoiding the trappings of their sudden fame; like Pearl Jam, they'd become almost as well known for their dogged political correctness as they were for their music. By 1993, though, U2 had largely made peace with their star status, and even as they lampooned their own fame with the flamboyant, tongue-in-cheek Zoo TV tour, they were also, quite unabashedly, enjoying its perks. Whatever message the stage show itself conveyed to U2's fans, behind the scenes the tour was virtually indistinguishable from any other Big Rock spectacle then traversing the globe, an opulent media circus booked into cavernous stadiums, with a huge entourage and no shortage of limos, four-star hotels, splashy parties, and celebrity hangers-on.

It was a scene Eddie would have professed to hate in any case, but to add insult to injury, U2's Italian fans gave Pearl Jam an indifferent reception. For Eddie, this was the rancid icing on the cake, and he did not bother to hide that during Pearl Jam's sets, especially at the shows in Rome. When fans in the first few rows pelted Pearl Jam with plastic bottles, yelling, "Fuck you," Eddie yelled right back at them. "Fuck me?" he asked peevishly. "Okay, you fuck me, and then Bono will come out and fuck *you*." He took an almost fiendish delight in baiting U2 from the stage, donning devil and fly masks in answer to Bono's onstage personas Macphisto and The Fly and duct taping "Paul Is Dead" (Bono's real name is Paul Hewson) onto his T-shirt.

Backstage during the Italian shows, things were equally tense. Pearl Jam barely got a sound check before the two Verona gigs—a situation that would be remedied after they complained to U2 drummer Larry Mullen, Jr., at an aftershow party—and in Rome, Eddie blew a gasket over an interview Dave wanted to do with *Modern Drummer*.

Just before the tour, in response to Eddie's concerns about the band's overexposure, Pearl Jam had agreed that they would only do interviews for a handful of magazines in promotion of *Vs.* But Dave had agreed to do the *Modern Drummer* interview, for a cover story that would appear in December 1993, months before the band decided to limit their press, around the same time that Stone and Jeff had been doing cover stories for *Guitar Player* and *Bass Player*. The way Dave saw it, he was entitled to do a solo interview just as Stone and Jeff had, and since he'd consented to the interview well before the antipress edict came down, he thought it only fair that he be allowed to honor the commitment. Eddie, however, did not agree.

According to Dave, Lance Mercer had taken photos of him during the

U2 shows in Verona for use in the *Modern Drummer* story, and he and Mercer were discussing shipment of the photos to the magazine when Eddie walked into the band's trailer and overheard them.

"I don't want you to do that cover," he says Eddie told him. When he protested, he recalls, Eddie left the room, returning a few minutes later with Kelly Curtis.

"Maybe it's not the best time for you to do this," Curtis said.

"Man, *everybody* knew I was doing this," Dave shot back. "Jeff did a cover, Stone did a cover, and this just happens to be when this one is coming out."

"Just call 'em and tell 'em no," he recalls Eddie saying. "Tell 'em to find somebody else, you'll do it in the spring."

"These guys are my friends, and this is an awesome thing," said Dave, irritated. "I'm not just gonna tell 'em to fuck off!" When he tried to enlist support from the other band members, the issue became a "huge huff."

"No one would deal with it," Dave recalls. "Everybody in the band was like, 'I don't want to hear it, just be neutral about it.'" When he made a last appeal to Kelly Curtis, he says, Curtis was far from encouraging: "Do what you think is right, but be prepared to suffer the consequences."

Given the pressure-cooker atmosphere and Curtis's rather ominous advice, it might have been wise to back down at that point. But Dave didn't. "I decided to go ahead and do it," Dave says, "because that *was* the right thing to do. The guy's deadline was just a couple of days away. Everyone knew it had been offered to me months and months before, and it was important to me. It wasn't about selling gear, and it wasn't about politics and bullshit. It was a magazine I'd read all my life. Eddie said it was a 'press thing,' that he didn't want us saturating the press. I told him, 'It's a *drum* magazine, for Christ's sake. It's only on one out of fifty newsstands that the guitar and bass player magazines are on!' You know, you have to *look* for these magazines. It was just some weird trip. For some reason, he didn't want *me* to do that interview."

Given the focus of Eddie's own interviews around that time, he may have been less concerned about the circulation of the *Modern Drummer* piece than he was about his inability to control its content. In stark contrast to Dave, who'd never made it a secret that he was enjoying Pearl Jam's good fortune, Eddie was still devoting most of the time he spent with reporters bemoaning Pearl Jam's popularity. By now, in fact, the singer's oft-repeated I-hate-fame sound bytes had begun to smell more

and more like spin control. Cameron Crowe, on hand during the Italian
shows to finish up his *Rolling Stone* piece, and Bill Flanagan, chronicling the Zoo TV tour for a U2 biography, both happened to observe Eddie during seemingly unguarded moments carping about the size of the
venues, and a few weeks later in Holland, the singer would welcome a
reporter from *Spin* with the same complaint. "I just spent the best of
what's left of my voice screaming at people back in America about booking us here," Eddie told the writer. "I mean, I may be shy about some
things, but not when it comes to the music. How can you have a religious experience watching a band in a place this size?"

Even if Eddie was as tortured by Pearl Jam's celebrity as he claimed
to be, his insistence on using every interview to drive that home often
made him seem more calculated—even self-aggrandizing—than candid.
Cameron Crowe wondered in his *Rolling Stone* story whether Eddie's
constant protestations were an "elaborate defense mechanism," a means
of preserving his punk credibility without actually having to turn his
back on the mainstream rock world, as his punk heroes had done.
Bono's conversations with Eddie had left him wondering the same
thing.

"He talks about how he only wants to play clubs," the U2 singer told
Bill Flanagan, "but he's not actually *playing* clubs, is he?

"The scene that they come out of has a lot of *rules*, actually," Bono reflected. "There's quite a code. Like with a lot of clubs, that can be quite
rigid. If you try to break out of it, even if you just want to see what's
across the road or around the corner, you can't do it. . . .

"He's not a rock & roll animal," Bono added. "He's come up from a
different place, a place that I prefer. But he's in a rock & roll band and
has to protect himself. He probably doesn't think he's got a mask, and so
he might not have figured the various masks of Zoo TV. But he has a
mask, and that's okay, because the important place not to be wearing
masks is in the songs."

✕◇✕

Back in the States that September, "Jeremy" swept the 1993 MTV Video
Music Awards, snagging moon-man statuettes for Video of the Year, Best
Group Video, Best Metal/Hard Rock Video, and Best Direction in a
Video. During the band's trips to the podium to collect the awards, Ed-
die—who'd turned up for rehearsals wearing one of his monster masks
and a sarcastic I ♥ GRUNGE T-shirt—struck the same notes he'd been hit-

ting in interviews. "If it weren't for music," he said in a reference to the real-life Jeremy, "I think I would've shot *myself* in front of the class-room." Accepting for Best Group Video, he was typically dismissive. "Well," he shrugged, "we're a group, and I guess it was a video. I don't know how you could say it was the *best*. It's just a little piece of art. You can't really put art into a competition." He paused to inspect the statue he held, mumbling, "Looks like Bono."*

Pearl Jam also served as musical guests at the ceremony, performing "Animal" and teaming with Neil Young to play "Rockin' in the Free World." The segment, which drew the night's only standing ovation, would be singled out in the following day's newspapers as a highlight of the show, but behind the scenes, it would give rise to yet another round of head butting between Eddie and Dave.

By this time, Eddie was moving into what some observers referred to as his Jim Morrison phase. He'd lopped his hair into a blunt, unflatter-ing chin-length mass and had begun to put on weight; he'd also taken to carrying a bottle of wine around with him on stage, and although the wine was apparently more a prop than anything else—his band mates later noted during an interview with this writer that Eddie would carry the same bottle around for hours and sometimes days with no substan-tial change in the level—it contributed to the rather disheveled picture he presented, fueling rumors that he'd developed a drinking problem and heightening the Morrison comparisons. Eddie had his wine with him on this night, too, and his showing during the broadcast was fairly standard for that period, more an emotional performance than a physi-cal one. For the most part, he was content to stand stock-still, belting out the song with his arms either folded across his chest or hanging limply at his sides.

Although the audience didn't seem to mind, Dave was annoyed by what he calls "the whole drunk-guy routine," feeling that Eddie had sac-rificed the band's performance to pump up his Morrisonesque mystique. The drummer claims that although Eddie appeared to be half-crocked that night, it was all an act; Eddie, he says, told him as much just after

---

*Just after this speech, Eddie had a fit of conscience and sought out U2's Edge back-stage, concerned that Bono might hear about his quip and take it as an insult. When he found Edge in his trailer, Eddie asked for Bono's phone number, saying that he wanted to call and apologize. Edge considered this. "I just hung up with Bono," he intoned solemnly. "And Eddie, he was crying." A few tense moments passed for a stricken Eddie before the guitarist broke up laughing and let him off the hook.

the segment, when the band was herded into the press tent to pose for photographers.

"He had two beers in his hand, and I said, 'Why don't you give me one of those, you look kind of silly,'" Dave recalls. "And he looked me straight in the eye, sober as can be, and said, 'No, man, I want people to think I'm fucked-up and drunk.' And then went *right* back to being drunk. I just stood there going, *holy shit*. At that point, I was way past saying anything to him."

Although one wonders why Eddie would go on a counterfeit drinking binge and then confess it to the one member of Pearl Jam with whom he felt the least kinship, his later comments to a *Kerrang!* reporter about the event were rather intriguing in light of Dave's claims. "In Los Angeles, 'fake' really becomes a problem," Eddie told the writer. "People were asking me at the MTV thing, 'What's wrong with you—are you drunk? Is something wrong?' They were all acting the same, like rock stars. If you don't act like a star or you don't look like a star, they think something's wrong."

Just after the photo session, Dave and Eddie clashed again. At most awards shows, the actual statuettes are reclaimed after publicity photos are taken so that they can be engraved with the artists' names. This was the case with the MTV Awards, and as Dave tells it, when Pearl Jam emerged from the press tent and an MTV intern attempted to relieve Eddie of his award, Eddie refused to hand it over.

"The guy said, 'I need that back,'" Dave recalls, "and Eddie said, 'No, you can't have it—you're gonna send me some cheap plastic one, I'm keeping this one.' I grabbed Eddie's arm and said, 'Man, this is his *job*.' You know, the kid's just standing there, just totally like, *huh*? Eddie jerked his arm away from me and said, 'Fuck you,' and just walked off."

Later that night outside Sony's post-awards bash, the drummer says, he spied Eddie and his skateboard buddies kicking the award around in the street like a hockey puck. "I'd just had it at that point," he sighs. "That was a *bad* night. And *Mike* . . . Mike was so drunk that night, he couldn't even stand up."

In a development that had escaped the attention of the fans and the press—perhaps because all the speculation was focused on Eddie's supposed battle with the bottle—Mike was really in trouble.

The guitarist had been struggling to overcome his alcohol dependency since the band's first tour, and his binges were legendary. Mike was far from being a mean drunk; if anything, he grew overly affectionate when he was drinking. But he was also unpredictable and uncontrollable, prone to wandering off and getting into trouble or causing embarrassing public scenes that required the intervention of his band mates.

On one occasion, at a party for Metallica in New York City, Kelly Curtis had been in a huddle with Metallica's attorney and a few other bigwigs talking business, when he looked up to see Mike hurtling unsteadily toward him.

"I *love* you, man," said Mike, tackling Curtis with almost enough force to knock him down and giving him a big sloppy buss on the lips before wheeling backward and upsetting the drink held by Metallica's startled manager. The others recognized the danger signs and shepherded Mike out of the party, but not before he'd flung a beer bottle against the wall, causing a brittle crash and an explosion of glass that sent a small knot of party goers scattering like roaches.

More recently, during an outing with Neil Young in Dublin just after Pearl Jam's Italian gigs with U2, Mike had fallen off the wagon big time, supplying the hotel-lobby autograph hounds with a story they would probably repeat for years. Dave had gone out for a bite to eat that night, and when he returned to Pearl Jam's hotel, a couple of teenage girls approached him in the street outside. As Dave signed autographs for them, they asked where Mike was, his signature being the only one they'd yet to collect. Assuming that the guitarist was following his usual M.O.— when he was trying to avoid drinking, Mike preferred holing up in his room to going out with the others—Dave told the fans that Mike was "probably upstairs just taking it easy." No sooner were the words out of his mouth than a man and a woman shuffled into view, a clearly besotted Mike propped up between them like a life-sized ventriloquist's dummy. Mike spied his band mate and let out an overjoyed whoop.

"Ockus!" he shrieked. Then all hell broke loose.

"He ran at me, simultaneously pulling his pants down, and dove on top of me and these two girls," says Dave, "and started humping me and yelling 'I'm gonna fuck the Ockus.' I grabbed him and got his pants up, and grabbed his belt and pulled it as tight as I could and held it, trying to get him to calm down. Every time I'd let him go for a second, his pants would come down and he'd start running around the street, screaming. He was totally out of control."

About that time, some of the crew came walking up the street, and Dave asked them to keep an eye on Mike. He then hurried upstairs to find Eric Johnson, arriving in the tour manager's room looking out-of-breath and panicked.

"What's going on?" Johnson asked.

"Look," said Dave, pointing out the window.

Johnson moved to the window and peered down into the street. The entire crew stood on a corner laughing. Mike, a few yards away, was running around in circles with his pants down around his ankles.

"We ran down there and grabbed him," Dave recalls. "Then it was the duty of taking him back to the hotel room and smoking pot with him until he passed out. You'd smoke a bunch of pot with him, then he'd get sick and you'd know he was fine, that he wasn't gonna go to sleep and throw up and drown in it. Once he passed out, you'd know he was down for the night and that he was safe."

By now, the others had made numerous attempts to communicate to Mike that they were worried about him. "We had a lot of meetings where they would say, 'Hey, Mike, you're getting way too fucked-up,'" the guitarist recalled in 1995. According to Dave, there were also several meetings about the problem during which Mike was not present and the others considered firing him. "They'd sit around and talk about, 'Well, do we just fire him, or do we wait, or what?'" the drummer recalls, "and then somebody would take him aside and talk to him. Usually me or Stone. He'd stop for a couple of weeks, but then he'd find an excuse to fall off the wagon."

Later, Mike would reflect on this time and say that his drinking had been a response to a variety of stresses, both internal and external. "I didn't have a lot of confidence," the guitarist said. "I was literally afraid of everybody. I didn't know how to relate to Eddie, and after the band really took off, I went off in my own world. . . . When everything blew up, everybody kind of lost their minds. Actually, Jeff and Stone had a pretty good hold on it throughout, and I think Eddie did, too. But everybody had their own ways of dealing with it. And mine, for a long time, was getting fucked up."

It would be nearly a year before Mike realized that he couldn't beat his addiction without professional help and entered a rehab facility for treatment. When he did, it would be entirely on his own initiative, not because he'd been issued an ultimatum. "I think they actually thought I was going to die," he reflected later, "but they never took steps to kick me out of the band, which I can't believe, because I fucked up so many times."

Mike's comments suggest that he viewed Pearl Jam's reluctance to fire him during this period as an act of pity or charity. Perhaps those things played a part to a certain extent—it's obvious that the others cared about him, and surely they didn't relish the idea of adding a pink slip to the problems he was already dealing with.

But they also *needed* him. Mike's unique, fluid style was a vital element of what made Pearl Jam work. Far from being a generic, interchangeable hired gun, he was the keeper of the band's blues spirit, his inventive leads a crucial foil for Stone's rhythm work and as much a factor in Pearl Jam's instantly recognizable sound as Eddie's distinctive vocals. Without Mike, the music would be hollow—and making it would be a lot less fun. Firing him was a decision they simply weren't prepared to make.

All they could do was keep an eye on him and hope that he got a handle on his addiction before they were forced to choose between his health and the band's needs. With *Vs.* due for release and a full-scale tour already booked, the Pearl Jam machine was in high gear. By now, that machine was large and powerful enough to steamroller right over a band member with a drinking problem.

XØX

Vs. stunned the record industry and the media the first week of its release, selling a whopping 950,000 copies and trouncing a one-week sales record formerly held by Guns n' Roses. Anticipation for the album was so high on the day of its release that at one Wisconsin store during a special midnight sale, some three hundred impatient fans rushed the doors and crashed through a display window, causing $15,000 worth of damage and leaving three eager record-buyers injured. The store later reported selling eight hundred copies of *Vs.* in forty minutes.

That *Vs.* blew out of stores so briskly despite lack of an accompanying video on MTV or the release of an advance single to radio—not to mention the nearly unheard-of concept of a popular mainstream artist spurning such traditional avenues of promotion—enchanted the monoliths of the mainstream media. CNN ran a segment on Pearl Jam the week after the album's release, gushing about the sales record set by "these reluctant self-promoters." *Time* slapped a snarling live shot of Eddie on its cover under the headline "All the Rage," making him the focus of an intro-to-grunge feature analyzing "Rock's Anxious Rebels." Alternative musicians, *Time* informed its readers with the repeat-after-me air of an anthropologist giving a lecture, "reject show-biz glitz. They support progressive social causes. Many of them avoid dating groupies and models. Their music is usually guitar-driven, with experimental touches." *Billboard*, the record industry's bible, ran its own piece emphasizing Pearl Jam's low-key personal style and promotional stance. "The band and Epic wanted to lead with the music," Epic's vice president of product development, Dan Beck, told writer Melinda Newman. "The audience is too intelligent not to do it that way. Everybody gets very suspect to hype, and we have no reason to hype this record."

Critics of the band would always guffaw over statements like this, pointing out that, in fact, Pearl Jam's much-lauded distaste for hype *was* the hype. Bill Gamble, then program director of Q101, the Chicago station that became a thorn in Eddie's side after enlisting his mother to do promotional spots, said in 1995 that he believed some of the hottest acts of the next decade would be acts who had taken a lesson from the way Pearl Jam had been "marketed—or *not* marketed—into becoming the biggest commercial property in the music business.

"This band has just not missed a beat to market itself perfectly," Gamble reflected. "They did things at the right time. They didn't do the videos, they created demand. *Everything* was the right move."*

✖◈✖

Indeed, whether it was due to calculation on Pearl Jam's part, or just plain serendipity, nearly every move the band made at this stage of their career only served to fuel their legend and increase their appeal.

On the eve of the *Vs.* tour, Eddie made headlines and charmed fans nationwide when, during an appearance on the syndicated call-in program "Rockline," he gave out his home phone number on the air. He and the other members of Pearl Jam spent a few days answering calls and chatting with those who got through, a move that chiseled the Eddie-as-regular-guy myth into the minds of fans more deeply than anything the band had ever done. What the fans didn't know was that Eddie had only given out his number so that the constant ringing would annoy a downstairs neighbor.

"I had this little apartment," he later laughed to an Australian radio

---

*Even close friends of the band have been known to roll their eyes over the notion that Pearl Jam's rise to fame was as organic as legend would have it. In 1997, during a panel on music management at the North By Northwest festival in Portland, Oregon, Epic staffer Andy Schwartz made the mistake of boasting, in the presence of Soundgarden manager Susan Silver, that Pearl Jam had no image. Silver, always one to call a spade a spade, replied with an exasperated, "That *is* the image, Andy."

deejay, "and the woman who moved in downstairs was just awful, terrible. Wouldn't let us play our music, even at volume three. . . . I was kind of bothered by this. So when we were finally moving out, I [decided] we'd turn the answering machine all the way up, and put the phone on four rings, and give the number out. Poor woman, I don't feel sorry for her at all. . . ."

Once the tour got rolling, newsmaking incidents came fast and furious. In Indio, California, during an infamous gig that later became known as the "Shoe Show," Eddie stopped the proceedings to square off with a mob of angry fans who'd been pelting the band with footwear, announcing that he and Jeff were going to wait by the exit gates and "beat the shit out of every barefoot person."

"Mmmmmmm," the singer breathed, licking the sole of a thrown sneaker. "Your dirt is my fucking *food*, don't you understand that by now?" When he jokingly announced that all the shoes would be donated to charity, a new rain of sneakers and sandals began. Eddie simply stood there, egging the offenders on. "Thanks *so* much," he said sarcastically, occasionally reaching out to swat away shoes that threatened to hit him in the head. "All *right*, more shoes! Shoe the shoeless!"

During the second of two benefit concerts in Mesa, Arizona, for Native American activist groups, the Apache Survival Coalition and the Mount Graham Coalition, the band made the MTV news feed when they draped a University of Arizona sweatshirt over a mike stand and set it on fire during their set, in protest of the school's plans to erect an observatory on Mt. Graham, a sacred site to the San Carlo Apaches. During the Mesa stop, Eddie also made a friend for life in Bill Miller, a Mohican singer-songwriter who'd been invited by Pearl Jam to open the shows, and who was treated abominably by the band's fans.

During Miller's set on opening night, an experience he later described as "just sickening, the longest thirty minutes of my life," the impatient grunge kids had booed him, spit on him, and thrown things at him. After the show, as he was putting away his guitar in disgust, Miller noticed "this little scraggly guy standing there, just sort of checking me out."

Miller, taking the stranger for a roadie, asked him, "Can I help you?"

"Yeah, man," his observer replied shyly. "Can I talk to you?"

"This guy was going on and on about my show," Miller recalled. "He was telling me how much the songs had moved him, and how I'd really touched his heart. He had tears in his eyes, and he told me not to worry about how the crowd had reacted. It made me feel better that at least someone on the tour was paying attention. So I asked the guy what his name was, and he said, 'I'm Eddie Vedder. I'm the lead singer for Pearl Jam.'

"The next night, he came out on stage before the concert started and screamed at the audience for about ten minutes, and told them to listen to me," Miller remembered. "And they did. The place went crazy. It was one of the best shows I'd ever played."

This was the side of Eddie that the fans so loved. What other rock star would be so hurt to see a fellow performer humiliated by a crowd— or take such pains to rectify the situation? Unfortunately, by the time the tour rolled into New Orleans in mid-November, Eddie's sensitive side was in remission. This time around, the news coverage—including a *People* item under the headline "Just Call Him Axl Rose"—would not be as flattering.

The trouble started after the first of Pearl Jam's three sold-out shows at the Lakefront Arena. Eddie had gone drinking in the French Quarter with some friends that night, among them Chicago White Sox pitcher Jack McDowell and members of opening act Urge Overkill. At around 4:30 A.M., as the group was winding up the evening at a punk bar called the Blue Crystal, Eddie got into a conversation with James Gorman, one of the club's waiters. As Eddie recalled later, by the time Gorman started bending his ear, he'd already spoken to around two dozen people in the bar—twenty of whose names he'd scribbled on his cocktail napkin so that he could add them to the guest list for the following night's show. He talked to Gorman for a few minutes, but when Eddie got up to leave, Gorman apparently made it clear that *he* would decide when the conversation was over. "We tried to walk on, but this guy, he wouldn't let it go," Eddie recalled. "He still had to have more. He still had to cover more points. And Blackie [Onassis, Urge Overkill's drummer] says, 'Look, man, just mellow out, we're going, you know.' And this guy's going, 'No, no, I got to say one more thing, we gotta talk.'"

Eddie, finally having had enough, pushed Gorman against a wall and spit in his face. A shoving match ensued, and when McDowell intervened, grabbing Gorman around the back in an attempt to get him away from Eddie, the brawl spilled out into the street. During the fracas, the bar's bouncer reportedly took a swing at McDowell, who lost his balance and hit his head on the bumper of a parked Jeep.

"So here's this guy, a talented and well-respected friend of mine, who's lying on the ground unconscious because of this little dick who's saying to me, 'You're not my messiah, you're not my messiah,'" Eddie fumed to a *Melody Maker* reporter. "And I'm going, 'That's what I was trying to tell you, man. That's what I was trying to *tell* you. I'm not your fuckin' messiah.' "

The police arrived and hauled Eddie to the pokey, charging him with public drunkenness and disturbing the peace. He was released on $600 bond. Gorman later filed a battery suit—according to Eddie, the waiter sought $3 million in damages—but nine months later, Eddie was acquitted by a New Orleans judge, who noted that Gorman and the bar's bouncer, Anthony Martinez, both had criminal records and "left something to be desired" as credible witnesses. Eddie did not have to speak a word in his own defense. "I'm just disappointed I didn't get to tell my side of the story," he said after the brief hearing.

The tour rolled on. In Nacogdoches, Texas, on November 20, it was Dave's turn to buckle under the pressure.

The drummer had had a stressful week. He'd just learned that a close friend was dying of AIDS, and he was also in bad shape physically, fighting off the flu and pumped full of antibiotics. The band had not arrived in Nacogdoches until seven in the morning on the day of the show, and because a group of friends had come down from Dallas to meet him, Dave hadn't been able to get any sleep before the gig. By showtime, he was exhausted, and the process of getting his guests into the venue and making sure they were comfortable ate up all of his warm-up time. "I didn't get in any good head space or anything," he remembers. "Which is like just walking in off the street to the stage."

Dave thought he was fine until he got midway through "Deep," the fourth song in the set. At that point, he says, he had a "full-out anxiety attack, and fucking flipped out.

"All of my friends were there," he explains, "so of course I was giving it a little more than I had in me, and it was just one of those things— I lost feeling from the neck down, basically. It was like a bad acid trip. I just got this total panic attack–freakout, and I couldn't breathe. I played for another hour and fifteen minutes just completely out of my head, throwing up and everything else."

The drummer made it through the set closer, "Alive," but he collapsed backstage after the set, telling Eric Johnson he thought he needed to go to the hospital. While a nurse was giving him oxygen, he says, the others walked in, but "nobody showed any compassion." Sheri Fineman, who witnessed the incident, says, "I could tell that Stone and Mike were both concerned, but it was more like, 'So, Dave, are you gonna be able to do an encore?' "

"We're kind of freaking out right now, because something's wrong with Dave, our drummer," Eddie told the crowd a few minutes later. "He's kind of passed out in the back. All the excitement, you know, playing his hometown and everything." The band finished the show without Dave, doing a three-song acoustic set and then enlisting Blackie Onassis to help them out on "Rockin' in the Free World." Dave, meanwhile, was taken to the emergency room, where he spent the next three hours undergoing texts before a doctor diagnosed exhaustion. He was unprepared for the cold reception he received when he got back to the venue and boarded the bus. Fineman remembers that evening well.

"We got back on the bus, and the driver's like, 'Hey, buddy, you okay?'" she recalls. "And Eric said, 'Hey, how are you?' And *nothing* from anyone else. They were all sitting in the back lounge, and they all turned around and looked at him, and then turned back to what they were doing."

Dave spent a few minutes stomping around the bus, muttering, "Thanks for caring . . . glad you guys *give a shit* . . . glad you're my *friends*," before retreating to his bunk in frustration. One by one, Fineman says, all of the others approached her during the course of the evening to ask how Dave was doing, but "not one of them spoke straight to him.

"I was lying down reading," she remembers, "and Eddie came up and said, 'Hey, Sheri—how's Dave doing?' We started to have this great conversation, and I was thinking, 'Yeah, *this* is the Eddie I remember.' And then Dave walked up, and Eddie just stood up and walked off. Midthought, mid-sentence, mid-everything. Just walked off. I thought, 'Okay, obviously there's something going on here.'"

Dave would be plagued by panic attacks for the rest of the tour. "It was just having that one attack, and then feeling like I was completely alone, because nobody seemed to give a shit," he reflects. "I'd try to go on, and then as soon as I felt any sort of funkiness physically, it'd be, 'Oh my God, it's happening again.' It was awful.

"Every show, I was having these attacks," he recalls. "So I sat down with everyone in a room, and started describing what they were like— that I was having this big problem, freaking out and throwing up before gigs. I was telling them that I needed a couple of days off, that I felt like I was completely out of control and I just couldn't do it.

"In the middle of my telling them this, I looked up and there was nobody there. They'd all left the room."

For the rest of the tour, the drummer kept to himself. "I just stopped talking to all of them, and tried to function," he says. "I hid in my hotel room. I'd go to sound check and then go back to the hotel, and if the show was at eight-thirty, I'd have a runner pick me up at eight. After the show, I'd go straight to the hotel." Jimmy Shoaf, Jr., Dave's drum tech, began keeping a valium in his shirt pocket at gigs, so that if Dave felt another attack coming on while he was on stage, he could take one. "I very rarely did," the drummer says, "but just knowing it was there seemed to help."

The problem would resurface during the band's tour the following spring, but by that time, Dave knew better than to bring it up to the others. "They didn't give a shit," he says with a shrug.

"I talked to Kelly about it," he recalls. "His reaction was, 'Well, I hope it works out.'"

※◈※

The band got through three more shows—one-offs in Arkansas, Oklahoma, and Kansas—before controversy struck again, this time in the form of an abruptly cancelled late-November gig at the University of Colorado in Boulder. Pearl Jam had been booked for a three-night stand, and the first show, on a Friday night, went off without a hitch. When they took the stage on Saturday, though, the band members were angered to see teams of headset-wearing policemen wandering through the crowd; for seemingly no reason, the campus had augmented the venue's normal peer-group security force with dozens of stern-looking uniformed officers. Eddie, in fine Morrison tradition, took the opportunity to vent his displeasure over the unnecessary police presence during the last few minutes of the show, confronting a few of the cops present and reportedly grabbing one officer's headset. On the morning of the Sunday show, during a meeting with campus officials and promoter Barry Fey, the band insisted that the venue ease its security. "They basically said, 'We don't think this should be how our music is heard and how our fans are treated,'" Fey recalled. When the school wouldn't budge, alleging that Eddie's actions the previous night had "created some tension," Pearl Jam canceled the gig, promising to return in the spring at a different venue to honor the tickets held by disappointed fans.

In early December, the embattled band returned home to Seattle for a series of homecoming concerts at the Seattle Center Arena—only to find themselves embroiled in yet another contest of wills with the ever-present Ticketmaster.

Pearl Jam had earmarked $20,000 of their profit from the three Arena concerts, to be held December 7, 8, and 9, as a charitable donation to the Seattle Center Arts and Sciences Academy. The money raised would be used by the Academy to send two lucky teenagers to the private Northwestern School of the Arts, Stone's alma mater. As part of the benefit, Kelly Curtis later said, he had negotiated a deal with a Seattle Ticketmaster representative under which Ticketmaster would donate $20,000 to the Academy from its service charges on the show.

Just before tickets were to go on sale, Curtis said, the band's agent got a phone call from Ticketmaster chairman Fred Rosen, who insisted that the local rep's deal with Curtis had not been authorized and demanded that another dollar be tacked onto the Ticketmaster service charge to cover the company's donation.

According to Curtis, the band was furious and ordered Rosen to cancel the concerts. After an hour-long impasse—and a heated conversation between Rosen and the band's agent—Rosen relented somewhat, agreeing to contribute $14,000 to the charity without raising the service fee on the tickets, but refusing to ante up the promised $20,000. The tickets went on sale, but Pearl Jam took the betrayal very personally.

"The last minute nature of that episode was a real eye-opener for us," Curtis later told the *Los Angeles Times*. "Most people we deal with don't do business that way—especially when it involves raising money for a good cause."

As if another run-in with Ticketmaster wasn't enough to curdle Pearl Jam's Christmas eggnog, Eddie came down with the flu after the last Arena show, an unfortunate occurrence that required the band to pull out of a planned mid-December appearance with Nirvana at a taping for an MTV New Year's Eve special.

At the time of the event, which was to be taped December 13 on the Seattle waterfront, relations between Pearl Jam and Nirvana were still a favorite topic of the gossips. The waters had calmed a bit after Kurt Cobain's public offering of the olive branch to Eddie at the 1992 MTV Video Music Awards; after meeting Eddie, Cobain obviously felt guilty about the derogatory comments he'd made about Pearl Jam in the past. "I'm not going to do that anymore," he said in an interview later that year. "It hurts Eddie, and he's a good guy."

In the fall of 1993, Eddie and Kurt had agreed, through their respective representatives, to pose together for a Christmas cover planned by the British music weekly *Melody Maker*, but according to *Melody Maker*, the two then had a "further misunderstanding" over the "All the Rage" issue of *Time* featuring Eddie on the cover. Courtney Love—whom it should be noted had a tendency to attribute more resentment for Eddie to her husband than Kurt's own public comments ever suggested—also claimed that Kurt had been irritated by the *Time* story, implying that Eddie had double-crossed Kurt and hoodwinked *Time* into focusing the story on him.

"I hate to be Yoko, but I would like to see my husband on the cover of *Time*," Courtney fumed. "Eddie called Kurt and he's whining, 'Oh, I'm having nothing to do with the *Time* cover, Kurt, I love you!' And he did it anyway. Kurt hates him. He was like, 'Fuck you. Fuck you.'" (Apparently, Courtney had never actually read the article, the text of which poked her conspiracy theory all full of holes. Even a cursory reading makes it clear that Eddie was not interviewed for the piece, and the *Time* writer noted within the story that Eddie wasn't pleased about being on the cover.)

In any case, MTV's announcement of a New Year's Eve concert featuring both Pearl Jam and Nirvana had done much to squelch any remaining speculation about acrimony between the two bands—which is why Eddie's failure to show caused such a huge stink. MTV was said to have been furious, but even worse, Eddie's absence was interpreted as a very public snub of Cobain and Nirvana. Gossips had a field day, contending that Eddie's "illness" was a smoke screen—that the real reason he'd refused to appear was the Feud.

"That was the worst part of it all," Eddie said later. "Sitting at home fuckin' sick as a dog and sweating and shivering and watching the hours pass before this thing was going to happen and thinking, 'I'm fucked, man, I'm totally fucked. . . .' People were saying we pulled out because we wanted to headline, or we wouldn't appear. . . . We would have gone on first, second, or fuckin' third, where the fuck ever, you know? There was no problem with the order. I was really happy about playing with them. I even thought about writing them to say, 'Sorry, man, I was sick.' But then the rumors got to be fun to listen to."

In February, Eddie sparked a new round of rumors, when he traveled to New York to appear at a two-night Carnegie Hall birthday bash for the Who's Roger Daltrey. Performing solo on Who classics ("Squeezebox," "My Generation," "The Kids Are Alright") and an obscure Pete Townshend number, "Sheraton Gibson," Eddie was a standout on both nights, prompting a *San Diego Tribune* reporter to remark that he, "more than any of the other guests, captured the spirit and tone of this still vital music about youthful angst and adolescent confusion and aspiration."

If Eddie didn't accomplish that onstage, he certainly did backstage.

He was for the most part a well-mannered guest—he even presented Daltrey with a birthday cake—and he enjoyed meeting a few of his heroes at the shows, among them Pete Townshend and Joey Ramone. But by the second night, he had become less-than-enthralled with the commercial feel of the affair. Unbeknownst to Eddie, the concerts, billed as "Daltrey Sings Townshend: A Celebration," were being taped for later offering as a pay-per-view special, and after the organizers presented him with a release form, he decided it was time to inject a little rock & roll back into the proceedings. With his old Lollapalooza buddy, Jim Rose of the Jim Rose Circus Sideshow looking on, Eddie demolished his dressing room, causing enough damage that Carnegie Hall later said it was considering issuing a ban on rock events. In a finishing touch that likely went unappreciated by the house staff as they surveyed the wreckage, Eddie had scrawled "This is my generation, baby" on the dressing room mirror.

Later, the *Seattle Times* would whisper that he'd written the message in his own blood.

XOX

Back in Seattle, a few weeks after the "Daltrey Sings Townshend" show, Eddie left his house to get something to eat. While he was out, he happened by a newsstand, where the day's headlines left him stunned.

"I just freaked out, man," he said later. "I went home and made some phone calls, tried to find out what the fuck was going on. Then I started pacing the house and started to cry. I just kept saying, 'Don't go, man, just don't fuckin' go . . . just don't go.'

"I kept thinking, 'If he goes, I'm fucked.' "

Kurt Cobain, Eddie had learned, was in a coma in a Roman hospital, the result of an overdose on tranquilizers and champagne. Nirvana's management, Gold Mountain, was insisting that the overdose was accidental.

Cobain remained in the coma for twenty hours before he finally awoke and scribbled a request—"Get these fucking tubes out of my nose"—onto a notepad. A few days later, he was released from the hospital, and Seattle let out a collective sigh of relief.

When the scare occurred, Courtney Love had just completed an interview with the British monthly *Select*. While awaiting a plane at Heathrow airport on her way back to the States with Kurt after his release from the hospital, Courtney took a moment to phone the *Select* reporter with an update. Dutifully following the Gold Mountain party line, she told the writer that the overdose "was not a suicide thing."

"This was just a tiff between me and Kurt, okay?" she explained. "That's all it was. A tiff. He was just upset that he was in some awful place and I was away enjoying myself and shopping."

Just before she hung up, the ever-tactful Courtney offered a final thought.

"You know," she said, "I wish it had been Eddie. They'd have had a fucking candlelit vigil for him."

Seventeen

Pearl Jam vs. the Status Quo / Kurt Cobain, 1967–1994 / Pearl Jam and Mudhoney Invade the White House / No More Tour: Eddie Puts His Foot Down / Goin' to the Chapel / I Found My Thrill on Capitol Hill / Conference Calls and Poker Faces

By 1994, Pearl Jam were at the peak of their power within the industry, bolstered by the record-breaking sales of *Vs.* and their proven status as a top concert draw. As they launched their spring '94 tour and began laying plans for a larger-scale outing that summer, the band began flexing that power in their business dealings, seeking changes in their contracts with promoters, merchandising companies, and others in the touring industry that would not only result in a better deal for Pearl Jam when they hit the road, but also, they contended, for their fans.

"One really good thing is how much we've learned being on the road, in terms of the business aspect of it," Jeff enthused that March, "and how exciting it is to be changing the way that people perceive things from a financial point of view—actually being able to get cheaper tickets, and forcing promoters to deal with only taking 20 percent of the merchandising. This summer, if Ticketmaster's gonna do something with us, they're gonna have to come around, or we're gonna deal with this tour ourselves. Ticketmaster wants to charge $4 a ticket this summer to print [the tickets] and sell them. The tickets are going to be $18, but when you put a $4 service charge on it, it ends up being 22 percent of the ticket price, which is more than *we're* making. When things get to that point, it starts to get a little bit ridiculous. It's the same way with merchandising. All the promoters and record companies are in bed with the venues, so they allow each other to charge 35 percent or 40 percent of the T-shirt prices, when in a lot of instances, the bands are only making 30 percent. And the only way the band can make any money is by charging $24 a T-shirt. The one thing that's really, really great about being in the position we're in is having the power to go in there and fuck with those people. It's a beautiful thing."

Some of the promoters eager to book Pearl Jam for spring appearances resented the hoops they had to jump through in order to secure contracts. Not only did they have to take a smaller-than-normal cut on the merchandising, they were also required to forward videotapes of their venues for the band's review and to answer detailed questions faxed by Pearl Jam on various aspects of their operations, including their policies on ticket prices and their handling of seating and security. "They're telling people, 'We'll do it our way, and you'll have nothing to say about it,'" grumbled Bob Fox, whose company, Brass Ring, booked the Fox Theater in St. Louis, Missouri. Nonetheless, most of the promoters bidding for shows—including Brass Ring, which scored a two-night booking for mid-March—did their best to meet Pearl Jam's demands, not wanting to forfeit bookings that would be a sure sellout.

When Pearl Jam began to focus on Ticketmaster's service charges, though, they were met with immediate resistance.

Ticketmaster, which maintained exclusive contracts with the majority of promoters and venues in the country, was in a prime position to throw a serious wrench into Pearl Jam's plans. Not only did Ticketmaster's contracts prohibit venues or promoters who entered into them from allowing anyone else to sell their tickets, but the contracts also provided for a portion of Ticketmaster's service charges to be paid back to the venue or promoter.

This payment—which Ticketmaster politely referred to as a "concession" but most everyone else termed a kickback—often resulted in as much as $500,000 in additional annual revenue for entities willing to sign on the dotted line and help Ticketmaster freeze out its competition. It was a very clever economic lure, designed to ensnare the nation's choicest venues in a web of "legal" monopoly. Because of the way Ticketmaster's contracts with venues and promoters were structured, Pearl

Jam's attempts during their spring tour to negotiate lower service charges—and separate disclosure of those charges on the tickets—resulted in a tug-of-war that grew more and more heated as the tour progressed.

In Chicago, where Pearl Jam had booked shows at the Chicago Stadium and the New Regal Theater, Ticketmaster refused to reduce its service charge, insisting that it be kept at $3.75 per ticket. The band went along with this, but only after negotiating an agreement with Ticketmaster's general manager in Chicago that the service charge would be disclosed separately on the tickets.

Just before tickets were to go on sale, Pearl Jam would later contend, Ticketmaster reneged on the agreement, only backing down when the band threatened to move the shows to a different venue and even then making it clear that its separate disclosure of the service fee would not extend to shows outside Chicago. (Ticketmaster later denied that any argument had taken place, claiming that one of Pearl Jam's associates had misrepresented the terms of the agreement to the band.)

A week later in Detroit, Pearl Jam again felt Ticketmaster's sting. For the Detroit concert, held at the Masonic Theater, the band had attempted to circumvent Ticketmaster entirely, offering three hundred tickets to members of its fan club and selling the rest of the available ducats through a newspaper lottery system. Tickets were priced at $18, with a $1.75 service fee going to the promoter, Nederlander, and a $1.50 facility fee going to the venue. According to Pearl Jam, Ticketmaster, which had an exclusive agreement with Nederlander, threatened the promoter with a breach of contract lawsuit and also "temporarily disabled the promoter's ticket machine so that it could not print tickets for the concert." Yet another last-minute squabble ensued, with Ticketmaster finally agreeing to fire up the ticket machines in exchange for Nederlander's forking over a portion of its $1.75 service charge.

Similar sparring erupted in mid-March, over shows planned for April 10 and 11 at the Boston Garden and April 12 at that city's Orpheum Theater. When Ticketmaster pushed for a service charge between $3 and $4, Pearl Jam countered with a threat to stage another newspaper lottery. This time around, surprisingly, Ticketmaster was cooperative, not only lowering its service charge for the shows to $1.80, but even agreeing to contribute $.20 from each ticket, the same amount Pearl Jam had pledged, to a local charity, the New England Home for Little Wanderers. "Ticketmaster fought us in Detroit," Kelly Curtis told the *Boston Globe* on March 16, "but they came to the party in Boston."

As it turned out, the victory was misleading. Around this time, Kelly Curtis, acting through the band's agent at William Morris, informed promoters of Pearl Jam's requirements for the summer tour. Tired of the constant back-and-forth with Ticketmaster, the band was now firm on three major points related to ticketing: They would only play venues where the per-ticket service charge was limited to 10 percent of the ticket price, the service charge must be disclosed separately on the face of the tickets, and the backs of the tickets were to carry no advertising—another prime source of revenue for Ticketmaster. Promoters were urged to find ways to work with the band, Curtis making it clear that Pearl Jam would just as soon not play as compromise on any of these key points.

The response was swift. On March 24, Ben Liss, executive director of the North American Concert Promoters Association, sent a memo to all of the organization's members. "Pearl Jam is putting out feelers once again to require promoters to bypass Ticketmaster on their dates later this summer," Liss wrote. "Ticketmaster has indicated to me they will aggressively enforce their contracts with promoters and facilities."

On the following day, Liss issued another, stronger warning to NACPA members. "Fred [Rosen] has indicated that he intends to take a very strong stand on this issue to protect Ticketmaster's existing contracts with promoters and facilities, and further, Ticketmaster will use all available remedies to protect itself from outside third parties that attempt to interfere with those existing contracts. . . . I urge you to be very careful about entering into a conflicting agreement which could expose you to a lawsuit."

War had officially been declared.

※◈※

According to Dave, it was on March 26 when it became clear that Ticketmaster was not going to be the only obstacle Pearl Jam faced in mounting a summer tour.

The band was in Murfreesboro, Tennessee, at the time, gearing up for a memorable show in which they would be joined by Memphis legend Steve Cropper for a cover of Otis Redding's "Dock of the Bay." Backstage just after the sound check, the drummer recalls, there was a tense band meeting.

"It started out about Mike's drinking, and then turned into a communication thing," says Dave. "Mike said something about the fact that he and I weren't included in band decisions, and they told us the reason we weren't included was because we weren't assertive enough, that we had to fight for our views. I got really pissed, and I told Eddie, 'Look, I can't fucking declare my artistic intent on the moment. I'm not gonna stand up and fight for something that I haven't thought out.'"

The meeting degenerated into a round of yelling and finger pointing, Dave says, before Eddie made a move that plunged the room into silence and instantly put the argument on a back burner. Calmly folding his arms across his chest, the singer glanced around at his band mates and announced, "I don't know if I want to tour this summer."

According to Dave, he and the others—including Kelly Curtis—responded with a collective, stunned "*What?*" and launched into an indignant joint tirade about all the planning they'd put into the tour, the months of hard work and frustration they'd endured in scouting out alternative venues to get around the Ticketmaster headache. After a few moments of this, the drummer says, Eddie threw up his hands, mumbling, "Forget it . . . whatever."

When the meeting broke up, Pearl Jam's summer tour was still on—but it would not be for long.

✕◈✕

By April 2, when Pearl Jam arrived in Atlanta to play a two-night stand at the Fox Theater and do some recording for the follow-up to *Vs.*, what had started as a few worried whispers among well-placed insiders had filtered through Seattle's music infrastructure, leaving in its wake an awful, communal sense of foreboding.

Kurt Cobain was missing.

Ever since Cobain's overdose in Rome, word had been leaking out of the Nirvana camp that all was not well. The band, slated to headline the Lollapalooza tour that year, had dropped out unexpectedly, amid rumors of a breakup. There had been news of several domestic disputes at the Cobain residence; on March 18, Love had summoned police to the couple's home on Lake Washington Boulevard, telling them Cobain had locked himself in a room with a revolver and threatened to kill himself. The officers had confiscated two handguns, a rifle, and twenty-five boxes of ammunition but left without taking Cobain into custody.

On March 25, ten of Cobain's friends, concerned about the singer's heroin use and self-destructive behavior, had staged an intervention at the Lake Washington house. During the five-hour confrontation, Love threatened to leave Cobain if he didn't get help; two of his band mates,

Krist Novoselic and Pat Smear, told him they were prepared to break up the band unless he checked into a rehab. At the end of the tense session, Cobain had agreed, but later that day, he'd balked at the airport. The singer had spent another five days in Seattle before agreeing to travel to Marina Del Ray, California, for treatment at the Exodus Recovery Center. Krist Novoselic drove him to the airport on March 30, unaware that earlier that day, Cobain had purchased a 20-gauge shotgun and stashed it in a closet at the Lake Washington house.

Cobain had stayed at Exodus for two days, last speaking to his wife on April 1. On the same evening, around 7:30, he'd told the Exodus staff he was going outside for a smoke, scaled the six-foot wall that surrounded the treatment center's patio, and disappeared into the night. By 1:00 A.M., he'd returned to Seattle on a Delta flight. Michael DeWitt, the nanny who kept Kurt and Courtney's daughter, Frances Bean, later reported seeing Cobain shortly after he got home. DeWitt recalled that Kurt looked ill and that his behavior had been odd.

Now, nobody knew where the singer was. The day after he'd fled the rehab clinic, Love had canceled his credit cards and hired a private investigator to track him down; according to Screaming Trees singer Mark Lanegan, a number of Cobain's friends were searching for him that week, but he hadn't returned any calls. "I had a feeling that something real bad had happened," Lanegan said later.

By April 3, the night Pearl Jam played their second show at Atlanta's Fox Theater, a missing-persons report had been filed on Cobain, and the Seattle community was buzzing with speculation about the singer's whereabouts and well-being. That evening, Pearl Jam's concert at the Fox was broadcast via satellite to radio stations nationwide. Afterward, spinning his favorite records on the air during an impromptu forty-five-minute deejay session, Eddie made reference to the unfolding crisis that few outside Seattle were aware of.

"Kurt Cobain," he said, "hope he's all right. Please be all right."

Just before nine in the morning on April 8, 1994, Gary Smith, an electrician who'd been hired to install a security system at Cobain and Love's home, arrived at the Lake Washington Boulevard house and discovered a body lying on the floor of the room over the garage. At first, Smith thought it was a mannequin. Then he saw the shotgun, and the blood.

Smith paged his boss at Veca Electric, then phoned the police. By the time the police arrived at Cobain's home, KXRX, a local FM station, had been tipped off by a Veca employee and was already reporting that a body had been found at the Cobain house. Before long, the Associated Press had picked up the story, and radio and television stations across the United States began broadcasting speculative reports. That afternoon, the medical examiner issued a statement confirming that the body was Cobain's. Officials later determined that he had been dead for two and a half days.

Cobain had obviously not wanted any mistakes made about his intentions. Before he pulled the trigger, he'd written a note, directed for the most part to his fans. But ultimately, the note would introduce more questions than it answered.

This note should be pretty easy to understand. All the warnings from the Punk Rock 101 courses over the years, since my first introduction to the, shall we say, ethics involved with independence and the embracement of your community [have] proven to be very true. I haven't felt the excitement of listening to as well as creating music . . . for too many years now. I feel guilty beyond words about these things. . . . The fact is, I can't fool you, any one of you. It simply isn't fair to you or me. The worst crime I can think of would be to rip people off by faking it and pretending as if I'm having 100% fun. Sometimes I feel as if I should have a punch-in time clock before I walk out on stage. I've tried everything within my power to appreciate it (and I do, God, believe me I do, but it's not enough). I appreciate the fact that I and we have affected and entertained a lot of people. I must be one of those narcissists who only appreciate things when they're gone. I'm too sensitive. I need to be slightly numb in order to regain the enthusiasm I once had as a child. On our last 3 tours, I've had a much better appreciation for all the people I've known personally and as fans of our music, but I still can't get over the frustration, the guilt and empathy I have for everyone. There's good in all of us and I think I simply love people too much, so much that it makes me feel too fucking sad. The sad little, sensitive, unappreciative, Pisces, Jesus man! Why don't you just enjoy it? I don't know. . . . I have it good, very good, and I'm grateful, but since the age of seven, I've become

hateful towards all humans in general. Only because it seems
so easy for people to get along and have empathy. Only because
I love and feel sorry for people too much I guess. Thank you
all from the pit of my burning, nauseous stomach for your
letters and concern during the past years. I'm too much of an
erratic, moody, baby. I don't have the passion anymore, and so
remember, it's better to burn out than to fade away.

Peace, Love, Empathy. Kurt Cobain.

XOX

Cobain's suicide stunned a community that had seen more than its fair
share of tragedy. Four other beloved locals—Andy Wood, poet Jessie
Bernstein, Stefanie Sergeant of 7 Year Bitch, and Mia Zappata of the
Gits—had been lost to Seattle in as many years, and those deaths had all
been painful to weather. But this one was different. The violent finality
with which the twenty-seven-year-old Cobain had shut out a world he
could no longer tolerate was just too much for his dazed compatriots to
process. Had it been an act of desperation and loneliness, or a grand,
punk "fuck all of you phonies"—an angry, defiant indictment of the living? Had Kurt won his battle, or lost it? There would never be answers.

"When Kurt did that, it just permanently changed my perception
about everything we've done for the past few years," Soundgarden's
Kim Thayil reflected a few weeks after Cobain's death. "And I don't
mean just me. I mean our band, and all the bands from here that play
with each other and support each other and watch each other's shows. It
just seemed to metaphorically put an end to everything.

"There's something weirdly martyrlike about what he did," Thayil
said. "It used to be like, we were watching each others' careers, and
everyone would go on about how wonderful it must be to live in Seattle—you know, grunge this and grunge that. And we all knew in the back
of our minds that it *wasn't* that wonderful. But the thrill really *was*.
Whatever the fraternal competition or the mutual support or affection
for each other was, one of those elements is removed. Everything feels a
lot less innocent, and more like a comic book. A rock & roll comic book.
It happened so quick. You barely had time to sit there in the afterglow. It
was like, boom, the light was out.

"If he'd overdosed, it would be different," Thayil mused. "It would be like, 'You fuck-up.' But he did something a lot of us have thought about."

※◇※

Pearl Jam were in a Washington, D.C., hotel, preparing for a show at the Patriot Center in Fairfax, Virginia, when they heard the news about Cobain. Eddie took it out on his room. "I just tore the place to shreds," he said later. "Then I just kind of sat in the rubble, which somehow felt right. . . ."

Like Soundgarden, who were on tour with Tad in Europe, Pearl Jam were on the road with friends from home when they learned of Cobain's death. Mudhoney—now sporting a major-label deal of their own and having long forgiven Stone and Jeff for their Green River–era commercial aspirations—were opening the shows on this leg of the tour. Their presence helped to ease some of the weirdness, but not all of it.

"I was just spinning," Eddie recalled of that day. "I was lost and didn't know if we should play, or if we should just go home, or if we should attend the services. I still have some regrets about that, even though in the end it was probably better that we played the last two weeks of the tour. I decided I would play those next two weeks, and then I'd never have to play again." From Pearl Jam's candlelit stage that night, a few songs into the set, Eddie—now left alone to wear the hated spokesman-for-a-generation crown he'd shared with Cobain—offered a single, eloquent comment on the tragedy.

"Sometimes, whether you like it or not, people elevate you," he said. "And it's very easy to fall. . . . I don't think any of us would be in this room without Kurt Cobain."

Later, Eddie would expand on this sentiment in interviews, aligning himself with Cobain in a manner that prompted some to charge him with dramatizing a relationship that had been tenuous at best. But cynics, Eddie insisted, were part of the problem.

"You know, all these people lining up to say that his death was so fucking inevitable . . . well, if it was inevitable for him, it's gonna be inevitable for me, too," the singer seethed to *Melody Maker*'s Allan Jones. "See, people like him and me, we can't be real. It's a contradiction. We can't be these people who just write these real songs. We have to live up to the expectations of a million people. And we can't do that. And then there's a cynical fuckin' media on top of that. Fuck that, fuck 'em. All along the line, they question your fuckin' honesty. No matter what you say, no matter what you do, they think it's an angle. . . . And when someone comes along who's trying to be real, they don't know the fuckin' difference. So if you say, 'No, I'm not playing your fuckin' game, I want out . . . I'm not doing this, I'm not doing that,' they still think you're part of it. They just can't accept that you don't want to be part of it, that you were never part of it."

Clearly, what bothered Eddie the most about his own relationship with Cobain was that so much time had been wasted on punk vs. rock finger pointing during Pearl Jam and Nirvana's early careers, time that the two men—who, as many have noted, had much more in common than their fame—could have spent trading war stories and helping each other deal with the madness.

"I wish that Kurt and I had been able to, like, sit in the basement a few nights and just play stupid songs together, and relate to some of this," Eddie told *Spin*. "That might've helped us to understand each other, that he wasn't the only one, or that I wasn't the only one. We kind of knew that in the back of our heads, but . . . we didn't really address that. Courtney told me later that he was so excited about a song he'd written with Pat Smear about beans. And that was exactly where I was coming from at the time.

"I don't want anything to do with this larger-than-life bullshit."

✖◈✖

If anything truly underscored the chasm between where Eddie wanted to be and where he was headed, circa 1994, it was the guest list for the Patriot Center show. Fugazi's Ian MacKaye, whose unimpeachable personal politics and avoidance of corporate checkbooks had years ago landed him on Eddie's most-inspired-by list, was a guest at the show; afterward, Eddie would spend the night at MacKaye's house. But also enjoying Pearl Jam's hospitality at the D.C. show were a number of White House staffers. Clinton's underlings had called to request tickets to the concert, and Kelly Curtis, who was said to have been beside himself with nervous excitement over the visitors, had graciously set aside the ducats. Eighty, to be exact.

The day after the show, the bureaucrats reciprocated, extending an invitation for Pearl Jam to tour the White House. At ten in the morning on April 9, Pearl Jam—minus Dave, who'd passed on the outing in favor of a visit to a local tattoo artist, and Eddie, who was still at MacKaye's house but would meet the group there—convened with Mudhoney, who were uninvited but had decided to tag along anyway, and headed for 1600 Pennsylvania Avenue.

Just getting there was nerve-wracking. In the van on the way over, the driver kept telling scare-stories about past White House visitors who'd been swarmed by the Secret Service and thrown into jail for insignificant offenses—one lady, he told them, had spent the night in jail after guards found a nail file in her purse. Matt Lukin, Mudhoney's bassist, had brought a joint with him to smoke on the way over, and he got paranoid after hearing the nail file saga, eating the joint and depositing his pocketknife behind one of the van's seats.

When they got to the White House, the driver balked at going through the gate. "No, sir, I can't do that," he told Eric Johnson. "I don't have the authority."

"Yes you do!" Eric insisted. "I have clear and distinct instructions to go through the goddamn gate!"

The driver wouldn't budge. Eric finally had to get out and find a Secret Service agent, who waved them through.

Once inside the gate, they met up with Eddie and Kelly Curtis, who'd arrived a few minutes earlier, and were escorted inside. Almost immediately, a trench-coat-wearing White House staffer swooped down on the Mudhoney contingent, introducing himself with a curt "Hi, my name's Henry, you're with me now," and planting himself between Mudhoney and Pearl Jam. As the luckless Mudhoney allowed themselves to be led away, clearly destined for the "B" tour, Mark Arm looked back over his shoulder at Stone, who was wearing a helpless expression Arm later described as "this same look that I've seen people give to doomed pups so often at the dog pound; the look that says, 'I'd help you if I could, really, I would.' "

While the members of Mudhoney were being escorted through the Press Room and the Situation Room, Pearl Jam were ushered into the Oval Office for a personal audience with Bill Clinton. Later, when they got back to the hotel with a stash of White House memorabilia, Dave asked them what they'd talked about with the president—and came away slightly disappointed over what he viewed as a missed opportunity.

"They talked about *basketball*," he says, laughing. "I remember saying, 'Well, did anybody ask him about, you know, legalizing pot, or any of that stuff?' And nobody did. I was bummed. Nobody asked him about anything real—they all just shot the shit. That was the big moment to say, 'Hey, how come this is the way it is, and what do you think about it really?' But nobody took it. All they talked about was a basketball game."

If Pearl Jam's obsession with basketball got in the way of the sweeping policy changes Dave had counted on them to facilitate during their brief chat with President Clinton, it also earned them an arch write-up in the *Boston Herald*, after they unwittingly resulted in the Boston Bruins being barred from their practice rink on the eve of the NHL playoffs. As a deal sweetener when the band's contract had been negotiated for shows at the Boston Garden on April 10 and 11, Garden president Larry Moulter had promised them time on the fabled Celtics' court, and he'd sent out a memo announcing that the court would be down on April 12 for Pearl Jam's use. Unfortunately, the Bruins never got the memo and arrived at the Garden that day for an important pre-playoff practice to find their ice rink covered by the Celtics' court and Pearl Jam happily immersed in a vigorous game of b-ball.

The *Herald*—perhaps a tad put off because one of its photographers had tried to shoot the band's game from courtside and been booted by Larry Moulter—chastized the band for pulling celebrity rank on the Bruins ("The Greatest Rock Band in History This Week Sure Has an Inflated Sense of Itself," the paper sniffed), but the Bruins themselves took the snafu in stride. Some of the team opted to shoot hoops at the end of the court not occupied by Pearl Jam for their workout, and the rest repaired to a surrogate ice rink in Wilmington. Eddie (whom the *Herald* noted had "a better outside shot than many of the Bruins") even managed to finagle an introduction after the Bruins returned to their locker room, shyly approaching the team's equipment man to ask if he could get a drink and then aimlessly loitering outside the locker room door until Bruins center Bryan Smolinski invited him in.

Eddie told the Bruins he was honored to play in a "building with such tradition," but chances are he neglected to mention that he'd helped himself to a souvenir to commemorate the occasion. On the previous evening, he'd sneaked into their locker room and smuggled out one of their hockey sticks.

XOX

Meeting President Clinton and the Boston Bruins may have helped to lighten Pearl Jam's mood that week, but it wasn't enough. Kurt Cobain's death had, as Kelly Curtis put it, "knocked the wind out of the band," and they were ready to go home.

Whether all of the band members were in agreement at this point as to how long they would *stay* home is uncertain. With only a few dates left on the spring tour, the others may have expected to spend a few months in Seattle and then head back out in July, when the summer tour was slated to begin. Planning was still underway for the tour; opening acts had been lined up, and the band's representatives were working with promoters to find venues that did not have exclusive contracts with Ticketmaster. But by the time Pearl Jam played their third Boston show, at the Orpheum Theater on April 13, Eddie's survival instinct had kicked in. He'd clearly decided he didn't want to do the summer tour.

"We had four shows left when I found out what happened in Seattle, and I didn't really think we should play the rest of those shows," he'd told MTV two nights earlier. "So as it is, I'm gonna get through these shows—it seems like it's the best thing for us, the best thing for the people coming to see the shows. It's been healthy for all of us, though incredibly difficult. After that, I—or we as a band—may not play for a very long time. As far as scheduling some monster tour or something, it's not gonna happen right now, because we need to protect the music and we need to protect ourselves."

After the sound check at the Orpheum, Eddie called a meeting and made it official. According to Dave, Eddie delivered the news to his band mates the same way he had in Murfreesboro prior to Kurt Cobain's death, when he'd first indicated his reluctance to do the tour. This time, though, Eddie wasn't just reluctant—he was firm. And this time, only Dave protested the decision.

"We'd spent so much time getting alternative venues going," the drummer says. "People were working so that we could do tickets through the mail and 800 numbers, and everything else. Then all of a sudden it's, 'I don't want to tour this summer,' and we aren't touring. Kelly told everybody, 'Don't tell the crew, because we don't want 'em to get bummed out before the end of this tour,' and I was just like, 'Man, this is *bullshit*.' You know, Rat Sound had already blown off other tours to do our summer tour—these people pay their *rent* from touring."

Dave, disgusted, walked straight down to the stage after the meeting and found his drum tech, Jimmy. "We're not touring this summer," he said sarcastically. "Hope it doesn't affect your *performance*, but I'd much rather you be pissed than think you have a job this summer when you don't."

It's uncertain how long it took word to filter out to the rest of the crew. Chances are they'd have known something was brewing anyway:

During the show that night, Eddie thanked them from the stage, a gesture typically reserved for the last gig of a tour.

After the show, Dave arranged for a car and departed alone for New York, where in a few days the band would make an appearance on *Saturday Night Live* and play the tour's final show at the Paramount Theater. On the way, he asked the driver to stop at a Burger King. As soon as he stepped inside the restaurant, fans began recognizing him, and within minutes, he'd drawn quite a crowd. The drummer bought them all dinner, ringing up a hefty tab.

Had he known what lay in his immediate future, he might have given that some more thought.

※◈※

Pearl Jam kicked off the *SNL* appearance on April 16 with "Not for You," a new song they'd recently begun playing live. A vicious harangue in the finest Us vs. Them tradition, set off by jagged riffs straight out of the Neil Young songbook and directed at intrusive fans and moneygrubbing industry middlemen, "Not for You" would in a sense set the tone for the next few years of the band's career. In a concession reserved for staff favorites, *SNL* had allotted Pearl Jam airtime for three songs, and they used it well, turning in performances of "Rearviewmirror" and "Daughter" that were all the more powerful to an audience still reeling from the shock of Kurt Cobain's death. Eddie mumbled a few lines from Neil Young's "My My, Hey Hey" before the coda of "Daughter," but stopped short of repeating the lyric Cobain had quoted in his suicide note ("it's better to burn out than fade away"). Instead, he made his statement during the show's closing segment, opening his jacket to reveal a "K" he'd drawn on his T-shirt over his heart, and pressing his hand over it in a subtle, wordless expression of loss and respect.

The Paramount show was an edgier affair. Wanting to end the tour on a positive note, the band had planned the surprise show as a special treat for fans, a gesture they would repeat often in the coming years. The concert wasn't announced until a few days before the show, with New York fan club members getting first crack at tickets and the remainder distributed through radio promotions and sold directly from the Paramount box office. But once again, Ticketmaster emerged as a killjoy. According to the band, Fred Rosen and his henchmen wasted no time in threatening the Paramount's promoter with a lawsuit over the alternative ticket-distribution method Pearl Jam had devised for the show.

Meanwhile, Eddie had worked himself into a lather backstage before the gig, talking to *Melody Maker*'s Allan Jones about his confusion over Cobain's suicide and over the public's expectations of celebrities in general.

"You know what I really need right now?" he told Jones. "I need to know what people want from me. I feel like there are all these contradictions about what people want, you know. And in the end they want too much. They want you to be a leader. They want you to be a victim. They want your fuckin' soul. They want everything. And some of them, they don't give up, they're relentless. And why should I care? I shouldn't even fuckin' care, man. I should be strong enough to say 'I don't give a fuck. Fuck you all, I don't give a fuck, you fuckin' bastards.' And then I'd really be a 'spokesman for a generation.' Because there are a lot of people out there, man, going 'Fuck this fuckin' shit. Fuck it.' They're ignorant and they're happy and they don't give a fuck about anything. I see a lot of people out there, man, and they're beyond fucked up. So maybe I should care a little less about them, because it looks like they don't care about me."

This less-than-subtle resentment for the hungry public would spill over into the show later in the evening. During a break in the set after the band played "Jeremy," Eddie, getting ready to launch into a monologue, told the crowd he hoped they wouldn't be offended, but that he was "going to say the word 'fuck' about eight times in the next thirty seconds." When the house responded with the predictable deafening roar, Eddie got annoyed with them for cheering.

"Okay," he said caustically, "so now it's like we can stand up here and just say the word 'fuck,' and that's enough, eh? We don't even have to play songs anymore. Well, that's gonna be a lot easier on my throat." He softened the blow a moment later, telling them, "What I wanted to say about the last song we did was, if you ever feel like saying, 'Fuck this, I'm getting the fuck outta here, just remember: Living is the best revenge."

But when a female fan called, "I love you, Eddie!" the sarcasm crept into his voice again. "You don't love me," he scolded. "You love who you *think* I am, the image you've created in your mind. You can't love me, 'cause I'm already in love. Did you know my ten-year anniversary with my girlfriend, Beth, is next month? That's the longest relationship of anyone in the band, unless you count Stone and Jeff."

Pearl Jam kicked into "Satan's Bed," a track from the forthcoming album that addressed issues of temptation and fidelity. At the side of the stage, Henry Rollins, another of Eddie's longtime heroes, stood watching all of this with an inscrutable expression. The Rollins Band had been asked to open some dates on Pearl Jam's summer tour, and Henry, who'd been told that Eddie was looking for him, had dropped by the show to talk to the singer. To someone like Rollins, a no-nonsense road hog who'd spent years crisscrossing the country in a dilapidated van with Black Flag and now plowed through grueling tour itineraries that often hit upward of two hundred dates a year, Eddie's intro to "Satan's Bed" seemed a little heavy-handed.

Backstage after the show, Rollins spent about twenty minutes with Eddie in the band's dressing room while the others went to an end-of-tour party. Eddie had wanted to tell Rollins personally that the summer tour was canceled, but he devoted most of the conversation to how tired and confused he was, speaking at length about the pressure he felt and his uncertainty over how to handle it.

Rollins liked Eddie, and he tried to be kind. But he wasn't one to mince words, and his advice was probably not what Eddie wanted to hear. In short, the punk veteran told Eddie to have more fun—that complaining about fame to an audience who could only see it as a privilege was the quickest way to lose them.

✖◈✖

When reports first surfaced that Pearl Jam had canceled their summer tour, the primary reason given by Kelly Curtis was that the band was distraught over the death of Kurt Cobain and needed a rest. This news didn't raise many eyebrows; by the time Curtis officially announced the cancellation, Eddie had already indicated as much to several reporters, saying that after the band finished its spring dates, he did not plan to tour again for some time.

Starting in late April, though, the focus of the news stories began to shift. Speaking to writer Melinda Newman for an item appearing in the May 7, 1994, issue of *Billboard*, Curtis was still attributing the cancellation of the tour to Cobain's death, which he said "threw everyone for a loop." But he added that the band's ongoing problems with Ticketmaster had also been a factor in the decision. "The band's committed not to tour until they find an alternative," he said.

Before long, it would be all but forgotten that there had ever been any reason for the cancellation *but* Ticketmaster, thanks to a behind-the-scenes development that much of the public would never be aware of:

Pearl Jam had been approached by the Justice Department and asked to make a formal complaint about Ticketmaster.

Although it's been widely reported that it was Pearl Jam's complaint about Ticketmaster that first drew the Justice Department's attention to the company's business practices and initiated the antitrust investigation that would later become such a cause célèbre with rock fans, the Justice Department was apparently already toying with the idea of an antitrust investigation against Ticketmaster, and had simply seized on Pearl Jam, in the wake of published comments by the band on their disputes with the ticket giant, as a high-profile wedge they could use to push the inquiry through.

"Actually, they contacted us," Kelly Curtis said during an October 1994 interview on Chicago's "Sound Opinions" radio show. "They'd been reading some press articles, and we just told them the experiences we'd had, and they kind of went on their own. . . . We did a few interviews, with the *Boston Globe* and the *Denver Post*, I think, just complaining about not having any choice . . . and that's really what it was all about."

Before leaving New York after the Paramount show, Pearl Jam took the Department of Justice up on its invitation and hired Sullivan & Cromwell, a white-shoe law firm known for its representation of corporate giants like Exxon, to draft a memo detailing their experiences with Ticketmaster. In the document, which was filed with the Antitrust Division of the Department of Justice on May 6, the band accused Ticketmaster of exercising a virtual monopoly over the concert ticketing business, claiming they'd been forced to scrap their summer tour after Ticketmaster successfully pressured promoters into a boycott.

Pearl Jam's complaint sent shock waves through a concert industry that relied heavily on Ticketmaster to keep its wheels—and its palms—greased, sparking a heated press debate between the principals and sending the industry players at the sidelines—among them promoters who stood to gain from their relationships with both Ticketmaster and Pearl Jam—scurrying into off-the-record corners.

From the beginning, Ticketmaster maintained that it operated fully within the confines of the law and dismissed Pearl Jam's complaint as a brilliant marketing ploy devised to sell more copies of their forthcoming album. "What you have here is a band that refuses to release singles or music videos and has now decided not to go on tour," Ticketmaster spokesman Larry Solters told the *Los Angeles Times*. "What better way

to generate publicity for a new album than to go after a convenient target and stir up some controversy?"

Some promoters concurred, though always under a cloak of
anonymity. "A lot of this is about getting the kids to rally together," one
promoter told a reporter from the Knight-Ridder newspaper chain.
"Pearl Jam is saying, 'Look, we're anti-establishment. We're fighting for
you. We'd rather not tour than deal with Ticketmaster and have you
ripped off.' It makes great press."

Pearl Jam, through Dan Klores, the publicist Kelly Curtis had hired to
field inquiries on the controversy, maintained that Ticketmaster's accusations were ridiculous. "I think a better way of promoting an album
would have been touring," Klores opined to the *Chicago Sun-Times*.
Kelly Curtis also laughed off Ticketmaster's assertion that the band was
less interested in lowering ticket prices than it was in taking its fans on
an unwitting ride on the P.R. train.

"That would make me a pretty smart guy, definitely," he told listeners during the "Sound Opinions" radio program. "I mean, there are a lot
easier ways to generate publicity." Adding that Pearl Jam had had "no
idea what we were opening up Pandora's box wise" when they took on
Ticketmaster, Curtis pointed out that if the band had intended the move
to garner publicity, "Eddie Vedder would have been on the cover of
every magazine talking about this thing." That the band's feud with
Ticketmaster had become a matter of such fervent debate in the press,
Curtis asserted, was simply because "it's an important issue."

The public and most of the press clearly thought so, embracing Pearl
Jam's stand against Ticketmaster as a matter that had long needed to be
addressed—a kick in the teeth to the corporate boogeymen whose greed
threatened to make concert tickets unaffordable for the average fan.
Even the White House joined the chorus of support for the band's efforts, although as is customary, the official statement allowed room for
later backpedaling. "The White House is impressed by Pearl Jam's commitment to its fans," senior Clinton advisor George Stephanopoulos told
the *Los Angeles Times*. "We want to make it very clear that we can't
judge the merits of the band's allegations against Ticketmaster or pre-
judge the Justice Department action in any way. But that said, we think
the goal of making concert ticket prices affordable is a laudable one. It's
something we believe in."

The Washington ranks overseeing the June 30 House Subcommittee
hearing on the matter, however, seemed to view the occasion more as a

platform for proving how "with it" they were than anything else, spending much of the hearing cooing over Stone and Jeff, who had appeared to testify, and prattling on about their own rock & roll glory days. The subcommittee chairman, California Democrat Gary Conduit, couldn't resist comparing the proceedings to a concert as he reminded those present to comport themselves with decorum. "No bottles, no cans, no Frisbees," he warned. Collin C. Peterson, a Democratic representative from Minnesota, puffed out his chest and trumpeted his background in country music ("I'm the only card-carrying member of a musician's association on this committee"), confessing that he'd "tried to learn a few Pearl Jam songs, but it was beyond my repertoire." During her own moment in the spotlight—one that elicited more than a few groans from the gathered observers—California Democrat Lynn Woolsey peppered Stone and Jeff with unrelated questions ("What does Pearl Jam *mean*?") and pledged her allegiance to the cause by declaring that "the music won't rock if the consumers are rolled." At one point, she leaned into her microphone and gushed, "I want to tell you, you are just *darling* guys."

Stone and Jeff did their best to keep the hearing focused on the issue at hand, although it was obvious they both found the proceedings a little surreal. On the following day, newspapers across the country would carry photos of the two being sworn in for their testimony, both garbed in the same casual clothing they wore on stage, Stone unable to suppress a half-exhilarated, half-embarrassed grin as he raised his right hand.

"As most or all of you are aware," Stone began, reading from the band's prepared statement, "in early May of this year, our attorneys at Sullivan & Cromwell filed a memorandum with the Antitrust Division of the Department of Justice in which we brought to the Government's attention certain conduct by Ticketmaster that we believe is unlawfully interfering with our freedom to determine the price and other terms on which tickets to our concerts will be sold. . . .

"Many of Pearl Jam's most loyal fans are teenagers who do not have the money to pay the $50 or more that is often charged today for tickets to a popular concert. Although, given our popularity, we could undoubtedly continue to sell out our concerts with ticket prices at that premium level, we have made a conscious decision that we do not want to put the price of our concerts out of the reach of many of our fans. . . . All of the members of Pearl Jam remember what it is like not to have a lot of money, and we recognize that a teenager's perceived need to see his or her favorite band in concert can often be overwhelming."

After a discussion of how Pearl Jam's policies with regard to ticket prices had put it at odds with Ticketmaster, the band's statement addressed Ticketmaster's hold on the industry.

"The reason that a band like Pearl Jam has been required to deal with Ticketmaster is because Ticketmaster has exclusive contracts with most major venues for concerts and with almost all significant promoters of concerts in the United States. In essence, if you play any of these venues or if you deal with these promoters, Ticketmaster will claim that its contracts give it the exclusive right to distribute tickets for your concert. This affords Ticketmaster tremendous power in this business. By locking up all of the suitable venues and promoters with arrangements of this type, Ticketmaster has effectively thwarted competition and left most bands without any meaningful alternative for distributing tickets. This absence of any alternative, in turn, gives Ticketmaster the power to exercise virtual control—to the exclusion of the views of the band—over the level of service charge imposed on tickets for that band's concert that are sold anywhere but at the box office. . . ."

Elsewhere, the statement attacked Ticketmaster's practice of "kicking back" a portion of the service charges it collected to promoters and venues, which made it advantageous for promoters to sign the exclusive contracts so that they would enjoy a portion of the Ticketmaster service fees. "Bands like Pearl Jam receive no part of the service charge collected by Ticketmaster," Stone read. "And let us make it quite clear that Pearl Jam seeks no portion of those service charges. As a result, a band like Pearl Jam, which is concerned about keeping the price of its tickets low, almost by necessity finds itself on the opposite side of Ticketmaster, which has every economic incentive to raise the price of the tickets it sells."

He went on to describe the series of run-ins with Ticketmaster that had led to the band's complaint, beginning with the "Drop in the Park" show in Seattle and winding up with the dispute over the New York show at the Paramount. Throughout, the statement alleged, Ticketmaster had "attempted to threaten and intimidate us" and had "urged promoters to refuse to deal with Pearl Jam."

"We do not consider ourselves to be crusaders," Stone read in closing. "And while we recognize that the issues we have raised have implications that go beyond Pearl Jam, our interest is really quite narrow. We simply have a different philosophy than Ticketmaster does about how and at what price tickets to our concerts should be sold. We do not want to force Ticketmaster to do business on our terms, but we believe we should have the freedom to go elsewhere if Ticketmaster is not prepared to negotiate terms that are acceptable to us. That is the essence of competition. As we learned in attempting to arrange a tour this summer, given the current state of Ticketmaster's dominance of the industry, that may well mean that we must play non-traditional venues and use non-established promoters or promote our own shows. . . . Something is vastly wrong with a structure under which a ticket distribution service can dictate the mark-up on the price of a concert ticket, can prevent a band from using other, less expensive, methods of tickets, and can effectively preclude a band from performing at a particular arena if it does not accede to using Ticketmaster."

After they'd made their statement, Stone and Jeff took questions from the gathered lawmakers. Most of the inquiries were polite and relevant, but not all of them. One annoying Republican congressman insisted on grilling the two about Pearl Jam's finances until Stone finally cut him short. "I think this line of questioning is strange," the guitarist said, exasperated. "It has nothing to do with whether Ticketmaster is a monopoly." Jeff, who was also irritated, grabbed the mike. "They told us we were going to be here, like, an hour," he said. "Actually, I have to go to the bathroom. I'll be right back." With that, he rose from the witness table and walked out of the room, not bothering to wait for permission.

Fred Rosen's statement at the hearing, in defense of Ticketmaster, was predictable. Pearl Jam, Rosen stated, had mounted a "concerted public relations campaign . . . to discredit Ticketmaster," the linchpin of which was the Sullivan & Cromwell memo to the Justice Department. Rosen described the memo as a "work of fiction."

"Sullivan & Cromwell has attempted to create the impression that Pearl Jam could not have put on a rock concert tour without dealing with Ticketmaster," Rosen said in his statement. "This is simply false. There are venues all across the country in which Pearl Jam could have performed without ever dealing with Ticketmaster. There are promoters who have no relationship with Ticketmaster, and who could have—and, we are told, were willing to—put on such a tour.

"Earlier this year, Pearl Jam indicated that they wished to go on a concert tour and that they wanted their fans to pay no more than $20. Ticketmaster had no objection. . . . Ticketmaster has nothing to do with setting ticket prices. If the band wishes to price its ticket at $5, $20, or $350, that is a decision for them to make. What the band did, however, was to set about dictating terms to others. The band decided that their ticket price would be $18, and dictated that the service charge be no more than $1.80. . . . When Ticketmaster became aware of Pearl Jam's

demand, Ticketmaster indicated to promoters that it was prepared to compromise: notwithstanding its contractual rights, Ticketmaster was prepared to provide ticketing services for a convenience charge of $2.25 to
$2.50. . . . A compromise would have worked if the Pearl Jam members
were willing to take $17.50 to $17.75 for themselves, rather than $18.
With a $2.25 convenience charge, no fan would have paid more than $20.

"Pearl Jam's advisors," Rosen pointed out, "responded by stating that
the terms dictated by the band were 'not negotiable. . . .' We will leave it
to this Committee, on these facts, to consider who was being unreason-
able or coercive.

"Pearl Jam decided not to go on tour. Their true reasons for doing so
are known to them and no one else. Whatever the reasons, however,
they decided to blame Ticketmaster. . . ."

On the surface, Rosen appeared to be adequately refuting the key accusations Pearl Jam had made against his company, asserting that there
were alternatives available for fans who wished to avoid paying service
charges as well as for artists who wished to avoid working with Ticketmaster. But to anyone familiar with the realities of staging a tour and
selling concert tickets, Rosen's comments seemed incredibly evasive
and misleading. The "alternatives" he suggested, while they did in fact
exist, were practical impossibilities.

Fans could avoid paying Ticketmaster service charges, Rosen
pointed out, by purchasing tickets at venue box offices as opposed to ordering them by phone. Technically, this was true. But Rosen neglected
to mention that some prominent venues did not even *maintain* box offices, or that even at those who did, box office tickets generally weren't
available until well after Ticketmaster had already begun selling them
by telephone and at its remote outlets. Most venues, in fact, didn't offer
box office tickets until the day of the show—by which time, of course,
most popular events had already been long sold out by Ticketmaster.
The reality was that any fan who took Rosen's advice and tried to purchase tickets for a popular concert at a venue box office would either go
home empty handed or wind up at the mercy of a scalper.

There was "absolutely no truth," Rosen contended, to Pearl Jam's
charge that "Ticketmaster has within its power to prevent Pearl Jam
from doing a concert tour. Any rock band can put on a concert of any
size anywhere in this country and never deal with Ticketmaster." Again,
while this claim might have been true on paper, in real life, any band
that attempted to tour without Ticketmaster would be faced with a logistical nightmare.

As Rosen claimed, Ticketmaster did not have a lock on every venue in the country. But Ticketmaster *did*, in fact, have exclusive contracts sewn up with most of the *preferred* venues in the country—the established network of safe, conveniently-located, well-run, acoustically suitable halls, amphitheaters, and arenas that booking agents had routinely routed their top artists through for years, the ones that consistently dominated the itineraries of major touring bands. Sure, "any rock band" could play a show "anywhere in this country and never deal with Ticketmaster." But only if that band was prepared to put its fans and its reputation at risk by playing mostly venues that might be either unproven or unsuitable for rock shows—the poorly managed, unsafe, inconveniently located, and acoustically shoddy venues that most artists avoided like the plague. To anyone who knew the industry ropes, Rosen's portrait of a level playing field was a fairy tale.

Several prominent music-industry figures took Pearl Jam's side of the argument and offered negative statements about Ticketmaster at the hearing—among them R.E.M. attorney and comanager Bertis Downs and Aerosmith manager Tim Collins. But however much other top artists and their managers resented Ticketmaster's presence in the profit equation—and however many of them would go on to voice support for Pearl Jam's stance in the press—none of them would be willing to endanger their livelihoods or their comfort by attempting to stage tours without Ticketmaster. A few artists, in fact, would toss criticism Pearl Jam's way, blaming them for upsetting the apple cart and making all the other apples look wormy by comparison.

Mounting a full-scale tour without Ticketmaster was not impossible, but it was, as Kelly Curtis later put it, an "incredible pain in the ass." In the end, after the hubbub over the subcommittee hearing died down and the industry settled into another summer tour season, only Pearl Jam would walk it like they talked it and refuse to do business with Ticketmaster. To the nation's concertgoers, this would make them heroes, but the title would come at a major price. Pearl Jam had just painted themselves into a corner that would be nearly impossible for them to get out of.

XX

As Pearl Jam's public battle with Ticketmaster continued to play out in the press, the band members saw to their private lives. In early June, Eddie and Beth had traveled to Rome, where they were married. Stone be-

gan laying plans for the launch of his own record label, Loosegroove, a
Sony imprint on which he would release recordings by his side band,
Brad, and other local artists he favored. Mike, who had fallen off the
wagon again after Cobain's death, made a move that was heartily supported by his band mates, traveling to Minneapolis in July and checking
into the Hazelden Clinic for rehab treatment.

Meanwhile, the band was gearing up to address another outstanding
piece of business.

In mid-August, the day Eddie was leaving for New Orleans to make
a court appearance related to the November bar brawl, Dave phoned
Kelly Curtis to check in. Curtis, he says, was friendly and happy to hear
from him—nothing seemed amiss. Just before they hung up, the drummer says, Curtis casually told him, "Oh, I think Stone wanted to talk to
you. You should give him a call." When Dave got in touch with Stone,
the guitarist asked him if he wanted to go have breakfast the next morning. Dave agreed, and the two made plans.

On the following day, just after Dave left the house, Sheri Fineman
says she received a call from Stone's ex-girlfriend, Donya Wittenborne.
Stone had broken up with Donya about three days prior, and she'd
moved out of Stone's house after the breakup.

Donya, according to Fineman, had recently mentioned walking in on
a meeting between Jeff, Stone, and Eddie in which it was clear to her
that something heavy was being discussed—they'd all looked startled
and fallen silent when she entered the room. On this morning, Fineman
says, Donya had more strange news.

"She'd called Stone's house to check and see if she had any messages
on his machine," Fineman recalls, "and there was a message from Kelly
on the machine that said, 'Just calling to check in and see if you dealt
with everything yet.' There was a call from Mike, too. She was really
freaked out, and she called me and said, 'Sheri, what's going on?'"

Fineman told Donya that Dave was out having breakfast with Stone
as they spoke.

"Oh, my God," she says Donya replied. "I think he's gonna get fired."

Eighteen

Blues for Breakfast / Mutual and Amicable All-Out War / Enter Jack
Irons / Bigger than the Beatles / Self-Pollution Radio / Summer
Tour, Take One / Bad Press in Boise / Can't Go Home Again: Pearl
Jam vs. the San Diego Sheriff's Department / I Won't Back
Down . . . Or Will I? / Backlash, Backpedaling,
and the Fury of Mother Nature

Dave remembers the conversation in the diner that day as being "very emotional." Stone, he says, was in tears when he broke the news that Pearl Jam were looking for a new drummer. At one point during their talk, Stone looked down at the nylon bracelet he was wearing, one of the pair that he and Dave had bought at the Public Market together in 1991 during Dave's first trip to Seattle to audition for the band.

"He was kind of playing with it, and he said, 'Look, I've still got it,'" Dave recalls. "I was just like, 'So what, you've still got it—you just *fired* me, what does *that* mean?'"

About a week after Dave's meeting with Stone, Kelly Curtis issued a brief press statement, saying that the drummer had left the band and calling the split "mutual and amicable." Dave, Curtis later claimed, had agreed to the statement before it was released. But after Curtis's statement hit the news wires, Dave released his own missive, one that left Pearl Jam with major egg on its face.

"There are different philosophies and personalities that make up

Pearl Jam," Dave said in a statement on August 26. "For reasons that I don't completely understand, the other members decided it was neces- sary to fire me in order to pursue a philosophy which they perceive as incompatible with mine. I was not involved in their decision, but I ac- cept it and am proud to have been a part of what Pearl Jam was."

"When I heard everyone saying I left the band to 'study music' or whatever, it hit me wrong," the drummer said at the time of his decision to divulge the real reason for his departure. "It made me feel like I was the one who had no responsibility to what the music meant to people. I just felt I'd rather have the truth out."

Curtis, asked at the time why Dave was fired, said he was "hoping not to have to say anything about it, because it's no one's business." The move, he insisted, "was a band decision—it wasn't Eddie Vedder, it wasn't any one person." But Dave and Fineman, along with others close to the band, have always maintained that the move had Eddie's fingerprints all over it. He is the only member of Pearl Jam who did not phone Dave after he was fired to express his regret. Fineman still seethes over a phone call she received from Eddie a week after Dave was dismissed. The singer was so reluctant to face Dave, Fineman claims, that before he phoned her, he had Kelly Curtis run interference to make sure that Dave wasn't home.

"Dave was out of town," Fineman recalls, "and Kelly called first to ask for the number of the hotel where Dave was. Two seconds later, the phone rings, and it's Eddie: 'Hey, Sheri, how's it going, how you holding up.' He said, 'I've been thinking about you—it's not that I didn't want to talk to Dave, I just didn't want to bring all this negative energy up, it's just not healthy.'

"Then he was trying to blame the whole thing on Stone," she says. "He told me, 'We were all in the meeting talking about it, and I was on my way home thinking, "Wow, what just happened, this is so heavy," and I didn't know what was gonna happen, but you know how Stone is—he just grabs the bull by the horns, and the next morning, Dave got fired.' You know, as if he had nothing to do with it. Which is *such* a crock of shit. I was just so pissed at him. The whole thing of blaming it on Stone—I had already seen Stone in person at that point. He'd come into my office just to say hi, and when he was talking about it, he looked like he was going to cry.

"Stone's whole excuse for firing Dave was that they needed to move on to the next level, and everyone needed to be happy," Fineman re- flects. "But I don't think it was his choice. I got the distinct impression that it was something he was going along with that he didn't necessarily agree with. I know Mike is like that. Mike goes along with what everyone else says, period. And I could see Eddie convincing Jeff that it was the best thing to do. I think Eddie laid down an ultimatum. I don't think he came right out and said it—I think he implied it. Eddie would never come out and say anything straight out. He's one of those people who doesn't ever physically *do* anything. He's never the one who does it. It's more like, 'It was out of my control.' You know, 'I don't know why things happened.' "

Dave claims Jeff told him the night after he was fired that part of the band's rationale was his inability to communicate with Eddie. While he doesn't deny that he and Eddie had a communication problem, he says it certainly wasn't for lack of trying on his part. "There were definitely a lot of arguments with me saying, 'I wish I could talk to Eddie,' and everybody getting pissed. Their advice to me was always, 'Wait for him to talk to you.' When I tried to talk to him, he'd say, 'Uh, not now, man,' and just leave. He'd do that a few times, and then I'd just say, 'Fuck it.' You know, 'Why do we have to treat him so delicately when he makes demands of everyone?' "

Fans were stunned to learn that Dave had been fired. The one member of Pearl Jam who had unfailingly found time to sign autographs or stop to talk to concertgoers, the drummer had long been a favorite, and to fans who were unaware of the tension that had been brewing between Dave and Eddie nearly from the beginning, his ouster seemed sudden and unjust, tarnishing the band's one-big-happy-family public image. Three years later, debates would still be erupting regularly on the alt.music.pearl-jam Usenet group over why the drummer was fired, with fans yet to reach a consensus as to whether Dave's replacement had adequately filled his shoes.

Compounding the fans' confusion, the other members of Pearl Jam were tight-lipped about the drummer's departure for months afterward, either refusing to comment at all or offering the sort of diplomatic, airbrushed sound bytes that feuding musicians have fed the curious public for decades. After Dave had lobbed a few unrepentant postfiring spitballs at them in the press, though, the others began to be more explicit when they were asked about their reasons for the decision.

"I can't say that we bought into that whole 'being a star' thing, and I think he was into being a star," Jeff told the *Minneapolis Star Tribune*. "There's nothing wrong with that; it just wasn't right for our band."

This was, of course, the ultimate put-down in alternative circles—one that Jeff had been scorched with a number of times himself. Dave has never argued that his views about success clashed with those of his band mates. Rather, he has always maintained he just found it ridiculous that, in merely being seen to enjoy his good fortune—as opposed to spending every waking moment publicly complaining about it—he was committing a punk felony. He still contends that, more than anything else, what drove a wedge between him and Eddie was the singer's fear of anything that might cause him to be outfitted with the dreaded "rock star" tag.

"I guess it's his insecurities that do that to him," the drummer says. "I mean, above anything else, I think he's an incredible singer, an incredible performer, and an incredible writer. I also think his politics are commendable—where he stands on a lot of issues. But that was never enough for him.

"It's weird, because Eddie's the kind of guy who, like me and like so many other musicians I know, was driven to music because of what it said to him when he was little. And there's millions of people who feel the same way about Eddie that he felt about Pete Townshend. I'm sure his words and his actions have changed and shaped a lot of lives, but he can't see it.

"I always thought, 'Well, *I* like it, so that's good enough for me, and obviously a few million other people like it, so it must be good.' It didn't matter to me what Henry Rollins thought about it, or what Ian MacKaye of Fugazi thought about it. They had their thing, and we had ours. But it just seemed like the only way Eddie could consider himself a success was if all the people that he idolized thought he was cool. All of a sudden, there were parameters on what the people around Eddie could be, because of what he'd turned *himself* into. You know, how are people gonna believe in his shtick if they look over his shoulder and there's someone who's the anti-Eddie? Someone who enjoys success, someone who isn't embarrassed to say, 'Yeah, I made a good amount of money last year.'

"Eddie dressed up like Kiss just like everybody else," Dave says after a pause. "And he didn't do that imagining himself standing in his hallway. He did it so he could close his eyes and picture the world in front of him. I dreamed of that, we *all* dreamed of it.

"But all of a sudden it wasn't politically correct to admit it. It just wasn't part of the marketing plan."

XOX

Fineman says she received a second phone call from Eddie not long after Dave made an appearance at the Sam Ash music store in New York
City, on September 9. The in-store had been scheduled before Dave was
fired, and Eddie apparently disapproved of the drummer's decision to
go through with it.

"He called and said, 'Sheri, what in the fuck is that guy thinking,
what's *wrong* with him?'" Fineman remembers. "He was yelling. Can
you even imagine Eddie yelling? He said, 'I don't even know if this is
true, so I shouldn't get mad, but I heard Dave was signing autographs in
New York at some Sam Ash thing.'* I said, 'Yeah, he was,' and Eddie
says, 'How could he do something like that—I don't know what his
problem is, I don't understand it.' He said, 'How can he even show his
face in public? I wouldn't even want to show my face in public after
what happened.' Then he was like, 'Signing autographs. Doesn't he
know the public will suck the life right out of you?'

"I said, 'Well, I don't think Dave sees it that way. I think Dave sees it
as making someone happy, and he gets off on that.' And at that point, I
could almost hear him thinking, 'Oh, wow, she's fucked up, too.' Finally
I just said, 'Eddie, I don't want to be in the middle of this anymore. It's
not fair for you to do this, you need to talk to Dave, here's his car phone
number, I think the two of you just need to talk.' He said, 'Yeah, we're
gonna have to do that. I have this friend coming to town, so it'll have to
be in a couple of days, but I'll call him and set that up.'"

Eddie never called again after that, Fineman says. But she never expected him to. She already knew that the friend he mentioned during
the call was Eleven drummer Jack Irons.

Dave says that Jeff finally admitted to him during a March 1995
phone call that one of the reasons he'd been fired was because Eddie
wanted to recruit Jack. "He told me that when he and Stone started the
band, they'd pretty much picked who they wanted to be in it, and that

*The day after Dave's Sam Ash appearance, a fan posted a revealing anecdote on an
America Online bulletin board devoted to Pearl Jam that Eddie has been rumored
to frequent. During the in-store, the fan on AOL reported, someone had passed Dave
a *Vs.* CD to sign. The drummer had opened the CD booklet, flipped to the page featuring a group photo of Pearl Jam, and drawn a bold circle with a diagonal slash—
the universal symbol for "No"—around Eddie's picture.

Eddie felt he should be able to pick who *he* wanted," the drummer recalls. "And he wanted Jack."

Even before that conversation, though, neither Dave nor Sheri had been surprised when they learned that Irons was in Seattle. Dave had suspected that Eddie had been angling behind the scenes to get Jack in the band ever since 1992, when Eleven had opened a run of shows for Pearl Jam. During that tour, word had filtered back to Dave that Eddie had issued Jack an open invitation, telling him, "Hey, if you ever want to be in the band, just let me know." Jack's band mates in Eleven, Natasha Schneider and Alain Johannes, also saw the development as inevitable.

"Even before he was asked, we knew there would be a time when he was asked," Schneider said later. When she and Johannes learned that Dave had been fired, she added, they simply called Jack and told him to "get ready for a phone call." (Jack's departure would come at an especially bad time for Eleven, who were preparing to record their album *Thunk.* Ultimately, Soundgarden's Matt Cameron would step in to help them complete the recording.)

While Schneider and Johannes were steeling themselves for the loss of their drummer, the rest of the world was betting on Nirvana's Dave Grohl to step in and fill the Pearl Jam vacancy. Pearl Jam denied from the beginning that Grohl was a candidate, but some chose to cling to the rumors anyway—among them, apparently, Courtney Love. In the wake of her husband's death, Love had taken to communicating directly with her fans via haphazardly typed stream-of-consciousness missives she either posted herself on America Online or forwarded to a friend for distribution on Usenet. On September 4, at the height of the Dave Grohl rumors, Love's Internet emissary, Carol Mariconda, received a typical screed from Love's E-mail address. Mariconda, as she always did with Courtney's messages, promptly forwarded it to Usenet.

Sun, 04 Sep 94 07:30:10 EDT

uhhh . . . grohl has JOINED PEARL JAM. this will undoubetly [. . .] be pubished but i dont fucking care,fyi, Kurt was not on speaking terms w/Dve Iscariot anyway 4 over a year, fuck him, yeah fuck you dave, ill be yr fuckin Yoko nightmare you fucking traitor [. . .] get those Jeremy royalties dave, Fuck you, why didnt you just join the fucking cult . . . God you are LOW and KC would juest shrug ,im sure he wouldnt be surprised anyway . . . i like doing this on the Void, better thanever speaking to you again. . . . im going w/Stipe to the aewards, lets maake those rumours finally cum true,uck you dave,shoot some hoop w/jeffy ok? fucker.

Nobody who had read any of Love's earlier Internet posts had reason to doubt the authenticity of this one; it was standard Courtney, right down to the careless typing and compulsive name dropping. But two days later, Mariconda posted a second E-mail she'd received from Courtney's address, this one denying responsibility for the previous post. Perhaps, Love mused, someone had guessed her password and used her account. She loved Dave Grohl, really she did—and now he was mad at her because of this "faux Courtney" posting. Honestly, if he wanted to join Pearl Jam, she didn't care, but she hadn't—repeat, hadn't—written that post. (One can only guess that the mysterious online impostor had also hacked into Love's appointment book: On September 8, four days after the "fraudulent" post in which "Faux Courtney" let it slip that she would be "going w/Stipe to the aewards," Real Courtney did show up at the MTV Awards with R.E.M.'s Michael Stipe.)

Thanks to the red tape involved in freeing Jack Irons from his contract with Eleven's label, Hollywood Records, it would be another two months before Pearl Jam put the Grohl-fixated gossips out of their misery and announced that Irons had joined the band. Unofficially, though, Irons began working with Pearl Jam almost immediately, sitting in with them during an early October appearance at Neil Young's annual Bridge School benefit and also lending his talent to their forthcoming album. Pearl Jam's third release, *Vitalogy*, had been in the can for months by the time Dave was fired, but now, Eddie went back into the studio with Jack and cut a new track, "Stupid Mop," the disjointed hodgepodge of tape loops, feedback, and scattershot drumming that would form the album's coda.

The eleventh-hour addition probably left the folks at Epic tearing their hair out. The release of *Vitalogy* had already been pushed back because of delays with the artwork, as Pearl Jam's concept for the packaging of *Vitalogy*—named after and inspired by an 1899 health encyclopedia Eddie had picked up during his travels—was much more ambitious than it had been for any of their other releases. It was also more expensive, requiring Pearl Jam to work out a deal with Epic in which they shouldered half of the additional production costs so that the label wouldn't jack up the album's retail price and pass the expense on to fans.

As opposed to the typical plastic jewel box, the band wanted to house the album in a cardboard digipak designed to look like the original *Vitalogy* volume, with a thirty-four-page booklet featuring lyrics and notes, along with excerpts and photos from the text of the book. The CD itself was to be inserted into a folder at the end of the booklet, which meant that it had to be hand-packed at the pressing plant rather than processed by machine. For the album's title, which was to be silk-screened onto every copy, the band had selected an unusual gold ink that was so volatile it had to be used within forty-eight hours or it began to separate. In a move that was as much a nostalgic indulgence for the band members as it was a concession to collectors and audiophiles, Pearl Jam had also insisted on a limited-edition vinyl pressing of *Vitalogy*, to be released a week prior to the CD and cassette versions.

"The band feels strongly about giving people a package that means something instead of just a regular plastic jewel box," Kelly Curtis told the *Los Angeles Times* that October. "It's kind of like albums used to be, definitely something of value."

Just as cynics had speculated that Pearl Jam's press-shyness was a clever ploy, geared more toward increasing the band's fame than limiting it, so would they seize on Pearl Jam's release of *Vitalogy* on vinyl a week prior to the CD release, pointing out that die-hard fans would likely feel compelled to buy both editions and that the move was just a moneymaking tactic. In many ways, though, the care Pearl Jam took with the packaging of their records sprang from the same place their antimedia tendencies did. Quite simply, they were trying to preserve for their own audience the kind of experience they themselves had had as rock fans in the Seventies.

"I heard a Talking Heads song today, and I was thinking about what a masterful songwriter David Byrne is and was, but more importantly how the band interacted, and how they seemed to grow over a period of the first five records," Eddie reflected not long after the release of *Vitalogy*. "I started thinking about how lately, there's a lot of bands that get to a certain level, and it just stops. They scrap it. Compare this to, say, the Rolling Stones or the Who, where they just continued on forever and are still playing, or they quit after twenty years. But Talking Heads, or Jane's Addiction, or the Police, or even Nirvana you could say, got to a point and then that was just it. I was wondering what the difference was between the early bands and these bands. . . ."

The difference, as Eddie touched on during the interview, was a host of industry-wide changes that had taken place in the late Seventies and early Eighties, among them the birth of MTV, the advent of the compact disc, and the growing proliferation of entertainment magazines and mainstream news outlets devoting coverage to a music that had formerly been relegated to a few fan magazines. All the members of Pearl Jam could remember what it had been like to be a rock fan prior to these changes—the delicious tactile ritual of a new album purchase, the fun it had been to pore over the artwork and liner notes in the days when the album packaging, and maybe a rare interview or two, provided the only means other than the music itself by which fans could gain insight into their idols. More than anything else, what Pearl Jam were attempting to do was turn back the clock and sidestep the *Future Shock* syndrome that had infected the careers of so many artists before them. They wanted their audience to be able to savor their work as opposed to merely consuming it—and them.

Vitalogy was a reflection of that goal, the sound of a band determinedly climbing out of its grunge pigeonhole and exploring its creative future. As many hours as fans would spend lovingly inspecting the *Vitalogy* packaging for insight into Pearl Jam's current mindset, the real clues lay in the grooves, fourteen tracks forming an intense personal document that was at once a meditation on the misery of celebrity ("Pry, to," "Bugs," "Corduroy," "Not for You") and a Rorschach of Eddie's view on the human condition—songs like "Last Exit," "Nothingman," "Better Man," "Whipping," "Satan's Bed," and "Immortality" exploring the rocky territory of love, sex, death, and everything in between.

Musically, the album was an incredibly diverse mission statement, taking on fast, almost mod garage rock ("Last Exit," "Whipping," and the ode-to-vinyl "Spin the Black Circle"); moody acoustic work ("Nothingman"); *Rust Never Sleeps* and *Harvest*-era Neil Young (respectively, "Not for You" and the dark "Immortality"); majestic, *Sgt. Pepper*-inspired psychedelia ("Tremor Christ"); and bristling, expertly crafted pop ("Corduroy," the album's hands-down standout track, and "Better Man," a gem rescued from Eddie's Bad Radio days). Sprinkled throughout were unusual instrumentals ("Aye Davanita") and experimental, avant-garde interludes like "Pry, to," "Bugs" (for which Eddie strapped on an accordion), and the eerie album closer, "Stupid Mop," a sonic collage on which a child was interviewed about discipline, sex, and suicide. Some of these forays were more successful on a performance-art level than a musical one, but they were never less than fascinating. All told, *Vitalogy* was a remarkable document of Pearl Jam's growth. Both a rumination on where they'd been and a declaration about where they wanted to be, the album offered a promising glimpse into the future of a band that wanted to continue challenging itself and its audience.

Pearl Jam weren't sure how *Vitalogy* would be received. As proud as they were of the record, they were also concerned that the record-breaking sales of their previous releases had left them with a lot to live up to, in the eyes of an industry that too often measured artistic viability by the number of units sold. "What if our new record doesn't sell a million copies the first week?" Eddie asked a *Spin* reporter in late October. "Are people going to be let down? Say it peaks at a half million or something. People are going to panic, say we've got to do some videos, we've got to get this band on the road. I mean, it's just music, what does it matter?"

He needn't have worried. The response to *Vitalogy*, from fans and critics alike, was overwhelmingly positive, and the sales were overwhelming, period. Not only did the CD version go platinum the first week of its release, barring even the hallowed Beatles (*Live at the BBC*) from the No. 1 slot in *Billboard*, but the vinyl release alone, issued a week earlier than the CD on November 22, debuted at a respectable No. 55 on the *Billboard* album chart as well, a feat that had not been accomplished by any other vinyl album since the advent of the compact disc.

For now, Pearl Jam could do no wrong.

In January 1995, the band commandeered the airwaves again, staging a nationwide satellite broadcast similar to the one they'd done in Atlanta but this time inviting all of their friends to participate. Billed as "Self-Pollution Radio"—a reference to a *Vitalogy* passage on the evils of masturbation and, perhaps, a tongue-in-cheek acknowledgment by the band of the program's more self-indulgent elements—the show was broadcast from a run-down Seattle apartment Eddie used as a rehearsal space, and unspooled as a sort of punk variety show-cum-political rally, featuring live performances by Pearl Jam, Soundgarden, the Fastbacks, Mudhoney, and Mad Season (the side project recently formed by Mike with Layne Staley of Alice in Chains and Barrett Martin of the Screaming Trees), as well as a spoken-word piece by Nirvana's Krist Novoselic. Eddie, in a rambling, often comical turn as deejay and master of ceremonies, spun records, officially named Jack Irons as the newest member of the band, played his and Beth's holiday answering-machine messages on the air, and put in phone calls to a number of musician friends, among them Neil Young (who wasn't home) and L7 drummer Dee Plakas (who discussed the feminist organization Voters for Choice, for which Pearl Jam, Young, and L7 would play a benefit in Washington, D.C., the following week).

By the time the broadcast wound down, with an impassioned reading by Eddie of a Voters for Choice memo chronicling the latest in an ugly rash of abortion clinic shootings, it clocked in at four hours and twenty-three minutes—almost an hour and a half longer than planned—and the word "fuck" had been uttered exactly forty-five times. For Pearl Jam and the other artists who'd participated, and for the fans who'd tuned in, it was a sloppy, fun, subversive triumph. Director Doug Pray, on hand during the broadcast filming footage for a forthcoming Seattle scene documentary, *Hype*, found the event fascinating.

"That was the result of a major label saying, 'Okay, you won't do videos, you won't do interviews . . . what will you do? Will you do anything?'" Pray remarked. "They have a huge budget to spend, so it turns into an accounting problem for them. The band's response, apparently, was, 'Okay, we want to set up in our practice room and have a bunch of our friends play, and we want to broadcast it to the whole world.' So they got this satellite dish—there's a shot of it in the movie—outside of the dingiest little practice room. This gigantic dish—what a visual metaphor—literally beaming all over the world. Los Angeles alone had four stations, a six-hour broadcast, no commercials. Just them playing music and every once in a while going, 'Is this thing on?' I mean, it was kind of bad in a way, but it was great. All these local bands they were promoting. If that isn't a radical example of do-it-yourself on a global scale, I don't know what is."

Pearl Jam spent their January paying homage to their pro-choice beliefs—and to Neil Young. On January 12, the band joined Young and Crazy Horse on stage at the annual Rock & Roll Hall of Fame dinner. Eddie, asked to give a speech inducting Young, turned up at the ceremony in a jovial mood, not only outdoing himself in his praise of Young but also leaving the industry crowd in stitches when he wondered at the podium who the "smartass" was who'd seated Pearl Jam next to the Ticketmaster table. Two days later, Pearl Jam and Young were in D.C. for the Voters for Choice benefit concert—an event that was marred somewhat when fans, always fond of Dave Abbruzzese, booed Jack Irons upon his introduction, prompting Eddie to point out that Irons had "saved the life of this band." In late January, they repaired with Young to Seattle, setting up at Bad Animals to begin recording *Mirror Ball*, a loose, well-received collaboration on which they served as Young's backup band. Just before they left town for a tour of Asia, Australia, and New Zealand, Young sat in with them during the second of two warm-up shows at Seattle's Moore Theater, debuting one of the newly recorded tracks, "Act of Love."

Aside from a mini riot caused by a ticket shortage in Melbourne and a brief scare in New Zealand when Eddie, surfing with former Split Enz member Tim Finn, got caught in a rip tide and had to be rescued by lifeguards (who later beat a path to reporters and tattled that the singer had not thanked them profusely enough), the month-long tour was blessedly hassle free. Once Pearl Jam returned to the States, though, aggravations began accumulating.

Eddie's wife, Beth, had formed her own band, a spacy, experimental outfit called Hovercraft, and Eddie had been filling in on drums until a permanent percussionist could be found.* Hovercraft, along with Dave Grohl's new band, the Foo Fighters, had been invited to open some April and May dates for former Minutemen bassist Mike Watt's band, and Eddie agreed to go along, assuming drum chores for Hovercraft and also appearing as a side man in Watt's band. Wanting to maintain a low profile on the tour, Eddie appeared onstage in a wig and dark glasses, but after the first show of the tour in Tempe, Arizona, MTV alerted fans to his presence on the outing, kicking off a round of Eddie-skewed media coverage that largely ignored everyone else on the bill and, apparently, resulted in some tension between husband and wife over the erroneous perception that Hovercraft was Eddie's band. In mid-May, fuming over *Rolling Stone*'s singling him out in its report on the shows, Eddie pulled off of the tour. Not long afterward, Epic released a testy statement by the singer clarifying Beth's position as the rightful leader of Hovercraft.

"Hovercraft is a band I played in during the Mike Watt/Foo Fighters/ Hovercraft tour, as well as various other occasions in the past," Eddie said in the statement. "I am not currently playing drums with them, so I shouldn't be considered a member nor should it be considered my side project. Hovercraft is its own creation and doing quite well at that. May this set the record straight for Hovercraft and all others involved. Hopefully this makes sense. If not, read it again."

---

*Ultimately, original Pearl Jam drummer Dave Krusen would fill the seat.

In June, after nearly a year of preparation and with the entire music industry looking on, Pearl Jam made their first tentative attempt to stage a tour that completely sidestepped Ticketmaster.

Back in April, the band had inked a deal with a spanking-new Ticketmaster rival called ETM, which would utilize a computerized telephone system to distribute the tickets, and announced a fourteen-date summer tour kicking off June 16 in Boise, Idaho. Speaking to reporters about the newly scheduled tour, Kelly Curtis was cautiously optimistic. "Pearl Jam is back, and we're trying something brand-new," Curtis told the *Washington Post* on April 4. "I hope the fans will be patient, because we're bound to have a few hiccups with this new ticketing system as the tour unfolds."

Unfortunately, the hiccups started even before the tour did.

A month after the band announced the dates, the very first show on the itinerary, scheduled at the Boise State University Pavilion, had to be canceled after a breakdown in contract negotiations that ultimately left Pearl Jam open to accusations of hypocrisy. Ticket sales at the Pavilion were normally handled by Select-A-Seat, a local agency that assessed a $.50 service charge per ticket. But Pearl Jam, pursuant to their contract with ETM, insisted during the negotiations that ETM be the sole entity responsible for selling tickets to the show. ETM's service charge, ironically, was $2 per ticket, plus an additional $.45 handling fee.

Kelly Curtis later claimed the show was canceled because ETM needed approval from the local government to operate at the state-run venue and could not obtain it before the show's on-sale date. But BSU Pavilion officials insisted that that had not been the case, charging that the deal breaker had been Pearl Jam's refusal to allow Select-A-Seat, with its lower service charge, to handle the ticket sales. "We're frustrated and disappointed," Charlie Spencer, assistant director of the Pavilion, told *Variety*. "Long before Pearl Jam made affordable ticket prices fashionable, we've worked hard to bring concertgoers the lowest ticket price possible. I'm surprised that Pearl Jam professed a certain ideology and then veered off from that stance."

Nobody else could understand the logic, either, and coming on the heels of a snotty April 10 commentary in the *Los Angeles Times* penned by Ticketmaster senior vice president Alan Citron, in which Citron pointed out that "ETM's fee structure virtually [mirrored] Ticketmaster's" and that Pearl Jam were "more interested in perpetuating the feud than in scheduling concert dates," the Boise cancellation fueled a growing perception among skeptical types that Pearl Jam's beef with Ticket-master had less to do with saving their fans money than it did with increasing their own slice of the pie. Not helping matters, punk upstarts Green Day had already put *their* money where Pearl Jam's mouth was, casually mounting a tour *with* Ticketmaster and still charging only $15 per ticket, $5 less than Pearl Jam's asking price.

"We take a lower cut than Pearl Jam," the band's drummer, Tre Cool, gloated to Alec Foege of *Rolling Stone*. "I'm not picking on them—I'm just saying that to anyone in general who's complaining about it. You don't want your tickets being $27 and shit? Take a lower cut, guys."

After the Boise flap, the band moved the tour's June 16 opening date to the Casper Events Center in Casper, Wyoming. In late April, the first real test of the ETM system, ticket sales for the Casper show went off without a hitch, as did sales for a pair of shows in Denver, ETM moving eighteen thousand tickets in seven minutes flat. By May, every date on the tour route had sold out, and with few complaints registered about the ETM ticketing process, Pearl Jam began to breathe a little easier. "There are small quirks, but it's working," the band's new publicist, Nicole Van-denberg, told *USA Today* on June 8, a week before the tour's launch. "People understand there's little benefit to the band and a lot to the fans."

A day later, though, Eddie's hometown would ring in with a surprise move, setting off a chain of events that effectively doomed the entire tour. On June 9, the *San Diego Union-Tribune* reported that the San Diego Sheriff's Department, citing security concerns, had asked Del Mar Fair officials to cancel two sold-out San Diego shows set for June 26 and 27 at the Del Mar Fairgrounds. This came as news to Kelly Curtis and the band, who'd been working with fair officials for two months on the shows and had not heard a peep out of the Sheriff's Department about any security fears.

"It disturbs me that the Sheriff's Department chose to release their concerns about safety and security to the media, rather than bringing them directly to us so that we could address them," Curtis said in a statement later that day. "I am unaware of their specific concerns, but had they made them known, we could have addressed them months ago. Now we're two weeks out from two sold-out shows for twenty-six thousand fans."

On June 12, three days after the *Tribune* article appeared, Curtis issued a second statement cancelling the shows, claiming that the "unprofessional and unproductive approach" taken by the Sheriff's Department had forced the band's hand. Eddie, too, had a statement to make, although it would be edited before most papers printed it.

"We did our job, set up the show, sold tickets," he said. "It's a long process. We're obviously ready to play. Not to make enemies, but it seems the officials in San Diego have overreacted, creating an impossible situation. It's a shame, really. Have a little more faith, assholes."

The cancellation resulted in a round of finger pointing in the *Tribune*, with Del Mar Fair officials and the Sheriff's Department claiming that they'd been willing to work out the snags in the show but that Pearl Jam would not make any compromises. "I don't want to be perceived as someone who is trying to hurt the public by preventing them from seeing entertainment they want to see," said Captain Chuck Wood, supervisor of the Encinitas Sheriff's substation. "We didn't cancel it. They did. Sorry." Jill Esterbrooks, spokeswoman for the Del Mar Fair, said that fair officials had sent a letter to the Sheriff's Department on June 10 addressing their concerns and offering to make a number of changes— among them banning alcohol, increasing security, staging the show in the daytime, and even cutting the opening act, Bad Religion, from the bill—that would ostensibly make the concerts more safe. According to Kelly Curtis, the suggested compromises were what had ultimately derailed the gigs. "Making it a daylight show, taking Bad Religion off the bill and adding three hundred extra security personnel was a draw," Curtis said. "The Sheriff's Department hasn't even accepted those proposals, and I know my band wouldn't."

San Diego fans reacted badly to news of the cancellation, phoning radio stations to air their opinions and lighting up the switchboard at the Sheriff's Department. ("They took their wrath out on dispatchers and basically cursed them out until about three A.M.," Lieutenant B. G. Davis told the Associated Press.) But the real fireworks began on June 13, when Kelly Curtis announced that Pearl Jam were reconsidering their anti-Ticketmaster stance.

"It took us a whole year to plan these summer dates, and we're not going to go through that again," Curtis told reporters. "We did want to make a point on how difficult it is to tour without Ticketmaster, and we made the point. . . . I think you'll find that the band is going to do whatever it takes to just play. And if that means they're going to have to play some Ticketmaster shows, they're going to play Ticketmaster shows."

On the following day, the controversy heightened, when Curtis announced that Pearl Jam had moved the two canceled San Diego shows to the San Diego Sports Arena—a venue that had an exclusive contract with Ticketmaster.

Although no tickets would actually be sold by Ticketmaster for the rescheduled shows—the Sports Arena would simply honor the Del Mar tickets previously sold by ETM—the venue had had to obtain approval from Ticketmaster allowing the ETM tickets to be honored for the shows. According to Ernie Hahn, the Sports Arena's business manager, Ticketmaster had granted the venue a contractual waiver enabling the Pearl Jam shows to go on in return for an undisclosed fee that would be donated to charity. "Ticketmaster and the San Diego Sports Arena felt that it was in the best interest of Pearl Jam fans here to have the shows play in San Diego," said Hahn, who described the situation as "real delicate."

Asked about the Sports Arena shows by journalists, Kelly Curtis and the band's publicist, Nicole Vandenberg, as well as Ray Garman, president of Fillmore Mercantile, a private Philadelphia merchant bank that was the principal shareholder of ETM, all attempted to distance themselves from Ticketmaster's involvement with the shows, saying that the arrangements for the rescheduled concerts had been made between the Sports Arena and Ticketmaster and that the band itself had not signed or negotiated any agreement with Ticketmaster.

But Curtis continued to tell reporters that the band was admitting defeat in its standoff with the ticket giant. "I regret to say that it's impossible for a major rock group to put on a national tour under the current circumstances without Ticketmaster," he told a *Los Angeles Times* reporter on June 14, the same day the rescheduled Sports Arena shows were announced. "They've got a monopoly. We did everything we could over the past fourteen months to get around them and put this tour together, but we failed. It's up to the Justice Department now." He made similar comments to the *Seattle Post-Intelligencer* and also issued a formal statement: "If the Department of Justice rules in favor of the consumers and Pearl Jam, it will change the look of ticketing for the entire music industry. If the ruling is in favor of Ticketmaster, the band may be forced to perform in some Ticketmaster venues in order to reach their fans. The band has done all it can. We've raised awareness of the Ticketmaster monopoly, and although we will continue to work to keep our ticket prices low, we feel the fate of ticket industry reform now lies in the hands of the Department of Justice. As for Pearl Jam, it's time for the band to get back to doing what they do best: making music and playing for their fans."

Ticketmaster responded predictably, issuing a statement asserting that "the security and logistical woes that the band has blamed for its touring problems have nothing to do with Ticketmaster," and adding that the company was "pleased that Pearl Jam is doing something to benefit its fans" and "happy to work with anyone that wants to use our services."

Curtis's statements resulted in a firestorm of press coverage. Between June 13 and June 15, headlines like "Pearl Jam Ends Ticketmaster Feud" and "Pearl Jam Admits Defeat" popped up all over the country like poison mushrooms, and when fans got wind of the news, the backlash was immediate—and powerful.

Almost as soon as the news began breaking, fans—many of whom had adopted Pearl Jam's Ticketmaster vendetta as a personal crusade, launching letter-writing campaigns and even boycotting Ticketmaster-run concerts—began calling radio stations and crowding online bulletin boards to express their disbelief that Pearl Jam would wimp out at this late stage of the game. To many—who'd waited for over a year to see Pearl Jam because of the band's refusal to work with Ticketmaster, comforting themselves with the knowledge that the cause was worth supporting—it seemed a massive betrayal.

In the face of this uproar, Pearl Jam began furiously backpedaling. As soon as the band took the stage in Wyoming for the tour's June 16 kick-off show, Eddie took the bull by the horns. "I guess you've heard, they're saying in the papers that we surrendered to Ticketmaster," he said. "Well, that didn't happen. And take my word, that's not *going* to happen." His words were greeted by thunderous applause. Meanwhile, backstage, Kelly Curtis was trying to explain to Robert Hilburn of the *Los Angeles Times* why he'd just spent three days telling reporters Pearl Jam were going to reconsider working with Ticketmaster when Eddie was claiming otherwise.

According to Hilburn's account of the conversation the following Monday, Curtis told Hilburn he'd spoken out of turn—that without consulting Pearl Jam, he'd announced the band's capitulation to Ticketmaster out of frustration over the canceled San Diego shows. "Jeff and Eddie were furious after reading reports that we had changed our policy," Curtis told Hilburn, "because that was not their intention at all, and we are all in agreement that it is not what we are going to do."

Hilburn didn't seem to question this, but others, who had been following the daily news updates on the controversy with interest, suspected that Curtis was simply taking the rap for his clients. Few managers in the business, after the kind of protracted, high-profile media feud Pearl Jam had been fighting with Ticketmaster, would take it upon themselves to make such a powder keg decision without the full knowledge of their clients, and given the tight control Pearl Jam typically exercised over business matters, it seemed incongruous that Curtis, even out of frustration, would raise the white flag to Ticketmaster—not to mention discussing it with several reporters during interviews and then issuing a formal statement—without first discussing it with the band. What had likely happened, many believed, was that the band members had realized they were fighting a losing battle and decided to throw in the towel; that Curtis, with their authorization, had announced their decision to the media; and that later—after the headlines and the backlash hit, and it became apparent that the public was not going to let them abandon the Ticketmaster crusade without taking a lot of guff for it—Curtis had taken the fall so the band could save face. Whatever the truth, few of Curtis's peers envied his position.

After the Wyoming show, the tour seemed positively jinxed. In Salt Lake City, the second date on the itinerary, a torrential downpour forced another cancellation just before the band was to go on, leaving a drenched Eddie, armed with a bullhorn, to greet arriving fans and tell them to go home. "Thanks for coming out here," he hollered. "Please don't get sick. We're going to come back and play twice as long." Losing battles or not, you had to admire his heart.

The band wobbled on, managing to pull off three more successful shows—two in Denver on June 19 and 20, and a third in Sacramento on June 22—before pulling into San Francisco. There, on June 24, the chaos and controversy that had been hanging over the tour like a radioactive cloud finally caught up with them.

XOX

Message posted in America Online's Pearl Jam forum, June 26, 1995:

Subj: Re: SD
Date: 95-06-26 01:19:25 EDT
From: S0NGMAN

Sorry, there won't be no SD shows. Take your girl out to dinner. We'll be back.

Nineteen

Justice Drops the Ball / Summer Tour, Take Two / Thank You,
NARAS Voters / *No Code* and Beyond

". . . I'm just all fucked up. I think that might be it for me for a while. Lucky for you, Neil Young's here, so he's gonna take over for a bit. . . ."

A few hours after the infamous June 24, 1995 Golden Gate Park concert where Eddie quit the stage after seven songs, leaving his band mates to finish the set with Neil Young before fifty thousand angry fans, Kelly Curtis convened with Stone, Mike, Jeff, and Jack and asked them what they wanted to do.

"That was the day we acted as a band," Stone said later, of their decision to scrap the rest of the ill-fated tour. "In the past, we had kind of allowed Eddie to steer the ship in some ways, and it's still that way. You want him to feel good about the situation, because when he's feeling good about it, it makes the whole thing work. But that day you could see he was totally sick but still trying to push himself. When we saw what was happening, the band finally said, 'This is insane. We've got to stop. . . .'"

On the following day, Nicole Vandenberg issued the statement mak-

ing it official. "Pearl Jam regretfully announced today that they will cancel the remaining concert dates of their fifteen-date summer tour. The
cancellation was brought on by the business problems and controversies
surrounding the band's attempt to schedule an alternative tour. . . ."

The status quo—and the typical rock fan—were only so resilient, and
for Pearl Jam, the days after the cancellation were brutal. As radio stations across the country took calls from irate ticket holders, KLOS in Los
Angeles attacked the band with satire, whipping up an inspired parody
of *Vitalogy*'s "Better Man":

> *San Francisco / No one expected a Neil Young show*
> *San Diego canceled / Pearl Jam, what a hassle . . .*
> *I'm pissed off, I'm let down / Life's so hard in this town*
> *First the Rams, then the Raiders / What's with all you*
>   *entertainers?*
> *This whole thing could have been much faster /*
> *Next time, please use Ticketmaster . . .*
> *A million kids are feeling blue / Can't find the Vedder man*
> *I kinda feel like I've been screwed / Can't find the Vedder man*
> *I'd like to get my hands on you / Can't find the Vedder man*

Newsweek rang in with a withering commentary. "When Pearl Jam
played San Francisco's Golden Gate Park on June 24, there wasn't a
cloud in the sky, except for the little black one above Eddie Vedder's
head," the piece began. "Pearl Jam has done battle with a lot of things:
Ticketmaster, the record industry, MTV, the press. . . . Of course, all this
is business, and a band as powerful (and bankable) as Pearl Jam earns
the right to do whatever it damn well pleases. The tour cancellations are
another matter. This is the first time Pearl Jam has specifically managed
to exclude its most devoted fans."

Certainly, that hadn't been the band's intention, but many of their
followers did feel spurned. In the wake of the news that the tour had
been scrapped, some of Pearl Jam's most loyal supporters began to turn
away, angry and unable to understand why the band had persisted for so
long with what now seemed a pointless charade. Typical were the reactions of a handful of forlorn ticket holders interviewed by the *Austin
American-Statesman* on June 27. One fan, twenty-six-year-old Kim Han-
kins, described her happiness over obtaining tickets, as well as the subsequent letdown. "I felt like I had won something," she said. "I planned
my entire weekend around it. Pearl Jam started out trying to punish

Ticketmaster, but now they're hurting us." Nineteen-year-old Eman So-joodi felt similarly jilted. "What sets me off the most is that Pearl Jam was the band that decided to take a stand against Ticketmaster, but then they sell tickets that aren't that much cheaper, they say they are giving in to Ticketmaster after all, and then they cancel their tour," he said, adding that he'd placed more than sixty calls to ETM in order to secure tickets. "You feel like you are one of the select few who was able to get through for once in your life, and then you end up getting screwed."

Three days after they announced the cancellation of the remaining dates, Pearl Jam attempted to undo some of the damage, reinstating three early July shows in Milwaukee and Chicago. Although it would take them until November to do it, they would eventually make up every canceled date on the itinerary. But, in a sense, as eager as fans were to see the shows, and as smoothly as the shows ultimately went, the reinstated dates only seemed to heighten the public confusion over what Pearl Jam's stance *was,* and why they'd canceled the dates in the first place. Nobody could understand the band's blaming Ticketmaster for the tour cancellation, since the dates had already been booked and the tickets had already been sold.

"The Pearl Jam decision-making process is falling victim to an emotional rollercoaster," wrote Michael Goldberg in the respected electronic music magazine *Addicted to Noise.* "Flip-flopping on whether to continue to fight Ticketmaster or cave in, on whether to make up the San Francisco date or not, offer refunds for that show or not, complete all (or at least some) of the remaining tour dates, or cancel the tour demonstrates an indecisiveness and emotional instability that we've never seen before on the part of this great band. Just as bad, sending out vague press releases that attempt to rationalize these illogical decisions just compounds the problem."

At this point, there was only one thing that could possibly have added to the air of defeat surrounding the band, and on July 6, Janet Reno kindly stepped in and took care of it.

The Justice Department, Reno announced that Thursday during her weekly news briefing, had decided to abandon its investigation of Ticketmaster.

✄⟡✄

There was "a great deal of activity" in the ticketing business, Reno told reporters, and although the Justice Department would continue to monitor developments in the industry, it simply "did not seem an appropriate time" to pursue a case against Ticketmaster.

It seemed a frustrating, by-the-book approach to a unique situation. Officials at the Justice Department would not elaborate on Reno's terse announcement, or offer any clues as to whether the issue at the core of Pearl Jam's complaint against the corporation—the cut of the service charges that was paid back to the venues and promoters who agreed to use Ticketmaster exclusively—had factored into the decision at all.

In stark contrast to the barrage of media coverage that had been devoted to the launch of the investigation and Pearl Jam's high-profile role in it, the announcement that the inquiry was being dropped caused barely a ripple in the press. Aside from the disappointed editorials filed by a handful of reporters who'd been following the case, there was no media outcry over the decision—no debate over whether the government had explored Ticketmaster's business practices on more than a superficial level before dropping the probe, no real discussion of the logic behind the decision, or the kick in the face it represented to consumers. Case closed, plain and simple. Back to business as usual.

Pearl Jam issued a brief, impotent statement over the Justice Department decision—"Ultimately," the release pointed out, "those who will be most hurt by the Justice Department's cave-in are the consumers of live entertainment"—and attempted to shrug off the bad vibes and restore the focus to their music.

It wasn't easy. Americans have always taken perverse pleasure in the public stoning of their fallen idols, and Pearl Jam would not be spared the ritual. For the first time in their career, their path wasn't paved with gold, and a media and broadcasting community that had always been supportive now seemed to be baiting them every step of the way. In Chicago, Eddie's old friends at Q101 took a tip from their marketing department and erected a billboard featuring their new slogan—THIS IS NOT FOR YOU—near the entrance of Soldier Field, for the express purpose of getting a rise out of the singer during the Chicago concert. Eddie did not disappoint, making a thinly-veiled reference to Q101 during the show as he introed "Not For You." Bill Gamble, then the station's program director, later suggested that Eddie's humorless tendencies made him an easy target.

"You know, we understand the trials and troubles people go through, but on the other hand, part of being a celebrity is that you are a public figure," Gamble said. "Most of the people that we do things with have a great sense of humor. He just seems way too serious at times. It's great playing with your wife in clubs and indulging yourself and driving around in vans. But somewhere along the line, you do have a responsibility to the people that enjoy your music. There is that Peter Frampton syndrome you have to be careful about. People have short-term memories."

After the Soldier Field show, Pearl Jam remained in Chicago for a week to record tracks for their fourth album, once again working with producer Brendan O'Brien. Soon afterward, the band members scattered, Eddie staying in Illinois to spend time with relatives, and the others heading for Europe to back Neil Young on a run of festival dates. Throughout the summer, there was very little word from the Pearl Jam camp.

In September, the band returned to the road in the U.S., doggedly finishing the dates they'd reinstated from the canceled summer tour. Unlike the previous string of misfires, the shows went relatively smoothly, and though the media were not quite through using the Ticketmaster controversy and subsequent backlash to fill column space, the public appeared ready to forgive the band its past chaotic year. As 1995 drew to a close, even the sharp-tongued Courtney Love was eating her words, dropping a contrite retraction of her past statements about Pearl Jam into an article she penned for *Spin*. Among the things she wished her late husband had been around to see, Courtney wrote, was her "getting over putting down Pearl Jam." Kurt "would've been over it, too," she noted, before publicly offering the olive branch: "All apologies to Eddie. I was an asshole, and I'm sorry."

Eddie, too, seemed to be in better spirits around this time. As 1996 got underway, he was feeling downright sociable, turning up in Park City, Utah to jam with the Fastbacks at a post-premiere party for the film *Hype*, and even showing his face on television with a surprise Letterman walk-on in late February. For weeks, Paul Shaffer and the Letterman band had been using Pearl Jam's "Black" as an intro and outro for commercial breaks—Letterman himself had been supplying comical, glass-shattering vocals—and Eddie, in New York to see one of the final Ramones shows (the punk legends had just announced their retirement), rang up *The Late Show* to inform them that he'd been watching and wouldn't mind stopping by. Later that evening during the show, viewers were delighted when, during Shaffer and Letterman's running "Black" gag, Eddie walked on, sang a few bars of the song, and, just as quickly, disappeared again.

If the Letterman stunt saw the singer offering a badly-needed glimpse of his sense of humor, though, it was Eddie, the ungrateful punk of old who showed up at the 38th Annual Grammy Awards on the following night. Pearl Jam had decided it would be fun to attend the ceremony—*Vitalogy* had been nominated for Album of the Year, and "Spin the Black Circle" was in the running for Best Hard Rock performance—but they likely regretted the appearance later, given the bitter commentary it sparked.

Some fans were outraged that Pearl Jam even deigned to attend the ceremony at all, feeling the move was an unfitting embrace by the band of the mainstream, commercial aspects of the industry they'd always professed to hate. Even Randy Osenenko, co-editor of the Pearl Jam fanzine *Footsteps* and one of the band's most loyal champions, publicly condemned their decision to appear, calling the event "a fucking beauty contest voted on by out of touch assholes" and announcing that she would be boycotting the broadcast. But it was Eddie's comments during the band's acceptance speech for "Spin the Black Circle" that provoked the most ire, interpreted as smug and ungracious by fans, the NARAS voters, and a host of other industry observers.

"I hate to start off with a bang," Eddie, flanked by his band mates, said at the podium after "Spin the Black Circle" won in its category. "I'm going to say something typically 'me' on behalf of all of us. I don't know what this means . . . I don't think it means anything. That's just how I feel. There's too many bands, and you've heard it all before. But my dad would have liked it. My dad died before I got to know him, and he would have liked it. So that's why I'm here. Thanks, I guess."

Eddie had been saying this sort of thing since the earliest days of the band's career, to nary a raised eyebrow. That this particular recitation of the singer's trademark you-can't-give-awards-for-art speech bombed so royally was just one more sign of the public's shifting attitude toward the band. Just a few years back, Eddie's comments would have been lauded, or used by some reporter to buttress yet another fawning Eddie-as-antistar profile. But now, to an audience that had grown tired of Pearl Jam's perpetually embattled state, Eddie just seemed to be beating a dead horse. Did he have no awareness at all of how strident and humorless he sounded? Was he so compulsively driven to thumb his nose at every last music industry institution—every *authority figure*—that he couldn't remember what it was like to sit at home watching the Grammys, pulling for your favorite band and sharing in their happiness when they won? Couldn't he drop the preaching and enjoy *anything*, even for a *moment*?

Although a few devout supporters rose to his defense after the fact, the general consensus was that if Eddie truly felt the way he said he did, he should not have bothered to show up. Reporters had a field day with his acceptance speech in their recaps of the event, most of them paring his comments down to a curt, ungrateful, "This doesn't mean anything."

Virtually ignored in all the fuss was the lone aspect of Eddie's speech that wasn't drenched in antiestablishment sentiment—the only words he uttered that night that went straight to the emotional scars at the heart of his music *and* his success, and went a long way toward explaining why the accolades had always seemed hollow to him.

My dad would have liked it. My dad died before I got to know him, and he would have liked it. So that's why I'm here.

If anyone had thought it at all significant that Eddie would choose this most pivotal of moments—a moment considered by many to be the pinnacle of a music industry career—to point out to an audience of millions the central deprivation of his life, nobody mentioned it. There may have been an adult standing at the podium, but the words had been those of a grieving child.

Apparently, nobody had been listening.

✕◈✕

Throughout 1996, the band members appeared to be testing the solo waters.

Eddie had been first out of the gate, collaborating in January with Pakistani vocalist Nusrat Fateh Ali Kahn on the soundtrack for the Tim Robbins film, *Dead Man Walking*. Mike began yet another side project, Bumrush, with Pearl Jam photographer Lance Mercer; before the year was out, he would be playing with a third satellite group, Tuatura, an ever-shifting ensemble also featuring R.E.M.'s Peter Buck. Stone, focusing on his growing role as record mogul, attended to his Loosegroove label, which would part ways with Sony 550 in late July and strike out on its own. Jeff turned up in a side group called Three Fish with Tribe After Tribe vocalist Robbi Robb, and would release a well-received album in June and mount a three-week tour in July. Just before the album's release, he spoke of the contrast between Three Fish and his usual affiliation.

"Pearl Jam's a huge machine, bigger than any of us," Jeff told Sara Scribner of the *Los Angeles Times*. "It's been really great to step out of it. I can be objective. . . . It makes me realize I don't need Pearl Jam—that I can be perfectly happy making music on my own."

Comments like this, on the heels of the band's controversial last year, fueled a widening public perception that Pearl Jam was splintering. Although the band had completed a fourth album, scheduled for release in late August, the recording was rumored to have been tense. Eddie and Stone, the insider scuttlebutt had it, had been at each other's throats, Eddie dominating the sessions and pushing the band to focus on recording his songs, and Stone frustrated and threatening to call it quits.

Later, during the few interviews they did to promote the album, Pearl Jam would counter these rumors, maintaining that the sessions had been more familial than any they had ever enjoyed. By now, the band had become so insular and secretive that fans could only guess at the truth.

XOX

No Code, released in August 1996, bore the brunt of Pearl Jam's scarce touring and turbulent last year. The album sold 350,000 copies in its first week, a more than respectable showing by industry standards, but not for the biggest rock band of the Nineties.

Almost unheeded in the fuss over the album's sales was the music itself. Although *No Code* contained its share of patented Pearl Jam raveups (notably "Hail, Hail," "Habit," and the smile-inducing "Mankind," on which Stone did an engaging turn on lead vocals), the album's real impact lay in its dramatic maturity, the more sober, contemplative tracks ("Sometimes," "Who You Are," "Off He Goes," "Present Tense," "I'm Open," and the closing lullaby, "Around the Bend") imparting soothing undertones of a band reaching for self awareness, and a sense of peace or resolution.

In a way, *No Code* was the right album at the wrong time, a softening of the band's harder edges—both musical and philosophical—arriving a little too late to appease an audience that was still feeling wounded by the events of the past year. Fans that had been behind Pearl Jam, even respected them, for their career-defining decisions to stop making videos and limit their press, were much less forgiving about the band's flouting of tradition when it came to touring. Pearl Jam's fall 1996 U.S. tour in support of *No Code* consisted of only twelve dates, and while many of the shows—like a September 29 date on New York's Randall's Island, during which the band played for nearly three hours and seemed determined to work their way through their entire catalog—proved dazzling for the fans who managed to snag tickets, too few fans did. Pearl Jam's new ticketing system offered plenty of advantages—lower service charges, beautifully-designed tickets that made excellent souvenirs, and built-in measures to foil scalpers—but the meager itinerary and out-of-the-way venues Pearl Jam were playing because of their continued boycott of Ticketmaster meant that fewer fans actually enjoyed those benefits. By the end of 1996, there was a growing consensus that Pearl Jam's battle with Ticketmaster had hurt the band's fans more than helped them. Many wished they would just get over it already and do a proper tour, and it certainly didn't win them any brownie points when, during the few interviews they did that year, they made statements indicating that the abbreviated tour had been their preference, rather than a circumstance their feud with Ticketmaster had forced them into.

"I think touring is always going to be a compromise," Jeff told the *Los Angeles Times*. "Eddie and Jack are both married and they don't like to tour a lot, while some of us would probably like to tour more. I can go either way. . . . One thing that people should understand is that it's not Ticketmaster that's keeping us off the road. We are playing as much as we want to right now. I think we learned some things from the twelve shows we just did in the States that will make it easier next time. I know we made some mistakes in touring, but we were just trying to do what was fair to the fans."

Perhaps. But what fans really wanted was to see the band play, and Pearl Jam's seeming inability to mount a full-scale tour was, for many, a signal that it was time to move on.

By the time the band headed to Europe, where they would also play fewer dates than they had in their early days, pop culture in general was moving on. Record companies and the media were frustrated with artists who refused to promote themselves, and fans were growing bored with icons who insisted upon shucking the crown. The industry and the mainstream record buyers, tired of the endless angst and shoegazing that had always been the hallmarks of alternative music, were now embracing purveyors o' sunshine like Hootie and the Blowfish and the Spice Girls, the kind of amiable, uncomplicated pop artists who were always Happy to Serve You. Before long, think-pieces on The Death of Alternative Rock would be turning up in the media, most of them using the lackluster sales of *No Code* to illustrate the point, and at least a few going so far as to suggest that Pearl Jam's fifteen minutes of alterna-fame were up.

Leading the nail-in-the-coffin brigade was *Rolling Stone*, which in November 1996 ran a profile on Eddie that was undoubtedly the most damning piece of press Pearl Jam had encountered in their entire career. Although many fans believed the piece was written out of retaliation because Pearl Jam refused to grant an interview, *Rolling Stone* later denied that, claiming the band had consented to an interview but had wanted to exercise so much control over the outcome that the magazine had decided to pass.

"I guess [Eddie's] record label or his representatives were indignant that we wouldn't go along with their plans for how they wanted to see him covered," *Rolling Stone* editor-in-chief Jann Wenner told CNN a year after the infamous cover story hit the stands. "In our writing a piece about him, which was long overdue, we wouldn't pick the writer they selected and essentially give them approval over the story. We said, 'We're just not going to do that; we don't operate that way.'" It was ironic, Wenner added, that "in this case we're talking about Eddie Vedder. He is supposed to stand for being the antistar, the one who is against all this privileged treatment. Well, in my view, he is just a very, very wealthy, very spoiled guy."

It was this theory—that the private Eddie Vedder had little in common with the public one—that formed the backbone of the article in question. Drawn largely on interviews with anonymous Epic staffers and other inside sources, and boasting the cover headline, "Inventing Eddie Vedder: Pearl Jam's Mystery Man," the piece purported to be an exposé on the singer, painting him as a manipulative, careerist control freak, asserting that he'd manufactured his troubled childhood in order to boost his popularity, and implying that, contrary to his professed avoidance of celebrity, he'd spent years painstakingly molding himself into the quintessential grunge icon. The other members of Pearl Jam, the piece posited, were little more than cowed puppets, and the band was on its last legs as a result of Eddie's megalomaniacal behavior and slavishness to his Everyman image.

The story caused a huge uproar. Though a smattering of fans opined that it was the most interesting article they'd read on the band in the past year—at least, they reasoned, it revealed *something* new about their frustratingly secretive idol—the majority viewed it as an outrage and a cheap shot, and a number of Eddie's peers, among them Michael Stipe, Krist Novoselic, and Courtney Love, fired off angry letters protesting the piece.

Pearl Jam seemed much less disturbed by the article than their celebrity friends were. Eddie, in the one public statement he did make on the subject, swore that he hadn't bothered to read it.

"I know who I am," he told writer Robert Hilburn. "I don't need to read someone else's bitter take on it."

However negatively slanted *Rolling Stone*'s version of the truth might have been, the authorized press the band did around the same time ran so far to the opposite extreme that to some, it was equally suspect. After a year as turbulent as the one the band had just been through, could Pearl Jam possibly be as grounded—and as comfortable about their perceived loss of popularity—as they claimed they were? Asked during talks with both *Spin* and the *Los Angeles Times*—the only two interviews Pearl Jam consented to—about the disappointing sales of *No Code*, the band members said they were neither surprised nor bothered by the perception that they were slipping.

"I guess what has happened to us with this record shows that promotion really does matter, just like everybody told us," Eddie told the *Times*. "If you don't operate in that framework, which we don't, it's obvious that you won't sell as many records. And that's fine. We expected this to happen much sooner than it has." The singer echoed this during the interview with Craig Marks of *Spin*, even telling Marks that he found the album's slow sales "great."

"We can be a little more normal now," he explained.

In a sense, the widely contrasting state-of-the-union reports offered by *Rolling Stone*, on the one hand, and *Spin* and the *Los Angeles Times*, on the other, simply canceled each other out, sparking a number of new questions but in the end answering few of them, leaving fans as curious as ever about the band's stability and future direction. Just as it had always been with Eddie's lyrics, the details of Pearl Jam's life, as 1997 dawned, were oblique enough to lend themselves to more than one interpretation. The only thing anyone could seem to agree on was that if Pearl Jam wanted to maintain their hold on the rock audience, they had some heavy changes to make.

The question, of course, was what they really wanted.

Ж◇Ж

By 1997, the Seattle Scene—not to mention alternative music in general—had been pronounced dead by the industry tastemakers. Of the four bands who'd burst out of Seattle in 1991 and captured the attention of the mainstream, only Pearl Jam was still intact. All of the others had succumbed, in some form or another, to the side effects of stardom.

Nirvana had lost its leader to suicide. Alice in Chains, derailed by Layne Staley's heroin addiction, were missing in action, stuck on what appeared to be a perpetual hiatus. Soundgarden had broken up in July amid rumors of discord. Susan Silver, long one of the scene's integral players, had even taken down her management shingle.

Each in their own way, the musicians who'd helped to define a pivotal chapter in rock & roll history were cutting their ties with the past and forging their futures. Dave Grohl was now as well known for his new band, the Foo Fighters, as he had been for his tenure in Nirvana. Chris Cornell was on the cusp of what would surely be a promising solo career. Courtney Love had turned to acting—winning accolades for her role as Althea Flynt in the Hollywood hit *The People vs. Larry Flynt*—and had completely reinvented herself in the bargain, forsaking her trademark kinderwhore look for Versace gowns and enlisting high-powered publicist Pat Kingsley to buff up her tarnished image.

Dave Abbruzzese had gone home to Texas, hooking up with some old musical friends from his pre-Pearl Jam days and forming a new band, the Green Romance Orchestra. He had run into some problems when he began looking for a label for GRO's first release, the diverse and engaging *Play, Parts I and IV**—most of the record execs he spoke with were more eager to capitalize on his past affiliation than he was comfortable with—but all told, his experience with GRO had been a healing one, doing much to erase the bitterness he felt over Pearl Jam's pulling the rug from beneath him.

"I'll always wish the best for them," he told *The Rocket* in 1997 of his former band mates. "I don't have hard feelings about what happened anymore. At this point, it doesn't really matter very much . . . Without that experience of getting fired and the experience of being in the band all those years, I wouldn't have been able to look at things they way I do now. . . . It was a blessing in a lot of ways, even the way it ended."

✖✧✖

As for Pearl Jam, they'd come to a crossroads. Either they could content themselves with preaching to the converted, continuing to let them-

---

*After a limited-edition pressing sold by mail order, *Play, Parts I and IV* finally saw nationwide distribution in October 1997, on Dave's own Free Association label.

selves be led—and defined—by an image and a legend they had clearly outgrown, or they could reintroduce themselves, opening some of the doors they'd slammed shut in the past and reaching out to a new audience. Whichever path they chose, it was bound to earn them criticism from one world or another—the one they'd come from, which prided itself on being uncompromising, or the one that beckoned, where compromise was a necessary aspect of survival.

In October 1997, just after the news broke that they had completed a fifth, as yet untitled album, Pearl Jam offered the first clue as to their direction, accepting an invitation by the Rolling Stones to open two mid-November dates of the Stones' "Bridges to Babylon" tour at California's Oakland Stadium. Longtime fans who'd never expected to see a ripple in Pearl Jam's anticommercial stance could be heard screeching far and wide when the Stones shows—sponsored by Sprint and ticketed by Ticketmaster—were announced, but many of those same fans grabbed up the $65 tickets as soon as they were offered. Within a week, two more Oakland dates were added, Pearl Jam's star power having enabled the legendary Stones, for the first time on their tour, to play more than two nights in the same city.

If a generational torch was being passed, Eddie finally seemed ready to accept it. "This has been the best year of my life," he told the *Los Angeles Times* before the first Oakland show. "I feel like I've really gotten a lot of things together. I'm even looking forward to touring."

It remained to be seen whether Pearl Jam would reconsider their anti-Ticketmaster stance when it came to their own U.S. tour, slated for the spring of 1998 and, at least during the planning stages, expected to consist of thirty or forty dates, the most extensive outing the band had undertaken in three years. According to Kelly Curtis, they were not planning to use Ticketmaster at all on the upcoming dates, but a query sent by Epic to fans on its Pearl Jam Internet mailing list, asking them how they'd feel if Pearl Jam decided to play some Ticketmaster venues this time around, suggested that the band was at least putting out feelers with an eye toward ending their boycott. If that wasn't enough to pique the fans' curiosity, a title had been confirmed for the band's new album.

Pearl Jam were calling their fifth album *Yield*.

As 1998 approached, the excitement surrounding the release—and the speculation over how the band's experience with *No Code* might influence the way they handled the new album and tour—had begun to escalate. Pearl Jam made headlines when radio stations all over the U.S. began playing *Yield*'s first single, "Given to Fly," as well as other tracks from the album, a full month before the single's planned air date. By the time Epic issued the requisite cease-and-desist orders, at least one station, WKRL-FM in Syracuse, New York, had aired the album in its entirety, and a number of the *Yield* tracks had been encoded by radio listeners and made available on the Internet. The premature airplay that spawned the Internet outbreak was widely reported as a "leak," with Kelly Curtis and Epic expressing puzzlement as to how radio stations had obtained copies of the album. But more than a few observers, pointing to the militaristic timing of the incident, smelled a ruse. Welcome, the cynics chortled, to record promotion in the Nineties.

Just before Christmas, word began spreading that Pearl Jam had made another unexpected departure, when reporters began trotting out inside sources who claimed the band had shot a video for "Given to Fly." Epic denied that a clip had been made for MTV, claiming that the band had in fact made a short film which would be released on home video. But the rumors only fueled the growing belief that the band was gearing up for the kind of full-court promotional press they hadn't staged since the release of *Ten*.

In the wake of these developments, Pearl Jam's followers didn't seem to know *what* to believe. Some began to suspect that the band's anti-establishment stance had been little more than a seven-year pose—that Pearl Jam had taken such a financial beating on *No Code* that they were now desperate to sell out, if only someone was still buying. Others, the true believers, insisted that the recent developments were entirely organic—that Pearl Jam had deliberately underpromoted *No Code* to whittle their audience to a manageable level, and that having accomplished that, the band members were now more comfortable maintaining a higher visibility. Each emerging sign that Pearl Jam were breaking with their own tradition was greeted by a new round of debate, the skeptics gloating about the changes as if they were proof of unthinkable hypocrisy, and the true-believers genuflecting to rationalize them. Had Pearl Jam ever really stood for anything, or had it all been a marketing ploy? Were they *good*, or were they *evil*? Were they one of *us*, or were they one of *them*? Rock fans have always required that their heroes be perfectly heroic, their villains perfectly villainous. Legend makes no allowances for gray areas.

In truth, maybe Pearl Jam had just grown up enough to take an objective look at the battlefield behind them—and the horizon that stretched before them—and recognize that the key to survival was not just knowing when to fight, but also when to lay down the sword. Perhaps they'd simply decided to do what was right for *them*, circa 1998, regardless of the fans and critics who wanted to preserve them in their uncompromising past like a bug in lucite. Maybe they would peddle themselves silly this year, *and* tour with Ticketmaster, *and* shower MTV with videos, only to turn around next year and pick a celebrated fight with some other swindling music industry dinosaur. Who knew?

Sure, there would be answers eventually. But with Pearl Jam, the questions had always been the real draw.

Source Notes

Much of the material in this book was culled from interviews I conducted with the band members and other key figures in the story between 1991 and 1994 while researching articles for *Rolling Stone*. Given the premium on magazine column space, the majority of that material was never published and appears here for the first time. Any exceptions are cited below.

Throughout the book, I have used the convention of alternating between past and present tense verbs of speech to distinguish between quotations drawn from my early interviews or from other published sources, and those taken from interviews conducted specifically for this project. As a rule, the former appear with past tense verbs of speech; the latter appear in present tense.

Unless otherwise noted below, quotations of comments made by the band members during their stage performances, as well as during their radio and television appearances, were either taken from my notes on shows I attended or transcribed from recordings of the concerts or broadcasts. Excerpts from letters and court documents appearing throughout the book are taken from the originals or copies of the originals, with the sole exception of the sealed declaration written by Eddie that is referred to in Chapter Fifteen. Although Peter Mueller allowed me to inspect the document during a visit to his office, he was unwilling to provide me with a copy for later reference. As a compromise, he agreed to read portions of the declaration onto tape, after I had reviewed it myself, so that it could be accurately described here.

A few of the individuals interviewed for the book agreed only on the condition that their comments would be kept entirely off the record; others spoke freely of their recollections in general, but asked that they not be quoted on certain matters. Wherever possible, I have relied on the accounts of named sources. Quotations attributed to unnamed sources appear only when no other source for that information would agree to speak on the record and I believed that the material in question was true and constituted a significant addition to the story.

In a few instances, I have taken the liberty of reconstructing conversations between key figures in the story. In every such case, the quotations used in the dialogue are based on the recollections of at least one of the participants; in instances where the substance of a given conversation could not be confirmed with all parties involved, I've made every effort to clarify within the narrative the sources upon whose recollections the passages are based. In all cases, what appears is, in my opinion, well founded and true to the original meanings of the participants.

Prelude

page xvii: "How ya doin?"; comments by Young at Golden Gate Park: As quoted in Michael Goldberg, "Pearl Jam Dispatch from the Field #4," *Addicted to Noise*, June 25, 1995.

page xviii: "This band has spent the last year and a half trying to do right by you!": As quoted in Karen Schoemer and Yahlin Chang, "Nobody Knows the Troubles They've Seen," *Newsweek*, July 10, 1995.

One

page 5: "He gave me 'Help'"; comments by Jeff Ament on his early years, p. 5: As quoted in Karl Coryat, "Godfather of the 'G' word," *Bass Player*, April 1994.

page 7: "We moved out because we actually thought we would make it": As quoted in Kathy Tucker, "Grunge Music Now Uncool in Town of its Birth," Reuter, July 22, 1993.

page 9: "People today don't realize": As quoted in Manuel Mendoza, "'Seattle Sound' Sets the Beat for Future," *The Buffalo News*, December 13, 1992.

page 10: "He would show up wearing a black jumpsuit": P. S. O'Neill, as quoted in Clark Humphrey, *Loser: The Real Seattle Music Story* (Feral House, 1995).

page 10: "There were four guys": Author interview with Ben Shepherd, 1994.

page 12: "The scene at the time": As quoted in Richard Cromelin, "In Search of Superunknown Seattle," *Los Angeles Times*, June 17, 1994.

page 12: Crover: "Jeff was a *Venom* fan"; Arm: "worst band in Seattle," "spazziest, freaked out lead singer": As quoted in Jo-Ann Greene, "Intrigue and Incest: Pearl Jam and the Secret History of Seattle," *Goldmine*, August 20, 1993.

page 14: "When I met Stoney": As quoted in James Rotundi, "Blood on the Tracks," *Guitar World*, January 1994.

page 14: "We played a lot of shows at the Metropolis": Author interview with Shepherd, 1992.

page 14: "I was trying to have my second-rate Van Halen licks involved": As quoted in Matthew Amster-Burton, "Q & A with Pearl Jam's Stone Gossard," *San Francisco Chronicle*, September 1, 1996.

page 15: "There were a lot of rules that bands had to conform to": As quoted in Mendoza, "'Seattle Sound' Sets the Beat for Future."

page 16: "It was really bizarre": As quoted in Chris Nickson, *Soundgarden* (St. Martin's Griffin, 1995).

Two

page 18: "I want to be a rock star": As recalled by Kevin Wood in Richard T. White, "Like a Candle in the Wind," *The Rocket*, April 1990.

page 19: "When we opened for bands like the Silly Killers": As quoted in Dawn Anderson, "Malfunkshun," *The Rocket*, December 1986.

page 19: "Andy was just the greatest guy": Author interview with Sheri Fineman, 1995.

page 20: "He was scared about simple things": As quoted in Katherine Turman, "Life Rules," *RIP*, October 1991.

page 21: "In my mind, Andy and Malfunkshun were the originators": As quoted in White, "Like a Candle in the Wind."

page 21: "Everyone I knew who moved here from Park Forest": Author interview with Kim Thayil, 1992.

page 23: "Everyone had this bad-ass attitude": As quoted in Greene, "Intrigue and Incest."

page 24: "if we're in the right place at the right time with the right kind of money": As quoted in Dawn Anderson, "Walk This Way," *The*

Rocket, August 1986. (Anderson attributed the comment to "the band." It appears that Ament made the remark, as he was the only band member quoted elsewhere in the piece.)

page 25: "We infiltrated that place": As quoted in Michael Norman, "Grunge Puts Seattle on Map," *Plain Dealer*, August 20, 1995.

page 27: "I thought they sucked": comments by Jonathan Poneman on Green River record release party, p. 27: As quoted in Greene, "Intrigue and Incest."

page 28: "Some of the other members started getting the idea they could be popular": As quoted in Everett True, "Sub Pop: Seattle Rock City," *Melody Maker*, March 18, 1989.

page 28: "reeked of L.A.-ism, and of chicks who smelled money," Seattle musician Tor Midtstog: As quoted in Humphrey, *Loser.*

page 29: "Okay, cool": As quoted in Greene, "Intrigue and Incest."

Three

page 31: "Greg and I were walking on Capitol Hill": Author interview with Fineman, 1995.

page 31: "All of a sudden, everyone got real quiet": As quoted in Greene, "Intrigue and Incest."

page 33: Curtis: "whole new ball game"; comments by anonymous Geffen staffer: As quoted in Richard T. White, "The Art of the Deal," *The Rocket*, January 1989.

page 34: "There were dozens and dozens of the 'next Guns n' Roses'": Author interview with Chris Cornell, 1992.

page 34: "Not much. There's five of them, and four of us": As quoted in Everett True, "Mudhoney: Sub Pop, Subnormal, Subversion," *Melody Maker*, March 11, 1989.

page 38: Ament's comments on tension in Mother Love Bone and problems with Polygram: Author interview with Ament, 1991. Fineman's comments on tension between Ament and Gilmore: Author interview with Fineman, 1995.

page 39: "I never had experiences . . . of him doing drugs": As quoted in Turman, "Life Rules."

page 40: "I was like, 'Dude, you don't know me well enough'": As quoted in White, "Like a Candle in the Wind."

page 41: "They kept telling me, 'We're gonna be *huge*'": Author interview with Fineman, 1995.

four

page 43: "Everybody was pretty traumatized"; comments by Fineman on Mother Love Bone confusion after Wood's death, p. 43: Author interview with Fineman, 1995.

page 44: "I think Stone knew": Author interview with Ament, 1991.

page 45: "We put out *Bleach*, and gosh, it just kept selling": As quoted in Michael Azerrad, *Come As You Are* (Doubleday, 1993).

page 45: "Our European agent had a distributor," subsequent comments by Pavitt and Poneman: As quoted in Michael Walker, "Puget Sound," *Los Angeles Times*, June 14, 1992.

page 47: "With Mike, it's either joke after joke, or nothing at all.": Author interview with confidential source, 1995.

page 47: "Everything I know, I stole directly from Ace Frehley": As quoted in Jeff Gilbert "Prime Cuts: Mike McCready—The Best of Pearl Jam," *Guitar School*, May 1995.

page 48: "Basically, we weren't that great a band": As quoted in Rotundi, "Blood on the Tracks."

page 49: "Everybody was just kind of hanging out": Author interview with Ament, 1991.

page 49: "That night was the greatest I've ever seen him play": As quoted in Greene, "Intrigue and Incest."

page 49: "We got together with Matt": Author interview with Ament, 1991.

page 50: "It was horrible, because I couldn't talk about it": As quoted in Turman, "Life Rules."

page 51: "They got a new president": Author interview with Ament, 1991.

page 52: "Trying to talk to me about drugs": As quoted in Dave Thompson, *The Red Hot Chili Peppers* (St. Martin's Press, 1993).

page 52: "One of the last things we said"; "I know this one guy down in San Diego": Author interview with Ament, 1991.

five

page 53: "I was going to try, or die trying"; comments by Eddie Vedder on his San Diego years, pp. 53–54: Author interview with Vedder, 1991.

page 55: "There were two other singers who auditioned": As quoted in George Varga, "Memo to Vedder: Come Get Early Work," *San Diego Union-Tribune*, November 8, 1995.

page 56: "I was on my own pretty early"; comments by Vedder on Bad Radio, pp. 56–57: Author interview with Vedder, 1991.

page 57: "It was the weirdest thing": Author interview with Flea, 1994.

page 58: "I forwent my paycheck that night": As quoted in Gina Arnold, *Route 666: On the Road to Nirvana* (St. Martin's Press, 1993).

page 58: "Eddie *was* Jack Irons": Author interview with confidential source, 1995.

page 59: "It was so exciting . . . I was nicknamed 'Crazy Eddie' "; Vedder's comments on Yosemite trip and Irons's involvement in introducing him to Gossard, Ament, and McCready, p. 59: Author interview with Vedder, 1991.

page 59: "He gave us a tape of some of the stuff he'd done": Author interview with Ament, 1991.

page 60: "The sleep deprivation came into play"; Vedder's recollections on making the *Mamasan* tape: Author interview with Vedder, 1991. (An abbreviated version of Vedder's comments first appeared in author, "Right Here, Right Now," *Rolling Stone*, October 31, 1991.)

page 60: "I didn't think about it as being an opportunity"; beach anecdote: Author interview with Vedder, 1991.

page 61: "Stone, I may be totally whacked out": As quoted in Coryat, "Godfather of the 'G' Word."

page 61: Irons's answering machine message; "These guys are looking for you": As recalled by Vedder in interview with author, 1991.

page 62: Ament: "Everything happened so *quick*"; Vedder: "I'd written three more songs": Author interviews with Ament and Vedder, 1991.

page 62: Vedder's comments on the writing of "Release" and the band's decision to call themselves Mookie Blaylock: Author interview with Vedder, 1991.

page 63: Vedder's recollections of the Off Ramp show; comments on his return to San Diego, pp. 63–64: Author interview with Vedder, 1991.

Six

page 67: Vedder: "a beautiful way to be introduced to the whole family"; Ament: "We wanted to make a record": Author interviews with Vedder and Ament, 1991.

page 68: Sports section: "That was the ultimate": Author interview with Vedder, 1991.

page 68: "Inside the small house were Andy Wood's friends": As quoted in Cameron Crowe, "Making the Scene," *Rolling Stone*, October 1, 1992.

page 69: "Maybe that's more based on Mark Arm": As quoted in Phil West, "Insiders Wonder Whether Movie Will Change Seattle's Music Scene," *Seattle Times*, September 17, 1992.

page 70: "this stump-dumb rocker dude from Aberdeen"; "It just felt degrading": As quoted in Azerrad, *Come As You Are.*

page 71: "When Nirvana left, I cried for a long time": As quoted in Mike Rubin, "Swingin' on the Flippity Flop with Sub Pop," *Spin*, April 1995.

page 72: "I'd get frustrated": As quoted in Rotundi, "Blood on the Tracks."

page 73: "I knew a kid who brought a sawed-off shotgun to class": Author interview with Vedder, 1991.

page 74: "A little over a year after losing Andy Wood"; "Mookie Blaylock is now Pearl Jam": Crowe, "Making the Scene."

page 75: "We'd kind of been bouncing words around": Author interview with Vedder, 1991.

page 75: "I don't know where that came from": Interview with Troy Sorenson, conducted by Richard Price on behalf of author, 1995.

page 76: "He kept telling me how he was going to have to come up with something"; Fineman's comments on Vedder's reaction to *Ten* artwork: p. 76: Author interview with Fineman, 1995.

page 76: "Congratulations. You're in *Rolling Stone*"; detail and subsequent quotations regarding Vedder's first appearance in *Rolling Stone*: pp. 76–77: As recalled by Vedder in interview with author, 1991.

page 78: "I love that. Somebody who's listened to our fucking tape three times"; subsequent comments by Ament and Gossard on artwork meetings with Epic: Author interviews with Ament and Gossard, 1991.

page 79: "Just go watch *Spinal Tap*": Author interview with Ament, 1991.

page 79: "He had a *bad* drinking problem": Author interview with confidential source, 1995.

page 80: "I think that's why I got into pot at such an early age"; recollections by Dave Abbruzzese on his background, pp. 80–81: Author interview with Abbruzzese, 1995.

page 82: Ament: "You see so many videos"; subsequent comments by Ament, Vedder, and Abbruzzese on "Alive" video shoot, pp. 82–83: Author interviews with Ament, Vedder, and Abbruzzese in 1991 and 1993.

page 84: "We were kind of like, 'When's he going to start being an asshole?'"; comments by Gossard, Ament and Abbruzzese on their first meeting: Author interviews with Gossard, Ament, and Abbruzzese, 1991. (An abbreviated version of Ament's comments first appeared in author, "Right Here, Right Now").

page 84: Abbruzzese's recollections on his initial impressions of the band members and on being asked to join: Author interview with Dave Abbruzzese, 1995.

Seven

page 90: "How much worse can it get?": Author interview with Vedder, 1991.

page 91: "I don't have any heroes," Vedder's comments on Gossard and Cornell: Author interview with Vedder, 1991.

page 91: Vedder's comments on Fugazi: Author interview with Vedder, 1991.

page 93: "So, have you thought of any questions?"; subsequent detail in anecdote p. 93: Author interview with Vedder, 1991.

page 94: Vedder: "I can't philosophize about the band as an entity"; Fineman: "He had to be part of all of it": Author interviews with Vedder and Fineman in 1991 and 1995, respectively.

page 94: "I think Eddie really wants to be famous": As witnessed by author, Los Angeles, California, 1991.

page 94: Vedder: "It could be the greatest record, but you don't get to make another"; Gossard: "You can't just jump in and fucking plaster every magazine with Pearl Jam ads": Author interviews with Vedder and Gossard, 1991.

page 95: "That's the one it's gonna be," subsequent quotations and detail in "your life on toast" anecdote: As recalled by Vedder and Ament in interview with author, 1991.

page 96: "It was like, 'What kind of band do we come off as?'": Author interview with Abbruzzese, 1991.

page 98: "You don't have to read it now if you're taking notes": Author's notes on band rehearsal, 1991.

page 99: "You feel like going somewhere and talking?"; subsequent quotations and detail in Space Needle anecdote, pp. 99–101: Author interview with Eddie Vedder, 1991. (A number of Vedder's comments here first appeared in abbreviated form in author, "Right Here, Right Now.").

page 101: "I know that everything that led up to this . . . happened for a reason": As quoted in author, "Right Here, Right Now."

page 102: "Stone and Jeff really felt that way": Author interview with Fineman, 1995.

Eight

page 104: Comments by Ament and Vedder on crowd reaction: Author interviews with Ament and Vedder, 1991.

page 105: "Eric, Eddie scares me"; subsequent detail on Abbruzzese-Johnson conversation regarding Vedder's onstage antics; Kelly Curtis reaction to Seattle show; Abbruzzese, "It's just fucking amazing": As recalled by Abbruzzese in interview with author, 1991.

page 109: "Eddie had moved to Seattle and Beth hadn't": comments by Chris Cuffaro on unreleased "Jeremy" video, pp. 109–112: Author interview with Cuffaro, 1995.

page 115: "I can't wait"; "*Rock and ROLLLLL!*": As witnessed by author, Los Angeles, California 1991.

Nine

page 118: "The crowd on that tour": Author interview with Abbruzzese, 1995.

page 118: "It was quite funny to see that": Author interview with Cuffaro, 1995.

page 119: "I saw the drawing": As quoted in author, "Right Here, Right Now."

page 119: "There were always kids coming up and showing me their tattoos": Author interview with Abbruzzese, 1995.

page 120: "I just need to tell you that this meant so much"; detail and quotations in anecdote p. 120: As recalled by Vedder in Kira L. Billik, "Pearl Jam Finds Life in the Wake of Death," *Rocky Mountain News*, December 13, 1991.

page 120: "I'd like to keep this thing really small for a while"; "about me, fighting to stay small": Author interview with Vedder, 1991.

page 121: "No way, I don't want to go there"; subsequent detail in anecdote on Vedder meeting with Mudhoney, pp. 121–122: As recalled by Cuffaro in interview with author, 1995.

page 123: "You try your hardest not to be affected by that": Author interview with Jeff Ament, 1994. (An abbreviated version of Ament's comment first appeared in author, "Where Angels Fear to Tread," *Rolling Stone*, May 5, 1994.)

page 124: Vedder: "We're kind of a dichotomy"; Ament: "I like it simple. There's just a lot of it": Author interview with Vedder and Ament, 1991.

page 124: Cuffaro's comments on Vedder-Abbruzzese tension: Author interview with Cuffaro, 1995.

page 125: "All of a sudden here was all this success": Author interview with Abbruzzese, 1995.

page 126: "talked about his Great Grandma Pearl"; subsequent quotations in anecdote on Abbruzzese-Vedder joint interview: As recalled by Abbruzzese in interview with author, 1995.

page 126: "Beth took care of all the publicity stuff": Author interview with confidential source, 1995.

page 126: "When Dave first came up"; comments by Fineman pp. 126–127: Author interview with Fineman, 1995.

page 127: "There was a fill that he wanted in 'Release'": Author interview with Abbruzzese, 1995.

page 128: "We'd played this horrible show"; detail and quotations in Milwaukee anecdote: Author interview with Abbruzzese, 1995.

page 128: "When Stone was upset": Author interview with Fineman, 1995.

page 129: "You know that's for *life*, don't you?": Author interview with Abbruzzese, 1995.

page 129: "Well, you're in for the tour": As recalled by Ament and Abbruzzese in interview with author, 1991.

Ten

page 133: "We were convinced he was a serial killer": As quoted in Jeff Gilbert, "Alive and Kicking," *Guitar World*, September 1992.

page 133: "He had monkeys, and a fucking panther": Author interview with Abbruzzese, 1995.

page 137: "Mike gets this look in his eye": As quoted in Rotundi, "Blood on the Tracks."

page 137: "The album is like visiting an animal in a zoo": Author interview with Vedder, 1991.

page 138: "That was totally over the top. People were balancing on speakers": As quoted in Lauren Spencer, "We've Got a Feeling," *Spin*, June 1992.

page 140: "We just looked at each other"; subsequent quotations in McCready and Abbruzzese Den Haag anecdote, p. 140: As recalled by Abbruzzese in interview with author, 1995.

Eleven

page 142: "An acoustic show," comments by Gossard on *MTV Unplugged*: As quoted in Gilbert, "Alive and Kicking."

page 143: "When we got to Ohio": Author interview with Ament, 1994.

page 143: Gold record anecdote: Author interview with Abbruzzese, 1995.

page 144: "I found out that by simply apologizing to the audience": As quoted in Lenny Stoute, "How Pearl Jam Got Cult Status Before its Time," *Toronto Star*, April 2, 1992.

page 145: "Me and a buddy went in one of the dressing rooms"; subsequent comments by McCready on *SNL* appearance, p. 145: As quoted in Gilbert, "Alive and Kicking."

page 145: "The thing about Eddie was, he couldn't say no"; quotations and detail on Eddie's interaction with fan in Ventura, pp. 145–146: As recalled by Cuffaro in interview with author, 1995.

page 146: "Models! Models are coming!": As witnessed by author, New York, New York 1994.

page 147: Vedder's comments on Doherty: As quoted in Darby Romeo, "The Misfortunes of Stardom," *The I Hate Brenda Newsletter*, Issue #1, 1993; Doherty's comments on Vedder: As quoted in Margy Rochlin, "Shannen Doherty," *Us*, March 1993.

page 148: "I'm sure some kids bought our album after reading stories": As quoted in Dennis Hunt, "Pearl Jam: Grim, Hard-driving Sound," *Los Angeles Times*, May 9, 1992.

page 149: "We had people who knew what they were doing. This wasn't a fly-by-night thing": As quoted in Tom Phalen, "City Cancels Free Pearl Jam Concert," *Seattle Times*, May 21, 1992.

page 150: "red, white, and blue fat boys": As quoted in The Stud Brothers, "Eddie Vedder Takes on the World," *Melody Maker*, June 20, 1992; "Thanks for being vocal": Video footage shot by a fan at Gas Works Park, May 20, 1992.

page 151: Spectator: "He's beyond Bono"; Vedder: "I don't want to be Bono": As quoted in The Stud Brothers, "Eddie Vedder Takes on the World."

page 151: "I was about a hundred yards away": Author interview with Abbruzzese, 1995.

page 153: "Everybody was saying, 'Oh, the pressure must be *awful*'": Author interview with Abbruzzese, 1995.

page 154: "Hey, I think my bag's missing"; subsequent quotations on Melody Club and Roskilde appearances, pp. 154–156: As recalled by Vedder in Allan Jones, "The Vedder Forecast," *Melody Maker*, October 9, 1993.

page 156: "That's it. Let's go home": As reported by MTV Europe, 1992.

page 157: "I realize that this guy wants to write that I'm fucking crazy": As quoted in Jones, "The Vedder Forecast."

Twelve

page 158: "It was the worst show we ever played": Author interview with McCready, 1992.

page 159: "There's nothing revolutionary about playing for big commercialistic rock promoters": As quoted in author, "Lollapalooza '92," *Rolling Stone*, September 17, 1992.

page 159: "This whole tour is entertainment for the leisure class": As quoted in author, "Lollapalooza '92."

page 159: "Eddie was saying, 'Well, we have our crowd' ": Author interview with Mike McCready, 1992.

page 159: "I have to admit, there was probably a little bit of skepticism": As quoted in author, "Lollapalooza '92."

page 159: "Aw, c'mon, why aren't you at the fucking show"; subsequent detail on Vedder and Liebling's meeting with Hebrew students, pp. 159–160: As recalled by Vedder in interview with author, 1992.

page 160: "The coolest part was realizing that it didn't fucking matter": As quoted in author, "Lollapalooza '92."

page 160: "Jim Rose is amazing": As quoted in interview with Dave Kendall of MTV, *120 Minutes*, 1992.

page 161: "In Miami, the bus driver got stuck in a traffic jam": Author interview with Fineman, 1995.

page 161: "Eddie, we didn't know it was you": As recalled by Jim Rose in his memoir, *Freak Like Me* (Dell, 1995).

page 162: "Six! We got six!"; quotations and detail in bus anecdote: As recalled by Abbruzzese in interview with author, 1995. This incident was also reported by MTV News in 1992.

page 163: "It would be silly to make a record and then not want anyone to know"; comments by Cornell on *Temple of the Dog* hype, p. 163: Author interview with Cornell, 1994.

page 163: "If the band had its druthers, they might not want it out": As quoted in Steve Hochman, "The Mother Lode of the Seattle Rock Scene," *Los Angeles Times*, September 6, 1991.

page 164: "I can relate to people having animosity or suspicion": As quoted in Jones, "The Vedder Forecast."

page 165: Detail and quotations on MTV veto of "Sonic Reducer": p. 165: As recalled by Abbruzzese in interview with author, 1995.

page 167: "I want you to know that I think you're a respectable human": As recalled by Kurt Cobain in Azerrad, *Come As You Are*.

page 168: "might be perceived as jumping on the bandwagon"; subsequent comments by Crowe on *Singles*: As quoted in Steve Hochman, "'Singles' Scene Moves to Seattle's Rock Beat," *Los Angeles Times*, June 28, 1992.

page 169: "Acting was really uncomfortable": As quoted in West, "Insiders Wonder Whether Movie Will Change Seattle's Music Scene."

page 169: "If anybody at Warner Bros. made too much of the 'Seattle Scene'": As recalled by Vedder in Steve Hochman, "Eddie's New Jam," *Los Angeles Times*, October 18, 1992.

page 170: "I went hat in hand and begged them to do the show": As quoted in Bernard Weinraub, "Finding a Sports Agent's Head and Heart," *New York Times*, December 23, 1996.

page 170: "Just stupid, drunk as hell": Author interview with confidential source, 1995.

page 170: "The whole reason Eddie got so drunk was because he was frustrated": Author interview with Abbruzzese, 1995.

page 170: "an annoying, motorized fan": Author interview with confidential source, 1995.

page 176: "For a group to want to do a free show": As quoted in Mick Wall, *Pearl Jam* (Sidgwick & Jackson Ltd., 1994).

Thirteen

page 181: "Ten years old. That's the age my child would have been": As written by Vedder in Eddie Vedder, "Reclamation," *Spin*, November 1992.

page 181: "These are things I've witnessed"; Vedder's comments on abortion debate, recollections of Chicago X show, detail on Rock for Choice concert, pp. 181–182: Author interview with Vedder, 1993.

page 182: "And look, the seats warm up!"; detail and quotations in new car anecdote, pp. 182–183: As recalled by Abbruzzese in interview with author, 1995.

page 183: "Everything was cool. We got all dudded up"; detail in American Music Awards anecdote, pp. 183–184: As recalled by Abbruzzese in interview with author, 1995. Abbruzzese's acceptance speech and detail on Johnson's demeanor at the podium taken from a tape of the broadcast. ·

page 185: "paradise"; "old rockers"; "dinner music": As quoted in Cameron Crowe, "Five Against the World," *Rolling Stone*, October 28, 1993.

page 186: "Kept us focused, kept the basic tracks more live, and kept us working": As quoted in Rotundi, "Blood on the Tracks."

page 187: "He told me it was about his truck": Author interview with Abbruzzese, 1995.

page 188: "I think it's fair to say that Eddie was pretty outraged": As quoted in Allan Jones, "The Vedder Forecast."

page 189: Gossard: "That title represented a lot of the struggles"; exchange between Ament and Vedder, pp. 189–190: As quoted in Crowe, "Five Against the World."

page 190: "I remember an article somebody in Seattle wrote": Author interview with Abbruzzese, 1995.

page 191: "It was kind of joked about"; detail on taping incident: Author interview with Abbruzzese, 1995. The incident was also described to author by an Epic publicist just after it occurred.

page 191: Van conversation on change in publishing split: As recalled by Abbruzzese in interview with author, 1995.

page 192: "I talked to Cameron very frankly"; comments by Abbruzzese on *Rolling Stone* cover story, pp. 192–193: Author interview with Abbruzzese, 1995.

fourteen

page 199: "Ed was a cut above": Author interview with Peter Mueller, 1997.

page 200: "a broken-down old lounge act": As quoted in Crowe, "Five Against the World."

page 200: "Ed was hardly a lounge act": Author interview with Mueller, 1995.

page 201: "He had his shirt off"; quotations and detail in anecdote on Mueller-Severson fisticuffs: Author interview with Mueller, 1997.

page 202: "Her first letter to me": Author interview with Mueller, 1997.

page 203: "I was truly in love with Karen": Author interview with Mueller, 1995.

page 204: "He could not risk losing this one wonderful girl": Letter written by Inez Mueller, August 22, 1993.

page 204: "moved to another state"; "My divorce had already been a black mark on my name": As recalled by Karen Vedder in Eric Blau, *Stories of Adoption: Loss and Reunion* (NewSage Press, 1993).

page 205: "hugely shocked": Author interview with Mueller, 1997.

page 205: "She didn't want there to be any connection"; quotations and detail on the couple's departure for Houston: Author interview with Peter Mueller, 1997. Further detail taken from Karen Vedder's recollections in Blau, *Stories of Adoption*.

page 205: "I told her halfway down that I had brought her diamond ring": Author interview with Mueller, 1997.

page 206: "a wonderful, cute young family from up North": As recalled by Karen Vedder in Blau, *Stories of Adoption*.

page 206: "my daddy went bye-bye on a boat": Letter from Karen Vedder to Inez Mueller, December 1, 1966.

page 208: "I don't want to say 'She's wrong that I was insensitive'"; subsequent quotations by Mueller, p. 197: Author interview with Mueller, 1997.

page 208: "That's when she became real to me": As recalled by Karen Vedder in Blau, *Stories of Adoption*.

page 208: "Those months were very, very difficult": Author interview with Mueller, 1995.

page 209: "Karen believed Ed was gay"; "Karen pursued the adoption": Author interview with Mueller, 1995.

page 210: "I never really had a chance to talk to Ed then": Author interview with Mueller, 1995.

page 210: "He would literally stop people in the street"; "We were way up at the top": Author interview with Mueller, 1995.

page 211: "Somebody didn't show up for modeling": Author interview with Eddie Vedder, 1991.

page 211: "Shirley was ecstatic with him": Author interview with Mueller, 1995.

page 211: "I think they're going to want me to do that commercial": As recalled by Mueller in interview with author, 1995.

page 211: "You had to sign your kids up before they were *born*": Author interview with Mueller, 1995.

page 212: "Our marriage was dissolving"; quotations and detail on Florida trip, pp. 212–213: Author interview with Mueller, 1995.

page 213: "I went from being the older of two brothers": Author interview with Vedder, 1991.

page 214: "terrible unruliness"; "part of the glue"; subsequent comments by Mueller on the group home, p. 214: Author interview with Mueller, 1995.

page 214: "That's when I cracked open my first Motown records": Author interview with Vedder, 1991.

page 215: "in the plan to have Edddie and Ed know one another"; subsequent comments on the dinner with Severson: Author interview with Mueller, 1995.

page 216: "I remember him being really cool"; Vedder's recollections of Severson, p. 216: Author interview with Vedder, 1991.

page 216: "When Ed came to that first dinner"; "Karen and I both had good intentions": Author interviews with Mueller in 1995 and 1997.

fifteen

page 217: "indomitable spirit": Author interview with Mueller, 1995.

page 218: Mueller's recollections on Severson's visits: Author interviews with Mueller, 1995 and 1997.

page 219: "When I look back on it": As recalled by Karen Vedder in Blau, *Stories of Adoption.*

page 219: "The house had a separate wing where Ed could have lived"; comments by Mueller on the idea of Severson's moving in with the family, pp. 219–220: Author interview with Mueller, 1995.

page 220: "I just dropped in on him"; comments by Mueller on meeting with Severson: Author interview with Mueller, 1995.

page 221: "I made a little bit of money [modeling]": Author interview with Vedder, 1991.

page 221: "I tried for a year to save [the marriage]"; detail on rest home meeting with Severson: Author interview with Mueller, 1995.

page 222: "There would be these peaks and valleys"; "rip-roaring evenings"; Mueller's recollections of Chewbacca incident: Author interview with Mueller, 1995.

page 223: "Peter, I've tried a lot of cases"; "It sounds, Karen, like you're actually disappointed": As recalled by Mueller in interview with author, 1995.

page 224: "My sisters and I always knew Eddie would be famous": Author interview with Kerryanne Donohue, 1995.

page 224: "It was a big deal not to touch his records": Author interview with Scott Caesar, 1995.

page 225: "I knew about it, but he didn't want to talk about it": Author interview with Donohue, 1995.

page 225: "Peter had handled a case for me": Author interview with Sharon Donohue, 1995.

page 225: "I was hoping she'd say, 'Sure, come along'": Author interview with Mueller, 1995.

page 226: Christmas ornaments incident: Author interview with Mueller, 1995.

page 227: "He basically told me, 'Dad, I don't want you around'": Author interview with Mueller, 1997.

page 228: "Because of the circumstances, I felt it was in the best interest of the children and me to get out of the state": Deposition of Karen L. Vedder, August 16, 1983, *Mueller, Peter J.* v. *Cheatum, Kim, et al.*, Case No. 486437, San Diego County Superior Court, August 16, 1983.

page 229: "He enjoyed his intact family": Author interview with Mueller, 1995.

page 229: "He definitely wouldn't go with me"; "We were all upset": Deposition of Karen L. Vedder, *Mueller, Peter J.* v. *Cheatum, Kim, et. al.*

page 229: "She told me, 'Pete, if Eddie decides to stay with you'": Author interview with Mueller, 1995.

page 229: "I bet that just to keep Eddie [from staying in California], you'll tell him that he's adopted": Deposition of Karen L. Vedder in *Mueller, Peter J.* v. *Cheatum, Kim, et. al.*

page 230: "I talked to two doctors and a priest": Author interview with Mueller, 1995.

page 230: "I thought it was over": Author interview with Mueller, 1995.

page 230: "I had to explain to my teachers why I wasn't keeping up": As quoted in Robert Hilburn, "He Didn't Ask for All This," *Los Angeles Times*, April 16, 1994.

page 231: "I think the Seventies and Eighties were a really weird time for parenting," subsequent comments by Vedder, p. 231: As quoted in Steve Hochman, "Eddie's New Jam," *Los Angeles Times*, October 18, 1992.

page 231: "Rose had her own condominium"; "I had a divided requirement": Author interview with Mueller, 1995.

page 232: "On several occasions I spoke to Mr. Mueller": Declaration of Fred Perkins, February 3, 1983. *Mueller, Karen L. v. Mueller, Peter J.*, Case No. D 163009, San Diego County Superior Court.

page 232: "physically attacking his girlfriend on the school campus": Letter addressed, "To Whom it May Concern," written by Roy Risner, assistant principal, San Dieguito High School, September 28, 1982.

page 233: "I was trying to cautiously bring him back to some form of responsibility"; subsequent comments by Mueller on Easter incident, pp. 233–235: Author interview with Mueller, 1995.

page 235: "It made me want to cry": Author interview with Rose Mueller, 1995.

page 235: "Mr. Mueller indicated that his son"; subsequent comments by Dess pp. 235–236: Psychological report by Dess dated July 19, 1982, attached as exhibit to Declaration of William J. Dess, July 29, 1982. *Mueller, Karen L. v. Mueller, Peter J.*

page 236: "During July, 1982 I observed that Edward's behavior": Declaration of Fred Perkins in *Mueller, Karen L. v. Mueller, Peter J.*

page 236: "She came out with the specific purpose to tell me that this guy wasn't my father": As quoted in Crowe, "Five Against the World."

page 236: "I just explained to him the whole circumstances": Declaration of Karen L. Vedder in *Mueller, Peter J. v. Cheatum, Kim, et al.*

page 237: "During a July weekend in Big Bear": Declaration of Rosalinda Mueller, February 3, 1983. *Mueller, Karen L. v. Mueller, Peter J.*

page 238: "after he had moved out of Peter's house and he came to me confused and upset": Deposition of Karen L. Vedder in *Mueller, Peter J. v. Cheatum, Kim, et al.*

page 238: "She wanted to break up the relationship": Author interview with Mueller, 1995.

page 238: "Except during periods of discipline"; subsequent detail from Karen Vedder declaration: Declaration of Karen L. Mueller, a.k.a. Karen L. Vedder, August 16, 1982. *Mueller, Karen L. v. Mueller, Peter J.*

page 239: "told me not to see a doctor anymore"; "I was so nervous and fearful"; detail on Eddie's declaration: As read to author by Peter Mueller from Declaration of Edward Jerome Mueller, August 18, 1982. *Mueller, Karen L. v. Mueller, Peter J.* This document was sealed and expunged from the record on March 28, 1983, pursuant to an agreement between the parties.

page 239: "This was the product of an agenda": Mueller's comments on Eddie's declaration, pp. 239–240: Author interview with Mueller, 1995.

page 240: "one of the most hostile"; "marijuana"; "disturbed young man": Letter written by Roy Risner, September 28, 1982.

page 240: "sincerely interested in Eddie's welfare": Letter to attorney Michael Clark by James Fosnot, counselor, San Dieguito High School, September 24, 1982.

page 240: "destructive outbursts"; "problems with drug usage"; "problems in school": Letter to attorney Michael Clark by J. Roland Fleck, Ed. D., October 5, 1992.

page 241: "Eddie's positive response to our concern," subsequent comments by Rose Mueller, p. 241: Declaration of Rosalinda Mueller, February 3, 1983. *Mueller, Karen L. v. Mueller, Peter J.*

page 241: "I later withdrew the petition for Chris": Author interview with Mueller, 1995.

page 241: "Eddie was very upset when this was sealed"; comments by Mueller on Eddie's declaration, pp. 241–242: Author interview with Mueller, 1995.

page 243: "He called Eddie in"; "Rich and I had been friends for years": Author interview with Mueller, 1995.

page 244: Not "because I wanted to do him wrong": Author interview with Mueller, 1997.

page 244: "I resented everybody around me": As quoted in Hilburn, "He Didn't Ask for All This."

page 245: "try out living with me again"; "something developed for him in Chicago": Author interview with Mueller, 1997.

page 245: "I called a juvenile officer in Skokie": Author interview with Mueller, 1997.

page 245: "He was a guitar player": As quoted in "Pearl Jam Watch III," *Chicago Tribune*, March 18, 1994.

page 246: "There's a shopping mall called North County Fair"; Mueller's recollections of buying *Ten*; comments on Eddie's treatment of him in the press; divided loyalty experienced by Vedder's younger brothers: p. 246: Author interview with Mueller, 1995.

page 247: "Eddie's mom would call Carla"; subsequent comments by Bill Gamble: Author interview with Gamble, 1995.

page 247: "Obviously, this caused a huge rift between us": As quoted in Craig Marks, "Let's Get Lost," *Spin*, January 1995.

page 248: "This kind of thing happens in families all the time": Author interview with Mueller, 1995.

Sixteen

page 251: "We needed to see that": As quoted in James Rotundi, "Right-Hand Men: Stone Gossard Meets Steve Cropper," *Guitar Player*, July 1994.

page 251: "I'm happy to have an adult in my life who leads by example": "Rockline" radio broadcast, October 1993.

page 251: "That week was a nightmare": Author interview with Abbruzzese, 1995.

page 252: "Fuck me? Okay, you fuck me, and then Bono will come out and fuck you": As quoted in Crowe, "Five Against the World."

page 253: "I don't want you to do that cover"; quotations and detail in *Modern Drummer* anecdote, p. 253: Author interview with Abbruzzese, 1995.

page 254: "I just spent the best of what's left of my voice": As quoted in Jim Greer, "The Courtship of Eddie Vedder," *Spin*, December 1993.

page 254: "He talks about how he only wants to play clubs"; subsequent comments by Bono: As quoted in Bill Flanagan, *U2 at the End of the World* (Delacorte Press, 1995).

page 255: Footnote: "I just hung up with Bono. And Eddie, he was crying": As recalled by Bill Flanagan in Flanagan, *U2 at the End of the World*.

page 255: "the whole drunk-guy routine"; quotations and detail on MTV Awards incident, pp. 255–256: Author interview with Abbruzzese, 1995.

page 256: "In Los Angeles, 'fake' really becomes a problem": As quoted in Liz Evans, "Famous Last Words," *Kerrang!*, October 23, 1993.

page 257: "I love you, man"; quotations and detail on Metallica party and Dublin incidents, p. 257: As recalled by Abbruzzese in interview with author, 1995.

page 258: McCready's comments on band meetings related to his drinking, his lack of confidence: As quoted in Jeff Gilbert, "Alive," *Guitar World*, March 1995.

page 258: "They'd sit around and talk about, 'Well, do we just fire him?'": Author interview with Abbruzzese, 1995.

page 259: "reject show-biz glitz": As quoted in Christopher John Farley, "Rock's Anxious Rebels," *Time*, October 18, 1993.

page 260: "marketed—or *not* marketed—into becoming the biggest commercial property"; subsequent comments by Gamble p. 260: Author interview with Gamble, 1995.

page 260: "I had this little apartment and the woman who moved in downstairs": Fan tape of Vedder interview with an unidentified deejay from Australia's Triple J radio, conducted before Pearl Jam's show at the War Memorial in Rochester, New York, April 7, 1994.

page 261: "just sickening, the longest thirty minutes of my life"; recollections by Bill Miller on Mesa, Arizona shows: As quoted in Buddy Seigal, "Walking Tall Down 'The Red Road,'" *Los Angeles Times*, August 27, 1994; Butch Hause, "Bill Miller Taps Rich Roots for His Sound," *The Denver Post*, January 11, 1994.

page 262: "We tried to walk on, but this guy, he wouldn't let it go"; comments by Vedder on bar brawl pp. 262–263: As quoted in Allan Jones, "I'm Not Your F***in' Messiah" *Melody Maker*, May 21, 1994.

page 263: Judge: "left something to be desired"; Vedder: "I'm just disappointed I didn't get to tell my side of the story": As quoted in Scott Aiges, "Pearl Jam's Vedder Cleared in N.O. Fight," *The Times-Picayune*, August 17, 1994.

page 263: "I didn't get in any good head space or anything"; comments by Abbruzzese and Fineman on Nacogdoches incident, pp. 263–264: Author interviews with Abbruzzese and Fineman, 1995.

page 265: "They basically said, 'We don't think this should be how our music is heard'": As quoted in Natalie Soto, "Pearl Jam Cancels Concert in Security Flap," *Rocky Mountain News*, November 29, 1993.

page 266: "The last minute nature of that episode": As quoted in Chuck Philips, "Pearl Jam, Ticketmaster and Now Congress," *Los Angeles Times*, June 30, 1994.

page 266: "I'm not going to do that anymore": As quoted in Hilburn, "He Didn't Ask for All This."

page 267: "I hate to be Yoko": As quoted in Andrew Harrison, "Love and Death," *Select*, April 1994.

page 267: "That was the worst part of it all": As quoted in Jones, "I'm Not Your F***in' Messiah."

page 268: "I just freaked out, man." As quoted in Jones, "I'm Not Your F***in' Messiah."

page 268: "Get these fucking tubes out of my nose": As quoted in Neil Strauss, "The Downward Spiral," *Rolling Stone*, June 2, 1994.

page 269: "not a suicide thing"; "just a tiff"; "candlelit vigil": As quoted in Andrew Harrison, "Love and Death."

Seventeen

page 270: "One really good thing is how much we've learned": Author interview with Ament, 1994.

page 271: "They're telling people, 'We'll do it our way, and you'll have nothing to say about it.'": As quoted in Susan Whitall, "Pearl Jam's Demands Put the Squeeze on Promoters," *Detroit News*, February 1, 1994.

page 272: "Ticketmaster fought us in Detroit": As quoted in Steve Morse, "Pearl Jam Adds Third Local Date," *The Boston Globe*, March 16, 1994.

page 273: "Pearl Jam is putting out feelers"; quotations from NACPA memos, p. 273: As excerpted in Fred Moody, "Battle of the Band," *Seattle Weekly*, November 2, 1994.

page 273: "It started out about Mike's drinking"; detail and quotations in band meeting anecdote, pp. 273–274: As recalled by Abbruzzese in interview with author, 1995.

page 275: "I had a feeling that something real bad had happened": As quoted in Strauss, "The Downward Spiral."

page 276: Cobain suicide note: Excerpts taken from a copy of the original.

page 277: "When Kurt did that, it just permanently changed my perception"; comments by Kim Thayil on Cobain suicide, p. 277: Author interview with Thayil, 1994.

page 278: "I just tore the place to shreds": As quoted in Robert Hilburn, "He Didn't Ask for All This."

page 278: "I was just spinning": As quoted in Craig Marks, "Let's Get Lost," *Spin*, January 1995.

page 278: "You know, all these people lining up": As quoted in Jones, "I'm Not Your F***in' Messiah."

page 279: "I wish that Kurt and I had been able": As quoted in Marks, "Let's Get Lost."

page 280: "No, sir, I can't do that"; detail and quotations in White House anecdote, p. 280: As recalled by Mark Arm in Mark Arm, "The Executive Branch of the Federal Government of the United States of America vs. Mudhoney," *Grand Royal* No. 2, 1994.

page 280: "They talked about *basketball*": Author interview with Abbruzzese, 1995.

page 281: "The greatest Rock Band in History This Week"; detail on Bruins incident: As quoted in Michael Gee, "Caught in a Jam," *The Boston Herald*, April 13, 1994.

page 281: "knocked the wind out of the band": As quoted in Hilburn, "He Didn't Ask for All This."

page 282: "We had four shows left": As quoted in an interview with MTV's Vanessa Warwick for *Headbanger's Ball*, conducted in Boston, April 11, 1994.

page 282: "We'd spent so much time getting alternative venues going"; quotations and detail in band meeting anecdote: As recalled by Abbruzzese in interview with author, 1995.

page 283: Burger King: As reported by Susan Bickelhaupt, "Pearl Jam Fans Find the Good, the Bad, and the Hungry," *The Boston Globe*, April 14, 1994.

page 284: "You know what I really need right now?": As quoted in Jones, "I'm Not Your F***in' Messiah."

page 284: "You don't love me, you love who you *think* I am"; detail on Paramount show, meeting with Rollins, pp. 284–285: As witnessed by author, New York, New York, 1994.

page 285: "The band's committed not to tour": As quoted in Melinda Newman, "Pearl Jam Postpones Summer Tour of U.S.," *Billboard*, May 7, 1994.

page 286: "Actually, they contacted us": "Sound Opinions" radio program, WKQX-FM, Chicago, Illinois. Curtis made these comments during a broadcast hosted by correspondents Jim DeRogatis and Bill Wyman that aired on October 9, 1994.

page 286: "What you have here is a band that refuses": As quoted in Philips, "Pearl Jam, Ticketmaster, and Now Congress."

page 287: "I think a better way of promoting the album": As quoted in Jim DeRogatis, "Why Pearl Jam Decided to File its Complaint," *Chicago Sun-Times*, June 19, 1994.

page 287: "That would make me a pretty smart guy": "Sound Opinions," October 9, 1994.

page 287: "The White House is impressed": As quoted in Philips, "Pearl Jam, Ticketmaster, and Now Congress."

page 288: "No bottles, no cans, no Frisbees"; comments by lawmakers during hearing: As quoted in Les Blumenthal, "Pearl Jam Duo Tell Congress Ticketmaster Gouges Fans," *News Tribune*, July 1, 1994; Verne Kopytoff, "Grunge Meets Grins as Pearl Jam Testifies on Ticket Fees," *Baltimore Sun*, July 1, 1994.

page 288: "As most or all of you are aware"; quotations from Gossard testimony at hearing, pp. 288–290: "Prepared Statement of Pearl Jam to the Information, Justice, Transportation, and Agriculture Subcommittee of the House Committee on Government Operations," June 30, 1994.

page 290: "I think this line of questioning is strange": As quoted in Blumenthal, "Pearl Jam Duo Tell Congress."

page 290: "They told us we were going to be here, like, an hour": As quoted in Dave Marsh, "Ticket to Ride," *Playboy*, November 1994.

page 290: "a concerted public relations campaign"; quotations from Fred Rosen statement at hearing, pp. 290–292: "Statement of Ticketmaster Corporation Before the Subcommittee on Information, Justice, Transportation, and Agriculture, Committee on Government Operations, United States House of Representatives," June 30, 1994.

page 292: "an incredible pain in the ass": As quoted in Fred Moody, "Battle of the Band," *Seattle Weekly*, November 2, 1994.

page 293: "Oh, I think Stone wanted to talk to you"; quotations and detail on Curtis, Wittenborne phone calls, p. 293: Author interviews with Abbruzzese and Fineman, 1995.

Eighteen

page 294: "very emotional"; comments by Abbruzzese on breakfast meeting with Gossard: Author interview with Abbruzzese, 1995.

page 294: "There are different philosophies and personalities": Press statement issued by Abbruzzese, August 26, 1994.

page 295: Abbruzzese: "When I heard everyone saying I left the band"; Curtis: "hoping not to have to say anything about it": As quoted in author, "Pearl Jam Drummer Beats It," *Rolling Stone*, October 6, 1994.

page 295: "Dave was out of town"; comments by Fineman, pp. 295–296: Author interview with Fineman, 1995.

page 296: "There were definitely a lot of arguments"; comments by Abbruzzese on Vedder, pp. 296–297: Author interview with Abbruzzese, 1995.

page 298: "He told me that when he and Stone started the band": Author interview with Abbruzzese, 1995.

page 299: "Hey, if you ever want to be in the band": Author interviews with Abbruzzese and Fineman, 1995.

page 299: Usenet excerpt, "Grohl has joined Pearl Jam": Usenet posting by Carol E. Mariconda, September 1994, as archived on Usenet FAQ for the alt.fan.courtney-love newsgroup, maintained by Mariconda and dated January 22, 1995.

page 300: "faux Courtney": Usenet posting by Mariconda, September 1994, as archived on alt.fan.courtney-love FAQ.

page 301: "The band feels strongly": As quoted in Steve Hochman, "The Book on Vitalogy," *Los Angeles Times*, October 23, 1994.

page 301: "I heard a Talking Heads song today"; Vedder's comments on *Vitalogy*, p. 301: As quoted in Marks, "Let's Get Lost."

page 304: "That was the result of a major label saying, 'Okay, you won't do videos' ": As quoted in Cynthia Fuchs, "Believe the *Hype!*," *Addicted to Noise*, December 1996.

page 306: "Pearl Jam is back": As quoted in Chuck Philips, "Pearl Jam Finds a Way to Tour," *The Washington Post*, April 4, 1995.

page 306: "We're frustrated and disappointed": As quoted in Adam Sandler, "Tix Fee Flap Jams Concert," *Daily Variety*, April 24, 1995.

page 306: "ETM's fee structure virtually [mirrored] Ticketmaster's": As quoted in Alan Citron, "Pearl Jam's 'Crusade' was Pointless," *Los Angeles Times*, April 10, 1995.

page 307: "We take a lower cut than Pearl Jam": As quoted in Alec Foege, "Green Day," *Rolling Stone*, December 28, 1995.

page 307: "It disturbs me that the Sheriff's Department": As quoted in statement issued by tour publicist Nicole Vandenberg, June 9, 1995.

page 307: Curtis: "unprofessional and unproductive"; Vedder: "Have a little more faith, assholes": As quoted in statement issued by Vandenberg, June 12, 1995.

page 308: Wood: "I don't want to be perceived as someone who is trying to hurt the public"; Curtis: "Making it a daylight show," p. 308: As quoted in George Varga and Kelly Thornton, "Pearl Jam Bows out at Del Mar Fair," *San Diego Union Tribune*, June 13, 1995.

page 308: "It took us a whole year to plan these summer dates": As quoted in Chris Riemenschneider, "Pearl Jam to Reconsider Its Ticketmaster Boycott," *Los Angeles Times*, June 14, 1995.

page 309: "Ticketmaster and the San Diego Sports Arena felt it was in the best interest of fans": As quoted in George Varga, "Pearl Jam Shifts Fair Dates to Sports Arena," *San Diego Union Tribune*, June 15, 1995.

page 309: "I regret to say that it's impossible": As quoted in Chuck Philips, "Pearl Jam Throws in Towel in Crusade Against Ticketmaster," *Los Angeles Times*, June 15, 1995.

page 310: Vedder: "I guess you've heard"; Curtis: "Jeff and Eddie were furious": As quoted in Robert Hilburn, "Vedder Lowers the White Flag," *Los Angeles Times*, June 19, 1995.

Nineteen

page 312: "That was the day we acted as a band": As quoted in Robert Hilburn, "Working Their Way out of a Jam," *Los Angeles Times*, December 22, 1996.

page 313: "Pearl Jam regretfully announced": Statement issued by Nicole Vandenberg, June 25, 1995.

page 313: "When Pearl Jam played San Francisco's Golden Gate Park": Karen Schoemer and Yahlin Chang, "Nobody Knows the Troubles They've Seen," *Newsweek*, July 10, 1995.

page 313: Fan comments on tour cancellation: As quoted in Michael Corcoran, "Pearl Jam Bears Brunt of Concertgoers' Anger," *Austin American-Statesman*, June 27, 1995.

page 314: "The Pearl Jam decision-making process": As quoted in Michael Goldberg, "Pearl Jam: Milwaukee & Chicago Dates Are On! S.F. Refunds Offered," *Addicted to Noise*, June 28, 1995.

page 315: "You know, we understand the trials and troubles": Author interview with Gamble, 1995.

page 315: Courtney Love apology: As quoted in Courtney Love, "Summer of Love," *Spin*, December 1995.

page 319: "Pearl Jam's a huge machine, bigger than any of us": As quoted in Sara Scribner, "Three Fish Helps Put Life into Proper Scale for Pearl Jam Bassist," *Los Angeles Times*, July 7, 1996.

page 320: "I think touring is always going to be a compromise": As quoted in Hilburn, "Working Their Way out of a Jam."

page 321: "I guess [Eddie's] record label or representatives": As quoted in interview with CNN correspondent Mark Scheerer, November 3, 1997.

page 322: "I know who I am. I don't need to read someone else's bitter take on it"; comments by Vedder on *No Code* sales, p. 322: As quoted in Hilburn, "Working Their Way out of a Jam."

page 322: "We can be a little more normal now": As quoted in Craig Marks, "The Road Less Traveled," *Spin*, February 1997.

page 323: "I'll always wish the best for them": As quoted in Dan Johnson, "Green Romance Orchestra: Love Hurts," *The Rocket*, November 19–December 3, 1997.

page 324: "This has been the best year of my life": As quoted in Robert Hilburn, "A High 'Yield' Return," *Los Angeles Times*, November 17, 1997.

Index

Index